CliffsTestPrep™

TOEFL® CBT

by

Michael A. Pyle

Hungry Minds™

Best-Selling Books • Digital Downloads • e-Books • Answer Networks
e-Newsletters • Branded Web Sites • e-Learning

New York, NY • Cleveland, OH • Indianapolis, IN

About the Author

Michael A. Pyle earned a bachelor's degree in English in 1977 and a master's degree in Linguistics in 1979. He has been involved in the field of English as a Second Language since he began work on his master's degree in 1977. The original TOEFL test preparation book that he co-authored was created while Mike was teaching at the University of Florida's English Language Institute and Santa Fe Community College in Gainesville, Florida in 1982. He also wrote Cliffs Advanced Practice for the TOEFL in 1992. Although Mike no longer actively teaches for any institution, he periodically makes presentations to individual classes at Daytona Beach Community College and Embry Riddle Aeronautical University in Daytona Beach, Florida. He is a member of Teachers of English to Speakers of Other Languages (TESOL) and regularly attends its annual meetings. He has made presentations on teaching techniques related to TOEFL at TESOL annual meetings from time to time.

Publisher's Acknowledgments

Editorial

Project Editor: Joan Friedman

Copy Editor: Billie A. Williams

Editorial Assistant: Alison Jefferson

Special Help: Constance Carlisle, audio CD producer; ripple FX, audio CD engineering; Voice Scouts, audio CD talent; Brian Talbot, Becky Wilmes, and Chuck Campbell, audio CD narration

Production

Proofreader: Arielle Carole Mennelle

Hungry Minds Indianapolis Production Services

CliffsTestPrep™ TOEFL® CBT

Published by
Hungry Minds, Inc.
909 Third Avenue
New York, NY 10022
www.hungryminds.com
www.cliffsnotes.com

Library of Congress Control Number: 00-106743

ISBN: 0-7645-8609-2

Printed in the United States of America

10 9 8 7 6 5 4

1B/SW/QW/QR/IN

Distributed in the United States by Hungry Minds, Inc.

Distributed by CDG Books Canada Inc. for Canada; by Transworld Publishers Limited in the United Kingdom; by IDG Norge Books for Norway; by IDG Sweden Books for Sweden; by IDG Books Australia Publishing Corporation Pty. Ltd. for Australia and New Zealand; by TransQuest Publishers Pte Ltd. for Singapore, Malaysia, Thailand, Indo- nesia, and Hong Kong; by Gotop Information Inc. for Taiwan; by ICG Muse, Inc. for Japan; by Norma Comunicaciones S.A. for Columbia; by Intersoft for South Africa; by Eyrolles for France; by International Thomson Publishing for Germany, Austria and Switzerland; by Distribuidora Cuspide for Argentina; by LR International for Brazil; by Galileo Libros for Chile; by Ediciones ZETA S.C.R. Ltda. for Peru; by WS Computer Publishing Corporation, Inc., for the Philippines; by Contemporanea de Ediciones for Venezuela; by Express Computer Distributors for the Caribbean and West Indies; by Micronesia Media Distributor, Inc. for Micronesia; by Grupo Editorial Norma S.A. for Guatemala; by Chips Computadoras S.A. de C.V. for Mexico; by Editorial Norma de Panama S.A. for Panama; by American Bookshops for Finland. Authorized Sales Agent: Anthony Rudkin Associates for the Middle East and North Africa.

For general information on Hungry Minds' products and services please contact our Customer Care department; within the U.S. at 800-762-2974, outside the U.S. at 317-572-3993 or fax 317-572-4002.

For sales inquiries and resellers information, including discounts, premium and bulk quantity sales and foreign language translations please contact our Customer Care department at 800-434-3422, fax 317-572-4002 or write to Hungry Minds, Inc., Attn: Customer Care department, 10475 Crosspoint Boulevard, Indianapolis, IN 46256.

For information on licensing foreign or domestic rights, please contact our Sub-Rights Customer Care department at 212-884-5000.

For information on using Hungry Minds' products and services in the classroom or for ordering examination copies, please contact our Educational Sales department at 800-434-2086 or fax 317-572-4005.

Please contact our Public Relations department at 212-884-5163 for press review copies or 212-884-5000 for author interviews and other publicity information or fax 212-884-5400.

For authorization to photocopy items for corporate, personal, or educational use, please contact Copyright Clearance Center, 222 Rosewood Drive, Danvers, MA 01923, or fax 978-750-4470.

Hungry Minds™ is a trademark of Hungry Minds, Inc.

Author's Acknowledgments

Writing a book requires a considerable amount of research and work, and once it is completed, it is natural to feel a great relief. I only hope that you find it as helpful as students have found the two earlier texts I wrote. I very much appreciate the feedback I have received from students and teachers over the years on the original texts. I am grateful to Joyce Pepple and Greg Tubach for asking me to write another Cliffs book. I am particularly thankful to Joan Friedman for all the work that she and her staff did in the actual production, revision, and completion of the text itself.

My father-in-law, Dr. Manuel Lopez Figueras, of Merida, Venezuela, again helped me write a new passage about his specialty, lichens. My friend Dr. Arnold Vera, a physician specializing in endocrinology in Ormond Beach, Florida, assisted me greatly in writing the passage about diabetes. I also wish to thank Alejandro Muñoz and his family for taking us all over Mexico, including on a tour of the Don Julio Tequila processing plant in Atotonilco-Jalisco.

Nowadays, I am a lawyer with a busy law office. I very much appreciate those members of my staff who were sometimes affected by my work on the book, especially when they had to handle the legal work for clients because I was locked in my room trying to meet a deadline. Those employees are Trisha Dellinger, Stacey Rahm, Michelle Hall, Tracy Stafford, Kathy Strawn, and Sheila Semanisin. Sheila regularly had to fax and overnight documents. Tracy even stepped in to draw figures for me on short notice. And Steve Rahm has done a magnificent job creating our toeflcourse.com Web site.

I appreciate Verna Londoño and the administrators of Daytona Beach Community College and Embry Riddle Aeronautical University for inviting me to speak to their students from time to time so that I could gauge the quality of what I had written.

I also appreciate how open and cooperative Gena Netten and others in the TOEFL office have been with me and other TOEFL authors. Without information from them, we would all be guessing about what to present to the readers.

As always, I am grateful to my wife, Maria, and children, Michelle and Michael, Jr., for putting up with my working so many hours as well as providing ideas for sample items. I was even receiving and returning text via e-mail while on a cruise with the family in the Carribean.

And most of all, thanks to you, the reader, for choosing this book. I hope that you will find it useful and I welcome your feedback. Visit the Web site and e-mail me with your comments and questions.

Table of Contents

PART I: INTRODUCTION TO THE TOEFL COMPUTER-BASED TEST

PART II: ANALYSIS OF EXAM AREAS

PART III: DETAILED REVIEW OF ITEMS TESTED

PART IV: PUTTING IT ALL TOGETHER: PRACTICE TESTS

Preface

Your TOEFL (Test of English as a Foreign Language) scores are important in determining whether you are ready to study in a U.S. or Canadian college or university. Thorough preparation leads to better scores, so you need to make the most of your available study time. This guide is the most complete, precise, and accurate of all study products available.

In keeping with the fine tradition of *CliffsNotes,* this guide was prepared for you by an expert in the field of teaching English as a Second Language (ESL). The strategies, techniques, and materials presented in this book have been tested over many years.

This book is written specifically as a preparation text for the TOEFL Computer-Based Test (CBT), and the question types are based on the CBT format of the TOEFL test.

Part I of this book gives you basic information about the TOEFL test, as well as a successful overall approach to taking the test.

Part II includes complete analyses of each part of the test, including question types, test-taking techniques and strategies, and a patterned plan of attack for each question type.

Part III gives you more detailed information and practice items for each of the sections of the test, including a detailed review of item types, items tested, problem areas, and sample TOEFL test questions.

Part IV contains six full-length practice tests, very similar in content and difficulty to the actual TOEFL test, as well as answer keys and scoring sheets for the practice tests.

The Appendix contains scripts of listening comprehension passages you encounter in parts III and IV.

This book also contains a detailed table of contents so you can easily find the area of the text with the information you need.

Remember: Allow yourself as much time as possible to prepare for the TOEFL test. The more time you have, the better. While this book is a great tool for learning English, you will learn the language more completely by reading, listening, watching television and movies, writing, and surrounding yourself with as much English as you can. Good luck in your studies, your successful completion of the TOEFL test, and your future.

How to Use This Book

This preparation guide is ideal for either individual or classroom use.

To the Student

Study English slowly and methodically. American English speakers often use the verb "to cram" when describing their studies. "To cram" means to try to place something forcefully into something else. When American students talk about "cramming," they mean that they study very quickly and try to put as much information as possible into their minds. Cramming is not the way to prepare for the TOEFL test. Learn English completely. Read books and magazines, watch television, watch movies, listen to conversations, and write. Do everything you can to obtain a good foundation in English.

In addition to immersing yourself in English through these methods, use this book. Be sure to use it slowly and methodically; do not try to cram all the information I give you by reading the book cover to cover in a few days.

Part I of this book provides general information about the TOEFL test. Part II gives you an analysis of the various sections on the exam. Part III provides more detailed information about how to succeed on the different sections of the test. Part IV contains practice tests and the answers and explanations for the questions they contain.

This text is organized in the same order as the sections of the TOEFL test. The easiest way to study is to follow the order of the book. However, you may choose to focus on certain sections if you anticipate having particular trouble with them. For example, you may want to start with the sections on Listening if that is the area you struggle with the most.

To use this book most effectively, follow these steps:

1. Determine the date on which you expect to take the TOEFL test. If your English is not very advanced, and you do not actually expect to pass the TOEFL test on the first try, *do not cram*. Do the best you can, and create a long-term study schedule that will allow you to feel completely prepared the second time you take the test.
2. Based on how many weeks you can devote to each section of the test, follow the schedule outlined in the following table. No matter how many weeks you have to study, try to read a newspaper or magazine each week, and spend time watching TV or going to a movie each week.

	4–6 Weeks	7–9 Weeks	10–13 Weeks	14–16 Weeks
Week 1	Read Parts I and II of this book Read Part III through page 100 Read Part III, "Writing" Write one essay Take Practice Test 1	Read Parts I and II of this book Read Part III through page 88 Read Part III, "Writing"	Read Parts I and II of this book Read Part III through page 88 Read Part III, "Writing" Buy or rent a book on tape	Read Parts I and II of this book Read Part III through page 88 Read Part III, "Writing" Buy or rent a book on tape If possible, order TOEFL Sampler CD-ROM from ETS
Week 2	Read Part III pages 100 through 128 Take Practice Test 2 Call recorded messages on the phone Write one essay	Read Part III pages 88 through 100 Take Practice Test 1 Review Part III, "Writing" Write one essay	Read Part III pages 88 through 100 Take Practice Test 1 Review Part III, "Writing" Write one essay Continue listening to book on tape	Read Part III pages 88 through 100 Take Practice Test 1 Review Part III, "Writing" Write one essay Continue listening to book on tape
Week 3	Read Part III pages 128 through 181 Take Practice Tests 3 and 4 Write one essay	Read Part III pages 100 through 128 Take Practice Test 2 Write one essay	Read Part III pages 100 through 128 Write one essay Continue listening to book on tape (or get another)	Read Part III pages 100 through 128 Write one essay Continue listening to book on tape (or get another)
Week 4	Read Part III pages 181 through 206 Take Practice Tests 5 and 6 Write one essay	Read Part III pages 128 through 152 Take Practice Test 3 Write one essay	Read Part III pages 128 through 152 Take Practice Test 2 Write one essay Continue listening to book on tape	Read Part III pages 128 through 152 Take Practice Test 2 Write one essay Continue listening to book on tape
Week 5	Review	Read Part III pages 153 through 170 Take Practice Test 4 Write one essay	Read Part III pages 153 through 170 Take Practice Test 3 Write one essay	Read Part III pages 153 through 170 Take Practice Test 3 Write one essay
Week 6	Review	Read Part III pages 170 through 187 Take Practice Test 5 Write one essay	Read Part III pages 170 through 187 Take Practice Test 4 Write one essay Continue listening to book on tape	Read Part III pages 170 through 187 Take Practice Test 4 Write one essay Continue listening to book on tape

	4–6 Weeks	7–9 Weeks	10–13 Weeks	14–16 Weeks
Week 7		Read Part III pages 187 through 206 Take Practice Test 6 Write one essay	Read Part III pages 187 through 206 Take Practice Test 5 Write one essay Continue listening to book on tape	Read Part III pages 187 through 206 Take Practice Test 5 Write one essay Continue listening to book on tape If you purchased TOEFL Sampler from ETS, take practice test. Get a good book and read it.
Week 8		Review	Review Part III pages 39 through 100 Take Practice Test 6 Write one essay Continue listening to book on tape	Review Part III pages 39 through 88 Take Practice Test 6 Write one essay Continue listening to book on tape Continue reading book
Week 9		Review	Review Part III pages 100 through 128 Review practice tests Write one essay Continue listening to book on tape	Review Part III pages 88 through 100 Review practice tests Write one essay Continue listening to book on tape Continue reading book
Week 10			Review Part III pages 128 through 181 Review practice tests Write one essay Continue listening to book on tape	Review Part III pages 100 through 128 Review practice tests Write one essay Continue listening to book on tape Continue reading book
Week 11			Review Part III pages 181 through 206 Review practice tests Write one essay Continue listening to book on tape	Review Part III pages 128 through 152 Review practice tests Write one essay Continue listening to book on tape Continue reading book If you ordered materials from ETS, take the practice tests.

	4–6 Weeks	7–9 Weeks	10–13 Weeks	14–16 Weeks
Week 12			Review	Review Part III pages 153 through 170
				Review practice tests
				Write one essay
				Continue listening to book on tape
				Continue reading book
				If you ordered materials from ETS, take the practice tests.
Week 13			Review	Review Part III pages 170 through 187
				Review practice tests
				Write one essay
				Continue listening to book on tape
				Continue reading book
				If you ordered materials from ETS, take the practice tests.
Week 14				Review Part III pages 187 through 206
				Review practice tests
				Write one essay
				Continue listening to book on tape
				Continue reading book
				If you ordered materials from ETS, take the practice tests.
Weeks 15 and 16				Review

Obviously, when I suggest that you read a newspaper or magazine, watch TV, or listen to a book on tape, I mean to do so *in English*. Each time I indicate to write one essay, I mean to use one of the sample topics provided in the "Writing" chapter in Part III of this book or one of the ETS sample essay topics printed in the Bulletin or listed on the Web Site. You can order a Bulletin by calling 609-771-7100 or download it from the Web site, www.toefl.org/infobull.html. Write this essay *in addition to* writing the essays included in each practice test.

3. Have your essays graded by a writing teacher. If you don't know a writing instructor who can do this, you can use my Essay Grading Service. You can send an essay by mail along with a check or money order payable to TOEFL Preparation Course, LLC. The mailing address is

> TOEFL Preparation Course, LLC
> 1265 West Granada Blvd.
> Suite
> Ormond Beach, FL 32174 USA

The fee for reviewing one essay is $20. If you submit more than one essay at one time, you may deduct $2 per additional essay submitted. (That is, the fee for two essays is $38, for three $56, and so on.) The discount is only applicable for essays submitted together, and it does not matter whether the essays are written by the same student or different students. If you provide an e-mail address, the scoring will be sent to you via e-mail. Visit my Web site, www.TOEFLCOURSE.com, for up-to-date instructions for submitting essays.

To the Teacher

This book is designed for use by students individually, so it is effective for study and practice even if no TOEFL course is available. It can also be used as a classroom textbook. To use it in the classroom, you can base your schedule on the preceding table. You can grade students' practice essays and provide them with prompt feedback, which will speed up their course of study. You can also administer each of the six practice tests in this book in order to simulate the actual TOEFL test experience.

For additional resources to use in a TOEFL classroom, contact the Educational Testing Service by phone at 609-771-7100, by e-mail at toefl@ets.org, or via its Web site at www.ets.org.

Study Guide Checklist

❑ 1. Obtain, read, and study the TOEFL Information Bulletin for Computer-Based Testing. (To order, call 609-771-7100 or visit www.toefl.org/infobull.html.)

❑ 2. Become familiar with the general description and structure of the TOEFL test as described in Part I.

❑ 3. Familiarize yourself with the "Questions Commonly Asked About the TOEFL Test" in Part I.

❑ 4. Review Part II, "Analysis of Exam Areas."

❑ 5. Review Part III, following the timeframe you determine in the "How to Use this Book" section.

❑ 6. Write an essay and ask a writing instructor to score it according to the TOEFL test scoring criteria. (You can use my essay grading service if you wish, which is explained in "How to Use This Book.")

❑ 7. Take Practice Test I, using the audio CD included in this book for the Listening section.

❑ 8. Check your answers, analyze your results, and review areas of the test you need to improve.

❑ 9. Write another essay and have it graded.

❑ 10. Return to Part III and continue your study following the time sequence you have established.

❑ 11. When finished with Part III, take the other practice tests in order. Use the audio CDs for the Listening section of each test. After you take each test, check your answers and analyze your results.

❑ 12. Return to any weak areas and study them again.

INTRODUCTION TO THE TOEFL COMPUTER-BASED TEST

GENERAL DESCRIPTION OF THE TOEFL TEST

The Test of English as a Foreign Language (TOEFL) is an exam that determines whether a student whose native language is not English has strong enough English skills to succeed in courses at a college or university in the United States or Canada. The test, which is administered by an agency called the Educational Testing Service, contains four parts: Listening, Structure (which tests knowledge of grammar and mechanics), Reading, and Writing.

The length of the test and time allotted to take it vary at each administration and may also depend upon how many questions you answer correctly. The general tutorial lasts approximately 40 minutes, although there are portions that you can move through quickly. Each section also begins with a mandatory tutorial, which you can move through as quickly or as slowly as you wish. (Expect to spend at least a few minutes on each, though.)

The Listening section takes from 40 to 60 minutes, the Structure section takes from 15 to 20 minutes, and the Reading Section takes from 70 to 90 minutes. The length of each of these three sections depends on the number of questions at the particular administration. The Writing section takes 30 minutes. The time for the entire test, including tutorials, is between 200 and 280 minutes. Because you will be selecting score recipients immediately after you take the test, plan to be at the testing center for a minimum of four hours. (See the next chapter for further explanation of selecting score recipients.) Take your time and relax. Only look at the clock to get a sense of how much time you have left in a particular section.

How Colleges and Universities Use TOEFL Scores

Thousands of colleges and universities require TOEFL test scores. However, no school considers the TOEFL test the only criterion for admission. Schools may also consider your grades from previous studies as well as other criteria, including records from an intensive English program (if you have taken one).

Each school has its own criteria for the TOEFL test score that is acceptable for admission. The TOEFL test results you receive cannot indicate whether your score is considered passing, because a score that one school considers suitable may not be accepted by another school. In general, you do not help yourself by gaining admission to a school before your English is up to the necessary level.

Computer-Based versus Paper-Based Testing

Two basic types of the TOEFL test exist: a computer-based test (CBT) and a paper-based test (PBT). Until a few years ago, everyone taking the TOEFL test used a pencil and paper version. But now, the computer-based test is given almost everywhere in the world. This book gives you lots of information about how to take the computer-based test, because that is the version you will probably be required to take.

You can take a paper-based test (PBT) only in areas where the CBT is not available. The Supplemental TOEFL Administration Program provides the PBT in areas where the CBT isn't offered.

The questions asked on the CBT and the PBT are very similar. However, the method of answering those questions differs. On the PBT, each answer choice is assigned a letter: for example, A, B, C, and D. On the CBT, answer choices are not lettered; you simply click with your mouse on the correct answer choice. In this book, we use letters to label answer choices for clarity, even though you won't see those letters appear on the TOEFL test computer screen.

When you take the CBT, rather than take the test at a specific time and place with other applicants, you make an appointment at a testing facility and take the test on a computer. You have more control during the listening comprehension section than you would if you took the PBT. You can determine how much time you need to spend on each listening question (within the section's total time limit, of course), and you can set the volume level of the listening passages because you have individual headphones.

Another significant difference between the PBT and the CBT is that the listening comprehension and structure sections of the CBT are computer-adaptive. This means that the first question you're given in either of these sections is of medium difficulty. If you answer correctly, the next question you receive is more difficult; if you answer incorrectly, the next question is less difficult. Your score depends on the number of questions you answer correctly, but it also depends on the level of difficulty of your questions. The reading and writing sections are not computer-adaptive.

The CBT is scored quite differently from the PBT. The total number of points you can score on the CBT is 300. On the PBT, the top score is 677. Colleges and universities are informed of the version of the test you take, so they know the top score you can possibly receive.

CBT scores are reported to institutions within two weeks after taking the test. You can review your unofficial CBT score while sitting at the computer at the conclusion of your test. That score is "unofficial" because the writing section cannot be scored automatically; you can only determine how you performed on the other three sections of the test.

The CBT is more flexible than the PBT regarding the time it takes and the number of questions you must answer. The TOEFL Bulletin and the TOEFL Web site can give you the most up-to-date information about the test structure. You can order the Bulletin by calling 609-771-7100 or download it from www.toefl.org/infobull. html. The Bulletin also contains registration information.

Computer Tutorials

The TOEFL computer-based test contains a tutorial, which you can review at your own speed. The tutorial shows you exactly how to use the computer to answer questions and move from one question to the next.

You can purchase a CD-ROM that has a copy of the computer tutorial in advance of the test so that you are comfortable with the computer functions when you arrive at the test site. (To order the CD-ROM, use the contact information given in the previous section.) Even if you review the tutorial in advance, you will need to review it again on the day of your test; everyone who takes the TOEFL test must go through the mandatory tutorial immediately before starting the test itself as well as a short tutorial before each individual test section. When the CBT first became available, test-takers spent approximately 40 minutes going through the tutorial before starting the test. But if you go through the tutorial in advance, you probably won't need that much time to review it on the test day.

For a general introduction to the computer you'll use on the day of your exam, see the chapter "Computer Basics for Taking the TOEFL Test," later in Part I.

Institutional Testing Program (ITP)

Some institutions administer TOEFL exams for their own students. ITP tests are actually previously used TOEFL tests; tests that are no longer administered to TOEFL test-takers. Colleges and universities that participate in the ITP administer exams to their students in order to diagnose their level of proficiency or to gauge their progress in an intensive English program. Some schools actually use these scores for admission to the college or university itself, while others use them only for general information within their intensive English program. ITP scores obtained in an administration at one school are not permitted to be used for admission at another school.

You can register for the ITP at any institution that offers the test. You can't, however, register for the ITP through the Educational Testing Service (the agency that administers the TOEFL). Scores are provided only to the institution and cannot be used for any other purpose.

Format of the Test		
Subject Area	**Time**	**Number of Questions**
General tutorial	Up to 40 minutes	
Listening tutorial	Approximately 10 minutes	
Listening	40–60 minutes	30–50 questions
Structure tutorial	Approximately 5 minutes	
Structure	15–20 minutes	20–25 questions
Break	5 minutes	
Reading tutorial	Approximately 10 minutes	
Reading	70–90 minutes	44–55 questions
Writing tutorial	Approximately 5 minutes	
Writing	30 minutes	1 topic
TOTAL (excluding tutorials)	155–200 minutes	94–130 (plus essay)

Note that the time range shown in this table doesn't include the time you spend on tutorials, because that can vary so widely. Plan to spend additional time after the test to view your scores and designate your score recipients. (You can choose up to four colleges and universities from a drop-down list on the computer screen.) The total possible time that this test requires, including tutorials and the post-test items, ranges from 4 to 4½ hours.

A clock appears on your computer screen during all sections of the test so that you know how much time you have left to complete each section. You can move through each section as quickly as you like, but the Listening section is more difficult to hurry through; you cannot control the speed of the passages you hear. Each section has a time limit.

The rest of this chapter provides a brief overview of each section of the test. For more in-depth information, be sure to review Part III.

Listening Section

The Listening section measures your ability to understand spoken English. This section is split into two parts:

- **Part A: Dialogues.** These are brief conversations between at least two people. Sometimes each speaker speaks only once, and sometimes one or both of the speakers speak more than once. After the conversation, you're asked a question, and you click the most appropriate answer choice. You must answer between 11 and 17 questions in this section.

- **Part B: Conversations and Talks.** The conversations in this section are longer than in Part A. Short lectures and academic discussions are included as well. Each conversation or talk is spoken only one time; you can't repeat it. Several questions are asked after each, and you must click the most appropriate answer choice for each question.

  You will hear two or three conversations in this section; each lasts less than one minute. After each conversation, you answer two or more questions. You will also hear four to six short lectures (approximately 2½ minutes each) and academic discussions (2 minutes or less each). There are generally three to seven questions for each short lecture and academic discussion.

Structure Section

The Structure section tests your understanding and usage of standard written English. You will answer two types of questions in the Structure section of the TOEFL test. The first type of question is an incomplete sentence with four choices of words or phrases to complete the sentence. The second type of question requires you to identify a word or phrase in a sentence that is incorrect. On the computer-based version of the TOEFL test, the two types of questions are interspersed throughout the Structure section.

Note: If you take the paper-based version of the TOEFL test, the two types of questions will be separated. Part A of the Structure section will contain only the first type of question. Part B will contain only the second type of question.

Reading Section

The Reading section measures your ability to read and understand academic passages typical of those you would read in a North American university or college. You will encounter various question types in this section, which are explained in detail in Part III of this book. Your understanding of vocabulary is tested in this section.

Writing Section

The Writing section measures your ability to compose in standard written English on an assigned topic. Your task in this section is to generate and organize ideas and to support them with examples and evidence. A list of possible essay topics is available in advance in the TOEFL Bulletin or on the TOEFL test Web site (www.toefl.org).

Q. How do I obtain a copy of the TOEFL Bulletin?

A. Order it or download it from www.toefl.org/infobull.html or call 609-771-7100.

Q. How do I know which form of the test to take?

A. The TOEFL Web site lists the locations where the different forms of the test are given.

Q. Can I choose to take either the paper-based test or the computer-based test?

A. No. You can take only the test that is available in your area.

Q. Can I take the TOEFL test more than once?

A. Yes, you can take the test as many times as you wish, but only once in one month. If you take the test twice in one month, your scores for the second examination aren't reported.

Q. What materials must I bring to the exam?

A. You must bring registration documentation if you applied for the test in a way that provides a written document. Otherwise, bring your confirmation number. Also, bring identification as specified in the TOEFL Bulletin.

Q. What other materials may I bring to the exam?

A. For the CBT, you may not bring anything else with you to the exam, including paper and calculators. Before you take the test, you're given a locker in which to place the contents of your pockets.

Q. Will I know my score when I finish the exam?

A. You will receive actual scores for the Listening and Reading sections. You will receive a range of possible scores in the Structure section. The reason you cannot get an exact Structure score on test day is because the Structure and Writing scores are combined. Therefore, that score cannot be finalized until the essay you create for the Writing section is read and graded (usually within two weeks after the exam).

Q. What do I do if I don't want my score reported?

A. You can cancel your scores after taking the exam when you're shown the scores on the computer. If you cancel your scores but change your mind within 60 days, you can reinstate them for a fee; see the TOEFL Bulletin for more information. If you don't cancel your scores, you can still choose not to report them to any institutions, simply by not choosing any institutions as score recipients.

Q. Do "computer-based" and "computer-adaptive" mean the same thing?

A. No. The entire TOEFL exam is called "computer-based" because it's given on the computer. Only two sections are computer-adaptive: Listening and Structure. Computer-adaptive means that every test taker is given a question of medium difficulty to begin each section. If you answer the first question correctly, you're given a slightly harder second question, and if you answer the first question incorrectly, you're given a slightly easier second question. This process continues throughout the exam. The level of question difficulty varies during the test according to whether you answer each question correctly. Therefore, your score is based upon not only the number of correct answers, but also the level of difficulty.

Q. Do I need computer skills to do well on the exam?

A. No. Studies have shown that knowledge of computers has virtually no effect on how well a test taker performs. But you should completely familiarize yourself with the computer instructions before you take the test.

Q. How can I prepare for the TOEFL test?

A. Practice with as much information as possible. If at all possible, take the tutorial provided through the TOEFL tests's Web site www.toefl.org/cbtutprq.html. Or, if you have time, purchase the PowerPrep software or TOEFL Sampler. Both of these packages include the tutorial, as well as practice tests and answers. These materials are superb for practice, although they don't provide explanation, analysis, and hints on passing the exam like this book. Call 800-446-3319 or visit www.ets.org/store.html to order these materials.

Q. Is the essay required on the computer-based test?

A. Yes. Unlike the paper-based test, in which the essay is provided at only certain administrations, the essay is a required part of the CBT. It accounts for 50 percent of your Structure score.

Q. Should I guess on the TOEFL test if I don't know an answer?

A. If you don't know an answer in the Listening and Structure sections, take a guess. Because of the computer-adaptive nature of the test, you must answer a question so the system knows what question to give next. In the Reading section, you can skip questions, but I recommend that you answer every question. If you have time remaining after you've finished the last question, you can return to previous questions and look at them in more detail.

Q. Is walk-in registration available?

A. Yes. Walk-in registration is available, but I advise that you make an appointment.

Q. Does scoring on the CBT differ from that of the PBT?

A. The scoring for these two test types is totally different. The score on the PBT ranges from 310 to 677, while the score on the CBT ranges from 0 to 300.

COMPUTER BASICS FOR TAKING THE TOEFL TEST

The computer program used for the TOEFL test is quite basic. Whereas you may use various computer keys to perform tasks in other programs, the program used on the TOEFL test is simplified. You perform most tasks on the TOEFL computer screen by clicking the left button on your mouse.

Scrolling means moving upward or downward in a document. Whereas you might use the "page up" and "page down" keys on other word processing programs, you use the mouse to scroll the information on the TOEFL test screen.

The items and icons that appear on the TOEFL computer screen are unique. For example, at the top left of each screen is a box that shows how many minutes you have left in a specific section of the test. If you don't wish to see it, you can click the clock (which says *Time*) at the bottom left of your screen and hide it. But in order to pace yourself, it's a good idea to have a general idea of how much time is left in a section. You probably won't feel rushed if you work through the materials deliberately and methodically.

At the top right of the TOEFL screen, you'll see the number of the question you're viewing and the total number of questions in the section. At the bottom right of the screen, you'll see the icons to click when you're finished with a section or area and ready to move on to a new section.

In all the Listening and Structure sections, there's an icon called *Next,* which you click when you're finished with a question. There's another icon to the left of Next called *Confirm Answer,* which you must also click before you can move to another question. The TOEFL test uses these icons because the Listening and Structure sections are computer-adaptive, meaning that your answer to one question leads you to a harder or easier question. In these two sections, you can't return to questions you've already answered, and you can't skip questions. In the Reading section, which is not computer-adaptive, you can skip questions and return to prior questions; thus, the *Previous* icon replaces the *Confirm Answer* icon in the Reading section.

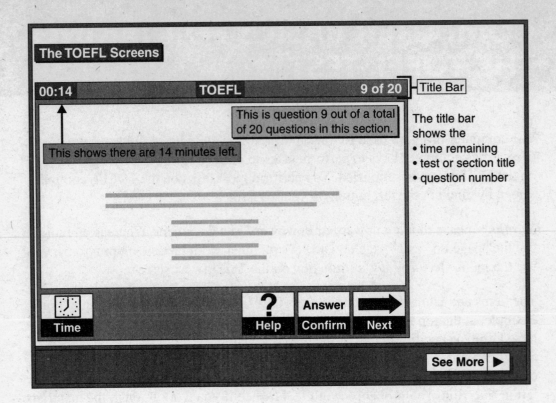

To answer a question, you click the correct answer with the left mouse button. Sometimes you click an oval bubble, sometimes a square, and sometimes a word or phrase. Whichever you click darkens so you know what you've chosen.

For the Writing section, the TOEFL test's word processor is much more rudimentary than what you may be used to. You can hand-write your essay if you wish. If you choose to type it, however, you type just as you would with any other word processor. If you want to move text, use the *Cut* and *Paste* keys. If you make a mistake, click *Undo*. The *Page Up* and *Page Down* keys also work in this section. The tab button does not work. Press the space bar five times or so to indent a paragraph, if you wish.

You should make every effort to experience the computer tutorial prior to taking the test. You don't want to waste time or become nervous trying to become familiar with the software while you're taking the actual test. You can obtain a copy of the TOEFL Sampler or purchase a copy of the PowerPrep program, both of which contain the tutorial (see the chapter on "Questions Commonly Asked about the TOEFL Test"), and practice at your leisure.

TAKING THE TOEFL TEST: A SUCCESSFUL OVERALL APPROACH

To score well on the TOEFL test, you must know English well and be able to apply what you know. You must also use your time wisely during the exam. Although your test results are important, don't let your nerves overwhelm you. If you don't achieve the score that you want or need the first time you take the test, you can always take it again. Try to relax as much as possible when you take the test.

Preparing for the Test

Absorb English by surrounding yourself with it as much as possible. Listen, read, write, and do everything that you can to learn English. Read magazines, newspapers, books, and anything else you can find. Pay attention to idiomatic expressions (sometimes called idioms) that you aren't familiar with and grammatical structures that you haven't seen before. (An idiomatic expression is a combination of two or more words that has a different meaning than the individual words would indicate. For example, *look up* can mean to "research," whereas *look* and *up* separately do not have meanings relating to research.)

Make the most of your preparation time. Complete the tables in the "How to Use This Book" section and plan your studies accordingly. Follow through in the order that this book suggests.

Become familiar with the test directions, techniques, and tutorials. To do so, use this book and review the TOEFL Bulletin, which you can order by calling 609-771-7100 or visiting www.toefl.org/infobull.html.

The Day of the Test

On the day of the test, follow the same routine that you would on any other day. Eat the same amount, get the same amount of sleep, and make the test day as normal as possible. Don't try to cram last-minute study time immediately before the test.

Be sure you know how to get to the test center, and arrive in plenty of time so you won't be rushed. Bring your required identification and proof of admission.

During the Test

Use your time as wisely as possible during the test. One time-saving technique is to avoid reading the directions for the different sections. In order to accomplish this, you must become very familiar with the directions prior to taking the exam, and this book helps you do so. Another way to save some time is to familiarize yourself with the computer tutorials prior to taking the exam. You cannot avoid the tutorials altogether on the day of the test, but you can skip through them quickly if you're already familiar with them. See the "General Description of the TOEFL Test" chapter for information on ordering a copy of the tutorials.

As you encounter questions, remember the techniques that you learn in this book and apply them methodically. Here are a few hints to get you started:

- Keep in mind that you cannot skip questions in the Listening and Structure sections. In those sections, make your best effort on each question, applying the knowledge that you have obtained, and then go on to the next question. Don't dwell on any one question too long or become concerned that you answered a previous question incorrectly.

- In the Reading section, answer all questions by applying the techniques that I give you in this book, but keep track of any questions that you may want to return to if you have enough time.

- For the Writing section, decide before you take the test whether you're going to write the essay by hand or on the computer. Write the essay using the techniques that I include in this book.

The most important thing to do is remember that you have prepared adequately and that you know English quite well. Relax and do the best you can.

PART II

ANALYSIS OF EXAM AREAS

The first part of the TOEFL test that you take is the Listening section, and it consists of two parts, which I describe in this chapter. The Listening section tests your ability to understand and interpret spoken American English.

The Listening section contains between 30 and 50 questions and lasts from 40 to 60 minutes, not including the time that you spend on the tutorial. You will find out when you start working on this section how many questions you will receive. The time you are allotted for the section will depend on the number of questions you are given. On the computer-based test, you have your own headphones and the ability to control the volume, so the quality of what you hear on the test should be perfect.

Basic Skills Necessary

To score well in the Listening section, you must have a thorough knowledge of English and a strong ability to interpret what you hear. However, you can't develop these skills overnight. To constantly practice your listening abilities, you must listen to English and pay attention to idioms, grammatical structures, and vocabulary words that aren't familiar to you.

What to Expect

During the test, you will see pictures of each speaker or speakers, but these drawings do not provide any useful information. In the questions that you encounter in Part B (explained later in this section), you may also see drawings, figures, or charts that illustrate what is being said. The appropriate drawing, figure, or chart will automatically appear onscreen when the speaker mentions it. After the speaker has spoken, you will hear and see the questions you must answer. Using the left button on your mouse, click the correct answer that appears onscreen.

Part A consists of dialogues between two people. Sometimes a speaker will speak more than once, and sometimes each speaker talks only once. Most topics are school-related. That is, they are discussions about classes, homework, lectures, and exams. Only one question is asked about each dialogue.

Part B consists of longer conversations or talks. Usually, you will hear six such talks or conversations. Some of the talks or conversations may be followed by only two questions. Others may be followed by several questions. The talks may be about a famous person, a scientific process, or any other topic that would be appropriate for a lecture.

To succeed on this section of the test, you must be able to listen carefully. Try to grasp the overall concepts being discussed even if you are not familiar with the specific words or phrases being used.

The directions provided in this book are not direct quotations of the TOEFL test directions, but they contain the same information that you will see on the test. This is true of the practice test directions as well. You should not need to read the test directions on the day of the test.

Part A

Directions: In this part, you will hear short conversations between two people, who each may speak only once or more than once. After the conversation, you will be asked a question. Choose the answer that most accurately answers the question based on what the speakers state or imply in their conversation.

Sample

> **Man:** I am trying to find a book by author Sterling Watson. Do you know where I should look?
>
> **Woman:** He's a fiction writer, isn't he? Log on to this computer. Click on fiction, and then search by author name. See? Oh, he has written quite a few books, although I've never heard of him.
>
> **Man:** His books were never in the top ten, but I like his style. I took a class from him at the University of Florida.
>
> **Q.** What does the man say about Sterling Watson?
>
> **A.** He is required to read one of his books but does not like his writing.
>
> **B.** He has never read any of his works previously.
>
> **C.** He appreciates his writing style.
>
> **D.** He learned about his books from a computer.

The answer is **C**, "He appreciates his writing style."

Common question types heard in Part A are:

- What does the (man/woman) mean?
- What will the (man/woman) probably do (next)?
- What will the speakers do?
- What is the (man/woman) going to do?

- What does the (man/woman) plan to do?

- What does the (man/woman) imply about . . . ?

- What is the (man's/woman's) problem?

- What problem does the (man/woman) think the (man/woman) has?

- What are the speakers talking about?

- What does the (man/woman) suggest that the (man/woman) do?

- What does the (man/woman) say about . . . ?

- What does the (man/woman) think about . . . ?

- What had the (man/woman) assumed about . . .?

Part B

Directions: In this part, you will hear several conversations and talks. You will hear each conversation or talk only once, and then you will hear several questions. Answer the questions based on what the speakers state or imply in their conversations. Choose the best answer from the choices provided.

Conversations in Part B generally involve academic matters or student life. A man and woman will each speak several times, and then questions will be asked about the conversation.

Sample

> **Man:** I can't believe we have to read this entire book by Monday.
>
> **Woman:** Some teachers think you have nothing else to do besides prepare for their class.
>
> **Man:** Well, my boss thinks the same thing about my job — that it's the only thing I have to do.
>
> **Woman:** Oh, I didn't know you were working. What do you do?
>
> **Man:** I do bookkeeping work for a small company on Saturdays. This weekend, I have to prepare end of the quarter reports to give to the accountant on Monday.
>
> **Woman:** You'd better start reading soon.
>
> **1.** What does the man imply about the assignment?
>
> A. It is too much to read in such a short time.
>
> B. He has already read the material.
>
> C. He can read at work.
>
> D. The teacher knows that he has a job.

2. What does the man imply about some teachers?

   A. They are understanding.

   B. They give thought-provoking assignments.

   C. They act like taking their class is the only thing a student has to do.

   D. They are unprepared.

3. What does the woman suggest that the man do?

   A. Skip work

   B. Begin work on the assignment as soon as possible

   C. Quit the class

   D. Stay up all night

4. What does the man say about his work?

   A. He does manual labor.

   B. He dislikes his job.

   C. His employer is very understanding.

   D. He works with figures.

The answers are 1 **A**, 2 **C**, 3 **B**, 4 **D**.

Talks in Part B are meant to represent academic presentations. They could involve a professor explaining something to a class or a specialist explaining his or her area of expertise. The talks frequently include some kind of chart or diagram, which appears onscreen when the speaker mentions it.

Sample

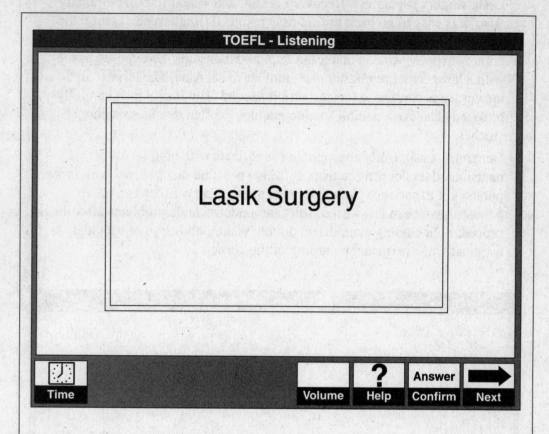

Lasik surgery is a new method of restoring certain kinds of vision loss. Lasik is an acronym derived from the word "laser" and some medical terms.

Unlike cataract surgery, which restores vision to eyes marred by a cloudy lens, Lasik is an elective procedure performed on healthy eyes. Generally, patients who choose Lasik surgery suffer from myopia, or nearsightedness, which means that their eyes cannot visualize distant objects. It also corrects farsightedness, the inability to see close objects, as well as astigmatism, which is a visual distortion that causes blurred vision. But the procedure does not correct presbyopia, the inability of the eye to focus that comes naturally with age.

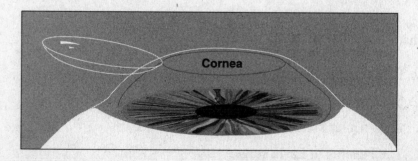

Lasik surgery is painless. Recovery is fast, and vision stabilizes quickly. Also, it is easy to go back to fine-tune results. Using a special knife, the surgeon slices a microscopically-thin hinged flap in the top of the cornea, exposes what is under the flap, and then zaps the exposed tissue with a laser for a preprogrammed number of seconds. The laser sculpts the cornea according to the correction needed. The flap is then carefully replaced. The eye's natural suction enables the flap to adhere without stitches.

Generally, Lasik is not appropriate for patients with high levels of nearsightedness or astigmatism. It is also possible that patients with large pupils will experience glare and halos after surgery. Likewise, some patients have been left with serious and uncorrectable problems after the procedure, including glare, haze, double vision, ghosting, or irregular astigmatism, a permanent warping of the cornea.

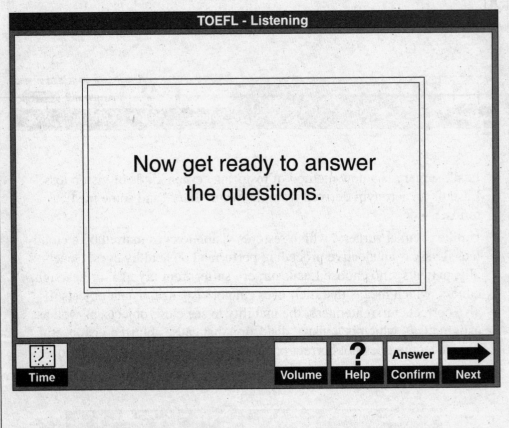

1. What is the talk mainly about?

   A. Different procedures for improving the eyes

   B. Several different eye defects

   C. A particular kind of eye surgery

   D. The benefits of Lasik surgery

2. Organize the following according to the order in which they take place during Lasik surgery:

   A. Apply the laser

   B. Slice the flap

   C. Replace the flap

   D. Expose the eye

3. The author contrasts cataract surgery from Lasik surgery by stating that Lasik surgery

   A. is not a surgery of necessity.

   B. is safer.

   C. is more important.

   D. is more useful.

4. Of the following types of eye problems, which would not be a likely candidate for Lasik surgery?

   A. Myopia

   B. Astigmatism

   C. Presbyopia

   D. Farsightedness

The answers are 1 **D**, 2 **B D A C**, 3 **A**, 4 **B**.

Common question types in Part B include questions about main ideas, details, purpose, and implication.

Main idea questions may include:

- What is the main idea of the talk?

- What is the talk mainly about?

- What are the speakers discussing?

- What would be a good title for the lecture?

Detail questions may include:

- What does the man/woman say about . . . ?

- What does the man/woman want?

- What does the man/woman suggest about . . . ?

- What is the man/woman describing?

Purpose questions may include:

- Why did . . . ?
- Why is . . . ?
- Why does the man/woman think . . . ?
- Why does the speaker mention . . . ?

Implication questions may include:

- What does the speaker imply about . . . ?
- What does the speaker infer about . . . ?
- What does the man/woman mean when he/she says . . . ?

Other questions in this part will ask you to choose a drawing, match questions, and organize or categorize answer choices. For example,

- You may be asked to pick out the correct drawing from what was described in words.
- You may be asked to match two concepts together.
- You may be asked to determine the sequence of events.
- You may be asked to categorize certain concepts.

All of these types of questions are demonstrated in the practice exercises and practice tests in this book.

Preparing for the Listening Section

As I say many times in this book, the best way to improve your English is to listen to as much English as possible. Use the following tips to listen to English daily:

- Watch movies and television, including news programs and weather reports. If a television isn't available, listen to the radio.
- Make telephone calls to recorded messages. For example, some newspapers have recorded information about local events and most movie theaters have recorded schedules of showings.
- Attend lectures in English if you can.
- Make use of a language laboratory if one is available. Check with a local university that has an intensive English program or with a Sylvan Learning Center in your area.

- Listen to books on tape. If you live in the United States, check out the tape program at Cracker Barrel restaurants, where you can exchange books on tape for a $1 rental charge. I prefer listening to unabridged books (meaning those with nothing omitted), so I get books on tape from Recorded Books, Inc. (www.recordedbooks.com). This company has a wide variety of books available for sale or rent.

- Take all the listening practice tests in this book. If you can obtain the TOEFL Sampler materials available, use them as well.

A Patterned Plan of Attack

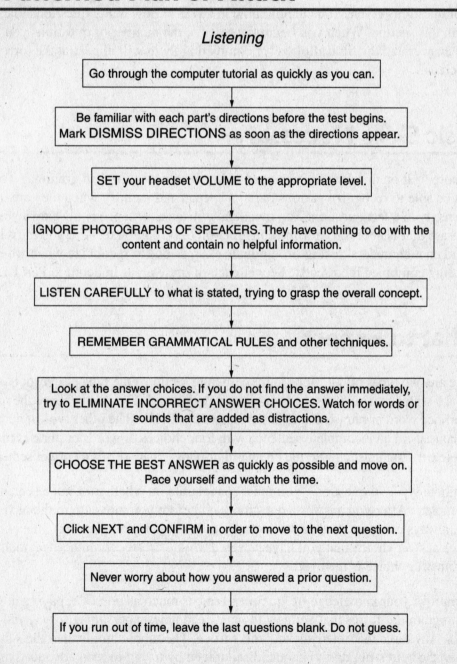

Listening

Go through the computer tutorial as quickly as you can.

↓

Be familiar with each part's directions before the test begins.
Mark DISMISS DIRECTIONS as soon as the directions appear.

↓

SET your headset VOLUME to the appropriate level.

↓

IGNORE PHOTOGRAPHS OF SPEAKERS. They have nothing to do with the content and contain no helpful information.

↓

LISTEN CAREFULLY to what is stated, trying to grasp the overall concept.

↓

REMEMBER GRAMMATICAL RULES and other techniques.

↓

Look at the answer choices. If you do not find the answer immediately, try to ELIMINATE INCORRECT ANSWER CHOICES. Watch for words or sounds that are added as distractions.

↓

CHOOSE THE BEST ANSWER as quickly as possible and move on.
Pace yourself and watch the time.

↓

Click NEXT and CONFIRM in order to move to the next question.

↓

Never worry about how you answered a prior question.

↓

If you run out of time, leave the last questions blank. Do not guess.

The Structure section of the TOEFL test measures your ability to recognize appropriate standard written English. This section includes questions that test your knowledge of grammar, idiomatic expressions, vocabulary, and other aspects of correct English.

The Structure section includes two question types (described in this chapter), which are interspersed. You will answer between 20 and 25 questions in 15 to 20 minutes. The time that you are given to complete the section depends on the number of questions given. You cannot know in advance how many questions to expect in this section. When you begin the section, the number of questions you must answer and the time allotted for completing them will appear at the top of the screen.

Basic Skills Necessary

To score well on this section, you need to know standard English grammar. You must be able to recognize various parts of speech and identify when they are used incorrectly in a test question. You must know when a sentence is missing a word or phrase that is necessary for the construction to be complete. And you must have a solid enough understanding of idiomatic expressions to recognize when words are being combined incorrectly. I cover each of these areas in detail in Part III.

What to Expect

There are two types of questions in the Structure section. One type of question shows a sentence with four words or phrases underlined. You must choose the one underlined word or phrase that is incorrect and click on it. The other type of question consists of an incomplete sentence with four choices of words or phrases that complete it. You must choose the one word or phrase that creates a correct sentence.

With both types of questions, you must concentrate on whether or not a sentence is complete. After you answer a question (and before you move on to the next one), always analyze whether the sentence as a whole is complete with the correction or answer choice that you have selected. If you create a sentence fragment, your answer choice is incorrect.

To improve your knowledge of grammar, read as much as possible, paying attention to grammar forms that are new to you. Read newspapers, magazines, and books. Any topic that interests you will suffice. The more complicated the subject matter, the better, but don't become discouraged by trying to read advanced magazines or complicated newspaper articles that are too far above your level.

Listening to books on tape is also a great way to improve your grammar (as well as your listening comprehension) if you can pay attention to the structure of sentences while also following the story.

Incomplete Sentences

Directions: You will be shown incomplete sentences with a blank indicating where a word or phrase needs to be added. Choose the word or phrase that most correctly completes the sentence.

Sample

> **Q.** While it is understandable that a going business with existing customers and name recognition will be purchased by another company, it is surprising that companies would purchase an internet domain name _____ in business for an incredible sum of money.
>
>   **A.** that it has never been used
>
>   **B.** that has never been used
>
>   **C.** that never been used
>
>   **D.** never to be use

A is incorrect because it contains the pronoun *it*, but the word *that* is a relative pronoun. **C** is incorrect because you cannot have a past participle of *be* (*been*) without an auxiliary *has*. **D** is incorrect because the word *use* is not in past participle form. Therefore, the correct answer is **B**.

Choosing the Incorrect Word or Phrase

Directions: You will see sentences with four underlined words or phrases. Choose the one word or phrase that is incorrect in standard written English.

Sample

> **Q.** After <u>create</u> [**A**] interest in automobile racing on the hard-packed sand of the beach in Daytona Beach Florida, William France, Sr. <u>built</u> [**B**] the Daytona International Speedway on property <u>leased</u> [**C**] from the county and lived to see it <u>develop</u> [**D**] into a major international attraction.

The answer is **A,** *create.* The sentence should read *After having created, After he had created,* or *After creating.* A verb in simple form cannot follow a preposition. Only a gerund (verb+*ing*) or a clause (subject + verb) can follow a preposition.

How to Prepare for the Structure Section

To improve your knowledge of grammar, read as much as possible, paying attention to grammar forms that are new to you. Follow these tips:

- Read newspapers, magazines, and books.

- Listen to books on tape, paying attention to sentence structures.

- Go through all the grammar rules in Part III of this book and become thoroughly familiar with them.

A Patterned Plan of Attack

Structure

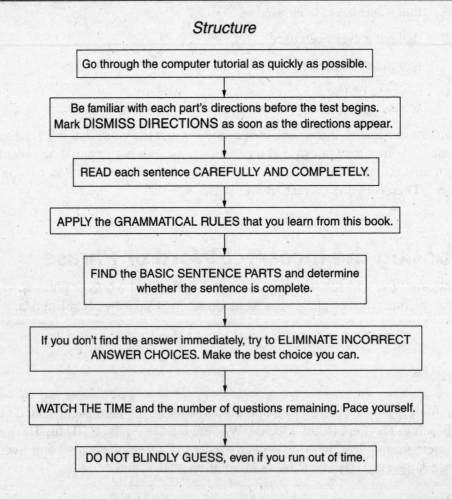

Go through the computer tutorial as quickly as possible.

Be familiar with each part's directions before the test begins. Mark DISMISS DIRECTIONS as soon as the directions appear.

READ each sentence CAREFULLY AND COMPLETELY.

APPLY the GRAMMATICAL RULES that you learn from this book.

FIND the BASIC SENTENCE PARTS and determine whether the sentence is complete.

If you don't find the answer immediately, try to ELIMINATE INCORRECT ANSWER CHOICES. Make the best choice you can.

WATCH THE TIME and the number of questions remaining. Pace yourself.

DO NOT BLINDLY GUESS, even if you run out of time.

The Reading section measures your ability to read and understand academic reading passages, including your knowledge of English vocabulary.

Basic Skills Necessary

To succeed in this section, you need to be able to read and understand English. You should have a sufficient knowledge of vocabulary and grammar to follow a fairly sophisticated passage, understand the difference between major ideas and details, and discern vocabulary definitions.

What to Expect

Reading section questions are based on major topics, subtopics, and details presented in a reading passage. Approximately 20 percent of the questions in this section are vocabulary questions, and all vocabulary words are contained in the reading passages.

Several question types exist in this section. You may be asked to pick out a correct answer from four possible choices, or you may be asked to click on a word in a passage that has the same meaning as another word. In addition, the Reading section frequently tests your understanding of pronouns and their antecedents. Sometimes four possible choices are provided, and sometimes you're asked to click on the word in the passage that is the antecedent of the pronoun in question. Occasionally, you're required to identify the most logical place to insert a new sentence into a paragraph in the reading.

Sometimes you're asked to choose a correct picture, word, phrase or diagram based on what the passage describes. Sometimes you also need to match pictures, words, phrases, or diagrams with other items similar to them. (However, there were no questions like this on a recent TOEFL test administration.) For example, you might be given the word *blue* and asked whether the word *color, shape,* or *size* best describes that word.

The quality of the passages in the Reading section may surprise you. They rarely consist of more than a couple of paragraphs, and generally, they don't have formal introductions and conclusions.

Concentrate on the topic sentence of each paragraph and read the entire passage, but don't spend too much time trying to understand it. Read the passage quickly and move on to the questions. You can return to the reading passage as you answer each question. The Reading section is not computer-adaptive, which means that everybody taking the test receives the same questions, regardless of whether they answered previous questions correctly or incorrectly. Therefore, you don't have a *Confirm* button on your computer screen during this section. Also, you can skip questions and return to them during the test, but there isn't a device on the computer screen to show you which questions you've skipped (which would make it easier to return to the questions you've skipped). Therefore, you have to click back through the questions in order to find the questions that you've left unanswered. Even though you're not required to answer each question in the Reading section before proceeding, I recommend that you do so.

Each reading passage appears on the screen, and then after you've read the entire passage, the questions relating to that passage appear. You can't skip any part of the reading passage. The computer system won't permit you to skip to the questions before the entire passage appears on your computer screen. Therefore, you should quickly read the entire passage before proceeding to the questions.

At the top of the reading passage, the words *Beginning, More Available,* and *End* appear. These words tell you your place in the reading passage. If you see *Beginning* at the top of the screen, you're seeing the very beginning of the passage. If you see *More Available,* you're in the middle of the text, and neither the beginning nor the end currently appears on the screen. If you see *End,* the last sentences of the passage appear on the screen.

To proceed through the passage, click the arrow button. If you click the bottom arrow, you'll slowly move through the reading passage. If you click within the bar that appears above the arrow, you'll move a page at a time. Because most readings are two screens long, usually clicking in the bar will bring you to the bottom of the passage. If you read to the bottom of the first screen and then click in the bar above the bottom arrow, you'll see the entire second screen of the passage.

The time that remains for you to read passages and answer questions is shown on your computer screen. Pay attention to the time. Before you begin the Reading section, you're told how many readings and questions you'll have and how much time you're given to complete the section. Divide the number of readings into the time that you're given so you can control how much time you spend on each set of passages and questions.

When you've finished reading a passage, click *Proceed*. You can still see the entire reading passage if you need it, and vocabulary and other questions that require you to view parts of the passage are generally presented in order. When questions that require you to review parts of the passage are asked, the area of the passage that it applies to will automatically appear to show the marked word or phrase. However, when the test asks a general question that doesn't refer to a portion of the text, the reading passage moves back to the beginning. You can scroll through the passage at that point if necessary.

In Part III of this book, you can practice answering the various types of reading questions that follow full reading passages. The following directions are very similar to those that you'll see on the TOEFL test:

Directions: This section measures your ability to read and understand written English similar to that which you may encounter in a college or university setting. Read each passage and answer the questions based on what the passage states or implies.

You'll encounter many varieties of questions in the Reading section. For example, you may be asked to do one of several things:

- **Click on the correct answer.** You must choose the single best answer to the question. On the computer screen, the answer choices are in the shape of ovals; the oval becomes filled in when you click on it. In this book, each answer choice is assigned a letter from A to D.

- **Click on the correct two answers.** You must click on the two best answers. On the computer screen, the answer choices are in the shape of squares; an *x* appears in each square when you click on it. In this book, each answer choice is assigned a letter from A to D.

- **Click on words or phrases in a specific order.** On the computer screen, you must click on highlighted words in a specific order. In this book, you will be asked to list answer choices in a specific order from A to D.

- **Click on pictures or drawings.** You're shown several images and asked to click on the one that depicts what the question asks. In this book, you'll be asked to choose among answers A through D.

Other questions in the Reading section require that you click on the correct answer in the passage, and you may be asked to do one of several things:

- **Click the word that means the same as another word.** Some vocabulary questions require that you click on the word in the passage that means the same as a word given in the question.

- **Click the referent of a pronoun.** To test your knowledge of pronoun antecedents, you must click on the noun or noun phrase in the passage to which a given pronoun refers.

- **Click the sentence in which a particular subject is discussed.** In this type of question, you're asked to identify where in the passage a particular issue is presented.

- **Click on the place in a passage where a specific sentence could fit.** You're given a sentence that does not appear in the original passage, and you must determine the most logical place for it in the reading passage.

Multiple-choice questions may require you to identify main ideas, significant points, inferences, details, vocabulary words, or referents. Questions that address main ideas may include:

- What is the passage mainly about?

- What aspect of . . . does the passage mainly discuss?

- What is a good title for the passage?

Questions that address significant points and inferences may read:

- All the following are mentioned about . . . except:
- All the following are reasons for . . . except:
- According to the passage, all the following factors affect . . . except:
- The passage supports which of the following statements about . . . ?
- In stating . . . , the author means that:
- The author mentions . . . as examples of:
- The author states. . . to imply that:
- The author mentioned . . . in the passage because:
- What can be inferred about . . . ?

Questions that deal with details in the passage may look like this:

- The main point that the author makes about . . . is that . . . :
- According to the passage, what/when/why/where/how . . . ?
- According to the passage, what is one effect of . . . ?

Vocabulary and referent questions may include the following phrases:

- The word . . . in the passage is closest in meaning to the word:
- The phrase . . . in the passage is closest in meaning to:
- The word . . . in the passage refers to:

Preparing for the Reading Section

The same methods that I suggest for improving your listening and grammar skills are also great for reading. Read, read, read. Read whatever you can, whenever you can. When you don't have time to read printed material, listening to recorded books is helpful, even for this section of the test. Read items that are as complicated as you are able to understand. Also, pay particular attention to new vocabulary words, including the use of prefixes, suffixes, and roots. Practice determining the meaning of a vocabulary word from its context. Likewise, learn to connect pronoun references to their antecedents. (Part III of this book provides detailed information about connecting pronoun references to their antecedents.)

A Patterned Plan of Attack

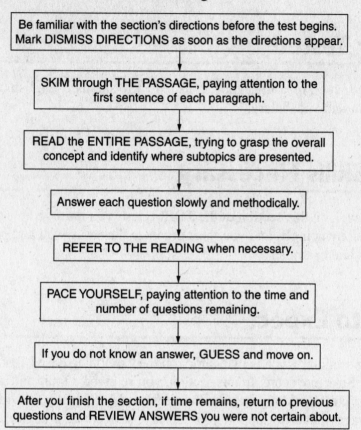

Reading

Be familiar with the section's directions before the test begins. Mark DISMISS DIRECTIONS as soon as the directions appear.

SKIM through THE PASSAGE, paying attention to the first sentence of each paragraph.

READ the ENTIRE PASSAGE, trying to grasp the overall concept and identify where subtopics are presented.

Answer each question slowly and methodically.

REFER TO THE READING when necessary.

PACE YOURSELF, paying attention to the time and number of questions remaining.

If you do not know an answer, GUESS and move on.

After you finish the section, if time remains, return to previous questions and REVIEW ANSWERS you were not certain about.

WRITING SECTION

Ability Tested

The Writing section measures your ability to write standard English using accurate grammar and vocabulary.

Basic Skills Necessary

To perform well on this section of the TOEFL test, you must be able to write clearly and convincingly, and you must organize the essay well and provide sufficient details and examples.

What to Expect

The Writing section, which is mandatory on the Computer-Based Test, makes up a part of your Structure score. In this section, you're given a topic and asked to create an essay. You should organize and write the essay carefully, providing sufficient examples and evidence to support your thesis. Use accurate grammatical structures as well as proper vocabulary. Don't try to use grammar or vocabulary with which you are not totally familiar. A mistake will cost you points. Rather, write simply and concisely. Complicated grammar and vocabulary are *not* required.

Examples of essays provided by the Educational Testing Service indicate that you don't need to develop an introductory or closing paragraph in as much detail as you might in a writing class, but you do need to develop the body paragraphs in the essay. Most writing teachers would say that you shouldn't use a single sentence as an introductory or conclusion paragraph, but for the TOEFL test, one sentence for each is probably sufficient.

You have 30 minutes to plan and write the essay. You may hand-write it or type it, but you're given a computer tutorial regardless of whether you want to write or type your essay. After taking the tutorial, you're asked a second time whether you want to type or hand-write the essay. The word processor used for the TOEFL test is rudimentary, but it's not difficult to learn. Make up your mind before you attend the test whether you are going to hand-write or type the essay.

You'll receive scratch paper on which you may organize your thoughts; do *not* bring your own scratch paper to the test. What you write on your scratch paper doesn't affect your score in any way, but you do have to leave the paper when you conclude the test. (The test administrators must ensure that you don't take information regarding the test with you.)

All possible writing topics are available in advance both in the TOEFL Bulletin and on the TOEFL Web Site. When you take the test, you receive only one topic; you will *not* have any options. There are so many possible topics that it's not worthwhile for you to write essays in advance on every topic.

Write several essays prior to taking the test, and try to have some of them scored. If you don't know a writing instructor who can do this, you may use my Essay Grading Service. You may send an essay by mail along with a check or money order payable to TOEFL Preparation Course, LLC. The mailing address is:

TOEFL Preparation Course, LLC

1265 West Granada Blvd.

Suite 1

Ormond Beach, FL 32174 USA

You may also visit www.toeflcourse.com to see whether I have added other possible procedures for submitting essays for grading.

The fee for reviewing one essay is $20. If you submit more than one essay at one time, you may deduct $2 per additional essay submitted. (That is, the fee for two essays is $38, for three $56, and so on.) The discount is only applicable for essays submitted together, and it does not matter whether the essays are written by the same student or different students. If you provide an e-mail address, the scoring will be sent to you via e-mail.

The essay is critical to your TOEFL test score. It makes up one half of your Structure score. For this reason, you won't receive a final Structure score immediately after you take the Computer-Based Test. The Structure score cannot be finalized until your essay is graded, which generally takes up to two weeks.

In Part III of this book, you can practice constructing essays for the Writing section of the test. The following directions are very similar to those that you'll see during the actual exam:

Directions: This section measures your ability to write in standard English, including your ability to organize ideas and support your thoughts with sufficient examples and evidence. You will be provided one topic and will be given 30 minutes in which to organize and write the essay. You may make notes on a separate piece of paper. Type or hand-write the essay.

How to Prepare for the Writing Section

The best way to improve your writing is to read and write as much as possible. Pay attention to what you read and how the author has organized thoughts and supported his or her thesis with details. Likewise, practice writing. Have somebody review your essays by comparing your writing to the TOEFL test criteria, as I discuss in detail in Part III.

To write a good essay, you must organize your thoughts. Before you write, make an outline showing the major topics that you'll tackle and the examples that you'll use to support these topics. You must address the essay question directly. The position that you take in your essay doesn't matter, but you must answer the question asked and not get sidetracked. A well developed introduction and conclusion is always helpful but not as important to your TOEFL score as well written body paragraphs.

A Patterned Plan of Attack

Writing

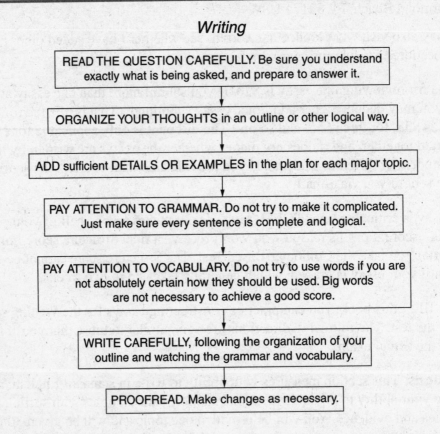

READ THE QUESTION CAREFULLY. Be sure you understand exactly what is being asked, and prepare to answer it.

ORGANIZE YOUR THOUGHTS in an outline or other logical way.

ADD sufficient DETAILS OR EXAMPLES in the plan for each major topic.

PAY ATTENTION TO GRAMMAR. Do not try to make it complicated. Just make sure every sentence is complete and logical.

PAY ATTENTION TO VOCABULARY. Do not try to use words if you are not absolutely certain how they should be used. Big words are not necessary to achieve a good score.

WRITE CAREFULLY, following the organization of your outline and watching the grammar and vocabulary.

PROOFREAD. Make changes as necessary.

PART III

DETAILED REVIEW
OF ITEMS TESTED

In this section, you get an overview of the items you should study to be prepared for the Listening section of the TOEFL test. Many grammar items are explained in greater detail in the Structure chapter that follows this one, so be sure to flip to that chapter for more information. This section treats the understanding of grammar structures whereas the structure section deals with the formal construction of some of the same items. For many of the items tested in the Listening section, sample questions are provided here that show you what a typical TOEFL test question might look like. If you know an English-speaking person, ask him or her to read these sample questions aloud. Hearing them will help you prepare for the test more effectively than just reading them.

Tenses and Time Indicators

On the Listening section, it's important to be able to recognize the different verb tenses.

Pay close attention to verb tenses, and watch for words that indicate time, such as after, before, while, when, next, once, and later.

Samples

Man: I haven't heard whether John is going on the cruise.

Woman: He'd made other arrangements before the cruise was planned.

Q. Narrator: What does the woman mean?

- **A.** John will attend the cruise.
- **B.** John is changing his arrangements.
- **C.** John still has to make his plans.
- **D.** John is not attending the cruise.

The answer is **D,** "John is not attending the cruise." The past perfect tense and the word *before* indicate the time.

Woman: Betty took the wrong bus and missed the meeting.

Man: I know. She showed up when it was over.

Q. Narrator: What do the speakers mean?

A. Betty is coming to the meeting.

B. Betty did not go to the meeting.

C. Betty might not come to the meeting.

D. Betty is on the bus.

The answer is **B,** "Betty did not go to the meeting." The sentence is in the past tense.

Man: Did Chuck call before or after the class?

Woman: He called during the class.

Q. Narrator: What did the woman say?

A. He did not call.

B. He called while the class was going on.

C. He called before the class.

D. He called after the class.

The answer is **B,** "He called while the class was going on," because *while* means the same as *during.*

Passive Voice

A sentence can be constructed either in the active or passive voice. In an *active* sentence, the subject performs the action. In a *passive* sentence, the subject receives the action. To create a passive sentence from an active sentence, the order of the active sentence is reversed. For the Listening section, you must be able to understand active versus passive voice so you can identify who performs the action and who receives the action.

Samples

> Woman: Where is David? I thought he was going to be here.
>
> Man: He was chosen to lead the committee, and it is meeting tonight.
>
> Q. Narrator: What does the man mean about David?
>
> A. He will be here soon.
>
> B. He chose the committee members.
>
> C. He has been appointed as the leader of the committee.
>
> D. He chose not to serve on the committee.

The answer is **C,** "He has been appointed as the leader of the committee," a passive sentence. Answer choice **B** might be tempting, but it reverses the order of who performed the action and who received the action.

> Man: What did Rafael tell the officer about the accident?
>
> Woman: He said the car was struck by the truck.
>
> Q. Narrator: What does the woman mean?
>
> A. The car avoided being hit.
>
> B. The truck hit the car.
>
> C. The car hit the truck.
>
> D. The truck took evasive action.

The answer is **B,** "The truck hit the car," which means the same as "the car was struck by the truck."

Appositives

An *appositive* is a reduced relative clause, which leaves a noun phrase. The noun phrase provides additional information about the noun. An appositive will often appear at the beginning of a sentence.

Gary Smith, *who is an excellent photographer*, will carry the weight.

relative clause

Gary Smith, *an excellent photographer*, will carry the weight.

reduced relative clause

An excellent photographer, Gary Smith will carry the weight.

appositive

Sample

> Woman: Do you know anything about the three students who are making the video display?
>
> Man: An excellent photographer, Gary Smith will carry the weight.
>
> Woman: You don't know the others?
>
> Q. Narrator: What does the man imply about the video producers?
>
>   A. One person will make it successful.
>
>   B. The group is made up of great photographers.
>
>   C. There is no hope for the video display.
>
>   D. Gary will load the equipment.

The answer is **A**, "One person will make it successful," because the appositive, "an excellent photographer," refers to Gary.

Modals

Modal auxiliaries are generally used to indicate something that is potential or uncertain. The modals are: *will, would, can, could, may, might, shall, should,* and *must*.

Sample

> Woman: Are you planning to go on the trip?
>
> Man: I may be able to.
>
> Q. Narrator: What does the man mean?
>
>   A. He is not sure whether he will go on the trip.
>
>   B. He will definitely go on the trip.
>
>   C. He will definitely not go on the trip.
>
>   D. He plans to go on the trip.

The answer is **A**, "He is not sure whether he will go on the trip," because the word *may* means the answer is unknown.

Conditional Sentences

A *conditional sentence* indicates that something will happen if another event happens first. In other words, one circumstance will occur under the condition that another circumstance occurs first. A conditional sentence can be *real* or *unreal*. If it's *real*, that means there is the potential for a result to occur in the future. If it's *unreal*, that means a result would have occurred already if a certain event happened, but in reality, the event didn't happen.

Conditional sentences each contain a clause beginning with the word *if*. This clause can appear as either the first or second clause in the sentence. A conditional sentence with a verb that's one step in the past means that it's contrary to fact, or *unreal*. That is, the opposite result occurred. Here is an example:

> If the bus hadn't already passed by, we would've been on time for our meeting.
> OR
> We would've been on time for our meeting if the bus hadn't already passed by.

If the bus hadn't already passed by means that the bus *did* pass by. This is a positive result because the clause is negative (the word *not* — contracted here as part of *hadn't* — makes it negative). Both of these sentences mean that the bus already passed by.

The other clause, *we would've been on time,* is also contrary to fact. It's a positive clause, so the idea is negative. It means we were *not* on time.

> If the bus had already passed by, there would be no people waiting.
> OR
> There would be no people waiting if the bus had already passed by.

The clause *If the bus had already passed by* is a positive clause, so it means that the bus did *not* pass by. The clause *there would be no people waiting* is a negative clause and, therefore, carries a positive meaning. It means there are people waiting.

> If the man had called the ambulance, the boy would've survived.
> OR
> The boy would've survived if the man had called the ambulance.

This means the man did *not* call the ambulance and the boy did *not* survive.

Notice the difference, however, when the verb is in the same tense as the context. This is called a *real condition* because the clauses don't have the opposite meaning.

If the bus arrives soon, we'll be on time for our meeting.

The bus still might arrive soon, and if it does, we'll be on time for our meeting.

If the man calls the ambulance, the boy can survive.

The man might call the ambulance, and the boy might survive.

Wish

The verb *wish* can convey the same concept as an unreal condition. It conveys a different concept from that of *hope*. Just like in the *unreal* conditional sentences you read above, the tense of the other verb in the sentence will be one step further in the past.

We *wish* the bus had arrived on time.

This means the bus did not arrive on time.

She *wishes* the man had called the ambulance.

This means the man did not call the ambulance.

Comparisons and Comparatives

Comparisons indicate degrees of difference or similarity.

Equal Comparisons

An *equal comparison* indicates that the two nouns or noun phrases in a sentence are (or are not) exactly the same.

This car is as old as that one.

This sentence means that the age of the two cars is equal.

This car is not as old as that one.

This sentence means that this car is newer than the other one.

In a *negative equal comparison,* you can substitute the word *so* for *as* without altering the meaning of the sentence.

His job is not *as* difficult as mine.

His job is not *so* difficult as mine.

Unequal Comparisons

Unequal comparisons imply that two or more entities are comparable to a greater or lesser degree. Some comparatives are formed by adding the suffix *-er* to the base adjective or adverb. Other comparatives are formed by adding the words *more* or *less* before the adjective or adverb. In general, it's more common to use *more* to create a comparative form from an adverb.

> John's grades are <u>*higher*</u> *than* his sister's.
> adjective
>
> He studies *more <u>frequently</u> than* she does.
> adverb
>
> This year's exhibit is *more <u>impressive</u> than* last year's.
> adjective

You can further intensify unequal comparisons by adding *much* or *far* before the comparative form. For example:

> This house is *far more expensive than* the others we've seen.
> This book is *much less interesting than* the one I read last month.

Double Comparatives

Double comparative sentences involve a comparative construction at the beginning of both clauses.

> *The sooner* we finish the project, *the sooner* we can start the next one.

This sentence means the same as, "As soon as we finish the project, we can start the next one."

> The more he ate, the hungrier he became.

This sentence means that as he ate more, he became more hungry.

Superlatives

The *superlative* compares three or more items, one of which is superior or inferior to the others. To form a superlative, add *-est* to an adjective or place the words *most* or *least* before an adjective or adverb.

> This is the *most powerful* car of the three.
> This house is the *least expensive* of all.

Superlatives that involve adverbs are generally formed by using *most* or *least* rather than *-est.*

That child behaves the *most <u>carelessly</u>* of all.
adverb

Negatives

In the Listening section, you must pay attention to whether a sentence is positive or negative.

The basic way to make a sentence negative is to add the word *not* to the phrase or to add the contraction *n't* to the verb.

Trisha is *not* ready to leave yet.
Trisha *isn't* ready to leave yet.

Other negative indicators include no, never, nobody, none, and nothing.

Limiting Words

Another way to create a negative sentence is to use limiting words and phrases.

Commonly used limiting words and phrases include hardly, seldom, never, barely, scarcely, rarely, no sooner, nowhere, not once, not often, not only, not until, only, only by, only then, only with, and under no circumstances.

When these words or phrases appear at the beginning of a sentence, they signal that the normal order of a sentence will be reversed. The normal sentence order is subject + verb. In a sentence that is begun by a limiting word or phrase, an auxiliary verb (a form of *have, be,* or *do*) appears before the subject.

She had *hardly* finished when she collapsed with exhaustion.
Hardly had she finished the race when she collapsed with exhaustion.

Both of these sentences mean that she collapsed as soon as she finished the race.

Never before have so many people been employed as they are now.

This sentence means that more people are employed now than have been in the past.

Under no circumstances will the judge reconsider her decision.

This means that the judge won't reconsider the decision under any circumstances.

No sooner had she completed the work than she went to sleep.

This sentence means that she went to sleep as soon as she completed the work.

Only with great care can the surgeon reconstruct the infant's heart.

This sentence means that the surgeon can reconstruct the infant's heart only if he or she uses great care.

Not often does a hurricane of this magnitude approach the coast.

This means that a hurricane of this magnitude doesn't approach the coast often.

Already and *Yet*

The word *already* indicates that a sentence has a positive meaning. The word *yet* is used to create a negative meaning.

Positive: Sandy has *already* finished work on her degree.
Negative: Sandy hasn't finished working on her degree *yet*.

Another way to use *yet* is to place it after the *have* and place the rest of the verb in the infinitive.

Sandy has *yet* to finish working on her degree.

Affirmative Agreement

To describe how two subjects perform or receive the same action, use *affirmative agreement,* in which the conjunction *and* is followed by a simple statement that includes either the word *so* or the word *too*. The word order of the second (simple) statement differs depending on whether you use *so* or *too*.

Pat is a professor, and Lynn is *too*.
Pat is a professor, and *so* is Lynn.

Both sentences mean that Pat and Lynn are professors.

She will work for me tonight, and he will *too*.
She will work for me tonight, and *so* will he.

These sentences mean that both people will work for the speaker tonight.

Susan drives a Lexus, and my sister does *too*.
Susan drives a Lexus, and *so* does my sister.

These sentences mean that Susan and the speaker's sister both drive a Lexus.

Negative Agreement

Sentences that contain negative agreement work much the same way as sentences that contain positive agreement. However, in order to indicate that the two subjects mentioned in this type of sentence have *not* done something, the words *either* and *neither* are used instead of the words *so* and *too*.

I didn't see Michelle this morning, and Joe didn't *either.*

I didn't see Michelle this morning, and *neither* did Joe.

These two sentences mean that both the speaker and Joe did *not* see Michelle this morning.

She won't be going to the meeting, and her colleagues won't *either.*

She won't be going to the meeting, and *neither* will her colleagues.

These sentences mean that both she and her colleagues will *not* attend the meeting.

Tag Questions

In a *tag question,* the speaker makes a statement but adds a brief question at the end that requests the listener to verify that the statement is true. The form is created by using the auxiliary from the main sentence (a form of *be* or form of *have*) or a form of *do* as the opening word of the tag question, and then repeating the noun or, more likely, replacing it with a pronoun. The auxiliary in the tag will be positive if the main sentence is negative and negative if the main sentence is positive.

Bob is a good student, isn't he?

The verb comes from the *is* in the sentence, and the pronoun comes from the noun.

Bob and Mary are good students, aren't they?

The verb comes from the *are* in the sentence and the pronoun comes from the nouns.

There are only 28 days in February, *aren't there?*

Notice in a sentence beginning with *there*, the pseudo noun *there* also appears in the tag.

You and I talked with the professor yesterday, *didn't we?*

You won't be leaving for another hour, *will you?*

Cause and Effect

There are several ways to show cause and effect that you need to be able to recognize to score successfully on the Listening section.

Because and *Because Of*

The word *because* and the phrase *because of* show cause and effect. The cause is shown immediately after the word *because* or the phrase *because of*.

> Jill quit her job *because* she was admitted to the university.
> Jill quit her job *because of* her admission to the university.

Both sentences show that Jill was admitted to the university, and the result was that she quit her job. You can also reverse the word order of either sentence:

> *Because* she was admitted to the university, Jill quit her job.
> *Because of* her admission to the university, Jill quit her job.

So

So means the same as *because* except that the result, not the cause, appears immediately after the word or phrase. For example:

> Jill was admitted to the university *so* she quit her job.

So is sometimes followed by *that* in a slightly different cause and effect sentence. In the following sentence, the word *that* is optional.

> Jill quit her job *so that* she could attend college.
> Jill quit her job *so* she could attend college.

The Reason . . . That

The phrase *the reason . . . that* also indicates cause and effect. The phrase *the reason* is used as the subject of the sentence, as shown in the following example.

> *The reason* she quit her job was *that* she was admitted to the university.

Other Phrases Indicating Cause and Effect

Sentences that show cause to the left of the verb and effect to the right of the verb contain verbs such as the following: **cause, lead to, result in, produce,** and **contribute to.**

Smoking *causes* cancer.

Driving a car in salt water or on a salty street can *result in* rust.

Sentences that show the result to the left of the verb and the cause to the right contain verb phrases such as the following: **be due to, result from, be caused by,** and **stem from.**

Cancer *results from* smoking.

This problem *stems from* their lack of preparation.

Other words that show cause and effect include **therefore, consequently, as a result,** and **thus.**

Marjorie didn't receive a response to her application; *consequently,* she applied for another job.

Causatives

Causative verbs are used to indicate that one person causes a second person to do something. A person can cause somebody to do something for him or her by paying, asking, or forcing the other person. The common causative verbs are **have, get,** and **make,** and each is explained in detail in the following sections.

Have and Get

Have and *get* both imply that the person who performs the task does so voluntarily. (The word *make,* discussed in the next section, is a stronger expression of force.) The clause that follows *have* or *get* may be active or passive.

Chuck *had* Maria complete the forms.

This active sentence means that Maria completed the forms because Chuck caused her to do so (either by asking or telling her to do so).

Chuck *got* Maria to complete the forms.
Chuck *got* the forms completed by Maria.
Chuck *had* the forms completed by Maria.

These sentences mean the same thing, but the first sentence is active while the second and third sentences are passive.

The judge will *have* the bailiff locate the parties.
The judge will *have* the parties located by the bailiff.

In both cases, the judge arranged for the bailiff to locate the parties. But again, the first sentence in this example is active while the second sentence is passive.

Make

Make can only be followed by a clause in the active voice. The verb *make* is stronger than the verbs *have* or *get*; it means *force*.

The thief *made* the man hand him the wallet.
The police officer will *make* the prisoners empty their pockets.

Words that Sound Alike

There's no sense in studying lists of words that sound like other words as you prepare for the TOEFL test. In fact, confusion of vowel and consonant sounds varies depending on your native language. People from some language backgrounds may confuse the sounds *p* and *b,* while people from other backgrounds won't have that problem. Likewise, others may experience difficulties with the sounds of *i* and *e,* such as in the words *feel* and *fill.* Although you should not try to memorize lists of words that sound alike, you should pay attention to the sounds that are similar as you learn and experience English.

Sample

Man: Did Holly complete the forms required for the university?

Woman: She wasn't feeling well, but she said she would fill them out tonight.

Q. Narrator: What does the woman say about Holly?

    A. She has already completed the forms.

    B. She doesn't feel like completing the forms.

    C. She intends to complete the forms.

    D. She feels like she should refuse to complete the forms.

The answer is **C**, "She intends to complete the forms." Don't confuse the words *feel* and *fill*.

You may also run into *homophones,* which are words that sound identical to other words but are spelled differently and have different meanings. For example, a few homophones are: *beat* and *beet*; *great* and *grate*; *whole* and *hole*.

Remember: Don't spend your study time creating lists of homophones. Your chances of seeing one particular word on a TOEFL test are slim. However, make sure that you pay attention to words that look and sound alike when you read and listen to English. If you aren't certain of a word's exact meaning in a particular sentence, look it up in the dictionary. Or, if you're listening to a conversation and aren't sure which word a speaker is using, ask that person to explain.

Idioms and Idiomatic Expressions

Sometimes, when words are used together, the combination of words has a meaning different from the meaning of each individual word. We use the terms *idiom* or *idiomatic expression* to identify those word combinations.

Just like studying lists of words that sound alike, it makes little sense to study lists of idiomatic expressions as you prepare for the TOEFL test. You learn the meaning of idioms by exposing yourself to English as often as possible. Some idiomatic expressions are used by people of certain ages or in certain geographical areas but not by other people. You'll likely come across some such expressions in all sections of the TOEFL test, so be sure to pay attention to them during your studies of English.

Sample

> Man: Should somebody deliver the papers to the Dean's office?
> Woman: Don't look at me.
>
> **Q.** Narrator: What does the woman mean?
>
>   **A.** She doesn't intend to take the papers to the Dean's office.
>
>   **B.** She saw the papers.
>
>   **C.** She went to the office.
>
>   **D.** She will take the papers to the Dean.

The answer is **A,** "She doesn't intend to take the papers to the Dean's office." The expression *Don't look at me* doesn't mean that anyone is looking at the speaker with their eyes. *Don't look at me* is an idiomatic expression that means, "I'm not going to do it."

Problem Items

Certain words and phrases are frequently confused by students because of grammar or usage that is unique, or because they are so similar to other English words.

No Sooner

Although the phrase *the sooner* often appears in double comparative sentences (explained earlier in this chapter), *no sooner* has a different usage. If the expression *no sooner* appears at the beginning of a sentence, an auxiliary appears immediately after it, and the word *than* introduces the second clause. The auxiliary is a form of the verb *do, have,* or *be* used along with a main verb, like the *have* in *have made.* The phrase *no sooner* means the same as "just as soon as."

> *No sooner* had the rain started *than* it stopped.

This sentence means the same as, "Just as soon as the rain started, it stopped."

Remember, Stop, and Forget

Certain words are followed by the infinitive or a verb + *ing.* The words *remember, stop,* and *forget* can be followed by either, with a difference in meaning.

> Georgia *remembered to call* her doctor.

This sentence means that Georgia remembered it was necessary to call her doctor, and she called him.

Georgia *remembered calling* her doctor.

This sentence means that Georgia remembered that she had called her doctor in the past.

Georgia *forgot to call* her doctor.

This sentence means she was supposed to call her doctor but didn't because she forgot.

Georgia *forgot calling* her doctor.

This sentence means that she called her doctor and subsequently forgot that she had done so.

Henry *stopped* to work.

A sentence like this implies that we know Henry was doing something else, and he stopped doing that other thing in order to start working.

Henry *stopped* working.

This means that Henry had been working, but he stopped.

Let and Help

The words *let* and *help* are similar to causative verbs (described earlier in this chapter), but they create a different meaning than the verbs *have, get,* or *make. Let* means *allow. Help* means *assist.*

The professor *let* the students leave early.

This means that the professor allowed the students to leave early.

We should *let* her make her own decision.

This means that we should allow her to make her own decision.

Ann Marie *helped* her daughter write the essay.

This means that Ann Marie assisted her daughter in writing the essay.

Used To and Be Used To

The phrases *used to* and *be used to* have different meanings. The basic difference between *used to* and *be used to* is that *used to* involves a past custom or habit and *be used to* involves a current custom or habit. The following examples show the difference in meaning.

Belinda *used to* swim every day.

This sentence means that in the past, Belinda swam every day.

Belinda *is used to* swimming every day.

This means that Belinda is currently accustomed to swimming every day.

Be used to can also be used for a past idea by changing the verb *be* to past tense.

Belinda *was used to* swimming every day.

However, the phrase *be used to* can also have a second meaning, as the following example illustrates.

A fork *is used to* pierce food and carry it to the mouth.

This sentence means that the purpose of a fork is to pierce food and carry it to the mouth.

Would Rather

Would rather is a commonly used idiom that means *prefer*.

Bill *would rather* fly directly to Indianapolis instead of stopping in Atlanta.

This means that Bill prefers flying directly to Indianapolis instead of stopping in Atlanta.

Henry *would rather* have gone to New York than to St. Louis.

This means that Henry went to St. Louis, but he wanted to go to New York.

James *would rather not* eat at that restaurant.

This sentence means that James prefers not to eat at that restaurant.

The phrase *would rather that* sets up a conjunctive idea when followed by either the simple form of a verb or the past tense. A conjunctive is a sentence in which one person wishes or requires another to do something, and the sentence structure "...*that*...verb in simple form" is used. This concept is covered more fully in the Structure section. *Would rather that* is followed by the simple form when it has a subjunctive meaning.

She *would rather that* you call her tomorrow.

This means that she wants you to call tomorrow instead of some other time.

We *would rather that* he take this class.

This sentence means that we want him to take this class.

Would rather that is followed by the past tense when the meaning of the sentence is contrary to fact, such as with unreal conditions and the verb *wish*.

Rafael *would rather that* his paper *were* complete.

This means that Rafael wishes his paper were complete, but it's not complete.

When the verb that follows *would rather that* is in the past tense instead of in simple form, you know that the sentence is discussing a situation that did not occur, or a "past contrary to fact" concept.

Michelle *would rather that* Sheila had come to work yesterday.

This means that Michelle is unhappy because Sheila didn't come to work yesterday.

Phrasal Verbs

Phrasal verbs, also known as *verbal idioms,* are idiomatic expressions that begin with a verb and contain one or more prepositions. As with idioms, memorizing lists of these particular expressions as you study is not important. Generally, paying attention to them as you become more familiar with the English language is much more important.

Samples

> Man: Why is the president so angry?
> Woman: The chairmen of the two companies *broke off* discussions regarding the proposed merger.
>
> **Q.** Narrator: What does the woman mean?
>
>   **A.** The companies are negotiating the merger.
>
>   **B.** One chairman broke his word.
>
>   **C.** The chairmen discontinued discussing a merger.
>
>   **D.** One company revoked its merger agreement.

The answer is **C**. The phrasal verb *break off* means to "discontinue."

> Woman: Are Stephen and Brenda still planning to change majors?
>
> Man: Brenda has decided to, but Stephen is still looking into his options.
>
> **Q.** Narrator: What does the man mean?
>
> **A.** Brenda hasn't decided whether to change majors.
>
> **B.** Stephen is investigating the alternatives.
>
> **C.** Brenda isn't going to change her major.
>
> **D.** Stephen is looking for a list of options.

The answer is **B**. The phrasal verb *looking into* does not mean that Stephen is physically looking at something. The phrase indicates that Stephen is considering his choices.

Following are a few other common phrasal verbs, definitions, and sample sentences:

- *Bring up* means "initiate."

  The attorneys for the developer are likely to *bring up* some new defenses.

- *Call on* means "ask," and it can also mean "visit."

  The constitutional law professor enjoyed *calling on* students in class.

  The banker is required to *call on* several customers every week.

- *Care for* means "like," and it can also mean "take care of."

  The boy does not *care for* beets.

  She earned extra money last year *caring for* several young children.

- *Check out* means "to remove or borrow temporarily," and it can also mean "investigate."

  Please *check out* the file from central records.

  The detective is still trying to *check out* all possible leads.

- *Come down with* means "become ill with."

  If you don't take a flu shot, you're likely to *come down with* the flu.

- *Count on* means "depend on" or "rely on."

  You should not *count on* receiving the scholarship.

- *Do away with* means "eliminate."

  Because of the increasing cost of gasoline, some companies have *done away with* reimbursement of travel expenses.

- *Figure out* means "interpret or understand."

  We are trying to *figure out* the annual budget.

- *Find out* means "discover."

  The scientists are trying to *find out* why the Mars explorer was lost.

- *Pass out* (or *hand out*) means "distribute," and it can also mean to faint or lose consciousness.

  The attorney *passed out* documents.

  The attorney *passed out* and fell to the floor.

- *Pick out* means "select" or "choose."

  Please *pick out* a book to read.

- *Point out* means "indicate."

  The victim *pointed out* the culprit.

- *Put off* means "postpone."

  Don't *put off* till tomorrow what you can do today.

- *Take over* means "substitute."

  The co-pilot had to *take over* when the pilot suffered chest pains.

- *Talk over* means "discuss."

  The men *talked over* their dinner plans.

- *Try out* means "test."

  A company must *try out* a new product before introducing it.

- *Turn in* means "submit."

  Please *turn in* your application.

Idioms of Suggestion

Frequently, Listening section questions on the TOEFL test involve suggestions and invitations. The questions may ask you something such as, "What does the woman suggest that the man do?" To successfully answer these types of questions, you should become familiar with idiomatic expressions that are used when someone suggests something to another person.

Sample

> Man: I don't have enough time to finish the research for my paper.
>
> Woman: Why not try outlining what you have now?
>
> **Q.** Narrator: What does the woman suggest that the man do?
>
> **A.** Finish his research
>
> **B.** Start planning the writing before finishing the research
>
> **C.** Give up on the project
>
> **D.** Don't use research

The answer is **B.**

Common idiomatic expressions that are used to show a suggestion include:

- Why not . . . ?
- Why don't you . . .?
- Have you considered . . .?
- You might want to . . .
- (Maybe) you could . . .
- Try . . .
- You'd better . . .

- You'd be better off . . .
- If I were you, I would . . .
- You should . . .
- Shouldn't you . . .?
- What about . . . .?
- How about . . .?
- What if you . . .?

Commands and Indirect Commands

You also need to be familiar with commands and indirect commands for the Listening section of the TOEFL test.

A *command* is a sentence that begins with a verb in simple form. In command sentences, the subject *you* is understood but not stated.

Close the door.

Please, *turn off* the light.

Negative commands generally use the word *don't* (or the phrase *do not*) before the verb.

Don't close the door.

Please, *don't turn off* the light.

An *indirect command* is a sentence in which one person reports that another person has given a command. The verb appears in the infinitive instead of the simple form.

Jill asked Robert *to close* the door.

Maria asked Mike *not to turn off* the light.

Practice Exercise

To work through the following exercise, you need to use the first audio CD that is included in this book. Starting with Track 1 of the CD, you will hear people having brief conversations similar to those you will encounter during Part A of the Listening section of the TOEFL test. At the end of a conversation, you will hear a question that you must answer based on your understanding of what the speaker(s) said. Each question is printed below, along with answer choices. Mark your answer choices as you go along.

After you have completed this exercise and checked your answers, turn to the appendix of this book. The conversations that you heard on the CD are transcribed there. If you had any difficulty understanding what a speaker was saying, listen to the CD again, this time reading what is being said at the same time you listen to it. Do not turn to the appendix until you have worked through this exercise at least once by just listening to the CD.

CD A, Track 1

1. What does the man say about the report?

   A. He wasn't impressed by it.

   B. He hasn't even seen it yet.

   C. He thinks it's worth studying by the whole class.

   D. He hasn't been able to review it in detail yet.

2. What does the woman say about her car?

   A. She just had it painted.

   B. The school bus damaged it.

   C. She struck a bus while driving the car.

   D. She had her bumper replaced.

3. What does the woman imply about Mr. Adams?

   A. He is a skillful instructor.

   B. He has years of experience but doesn't explain things well.

   C. He is very knowledgeable.

   D. He is arrogant and has no teaching experience.

4. What do the speakers imply about Thalía?

   A. The man admires her looks.

   B. The man dislikes her.

   C. She doesn't sing well.

   D. She is an excellent actress.

5. What does the man imply about the exam?

    A. He thought it was unfair.

    B. He didn't prepare as well as he could have.

    C. He studied very hard but didn't pass the exam.

    D. He couldn't have done better on the exam.

6. What does the woman imply about Jane?

    A. Jane wishes she had known about the surprise.

    B. The surprise was a bad idea.

    C. Jane was aware of the surprise beforehand.

    D. Jane didn't like being surprised.

7. What is the man's problem?

    A. He forgot to take the exam.

    B. He made a mistake, which cost him a number of answers.

    C. He turned in his paper too late, so it didn't get scored.

    D. He is angry about the testing format.

8. What do the speakers imply about the documentary?

    A. It was overrated.

    B. It was boring.

    C. It was extremely interesting.

    D. They missed it.

9. What do the speakers say about the accident?

    A. The children got through it okay.

    B. The speakers have forgotten about it.

    C. The speakers don't like thinking about it.

    D. The speakers are grateful that nobody was seriously hurt.

10. What does the woman say about Brenda?

    A. She didn't know what to do.

    B. She used an auto repair manual.

    C. She wishes she still had her old job.

    D. She has experience as a mechanic.

11. What is the woman's problem?

    A. She isn't sure whether to report something.

    B. She is distressed that somebody knows what she did.

    C. She is angry about a contract.

    D. She wanted to ask a question.

12. What do the speakers mean?

    A. They're tired.

    B. The woman is worried about the man's anger.

    C. They feel refreshed.

    D. They broke their table.

13. What does the woman suggest that the man do?

   A. Give Heather more freedom.

   B. Give up on Heather.

   C. Discipline Heather.

   D. Be more involved in Heather's life.

14. What do the speakers mean?

   A. The man is retiring for good.

   B. The woman is pleased that the man is leaving.

   C. The woman doesn't care for the current management.

   D. The man is temporarily turning things over to the woman.

15. What does the man mean about Jeff?

   A. He is studying.

   B. He hasn't made up his mind.

   C. He is very much against the issue that the man promotes.

   D. He isn't aware of what the man and woman are discussing.

Answers for the Practice Exercise

1. D.	6. C.	11. A.
2. B.	7. B.	12. A.
3. D.	8. C.	13. A.
4. A.	9. C.	14. D.
5. B.	10. D.	15. C.

The Structure section tests your knowledge of *standard written English*, which is not always the same as spoken English. This chapter provides you with general rules that describe how standard written English is typically used; to find the rules as you study, look for text with a shaded gray background. Often, when you are reading, conversing, or taking the TOEFL test, you'll be able to apply these rules to your use and understanding of English.

Part of the challenge of taking the TOEFL test is that its questions sometimes involve complex and multiple issues that aren't so easy to discern. A good strategy when taking the test is to ignore extra words in a sentence that make a particular rule hard to recognize. But remember also that the rules in this chapter describe only typical usage; like most rules, they can be broken on occasion. Try not to be alarmed if a rule doesn't seem to work for a specific sentence.

In this chapter, I use the following symbols:

- Parentheses ( ) indicate that a word or phrase is optional; a rule will still be true whether that word or phrase is included or not.

- Brackets { } indicate that you can choose between two or more words or parts of speech; whichever you choose, the rule will still hold true. A backslash separates the two choices.

Keep in mind that you learn a language by reading and communicating, paying attention to new usage, and studying slowly and methodically. Studying rules shouldn't replace the slow, methodical learning of the language. When you come across a rule during casual conversation or as you read, pay attention to it and how it works in the particular sentence. If you notice people disregarding the rule in conversational English, don't be alarmed. Sometimes spoken English is not the same as the standard written English that is the subject of the TOEFL test.

Structure questions typically test one of the following items:

- **Sentence structure.** The sentence structure questions test more than a word or two; they test your ability to make a sentence complete. A sentence must have a subject, verb, and perhaps a complement. Sentence structure questions also test your understanding of subordinate clauses, which must not be independent clauses.

- **Word order.** Word order questions are generally more detail-oriented than sentence structure questions. They test, for example, your understanding that an adjective should appear before the noun it modifies, not after it.

- **Word form.** These questions test your ability to recognize which form of a word should be used in a given situation. For example, a word form question might require you to determine that an adjective form of a word is being used when the noun form of the word is required. Word form questions also include recognizing which ending should be on a word. For example, you may need to recognize if a plural ending on a noun should be singular, a singular designation on a verb should be plural, a verb ending should indicate a different tense, and so on.

- **Word choice.** The word choice type of question tests your understanding of idiomatic expressions, of which prepositions to use with certain words, of problem words that are sometimes confused, and so on.

- **Missing or extra words.** The missing or extra word problems can sometimes overlap with some of the other categories, but I treat them separately because sometimes they are easier to recognize than some of the other question types.

Sentence Structure

To score well on sentence structure questions, you should have a strong understanding of basic sentence structures in standard written English and of parts of speech. The following sections help you strengthen your knowledge of sentence structure and provide sample questions so you can test yourself.

One of the most important subjects tested in the Structure section is the basic sentence structure in English. The first rule to remember about standard written English is this:

Every sentence must have a subject and a conjugated verb.

With this rule in mind, you may think that identifying an English sentence is easy. However, keep in mind that a clause also has a subject and a verb, and some types of clauses cannot be considered complete sentences. An *independent clause* can stand on its own as a sentence; it doesn't need another clause in order to be complete. But a *dependent clause,* despite having a subject and a conjugated verb, cannot stand on its own as a complete sentence; it contains a word that indicates it must be combined with an independent clause in order to create a complete sentence. For example, the clause *because she went to the doctor* contains both a subject, *she*, and a conjugated verb, *went*, but the word *because* indicates that it is a dependent clause and cannot stand on its own. Clauses are discussed later in this chapter in the "Phrases and Clauses" section.

If a sentence contains a complement or a direct object, it generally appears immediately after the verb or verb phrase. If there is a modifier, it generally appears after the complement. The following table illustrates the rule of this typical sentence structure.

Subject	Verb	Complement	Modifier of Place	Modifier of Time
The pilot	completed	his training	at Embry Riddle Aeronautical University	last year.
All students	must submit	their housing requests		by next week.
The boy	enjoys	fishing.		

Sentences that follow this rule may be simple or complex. Additional words and phrases can appear in these sentences without violating the basic rule.

Subjects

The *subject* performs the action in an active sentence. Every sentence and every clause must have a subject. The subject is usually a noun or noun phrase (explained in the following section), although it may consist of something else. Usually when a TOEFL test question asks you to identify the subject of a sentence, the sentence begins with a dependent clause or phrase, and you must recognize that the sentence subject is located in the independent clause.

> **Incorrect:** Without a doubt, is very important to study throughout the term rather than trying to cram at the end.
>
> **Correct:** Without a doubt, *it* is very important to study throughout the term rather than trying to cram at the end.

The first example is incorrect because it is a *phrase* — a string of words that is missing either a subject or a verb. In this case, the subject is missing; the subject *it* should appear before the verb *is*.

> **Incorrect:** Being a very abrupt and unfriendly man, did not have many friends.
>
> **Correct:** Being a very abrupt and unfriendly man, *Professor Stanley* did not have many friends.

The first example is incorrect because the subject, *Professor Stanley,* is missing.

Nouns and Noun Phrases

The subject of a sentence may be a single-word noun, such as *teacher* or *dog,* or it may be a noun phrase. A *noun phrase* is a group of words ending with a noun (but not beginning with a preposition). The noun phrase may contain one or more nouns, articles, adjectives, and conjunctions.

Following are examples of sentences that contain noun phrases as subjects.

> *A linguistics student* studies how languages are created.
>
> *Tall buildings* must provide safety mechanisms.
>
> *The greatest skiers* will compete in the show.

The noun phrase *A linguistics student* contains an article, *A,* an adjective, *linguistics,* and a noun, *student. Tall* is an adjective describing the noun *buildings.* In the last example, an article, *The,* an adjective, *greatest,* and a noun, *skiers,* combine to create the subject.

Other Types of Subjects

Although a noun phrase usually functions as the subject of a sentence, there are other possibilities. I describe many of these later in this chapter, and I simply mention them here to clarify that there are other possibilities.

> There is a car in the road. (The subject is actually *a car.*)
>
> It is important to read something every day. (*It* acts like a subject.)
>
> Knowing the essay topics in advance was helpful to him. (*Knowing,* a gerund form of a verb, is the subject.)
>
> To believe in yourself is very important. (*To believe,* an infinitive form of a verb, is the subject.)

Verbs and Verb Phrases

Every sentence and every clause must have a conjugated verb. By *conjugated,* I mean that the verb can't be a verb+*ing* alone, an infinitive alone, or a simple form alone. If the verb is one of these forms, it must be accompanied by an auxiliary or another verb form. The verb or verb phrase follows the subject in an active sentence and describes the action. In a passive sentence, the noun that served as a complement in the active voice sentence becomes the subject.

A *verb phrase* has an auxiliary in addition to the main verb. In general, the auxiliaries are :

- A form of *be*; in an active sentence, it is followed by a verb in the present participle: *be* + verb+*ing*

    Example: The bat *is flying* towards the light.

- A form of *have;* in an active sentence, it is followed by a verb in the past participle: *have* + verb+*ed.*

    Example: She *has completed* the project.

- A modal (*will*, *would*, *can*, *could*, *may*, *might,* or *must);* in an active sentence, it is followed by a verb in simple form

   Example: The team *must practice* more.

Keep in mind that the passive sentence construction is different. A sentence isn't correct if any of the three verb forms above appear without the auxiliary. Verbs are dealt with in more detail later in this chapter in the section "Form of Verb."

Complements

A *complement* completes the verb. Some verbs require a direct object; some may be followed by an object, although it's not required; and some can't be followed by an object. A verb that requires a direct object is a *transitive verb*. A verb that doesn't require a direct object is an *intransitive verb*. Most dictionaries indicate whether a verb is transitive or intransitive before the definition of the word by including "tr," "intr," or some such abbreviation. Sometimes a dictionary will show one definition as transitive and another as intransitive.

Determine is a transitive verb.

The group is trying to determine *the best course of action*.
complement

Swim is an intransitive verb.

The girl wants to swim *in the pool*.
no complement

The phrase *in the pool* is a place modifier, not a complement.

A complement may also consist of something other than a noun or noun phrase, such as a verb in the infinitive form or in the gerund (verb+*ing*) form.

They will probably consider *Atlanta* as the location for next year's meeting.
noun as complement

They will probably consider *calling* another meeting.
gerund as complement

They plan *to call* another meeting.
infinitive as complement

Modifiers

A modifier is not required in a basic standard English sentence, but if one appears, it generally follows the complement in the sentence.

If a sentence contains both a modifier of place and a modifier of time, the modifier of time usually appears last, unless it appears at the beginning of the sentence, before the subject.

Donna took the test *in Orlando* *yesterday*.

                modifier of place modifier of time

Yesterday, Donna took the test *in Orlando*.

modifier of time   modifier of place

The group ate dinner *at Bern's Steakhouse* *last month*.

               modifier of place   modifier of time

Normally, the modifier won't separate a verb from the complement.

Incorrect: Marjorie *cooked* *on the grill* *the chicken*.

               verb   modifier   complement

Correct: Marjorie *cooked* *the chicken* *on the grill*.

             verb   complement   modifier

The modifier can also appear between two parts of a verb; that is, after the auxiliary and before the main verb.

The boy *will* *probably* *go* to class today.

              modifier

The boy *is* *probably* *going* to class today.

              modifier

The boy *has* *probably* *gone* to class already.

              modifier

The man *was* *recently* *found* guilty of manslaughter.

              modifier

Phrases and Clauses

A *phrase* is a group of words that lacks a subject and verb. For example, *in the corner* is a phrase. Obviously, a phrase cannot stand alone as a complete sentence.

Clauses are groups of words that do contain subjects and verbs. *Independent clauses* can stand alone as complete sentences. *Dependent clauses* cannot stand alone because they contain words that make them dependent. If you remove the word that makes a clause dependent, the clause can stand alone as a sentence.

> *Although the bear is able to sprint rapidly,* it tires easily due to its weight.
>   clause

The underlined words in this example represent a dependent clause. On its own, *Although the bear is able to sprint rapidly* is not a complete sentence. However, the clause does contain a subject, *the bear,* and a verb phrase, *is able.* The word *Although* is the only thing preventing this clause from being independent.

> The bear is able to sprint rapidly.

With the word *Although* removed, the clause is a complete sentence.

Structure Quiz 1

Directions: The first type of question consists of incomplete sentences, with a blank line showing where information is to be filled in. Choose the word or phrase that most correctly completes the sentence. The second type of question consists of sentences with four underlined words or phrases. Choose the one word or phrase that is incorrect in standard written English. Mark your answer choices in the book or on a separate piece of paper.

1. The rain forest, _____ large trees that provide shade to the vegetation below, is home to unique flora and fauna.

    A. has

    B. with its

    C. and

    D. although has

2. Despite the polar bear's tremendous weight and height, _____ of sprinting at tremendous speed.

    A. it is capable

    B. is capable

    C. it is able

    D. ability

3. Having multiple sclerosis has diminished Mr. Wilson's physical condition,
       A   B

   but his ability to maintain a positive attitude and continue working an
        C   D

   inspiration.

4. The <u>huge</u> increase in popularity of specialty coffees <u>contribution</u> to the
   A   B
   success <u>of</u> Starbucks, Barney's and <u>other</u> coffee purveyors.
            C   D

5. Patients on Interferon are advised _____, so that they can sleep
   through the night without noticing the flu-like symptoms that are
   characteristic of the drug.

   A. just before going to sleep to inject themselves

   B. to inject themselves just before going to sleep

   C. to inject just before going to sleep themselves

   D. injecting themselves just before going to sleep

6. After it had <u>conclude</u> work on the budget, <u>the</u> legislature <u>adjourned</u> <u>until</u> the
                 A   B   C   D
   next session.

7. Even when <u>awarded</u> a scholarship, a student generally must still <u>paying</u> for
               A   B
   books, <u>living</u> expenses, and <u>other</u> costs.
           C   D

8. The U.S. government, along with a number of states, is <u>fight</u> a <u>protracted</u>
                                                           A   B
   legal battle with tobacco companies in order to <u>obtain</u> <u>relief</u> for the huge
                                                     C   D
   medical costs caused by smoking.

9. The leaders of the two countries _____ an agreement to avoid future
   conflicts.

   A. have recently reach

   B. recently reach

   C. have reached recently

   D. have recently reached

10. The teachers are <u>expecting</u> to call <u>tomorrow a meeting</u> in order to <u>review</u> the
                      A   B   C
    <u>disciplinary</u> problems.
     D

Answers and Explanations
for Structure Quiz 1

1. **B:** *with its. Has* is not correct because the clause between commas is a dependent clause and simply provides additional information. (The sentence, "The rain forest is home to unique flora and fauna" could stand alone, and the information about trees is not necessary to the meaning of the sentence.) Because *is* is a conjugated verb and the sentence isn't setting up a parallel structure sequence, a conjugated verb such as *has* makes no sense in the dependent clause. The answer *and* is not possible because it would make a plural subject, and the relative clause contained within the commas would be incomplete. The answer *although has* is incorrect because *although* would need to be followed by a subject and a verb, such as "although it has." *Although* also wouldn't make sense in the context of the sentence; the fact that the rain forest has large trees is a reason that it provides protection.

2. **A:** *it is capable.* The first clause is dependent because of the word *Despite.* Therefore, the second clause must be independent. There must be a subject and a verb. In this case, the subject is *it,* which is why the second answer choice is incorrect. Distracters appear in the other answer choices. Both *able* (adjective) and *ability* (noun) require *to,* not *of,* when followed by a preposition.

3. **D:** *working an.* The verb *is* or *was* needs to appear between *working* and *an.* The sentence is compound. Both parts of the sentence are clauses, which means that they both must have a subject and a verb. In the first part of the sentence, *having multiple sclerosis* is the subject and *has diminished* is the verb. In the second part of the sentence, the subject is *his ability,* which is modified by the complements beginning with infinitives (*to maintain a positive attitude and continue working*). The conjugated verb *is* or *was* is required to complete the subject/verb structure.

4. **B:** *contribution.* The sentence requires a conjugated verb. The subject is *The huge increase in popularity of specialty coffees.* Therefore, it must be followed by the verb *has contributed.*

5. **B:** *to inject themselves just before going to sleep.* The correct order is subject, verb, complement, modifier. The subject is *Patients.* The verb phrase is *are advised.* The complement is the infinitive and its complement, *to inject themselves.* The modifier of time is *just before going to sleep.* Choice **D** is incorrect because *advise* must be followed by the infinitive, not a gerund (verb+*ing*).

6. **A:** *conclude.* The verb is past perfect (*had* + verb in past participle), so the answer must be *concluded.*

7. **B:** *paying.* After the modal *must,* the simple form of the verb is required, so *pay* is correct. The word *awarded* is correct because it's the result of a reduced adverb clause, *when he or she has been awarded.*

8. **A:** *fight.* The verb structure *is fighting* is required because the verb *be* is followed by a verb+*ing* in an active sentence.

9. **D:** *have recently reached.* The modifier of time can appear between the auxiliary and main verb. Choice **A** is incorrect because the main verb is not in the past participle. Choice **B** is incorrect because the word *recently* sets up a time, so the simple present makes no sense. Choice **C** is incorrect because the modifier can not appear between the verb and the complement (*have reached an agreement*).

10. **B:** *tomorrow a meeting.* The order of a sentence is usually subject, verb, complement, modifier. The complement is *a meeting,* so the modifier must come after the complement — *a meeting tomorrow.*

Recognizing Unusual Subjects

Sometimes subjects and complements are not standard nouns or noun/adjective combinations. Several types of phrases and clauses can function as noun phrases. The point is to recognize the subject or complement so you can determine whether the sentence is complete and verify that the subject and verb agree.

Infinitives and Gerunds

> An *infinitive,* a verb in the form *to* + verb in simple form, can be the subject of a sentence.

Typically, an infinitive is part of a verb construction. Technically, it completes a verb construction, meaning that it introduces a complement construction. Sometimes the sentence is reversed and the infinitive appears as a subject. When used that way, the infinitive is a singular noun.

Pam wanted *a book.*

A book is the complement. What did she want? She wanted a book.

Pam wanted *to read another book.*

To read another book, an infinitive phrase, is the complement. What did she want? To read another book.

The sentence construction can also be turned around:

A book is what Pam wanted.

To read another book is what Pam wanted.

To learn piano requires considerable practice.

To be great musicians is their goal.

In the last three examples, infinitive phrases are acting as subjects of the sentences.

> **A gerund is a verb+*ing* that is used as a noun or part of a noun phrase. Gerunds act just like infinitives in a sentence construction.**

> Jennifer enjoys *good books*.

In this sentence, *good books* is the complement.

> Jennifer enjoys *reading good books*.

Here, the gerund phrase *reading good books* serves as the complement.

> *Reading good books* is what Jennifer enjoys.

In this case, the gerund phrase acts as the subject of the sentence. It is always singular, so the verb *is* agrees with the subject.

That Clauses

> **A clause that begins with the word *that* can also serve as the subject of the sentence.**

This sentence structure is the reverse of a structure that uses a *that* clause as a complement. Remember that a clause contains both a subject and a verb. If you are unsure whether a sentence contains a *that* clause (as opposed to a phrase, which does not contain a subject and verb), omit the word *that* and see if the rest of the clause can be a sentence on its own.

> It <u>was</u> a miracle <u>*that anybody survived the accident*</u>.
>   verb   complement
>
> <u>*That anybody survived the accident*</u> <u>was</u> a miracle.
>   subject   verb
>
> It <u>is</u> well known <u>*that the meat manufactured in those factories is unsanitary*</u>.
>   verb   complement
>
> <u>*That the meat manufactured in those factories is unsanitary*</u> <u>is</u> well known.
>   subject   verb

In the last example, don't get confused by the fact that the noun *factories* is plural, because *factories* by itself is not the subject of the sentence. The verb must be singular because the subject is the entire *that* clause.

> It surprised the doctor <u>*that the patient's condition had worsened so quickly*</u>.
>   complement
>
> <u>*That the patient's condition had worsened so quickly*</u> surprised the doctor.
>   subject

73

Question Words

A question word can serve as the subject of a sentence. Examples of these words include: *How, how long, how many, how much, how often, how soon, what, when, where, whether,* and *why*.

Just like infinitives, gerunds, and *that* clauses, question words can appear in the subject or object position of a sentence. When question words appear as part of a clause in the complement position, we say that the sentence contains an *embedded question*. An *embedded question* is one that is included within a sentence or another question. The word order is different from typical questions, except for subject questions. A *subject question* is a question in which the unknown item is the subject of the sentence:

> She is not certain *who* is in the room. (The question portion of the sentence is in the same order as it would be for a question.)

The word order for most embedded questions is: Subject + verb + question word + subject + verb + complement.

> The police are not certain *where* the suspect is hiding.
> The teacher learned *whom* the woman had called.

An auxiliary (a form of *be, have, do) cannot* appear between the question word and the subject. If the auxiliary would be a form of *do* in the question, there isn't an auxiliary in the embedded question.

> **Question:** *When will* the meeting *take* place?
> **Embedded question:** We haven't determined *when* the meeting *will take* place.

> **Question:** *Why did* the professor *cancel* the class?
> **Embedded question:** We don't know *why* the professor *cancelled* the class.

When the clause beginning with the question word appears at the beginning of the sentence, it becomes the subject of the sentence. Remember that the verb is singular because the entire clause is the subject. Don't be confused if a noun appearing immediately before the verb happens to be plural.

A typical construction for a sentence beginning with a question word is as follows: Question word + noun phrase + verb (complement) + verb + subject.

> *When* the play will begin is uncertain.
> *How many* fans attended the game is still unknown.

Complex Sentence Structures

Earlier in this chapter, I reviewed the structure of simple sentences. Not every sentence follows the same pattern as the simple structure. In fact, most of the sentences you encounter on the TOEFL test will be slightly more complex than those I presented above. This section helps you prepare for the types of sentence structures you need to know in order to score well on the Structure section.

Compound Sentences

Two simple sentences can be joined with conjunctions in order to create a compound sentence.

Coordinating conjunctions include *and, but, or, so,* and *yet*.

Conjunctions are used to join sentences in the same way they are used to join nouns, adjectives, and other parts of speech.

> The University of Florida *and* Florida State University both have excellent academic programs.

In this sentence, *and* joins two nouns to create a compound subject, *The University of Florida and Florida State University.*

> The University of Florida has a large *and* successful athletic program, *and* potential students are drawn to the school because of it.

In this example, the first *and* joins the adjectives *large* and *successful,* which both describe the athletic program. The second *and* joins two simple sentences to create a compound sentence.

> The scholarship was designed for students with high grade point averages, *but* it was adapted to A students from a particular geographical area.

In this case, the conjunction *but* is used to join two simple sentences. Notice that in the last two examples, the clauses that come before and after the conjunctions can stand on their own as complete sentences.

Passive Voice Sentences

A sentence can be constructed either in the active or passive voice. In an *active* sentence, the subject performs the action. In a *passive* sentence, the subject receives the action.

To create a passive sentence, the structure of an active sentence is reversed.

Active sentence with simple verb: *The bus struck the car*.

                   subject   verb in   complement
                               simple past

Passive sentence: *The car was struck* by the bus.

          subject form of *be* + verb
                   in past participle

In the passive sentence, the form of *be (was)* is in the same tense as the verb in the active sentence (*struck*, which is past tense). But here, the word *struck* is actually in the past participle, even though it looks identical to the past tense.

Active sentence with progressive verb: *A man was reviewing the artwork*.

                       subject   verb in   complement
                                past progressive

Passive sentence: *The artwork was being reviewed* by a man.

             subject   form of *be* + verb
                        in past participle

Active sentence with present or past perfect verb:

                      The bus has struck the car.

           subject   verb in   complement
                        perfective

Passive sentence: *The car has been struck* by the bus.

          subject   form of *have* + *been* +
                  verb in past participle

Active sentence with modal: *A man will review the artwork*.

                    subject   modal + verb in complement
                              simple form

Passive sentence: *The artwork will be reviewed* by a man.

            subject   modal + *be* + main
                  verb in past participle

Active sentence with modal in the perfective:

                  A man will have reviewed the artwork.

           subject   modal + *have* + verb   complement
                       in past participle

Passive sentence: *The artwork will have been reviewed* by a man.

          subject   modal + *have* + *been* + main verb
                      in past participle

Conditional Sentences

A *conditional sentence* indicates that something will happen if something else happens first. That is, one circumstance will occur only under the *condition* that the other circumstance occurs. A conditional sentence can be real, meaning that one thing will happen if the other thing happens, or unreal, meaning that something may or may not happen (or be happening right now). Whether or not the condition will occur is already determined.

A conditional sentence contains a dependent (or *subordinate*) clause and an independent clause. The Structure section questions presented on the TOEFL test will typically require you to determine whether the sentence is complete, with both the dependent and independent clause following the rules of standard written English.

The dependent clause can appear as the first or second clause in the sentence with no change in the meaning.

> If the bus had not already passed by, we would have been on time.
> We would have been on time if the bus had not already passed by.

The dependent clause is the clause that starts with *if.* The modal generally won't appear in the dependent clause. The *if* clause can appear as the first or second clause in a sentence.

> **For sentences that begin with an *if* clause, a typical structure is as follows:**
> ***If* + subject + conjugated verb + subject + modal + verb**
>
> **For sentences that end with an *if* clause, a typical structure is as follows:**
> **Subject + modal + verb + *if* + subject + conjugated verb**

> If the man had called the ambulance, the boy would have survived.
> The boy would have survived if the man had called the ambulance.

Real (Possibly True) Conditions

The *real* or *possible* condition is used when the speaker expresses an action or situation that usually occurs or will occur if the stated circumstances are satisfied. The tense (time) in the two clauses will generally be the same.

> The professor will grade the essays if he has time.
> (He will grade the essays unless he does not have time.)

> **Real conditional sentences are usually constructed in the future tense and contain a verb in the simple present tense in the dependent clause and *will, can, may,* or *must* + a verb in simple form in the independent clause.**

If she wants to study tonight, she will call you.

She will call you if she wants to study tonight.

Unreal (Not True) Conditions

The *unreal (not true) condition* expresses a situation (past, present, or future) that would take place or would have taken place if the circumstances expressed were or had been different. The tense will always be one step further in the past than what is logically the time of the sentence.

> **Unreal conditional sentences constructed in the present or future tense contain a verb in the simple past form in the dependent clause and *would, could, or might* + the verb in simple form in the independent clause.**

If she *wanted* to study tonight, she *would call* you.

She *would call* you if she *wanted* to study tonight.

The use of the past tense and past modal means that she doesn't want to study tonight and, therefore, won't call.

> **The past tense of the verb *be* is always *were* and never *was* in a conditional sentence, even when the subject is *I, he, she,* and *it.***

If Linda *were* here, she would know what to do.

Linda would know what to do if she *were* here.

This means that Linda is not here.

> **Unreal conditional sentences constructed in the past tense contain a verb in the past perfect in the dependent clause and *would, could, or might* + *have* + the verb in simple form in the independent clause.**

If she *had wanted* to study tonight, she *would have called* you.

She *would have called* you if she *had wanted* to study tonight.

This means that she didn't want to study and, therefore, didn't call.

Relative or Adjective Clauses

Two independent clauses that have the same subject can join into a single sentence through the use of a relative clause. (Some people use the term *adjective clause* instead of *relative clause,* but both terms refer to the same construction.)

To create a sentence joined with a relative clause, the subject of one of the independent clauses must be replaced with a relative pronoun.

The relative pronouns are *that, which, who, whom* and *whose*.

The clause that has the relative pronoun becomes a subordinate or dependent clause, which means that it must be joined to the independent clause in order to be correct. *Note:* A regular pronoun, such as *he, she,* or *it,* cannot appear with a relative pronoun.

Take, for example, two independent clauses that both have *Sally* as the subject.

> Sally is the secretary.
> Sally is in charge of the calendar.

To combine them, one of the subjects will drop out and be replaced by the relative pronoun *who*. The relative pronoun *who* cannot be combined with a regular pronoun, such as *she*.

> **Incorrect:** Sally is the secretary *who she* is in charge of the calendar.
> **Correct:** Sally is the secretary *who* is in charge of the calendar.

In the following example, the object of one sentence is the same as the subject of the next. A relative pronoun can be used to combine these sentences as well.

> Bill bought a boat. The boat cost $16,000.
> Bill bought a boat *that* cost $16,000.

The word *that* replaced *The boat* in the second sentence.

That and *Which*

The words *that* and *which* may seem to be interchangeable, but they are not. Their use in a sentence depends on whether a relative clause is restrictive or nonrestrictive. A *restrictive clause* conveys information that is essential for understanding the meaning of the sentence. A restrictive clause is like an adjective because it helps to define a noun. A *nonrestrictive clause,* on the other hand, contains information that isn't required to define the noun. A nonrestrictive clause is set off from the independent clause by commas; a restrictive clause is not.

ved *That* can be used only in restrictive clauses, and *which* is generally used only in nonrestrictive clauses.

> **Restrictive clause:** Palm-sized computers *that connect to the Internet* are becoming very popular.

The relative clause *that connect to the Internet* is required. If it were omitted, the sentence would have a different meaning. It would mean that all palm-sized computers are becoming popular, which is different from what the sentence says now. The clause is restrictive because it restricts the meaning of the noun phrase *Palm-sized computers*.

> **Nonrestrictive clause:** Seabreeze High School, *which is on the beachside*, is the rival of Mainland High School.

In this case, you can omit the relative clause *which is on the beachside,* and the sentence means the same thing: Seabreeze High School is the rival of Mainland High School. The location of Seabreeze High School is provided as additional information and doesn't define the school, so it is nonrestrictive.

Who, Whom, and *Whose*

Who and *whom* are also used in different ways, but either word can be used in restrictive and nonrestrictive sentences. The difference between these two relative pronouns is that one is used to replace the subject of a sentence, and one is used to replace the complement.

> *Who* is used to replace a noun phrase in the subject of the sentence. *Whom* is used to replace a noun phrase in the complement.

The TOEFL test probably won't test the distinction between these two words because even native English speakers often use them incorrectly.

> *The athletes* have scored the most points.
> subject
> *The athletes* will play on the all-star team.
> *The athletes who* have scored the most points will play on the all-star team.
> *Professor Allen* is the only instructor.
> She has consulted *Professor Allen* about the project.
> complement
> *Professor Allen* is the only instructor *whom* she has consulted about the project.

Note: If the noun in question could be replaced by the pronoun *him, her,* or *them,* then you need to use the relative pronoun *whom.*

Just as the complement form of a pronoun always appears after a preposition, so does *whom.*

> *The officers* are tired.
> The woman is talking to *the officers*.
> object of preposition
> *The officers to whom* the woman is talking are tired.

Whose is the relative pronoun that indicates possession.

The team consisted of *several players.*

The players' talent was incredible.

   possessive

The team consisted of *several players whose* talent was incredible.

The TOEFL test generally contains more complicated sentences, in which you may find it difficult to locate the relative clause. This is one of the ways in which the TOEFL tests your knowledge of sentence structure. If the relative pronoun is missing, if a regular pronoun appears after the relative pronoun, or if a verb or subject is missing, the sentence will be incomplete. The relative clauses must each contain a subject and conjugated verb. If you're unsure, remove the relative pronoun and make sure that the two clauses can be complete sentences if they stand alone.

Samples

> **Q.** Instructors who _____ teaching ability are prevalent at this university because publishing is one of the major criteria for tenure.
>
>   **A.** lack
>
>   **B.** without
>
>   **C.** do not
>
>   **D.** no have

The answer is **A,** *lack,* because that choice is the only conjugated verb. The main sentence, *Instructors are prevalent . . .* has a subject and verb, but the relative clause does not have one, unless you add *lack.*

Clause 1: Instructors are prevalent at this university because publishing is one of the major criteria for tenure.

Clause 2: Instructors lack teaching ability.

> **Q.** Not all textbooks that have been written on this subject _____ as detailed as this one.
>
>   **A.** with
>
>   **B.** to
>
>   **C.** be
>
>   **D.** are

The answer is **D,** *are.* The sentence contains a relative clause — *that have been written on this subject.* Thus, the independent clause is *Not all textbooks* _____ *as detailed as this one.* The word *detailed* functions as an adjective, not a verb, in this sentence. Therefore, a conjugated verb is missing, and *are* is the only choice. Choice **A** contains no verb, and choices **B** and **C** are not conjugated verbs.

> **Clause 1:** Not all textbooks are as detailed as this one.
>
> **Clause 2:** Textbooks have been written on this subject.

Q. The oldest tree in this part of the world is the redwood, _____ thousands of years old.

    A. which may be

    B. its age

    C. and which

    D. it is

The answer is **A,** *which may be.* The part of the sentence preceding the comma is an independent clause. The dependent clause following the comma must be preceded by a relative pronoun and verb to make sense. Choices **B** and **C** are incorrect because they lack a relative pronoun. Choice **D** is incorrect because it uses a regular pronoun (*it*) instead of a relative pronoun.

> **Clause 1:** The oldest tree in this part of the world is the redwood.
>
> **Clause 2:** The redwood is thousands of years old.

Reduced Relative (Adjective) Clauses

A *reduced relative clause* is a restrictive relative (or adjective) clause with the relative pronoun and the verb *be* omitted. Even though these words are removed, the reduced clause has the same meaning as the restrictive relative clause it comes from.

Before progressive (continuous) verb structures in active voice:
The nurse *who is completing* the charts is Donna Edwards.
              relative clause

The nurse *completing* the charts is Donna Edwards.
        reduced relative clause

Before passive voice:
The figure *that was obtained* from this formula is incorrect.
          relative clause

The figure *obtained* from this formula is incorrect.
        reduced relative clause

The contractor has completed construction on a home _that is equipped_ with a safe room.

relative clause

The contractor has completed construction on a home _equipped_ with a safe room.

reduced relative clause

Before prepositional phrases:

The car _that is in the garage_ has a flat tire.

relative clause

The car _in the garage_ has a flat tire.

reduced relative clause

Before noun phrases with nonrestrictive clauses:

Tracy Stafford, _who is a paralegal_, is considering enrolling in law school.

relative clause

Tracy Stafford, _a paralegal_, is considering enrolling in law school.

reduced relative clause

Adverb Clauses

An _adverb clause_ is another type of subordinate clause, which is identified by certain connector words that vary depending on the function of the clause. Just like adjective clauses, adverb clauses connect two independent clauses into a more complex sentence.

> Adverb connectors used to indicate concession include _although, even though, even if, though, whereas,_ and _while_. Concession means that something is true (or false) in spite of the fact that another thing is true (or false).

For example, consider the following two sentences:

She studied every day.
She didn't grasp the concepts presented.

These two sentences can be combined by using one of the connector words listed above to create an adverb clause.

Though she studied every day, she didn't grasp the concepts presented.

connector

She didn't grasp the concepts presented _though_ she studied every day.

connector

This means that it is true that she studied everyday, but even so she still did not grasp the concepts.

> **Adverb connectors that indicate time include *after, before, once, while, since, until,* and *when.***

Consider the following example:

> The students took the exam.
> The professor graded papers.

If these two events are taking place at the same time, you can use an adverb clause to show the relationship between them.

> *While* the students took the exam, the professor graded papers.
> connector
> The professor graded papers *while* the students took the exam.
> connector

Keep in mind that the words listed in this section do not always signal the use of an adverb clause. These connectors can also be used with noun phrases.

> *Since* the accident, he hasn't been himself.

In this sentence, *Since* is used with the noun phrase *the accident* rather than with an adverb clause.

> *Since* he was in an accident, he hasn't been himself.

This example indicates how *Since* can be used to create an adverb clause.

> **Adverb clause connectors that represent cause and effect are *as, because,* and *since.***

> *Because* her children are ill, she had to miss work today.
> She had to miss work today *because* her children are ill.

Reduced Adverb Clauses

Just as you can reduce an adjective clause, you can reduce an adverb clause by removing the auxiliary words. If there isn't an auxiliary, the verb must be converted to a verb+*ing* form, and the subject of both clauses must be the same. Following are several examples.

Active Verb

> When *they drive* cars, teenagers need to remember their lack of experience.
> When *driving* cars, teenagers need to remember their lack of experience.

While *she was reviewing* the materials, she was also trying to watch television.
While *reviewing* the materials, she was also trying to watch television.

Passive Verb

Although *it had been completed*, the report was not turned in on time.
Although *completed*, the report was not turned in on time.

Adjective

Although *she was exhausted*, she continued to work on the project.
Although *exhausted*, she continued to work on the project.

Structure Quiz 2

Directions: The first type of question consists of incomplete sentences, with a blank line showing where information is to be filled in. Choose the word or phrase that most correctly completes the sentence. The second type of question consists of sentences with four underlined words or phrases. Choose the one word or phrase that is incorrect in standard written English. Mark your answers on this page or on a separate piece of paper.

1. The oncologist studied the results of the biopsy and decided _____ additional tests.

    A. should order

    B. to order

    C. he should ordering

    D. ordering

2. That carcinogenic substances _____ in many common household items is well-known.

    A. are contained

    B. contained

    C. containing

    D. are containing

3. If the man <u>had transported</u> to the hospital <u>sooner</u> than he was, he <u>could</u> have
            A   B   C
<u>survived</u> the electrocution.
   D

4. Porpoises, which _____ actually mammals because they breathe air through an orifice in their heads, are playful and intelligent.

   A. is

   B. be

   C. being

   D. are

5. Florida's timberlands <u>suffered</u> <u>considerable</u> damage from the wildfires of
                           A   B
1998, <u>resulted</u> from <u>insufficient</u> rainfall.
       C   D

6. Whereas Internet proponents say that someday all computer programs and data will reside on an Internet server instead of individual computers, many individuals _____ afraid to lose control over their own documents.

   A. are

   B. being

   C. also

   D. very much

7. After _____ suspended for misbehavior, the student requested reconsideration.

   A. having been

   B. having

   C. have

   D. was

8. Why so many people die from this illness _____ unknown, but researchers have learned much about the source of the problem.

   A. is

   B. are

   C. widely

   D. has

9. The doctors have not been able to determine when _____ to lose her mental capacity.

    A. did the woman begin

    B. the woman began

    C. began the woman

    D. the woman was begun

10. The results must have already <u>be</u> received by the <u>examining</u> committee
                                      A   **B**
because the members <u>seem</u> to be <u>continuing</u> their determinations.
                       C   **D**

11. Ms. Henry insisted that the results of the research be presented to the panel before _____.

    A. was held the vote

    B. was the vote

    C. voted

    D. the vote was held

12. Knowing how to repair and install computer networks _____ Melissa a great advantage in her job, because she is the only person in the company with that knowledge.

    A. have given

    B. given

    C. giving

    D. has given

Answers and Explanations for Structure Quiz 2

1. B: *to order.* After the verb *decide*, when the complement is a verb, it must be the infinitive. The word *should* would have been correct if a choice had stated "that he should order" or "he should order."

2. A: *are contained.* The sentence is in the passive voice so the verb structure is a form of *be* + verb in past participle. It's also a *that* clause structure, so there must be a subject and a verb in the *that* clause.

3. A: *had transported.* The sentence is obviously a passive voice concept. The man didn't transport somebody else to the hospital; somebody transported him. Therefore, the structure must be *had been transported*. The sentence is also conditional, so the conjugated verb appears in the *if* clause and the modal structure appears in the other clause.

4. **D:** *are.* The relative clause has the same understood subject as the base sentence, *porpoises.* Therefore, the verb must be a plural conjugated verb.

5. **C:** *resulted.* The first part of the sentence is an independent clause. It has a subject, *timberlands,* and a conjugated verb, *suffered,* so the second clause must have a relative clause, a conjunction, or a reduced relative clause. The conjugated verb *resulted* makes no sense by itself. It would be correct, however, if it was *which resulted, resulting,* or *having resulted.*

6. **A:** *are.* The first clause is dependent because it begins with *whereas,* so there must be a regular conjugated verb in the second clause.

7. **A:** *having been.* It would also be correct if it said "after she was."

8. **A:** *is.* The subject is a question word clause, so the verb must be singular, and it must be a conjugated verb.

9. **B:** *the woman began.* In an embedded question, the order is question word + subject + verb.

10. **A:** *be.* The correct form for a present perfect passive with a modal is: modal + *have been* + verb in past participle.

11. **D:** *the vote was held.* The word *before* must be followed by a noun phrase (*the vote*), a subject + verb (*they voted*), or a verb+*ing* (*voting*). In this case, the verb is in the passive voice but follows the order subject + verb. Choices **A** and **B** are out of order and have no subject, and choice C is missing a subject or is in the wrong form.

12. **D:** *has given.* The subject is *knowing,* a gerund, so it determines the verb, and the verb must be conjugated.

Reverse Order Constructions

Certain types of sentence constructions involve reversing the normal sentence or clause order.

Reversed Conditional Construction

One type of reversed order construction is the past unreal conditional. As described earlier in this chapter, this is the sentence that contains the word *if* and a tense that is one step in the past beyond the meaning.

The typical sentence structure for a past unreal conditional sentence is as follows: *If* + subject + *had (not)* + verb in past participle + subject + modal + verb.

> A reversed conditional sentence construction for a past condition looks like the following: *Had* + subject + (*not*) + verb in past participle + subject + modal + verb.

> *If* the team *had* played more aggressively, it could have won the tournament. (Past unreal conditional sentence)
>
> *Had* the team played more aggressively, it could have won the tournament. (Reversed conditional sentence)

> *If* she *had not* lost the ticket, she would have gone to the concert.
>
> *Had* she *not* lost the ticket, she would have gone to the concert.

This same concept also applies to the verb *be* in a present time concept. It will be one step in the past — in the simple past for a present time concept. Remember that in an unreal condition, the verb *be* will always be *were* and never *was*. Also remember that positive and negative always appear to be the opposite. A negative clause means a positive idea and a positive clause means a negative idea.

The typical sentence construction for a present unreal condition is as follows: *If* + subject + *were* (*not*) + verb in present participle + subject + modal + verb + {noun/adjective}.

The reversed sentence construction for a present unreal condition looks like the following: *Were* + subject + (*not*) + verb in present participle + subject + modal + verb + {noun/adjective}

> *If* Rafael *were* studying, his television would not be so loud.
>
> *Were* Rafael studying, his television would not be so loud.

This means that Rafael is not studying.

> *If* Brandon *were* not a point guard, he would be in the game now.
>
> *Were* Brandon not a point guard, he would be in the game now.

This means that Brandon is a point guard.

> *If* Maria *were* tired, she would take a break.
>
> *Were* Maria tired, she would take a break.

This means that Maria is not tired.

Reversed Order Limiting Words

Some expressions can be reversed in order to show emphasis. Most of the words in the list below are negative concepts. As always, if the normal construction does not have an auxiliary, you must use a form of *do*. Remember that auxiliaries are a form of *be*, a form of *have,* or a form of *do*. *Be* and *have* are part of the verb structure, like *is going* or *has gone*. But in questions and negatives that do not have an auxiliary as part of the verb structure, *do* is inserted:

She wants to leave.

She *does* not want to leave.

Does she want to leave?

> **Commonly used limiting words and phrases include *hardly, seldom, never, barely, scarcely, rarely, no sooner, nowhere so, not once, not often, not only, not until, only, only by, only then, only with,* and *under no circumstances.***

The normal order of a sentence containing a limiting word would be as follows: Subject + (auxiliary) + limiting word + verb in past participle + balance of sentence.

She had *hardly* finished the race when she collapsed with exhaustion.

> **The reversed order construction of a sentence with a limiting word would look like the following: Limiting word + auxiliary + subject + verb in past participle + balance of sentence.**

Hardly had she finished the race when she collapsed with exhaustion.

In the following examples, a sentence that has no auxiliary is reversed, which requires an auxiliary:

She rarely attends meetings.

Rarely *does* she attend meetings.

Each of the following examples follows a reversed construction because each begins with a limiting word or phrase. Therefore, each requires an auxiliary.

Never before *have* so many people been employed as they are now.

Under no circumstances *will* the judge reconsider her decision.

No sooner *had* she completed the work than she went to sleep.

Only with great care *can* the surgeon reconstruct the infant's heart.

Not often *does* a hurricane of this magnitude approach the coast.

Appositives

An *appositive* is a type of reduced relative clause. Found at the beginning of a sentence, an appositive is a noun phrase that provides additional information about a subject or object.

Relative Clause: Dana, *who is an excellent student*, has won a scholarship.

Reduced Relative Clause: Dana, *an excellent student*, has won a scholarship.

Appositive: *An excellent student*, Dana has won a scholarship.

Relative Clause: The University of Miami, *which is a private university*, has a well-respected law school.

Reduced Relative Clause: The University of Miami, *a private university*, has a well-respected law school.

Appositive: *A private university*, The University of Miami has a well-respected law school.

Direct and Indirect Objects

Sentences that contain direct and indirect objects may be constructed in two different ways without changing the meaning. An *indirect object* is an animate object to whom or for whom something is done. A *direct object* may be animate or inanimate and is the first receiver of the action.

The indirect object normally appears after the direct object and is preceded by a preposition. The prepositions that generally precede an indirect object are *for* and *to*. But an indirect object may also appear before the direct object without being preceded by a preposition.

> **One typical sentence structure including both a direct and indirect object looks like the following: Subject + verb + direct object + {to/for} + indirect object.**

Larry gave *the insurance policy* to *Melissa*.
            direct object   indirect object

> **A second typical sentence structure including both a direct and indirect object looks like the following: Subject + verb + indirect object + direct object.**

Larry gave *Melissa* *the insurance policy*.
          indirect object   direct object

The insurance policy is the direct object because Larry grasped the insurance policy. The second action is that of handing it to Melissa, who is the indirect object as the recipient of the direct object.

Joy gave *the essay* to *her teacher*.
        direct object   indirect object

Joy gave *her teacher* *the essay*.
        indirect object direct object

He lent *some money* to *his brother*.
        direct object   indirect object

He lent *his brother* *some money*.
        indirect object   direct object

If the direct object and the indirect object are both pronouns, the first sentence structure is generally used.

> **Correct:** They gave *it to us*.
> **Incorrect:** They gave *us it*.

The verbs *introduce* and *mention* require the preposition *to* prior to an indirect object. You cannot use the second sentence structure with these verbs.

> I introduced *John to Dr. Jackson*.
> He mentioned *the party to me*.

Common verbs that take an indirect object include the following:

bring	get	owe	send
build	give	paint	show
buy	hand	pass	teach
cut	leave	pay	write
draw	lend	promise	
feed	make	read	
find	offer	sell	

Some of these verbs can be followed by either the preposition *for* or *to*, while others can be followed by only one of these words.

Illogical Participial Modifiers (Dangling Participles)

A participial phrase (a phrase that contains a verb+*ing* without auxiliaries) can combine two sentences with one stated subject and one understood subject. A participial phrase is actually a reduction in which a noun and auxiliary have been omitted.

> While *she was driving* too fast, she lost control of the car.
> While *driving* too fast, she lost control of the car.

With the reduced form, both the phrase and the independent clause must have the same logical subject. If they do not have the same subject, the result is illogical and incorrect.

> **Incorrect:** While driving too fast, the car spun out.

In this example, the actual subject of the verb *driving* is a person. Therefore, immediately after the comma, whoever is driving the car must be mentioned. The car is not driving itself, so it is illogical for *car* to be the subject of the independent clause.

Correct: While driving too fast, the girl lost control of the car.

This example is correct because *the girl* is the implied subject of the participial phrase and the stated subject of the independent clause.

The participial phrase may be preceded by a preposition. The following prepositions commonly precede participial phrases: *by, upon, before, after,* and *while.*

> **A typical sentence structure for a sentence with a participial phrase resembles the following: (Preposition) + (*not*) + verb+*ing* + (object) + subject + verb in any tense + remainder of the sentence.**

> After completing her homework, Michelle read a book.
> By not working long hours, you will feel better.

If only the verb+*ing* appears in the participial phrase, the time of the sentence is indicated by the tense of the verb in the main clause.

> **Present:** Practicing his typing regularly, Ken *hopes* to improve his word processing skills.
> **Past:** Needing a new car, Franklin *read* the newspaper ads.
> **Future:** Completing the assignment before midnight, Sally *will mail* it tomorrow.

The perfect form (*having* + the verb in past participle) shows that the action of the participial phrase occurred before the action of the main verb.

> **A normal sentence structure using the perfect form in a participial phrase appears as follows: (*Not*) + *having* + verb in past participle + (object) + subject + verb in any tense + remainder of sentence.**

> Having finished her homework, Trisha went to sleep.

This means that after Trisha had finished her homework, she went to sleep.

> Not having read the article, she could not answer the question.

This means that because she had not read the article, she could not answer the question.

The participial phrase can also be used to express an idea in the passive voice.

> **A sentence with a participial phrase in the passive voice usually has the following construction: (*Not*) + *having been* + verb in past participle + subject + verb in any tense + remainder of sentence.**

> Having been summoned by the court, the attorney arrived for the hearing.

93

This means that after the attorney had been summoned by the court, he arrived for the hearing.

> Not having been notified of the change in flight schedule, Franklin missed his flight.

This means that because he had not been notified of the change in flight schedule, Franklin missed his flight.

In the passive voice, the words *having been* can be dropped and the past participle can appear alone.

> Summoned by the court, the attorney arrived for the hearing.

Because/Because Of

The word *because,* when not followed by *of*, must be followed by a clause. Remember that a clause standing alone is a complete sentence. The phrase *because of* is followed only by a noun or noun phrase. *Because of* cannot be followed by a conjugated verb.

> He cancelled his appointment *because he was sick*.
>   subject   verb
>
> He cancelled his appointment *because of his illness*.
>   noun phrase

It is also possible for the *because* clause to begin the sentence.

> *Because* he was sick, he cancelled his appointment.
> *Because of* his illness, he cancelled his appointment.

Word Order

Word order questions on the TOEFL test require that you recognize if a word or phrase is placed in a position that is not correct. This type of question is similar to the sentence structure question, except that word order problems involve just a few words.

Order of a Superlative

Some TOEFL test questions ask you to determine the correct order of a superlative. The order should be *the* + superlative + noun:

Q. This is _____ on Broadway.

    A. longest-running play

    B. the longest-running play

    C. the play longest-running

    D. play longest-running

The answer is **B**, which follows the rule described above.

Order of an Intensifier

An intensifier will generally appear before the adjective it modifies. An intensifier adds more emphasis to an adjective or adverb. Examples are *too, quite, considerably,* and *very.*

    This book is *very* easy to understand.
    This book is *too* hard to understand.

The intensifiers *far, too,* and *much* can add even more intensity:

    This book is *far too* hard to understand.

Q. Her fever is _____ to ignore.

    A. too much high

    B. high too much

    C. too high

    D. so high

The answer is **C,** *too high.* The word *much* in the first two choices is not in proper order. It would be correct to say *much too high,* but that option is not given.

Order of Verb Modifier

Other TOEFL questions require you to know where to place a verb modifier. Any modifier of the verb will normally appear before the verb. Examples of verb modifiers include *always, never,* and *almost.*

    Susan *always* takes her medicine.

Q. Hurricanes _____ during this time of year.

    A. almost occur never

    B. occur almost never

    C. almost never occur

    D. never occur almost

The answer is **C,** *almost never occur. Almost never* is opposite in meaning but similar in word order to *almost always.*

Order of Adjectives and Nouns

An adjective normally appears before a noun, not after it.

Q. The professor was pleased with _____ of the students.

    A. progress remarkable

    B. remarkable progress

    C. the progress remarkable

    D. the remarkable progress

The answer is **D,** *the remarkable progress.*

Q. The _____ of this city are well secured.

    A. high-crime areas

    B. areas of crime high

    C. areas where is high crime

    D. highest criminal areas

The answer is **A,** *high-crime areas.* A noun can be used in combination with other words to make an adjective. For example, it is correct to write *four-story buildings.* The noun used inside the hyphenated adjective form is not made plural even if the other noun is.

Q. She has <u>scored</u> up to <u>five as much times</u> as Robert <u>on</u> <u>that</u> exam previously.
     A   B   C D

The answer is **B,** *five as much times.* The correct order of this expression is *five times as much.*

Enough

The word *enough* is unusual because it may modify a noun, an adjective, or an adverb, and its position differs depending upon which part of speech it modifies.

Enough follows an adjective or an adverb, as in the following examples.

> The skillet is not <u>*hot*</u> *enough* to cook the food.
>   adjective

> She writes <u>*well*</u> *enough* to be awarded a scholarship.
>   adverb

Enough precedes a noun, even if the noun is modified by an adjective.

> The company does not have *enough* <u>*liquid funds*</u> to pay its bills.
>   noun

> The group does not have *enough* <u>*food*</u> to provide for the injured people.
>   noun

Structure Quiz 3

Directions: The first type of question consists of incomplete sentences, with a blank line showing where information is to be filled in. Choose the word or phrase that most correctly completes the sentence. The second type of question consists of sentences with four underlined words or phrases. Choose the one word or phrase that is incorrect in standard written English. Mark your choices on this page or on a separate piece of paper.

1. Had the victim _____ able to find a telephone to contact authorities, she would have received assistance.

   A. been

   B. be

   C. would have been

   D. had been

2. An Alzheimer's victim, former president Ronald Reagan _____ in the spotlight even after the symptoms began to appear.

   A. stayed

   B. stay

   C. staying

   D. who stayed

3. Private couriers, <u>extremely</u> popular in large cities, <u>traveling</u> by bicycle
                           A   B

<u>carrying</u> packets containing documents and other items <u>from</u> office to office.
C   D

4. Loudly applauding the speech, _____ quickly left the stage.

    A. the speaker waved to the audience and

    B. the audience watched as the speaker

    C. the audience saw the speaker

    D. the speaker waving to the audience

5. The expenses were <u>too much</u> high for the program <u>to continue</u>, <u>so</u> the
                             A   B   C

administration decided <u>to terminate</u> some positions.
                        D

6. In a relay race, one runner runs a distance, hands _____, and that runner completes the race.

    A. other runner the baton

    B. the baton another runner

    C. the baton to another runner

    D. the baton other runner

7. <u>Because the</u> high risk of fire <u>during</u> the drought, the officials <u>ordered</u> that no
     A   B   C

outside fire of any sort could be <u>set</u>.
                                 D

8. Hurricanes almost <u>veer always</u> to the northeast at <u>some</u> point after <u>traveling</u>
                        A   B   C

in a westerly direction <u>across</u> the water.
                              D

9. Never before _____ in an earnest attempt to resolve their differences.

    A. have the leaders of these two countries met

    B. the leaders of these two countries have met

    C. have the leaders the two countries meet

    D. met the leaders of the two countries

10. The girl fell <u>into</u> the <u>water cold</u>, but was <u>rescued</u> <u>immediately</u>.
                       A   B   C   D

11. The professor has not written a book _____ to the masses to generate interest from a publisher.

    A. enough appealing

    B. appealing enough

    C. appeal enough

    D. enough appeal

12. During the entire <u>hour three</u> deposition, the witness <u>steadfastly</u> denied <u>having</u>
                           A   B   C
known the defendant <u>previously</u>.
                                D

Answers and Explanations for Structure Quiz 3

1. A: *been.* This is a reversed conditional sentence. The sentence could begin *If the victim had been able* or, as here, *Had the victim been able.* The word *been* completes the past perfect construction.

2. A: *stayed.* That answer choice is the only one that is a conjugated verb standing alone. The appositive, *an Alzheimer's victim,* is extra information and is dependent. There must be a complete clause as the dependent clause. The relative pronoun *who* cannot be used because it would make the second clause dependent too. At least one clause must be independent.

3. B: *traveling.* It would be correct as a conjugated verb, *travel.* That form is correct because the subject is plural, *couriers.* The two other words ending in *ing* are both correct because they are not functioning as the conjugated verb in the sentence. The clause *extremely popular in large cities* is a reduced relative clause or an appositive and is correct.

4. B: *the audience watched as the speaker.* The logical subject of the participial phrase that begins the sentence is *audience,* because they were applauding. So two answer choices are ruled out. The third answer choice is not correct because the verb *left* would have to be *leave* (simple form) after the verb *saw.*

5. A: *too much.* The correct order is *much + too +* adjective.

6. C: *the baton to another runner.* The order is direct object *+ to +* indirect object, or indirect object *+* direct object (*another runner the baton*).

7. A: *Because the.* The rule is *because +* clause or *because of +* noun.

8. A: *veer always.* The order is *almost + always +* verb. *Veer* is a verb, meaning to turn.

9. A: *have the leaders of these two countries met.* After the limiting words *never before,* the order of subject and verb is altered: auxiliary *+* subject *+* main verb.

10. B: *water cold.* The order is adjective *+* noun (*cold water*).

11. **B:** *appealing enough.* The correct order is adjective + *enough*. The word *appeal* is a noun. (The book is *appealing enough.* The book has *enough appeal.*)

12. **A:** *hour three.* The order is adjective-noun + noun (*three-hour deposition*).

Word Form

Word form questions test your ability to recognize when a sentence uses one form of a word but it should have another. *Note:* The TOEFL test will never use a word that is not a real word found in standard written English.

Using the wrong form of a word generally means that you use a noun when you should use an adjective, a verb when you should use a noun, a preposition when you should use a conjunction, and so on. For example, you may think that the word *major* belongs in a certain sentence, but the sentence calls for a noun instead of an adjective so you should really use the word *majority.*

Other word form questions may ask you to recognize that a word has an incorrect ending, even if it is the right part of speech for the context. For example, a sentence may have all the right parts of speech but contain a verb that is singular when it should be plural. The verb is in the wrong form, so you would need to identify that problem and know how to correct it.

Word form questions frequently ask you to look for parallelism or parallel structure in a sentence. For example, a sentence may contain a compound verb. If the two verbs are in two different forms, or if one is not a verb at all, that should signal you that one of them is incorrect.

Become familiar with common adjective, noun, and verb endings (suffixes) so that you can recognize that a word is in the wrong place even if you do not know the meaning of the word. The "Reading" chapter in Part III contains detailed information about common word endings.

Following are examples of word form questions similar to those you will encounter on the TOEFL test. Each question will have four underlined words or phrases. You must choose which underlined word or phrase is used incorrectly in the sentence. In this book, a letter from A to D is assigned to each possible answer choice. On the TOEFL CBT, you will simply use your mouse to click on the word that is in the wrong form.

Q. The <u>people</u> will likely <u>election</u> Ellen the <u>winner</u> of <u>the</u> race.
      A   B   C   D

The answer is **B,** *election. Elect* is the verb form required in this sentence. *Election* is the noun form.

Q. She was <u>convenience</u> <u>hidden</u> away <u>when</u> the social worker <u>visited</u>.
           A   **B**   **C**   **D**

The answer is **A**, *convenience*. The adverb *conveniently* should be used to modify the verb *hidden*. A noun makes no sense between two parts of a passive verb structure.

Q. Her <u>weigh</u> has increased <u>remarkably</u> <u>since</u> she began receiving treatment.
   A **B**   **C**   **D**

The answer is **B**, *weigh*. *Weigh* is a verb and makes no sense between a possessive pronoun and a verb. The noun required in this sentence is *weight*.

Q. <u>In spite</u> <u>of</u> her good <u>intentional</u>, she is not <u>well liked</u>.
     A   **B**   **C**   **D**

The answer is **C**, *intentional*. *Intentional* is an adjective and makes no sense in this sentence. The noun *intentions* is required.

Q. In an <u>irony</u> twist of <u>fate</u>, it was Jim <u>who</u> lived <u>through</u> the fire.
        A   **B**   **C**   **D**

The answer is **A**, *irony*. The word *irony* is a noun, but it is modifying a noun, *twist*. The adjective form that must be used is *ironic*.

Q. She was <u>solicitation</u> by the <u>group</u> <u>for</u> additional <u>services</u>.
          A   **B** **C**   **D**

The answer is **A**, *solicitation*. The form required to complete the passive voice structure is the past participle of the verb, *solicited*.

Need and *In Need of*

The verb *need* is followed by the infinitive (*to* + verb in simple form) when a living thing is the subject and the verb+*ing* or *to be* + past participle when an inanimate object is the subject.

Susan *needs to study* economics.
Melvin *needs to sleep* tonight.

In these examples, because Susan and Melvin are living things, the infinitive is necessary.

The composition *needs rewriting*.
The composition *needs to be rewritten*.

The composition is an inanimate object, so *needs* must be followed by the verb+*ing* or *to be* plus *rewritten*. The second choice above is more common and is actually a passive construction.

> In the phrase *in need of,* the word *need* is not used as a verb. This phrase must be preceded by a form of the verb *be* and followed by a noun or noun phrase.

Mike *is in need of* a liver transplant. (Mike needs a liver transplant.)

The organization *was in need of* funds. (The organization needed funds.)

So and *Such*

Generally, when these words appear in a construction ending in *that*, *so* modifies adjectives or adverbs and *such* modifies nouns.

> When the word *so* is used with an adjective or adverb alone, the sentence structure is as follows: Subject + verb + *so* + {adjective/adverb} + *that* + remainder of sentence.

She sang *so <u>well</u> that* she was asked to audition.
        adverb

The food was *so <u>good</u> that* he could not resist it.
        adjective

> When *so* is used with intensive modifiers (such as **much, many, few,** and **little**), the sentence structure is as follows: Subject + verb + *so* + intensive modifier + noun + *that* + remainder of sentence.

The man brought so *many* books *that* he needed assistance to carry them.

The cooks made so *little* food *that* some people were not served.

> When *such* is used with singular count nouns, the sentence structure is as follows: Subject + verb + *such a* + adjective + singular count noun + *that* + remainder of sentence.

It was *such* a hot day *that* several people fainted.

So could also be used in this circumstance, but the article (*a, an,* or *the*) must move in the sentence construction so it falls between the adjective and the noun.

When *so* is used with singular count nouns, the sentence structure is as follows: Subject + verb + *so* + adjective + *a* + singular count noun + *that* + remainder of sentence.

It was *so* hot a day *that* several people fainted.

When *such* is used with plural count nouns, one possible sentence structure is as follows: Subject + verb + *such* + adjective + plural count or noncount noun + remainder of sentence.

This is *such* sour juice *that* I cannot drink it.

They are *such* popular singers *that* they will likely win an award.

Adverbs and Adjectives

The TOEFL test often contains questions that ask you to identify when an adjective is being used instead of an adverb and vice versa. A review of the basic differences between these parts of speech is important.

Adjectives

Adjectives fall into two categories: descriptive and limiting.

Descriptive adjectives describe the color, size, or quality of a noun or pronoun.

Examples of descriptive adjectives include *large, small, happy,* and *sad.*

Limiting adjectives restrict the nouns or pronouns they modify in quantity, distance, possession, or some other way.

Types of limiting adjectives include: cardinal numbers (*one, two*); ordinal numbers (*first, second*); possessives (*my, your, his*); demonstratives (*this, that, these, those*); quantity (*few, many, much*); and articles (*a, an, the*).

Adjectives are unaffected by whether the noun is singular or plural, except for the adjectives *this, that, these* and *those.*

Adjectives normally precede the nouns they modify, but they follow linking verbs. Adjectives modify only nouns, pronouns, and linking verbs. Adjectives answer questions such as "what kind?" or "how many?"

This is a *good* movie. She is an *excellent* student.

Adverbs

Adverbs modify verbs (except linking verbs), adjectives, and other adverbs. Many descriptive adjectives can be changed to adverbs by adding the suffix -ly to the base. For example,

quick becomes *quickly*
adjective   adverb

bright becomes *brightly*
adjective   adverb

quiet becomes *quietly*
adjective   adverb

There are also irregular adjectives, which change the entire base in order to become an adverb. For example, the adjective *good* becomes the adverb *well.* Also, *fast* is unusual because the same word form acts as both an adjective and an adverb. An adverb answers the question "how?".

Alberto drives *carefully*. (How does Alberto drive?)

Michelle speaks Spanish *fluently*. (How well does Michelle speak Spanish?)

He was driving *fast*. (How was he driving?)

TOEFL test questions, of course, are never quite so simple as these examples. Following are some sample word form questions that are better representations of what you will encounter on the test.

Q. These flowers can be convenient grouped into types depending upon
                              A   B

how often they bloom.
C   D

The answer is **B,** *convenient,* because *grouped* is functioning as an adjective and it must be modified by an adverb. How can the flowers be grouped? They can be *conveniently* grouped. An adjective normally cannot be followed by an adjective unless they both clearly are modifying the same noun. For example: It was a cold, windy day. *Cold* modifies *day* and does not modify *windy*.

Q. They are a lively and interestingly group of musicians.
        A B   C   D

The answer is **C,** *interestingly. Lively* may look like an adverb, but it is an adjective, modifying *group. Interesting* is also an adjective, further telling what kind of group, and is the correct form.

Q. The preacher's sermon was viewed as moral reprehensible by his detractors.
                              A   B   C   D

The answer is **C**, *moral*. The word *moral* is incorrect because it modifies the adjective *reprehensible* and does not modify a noun. An adjective cannot modify another adjective, so the word should be *morally*.

Adjective Forms

The TOEFL test sometimes, but not often, requires you to determine if an adjective itself is in the correct form. Keep in mind that adjectives do not change depending on the number of the noun they modify. (In other words, the adjective modifying a singular noun will be the same if it is modifying a plural noun.)

> **Q.** This movie <u>has been</u> described as <u>a</u> masterpiece in <u>subtle</u> and <u>novels</u> images.
>   A   B   C   D

The answer is **D**, *novels*. The adjective should be *novel*, even though the noun *images* is plural.

Linking Verbs

I have noted in this section that adjectives modify linking verbs and adverbs do not. (Adjectives that modify linking verbs are normally called *predicate adjectives* because they are in the predicate area of the sentence; they complete the verb.) To clarify, *linking verbs* are a special category of verbs that connect (or *link*) the subject with the subject complement (the predicate adjective). These verbs do not show action.

> **Linking verbs include words such as be, appear, feel, become, seem, look, remain, sound, smell, stay, and taste.**

> Jeff *appears* ill. (*Ill* is the predicate adjective.)
>
> Sufferers of lung disease *become* tired quite easily. (*Tired* is the predicate adjective.)
>
> The food *tastes* good. (*Good* is the predicate adjective.)

Parallel Structure

Parallel sentence structure is a common source of confusion involving the wrong form of a word. The TOEFL test often contains word form questions that ask you to recognize that a sentence should have a parallel structure but doesn't.

Parallel structure means that when information in a sentence is given as a list or a series, all components of that list or series must be grammatically parallel or equal. There may be only two components, or there may be more than two components in a list. For example, if the first item in the list is a noun, the rest must be nouns. If the first item is a verb in infinitive form, the rest must also be infinitives. Consider the following sample question:

Q. The bears <u>have</u> <u>become</u> more active, <u>aggression</u>, and angry <u>than</u> before.
            A   B   C   D

The answer is **C,** *aggression,* which is incorrect because the other two words in the list (*active* and *angry*) are adjectives. *Aggression* is a noun. The adjective form of this word would be *aggressive.*

Q. The astronauts <u>on</u> this mission expect <u>to dock</u> with the space station,
                A   B

    <u>performance</u> a space walk, and <u>repair</u> the Hubbel telescope.
    C   D

The answer is **C,** *performance. Performance* is a noun, but *dock* and *repair* are verbs. *Perform* would be the correct form of the word to use.

Q. The Dean demanded <u>thorough</u> research, complete <u>investigate</u>, and a
                    A   B

    <u>well-written</u> <u>report</u>.
    C   D

The answer is **B,** *investigate. Investigate* is a verb, while *research* and *report* are nouns. *Investigation* would be correct.

Pronoun Forms

A common type of question on the TOEFL test asks you to recognize when the incorrect form of a pronoun is being used. This section outlines the various types of pronouns and their functions in a sentence.

Certain pronouns are *subject pronouns,* which means that they should appear in the subject position of the sentence or after a form of the verb *be.*

> **The subject pronouns are *I, you (singular), he, she, it, we, you (plural),* and *they.***

    She is studying for an exam.

    They have left for work.

    It was *she* who arrived late. (The subject pronoun appears after the linking verb *be.*)

Other pronouns are *object pronouns,* which means that they should appear in the object or complement position or after prepositions.

> **The object pronouns are *me, you (singular), him, her, it, us, you (plural),* and *them.***

The doctor prescribed some medication for *him*. (after preposition)

Dr. Williams called *them* last night.

To *him*, it appears to be hopeless. (after preposition)

Two types of pronouns can be used to indicate possession. The first type are used as adjectives because they must be followed by a noun.

Possessive pronouns used as adjectives are *my, your (singular), his, her, its, our, your (plural),* and *their*.

I broke *my* leg.

The bird abandoned *its* nest.

He is working on *his* report.

The other type of possessive pronoun is used in place of a noun.

Possessive pronouns that replace nouns are *mine, yours (singular), his, her, its, ours, yours (plural),* and *theirs*.

She broke her leg once. I broke *mine* too. (*mine* = my leg)

He is working on his report. She is working on *hers* too. (*hers* = her report)

Reflexive pronouns follow verbs and show that the subject is both giving and receiving the action.

The reflexive pronouns are *myself, yourself, himself, herself, itself, ourselves, yourselves,* and *themselves*.

The bird cleaned *itself* in the bird bath.

We taught *ourselves* how to use the Internet.

He hurt *himself* when he fell.

Reflexive pronouns can also be used to show emphasis.

She prepared the entire report *herself*.

She *herself* prepared the entire report.

You *yourself* must decide whether you are ready to make the commitment.

On the TOEFL test, a question may use one of the pronoun forms in place of another. You must be able to recognize when the wrong form of a pronoun is used.

  Q. The disagreement is between we.
    A   B   C   D

The answer is **D**. *We* is incorrect because after a preposition, the complement form of the pronoun (*us*) is appropriate.

> **Q.** <u>She</u> is <u>known</u> for <u>herself</u> contributions <u>to</u> art.
>   A   B   C   D

The answer is **C.** *Herself* is incorrect. The pronoun is used as a possessive adjective here, so the form should be *her.*

> **Q.** After a <u>difficult</u> ordeal, <u>her</u> and Robert <u>felt</u> great <u>relief</u>.
>   A   B   C   D

The answer is **B.** *Her* is incorrect. The initial phrase is a prepositional phrase, so the pronoun is in subject position and should be *she.*

Noun/Pronoun Agreement

A common type of pronoun error results from an agreement problem. A pronoun must agree with the noun it refers to, both in terms of gender and number.

> **Incorrect:** Rafael purchased a new car but then decided *he* did not like *them.*
> **Correct:** Rafael purchased a new car but then decided *he* did not like *it.*

In the first sentence, *them* is incorrect, because it is a plural pronoun that refers to a singular noun, *car.* In the second sentence, both pronouns agree correctly with the nouns they replace. *He* refers to *Rafael,* and *it* refers to *car.*

> **Incorrect:** The heavy structures began to weaken, but *it* is still standing.
> **Correct:** The heavy structures began to weaken, but *they* are still standing.

In the first sentence, *it* is incorrect, because the noun, *structures,* is plural. The second sentence shows a correct use of the pronoun *they.*

The following sample question represents what you might encounter on the TOEFL test:

> **Q.** <u>These</u> principles of law, which <u>originally</u> developed under English Common
>   A   B
> Law, are still <u>widely</u> followed today, although <u>it has</u> not been followed by
>   C   D
> California courts.

The answer is **D,** *it has.* If you eliminate the relative clause between the first two commas and examine what the antecedent of the pronoun *it* is supposed to be, you will see that it refers back to *These principles.* The prepositional phrase *of law* should be ignored when determining the subject of the sentence. *It has* should actually be *they have* in order to agree with the noun.

Another type of TOEFL test question asks you to recognize that a pronoun does not have a logical referent. In other words, if you cannot clearly identify the noun that a pronoun refers to, that indicates there is a problem with the pronoun.

Q. James was <u>dismissed</u> from <u>his</u> job because <u>they</u> were unhappy <u>with</u> his work.
                     A   **B**   **C**   **D**

The answer is **C,** *they,* because that pronoun does not have an antecedent in the sentence. We might assume that *they* refers to James's employers, but we cannot be certain because that information is not provided. The sentence would be correct if it were written: "James's employer dismissed him from his job because <u>she</u> was unhappy with his work."

Q. Dawn <u>dislikes</u> <u>politics</u> because <u>she</u> believes that <u>they</u> are interested only in fame.
            A   **B**   **C**   **D**

The answer is **D.** The pronoun *they* does not have an antecedent in this sentence and is therefore incorrect. The word *politics* is singular and generic, so *they* cannot refer to it. The sentence would be correct if it were written: "Dawn dislikes politicians because she believes that they are interested only in fame."

Verb Forms

A verb must agree with the context of a sentence in terms of time and who is performing or receiving the action. The verb form completes the sentence construction set up by an auxiliary. The following sections help you become familiar with the basic verb structures.

Basic Verb Rules

Certain verb constructions appear as a single word, while others appear with auxiliary words. The following examples are in the active voice.

- **Simple present:** Birds *fly.*
- **Simple past:** The bird *flew* around the tree.
- **Present progressive:** The bird *is flying* away.
- **Past progressive:** The bird *was flying* away.
- **Present perfect:** The bird *has flown* away.
- **Past perfect:** The bird *had flown* away before the cat could catch it.

You should be able to recognize a verb form from its appearance. Simple present tense is the verb by itself, which will be followed by *-s* in the third person singular form. (The bird *flies.*) On the following pages, you will find more detail on the various verb forms. The last two forms (present participle and past participle) *must* appear with an auxiliary when they are functioning as a verb. Sometimes they function as an adjective, in which case they will not be preceded by an auxiliary.

Auxiliary required: The baby *is crying*.

Auxiliary not required: The *crying* baby needs to eat. (*Crying* is acting as an adjective, not a verb.)

Auxiliary not required: The baby *crying* the loudest needs to eat. (*Crying* is part of a reduced relative clause.)

Regular Verbs

A regular verb follows standard rules. The past tense of a regular verb ends in *-ed,* as does the past participle form. All verbs end in *-ing* in the present participle. The following table shows examples of regular verbs.

Simple Present Tense	Simple Past Tense	Past Participle	Present Participle
walk	walked	walked	walking
study	studied	studied	studying
type	typed	typed	typing

Irregular Verbs

Irregular verbs are, obviously, less predictable than regular verbs. Various rules apply to irregular verbs depending on the ending of the base verb. Studying lists of irregular verbs is not as helpful as paying attention to their use as you read English and listen to English conversations. The following table offers some examples of irregular verbs.

Simple Present Tense	Simple Past Tense	Past Participle	Present Participle
begin	began	begun	beginning
find	found	found	finding
eat	ate	eaten	eating
ride	rode	ridden	riding

Simple Present Tense

The simple present tense is not used very frequently to indicate present time in standard written English. Generally, the present progressive tense is used to indicate that something is happening in the present time. Verbs in simple present tense usually indicate that an action is habitual or repetitive.

Birds *fly*.

This means that birds fly in general, or regularly. It does not indicate that birds are flying now.

Harry *swims* every day.

This means that Harry regularly swims, not that he is swimming now.

However, some verbs are used in simple present tense to indicate that something is happening in the present time. These verbs as known as *stative verbs*.

Common stative verbs include *know, believe, hear, see, smell, wish, understand, hate, love, want, appear, own, have, sound, need, taste,* and *like.*

I *believe* you.

This means that I believe you now. In this case, the present progressive tense ("I am believing you") would sound strange.

This *seems* like an interesting movie.

This means that the movie seems interesting right now. Again, the present progressive tense ("This is seeming like an interesting movie") doesn't work with this verb.

Present Progressive Tense

The present progressive form of a verb always consists of a present form of the verb *be* and a verb+*ing*. The present progressive is generally used to indicate an action occurring in the present time.

A typical sentence construction using the present progressive is as follows: Subject + {*am/is/are*} + verb+*ing*

Lisa *is reading* a magazine.
Maria *is writing* a paper.

By adding a word or phrase that indicates the future, the same verb structure can be used to describe a future action.

Lisa *is cooking* tonight.
Maria *is writing* her paper tomorrow.

In the above examples, *tonight* and *tomorrow* signal that the action will take place in the future.

Simple Past Tense

The simple past tense (formed by adding –*ed* with regular verbs) indicates that a completed action happened in the past at a specific time.

> The fireman *pulled* the hose across the street.
> Gina *bought* a new coat.

Past Progressive Tense

The past progressive indicates that an action was occurring for some time in the past until it was interrupted by another action.

> **A typical sentence structure using the past progressive tense is as follows: Subject + {*was/were*} + verb+*ing* + remainder of sentence.**

> The professor *was grading* papers until the student arrived for a conference.
> The boys *were studying* before the game.

Present Perfect Tense

The present perfect is used to indicate that an action happened at an indefinite time in the past or began in the past and still is occurring in the present.

> **The normal sentence construction using the present perfect tense is as follows: Subject + {*has/have*} + verb in past participle form + remainder of sentence.**

> The students *have completed* the project.

When the students completed the project is not indicated. Compare this sentence to "The students completed the project last night."

> Susan *has written* a letter of complaint to the car company.
> Kristin *has lived* in Atlanta for three years.

Present Perfect Progressive Tense

The present perfect progressive construction is used to show that an action began in the past and is still occurring in the present.

> **The typical sentence construction using the present perfect progressive tense is as follows: Subject + {*has/have*} + *been* + verb+*ing* + remainder of sentence.**

She *has been waiting* all day for a call from the doctor.

The students *have been working* on the project.

Past Perfect Tense

The past perfect is usually used with *before, after,* or *when.* Generally, it cannot appear as a single clause because the tense is used when one action happened before or after another. Both actions have to be stated in the same sentence or in adjacent sentences.

> **A typical sentence construction indicating past perfect tense is as follows: Subject + *had* + verb in past participle + {*before/when*} + subject + verb in simple past form + remainder of sentence.**

The students *had completed* the project *before* they *went* to the movies.

> **Another past perfect tense sentence structure is: Subject + verb in past tense + *after* + subject + *had* + verb in past participle + remainder of sentence.**

The students *went* to the movies *after* they *had completed* the project.

Past Perfect Progressive Tense

The past perfect progressive tense is similar to the past perfect tense except that the action is progressive (or ongoing).

> **A typical sentence construction indicating past perfect progressive tense is as follows: Subject + *had been* + verb+*ing* + {*before/when*} + subject + verb in simple past form + remainder of sentence.**

The students *had been working* on the project *before* they *went* to the movies.

Another option is to use a gerund in place of the second subject and verb.

The chef *had been studying* for five years *before opening* a restaurant.

Modals

The modal auxiliaries are generally used to indicate something that is potential or uncertain. A modal is an auxiliary, so it is never used with another auxiliary verb. An auxiliary is simply a helping word, which is used along with a main verb. Other auxiliaries include forms of *be, have,* or *do.* A modal is an unusual type of word in that it indicates a condition or an unknown situation.

I *am* going to the movies.

I *am* not going to the movies.

Both of the above sentences are certain. They describe actions that we know will or will not happen.

I *may* go to the movies.

I *may* not go to the movies.

The use of the modal *may* makes both of these sentences uncertain.

The modals are listed in the following table.

Present Tense	Past Tense
will	would
can	could
may	might
shall	should
must	

A modal is always directly followed by the simple form of the verb. After a modal, there can never be a verb+*ing,* a verb ending in *s,* a past tense or past participle form of a verb, or an infinitive form of a verb (*to* + verb).

The typical sentence structure for a sentence that uses a modal is as follows: Subject + modal + verb in simple form + remainder of sentence.

The woman *must go* to the doctor today.

To indicate the past time when using a modal, the word *have* in the simple form appears after the modal, followed by a verb in the past participle.

The sentence structure for the past time with a modal is as follows: Subject + modal + *have* + verb in past participle + remainder of sentence.

Julie *could have hurt* herself in the accident if she had not been wearing her seat belt.

Subject/Verb Agreement

The subject and verb in a sentence must agree in person and number, as the following examples show.

The bridge *opens* every hour.
   singular   singular

The bridges *open* every hour.
    plural   plural

Noun Endings

The endings on a noun in English indicate whether they are singular or plural. The verb or other parts of a sentence offer clues as to whether a noun should be singular or plural.

> The scientists are studying a new compound.

In this example, *Scientists* must be plural because the verb *are* is plural.

A typical TOEFL test question might look like this:

Q. Ten to twenty <u>year</u> after <u>transferring</u> files to new media, the files should <u>be</u>
              A   **B**   **C**

checked <u>for</u> compatibility.
     D

The answer is **A**. The word *year* should be plural because it is modified by the words *Ten to twenty*.

Distracting Words and Phrases

On the TOEFL test, it is often difficult to determine which word is the subject when the subject and verb are separated by a word or phrase. Because of that, it can be hard to determine whether a subject and verb agree in form.

> **Prepositional phrases and other parenthetical information have no effect on the form that the verb should take. Whenever anything appears between the subject and the verb, try to block out the additional information and locate the verb.**

One common distraction is a prepositional phrase between the subject and verb.

The students, with 20 classes left in the semester, *intend* to attend all the
plural subject   plural verb
remaining classes.

The study of language *is* known as the science of linguistics.
singular subject   singular verb

The scales on the fish's body *help* to protect it.
plural subject   plural verb

Poor *visibility* from fog and forest fires *causes* accidents.
   singular subject   singular verb

Another common distraction is a relative clause or reduced relative clause between a subject and verb.

<u>The students</u>, who have 20 classes left in the semester, <u>intend</u> to attend all the
  plural subject   plural verb
remaining classes.

<u>Diabetes</u>, which may be caused by one of several different conditions,
singular subject
<u>affects</u> many people each year.
singular verb

A participial phrase between the subject and verb can distract you as well.

<u>The students</u>, believing that Professor Jones will not take roll, <u>intend</u> to skip
  plural subject   plural verb
class.

Finally, remember that phrases that begin with *together with, along with, as well as,* and *in addition to* have no impact on the subject and verb.

<u>Professor Byrd</u>, along with several colleagues, <u>travels</u> to a national
   singular subject   singular verb
conference each year.

For practice, underline the correct form of the verb in parentheses in the following sentences.

1. The effects of cigarette smoking (is/are) known to be quite harmful.

2. The use of bank debit cards to obtain cash (have/has) become very popular recently.

3. Commercials shown during the Super Bowl (cost/costs) a considerable amount of money.

4. The degree of intoxication after ingesting alcohol (vary/varies) from person to person.

5. The photograph of the race's final moments (has/have) been awarded first place.

The answers are as follows: **1,** *are;* **2,** *has;* **3,** *cost;* **4,** *varies;* **5,** *has.*

A Number of or The Number of

Although these two phrases look and sound very similar, they have a different impact on verbs that follow them in a sentence. *A number of* has a meaning similar to *many*. It is a plural concept and requires a plural verb. *The number of* is a way to describe an amount. It is a singular concept and requires a singular verb.

> <u>*A number of boys*</u> <u>*have*</u> arrived for the meeting.
>   plural subject   plural verb
>
> <u>*The number of boys*</u> coming to the meeting <u>*is*</u> nine.
>   singular subject   singular verb

The following sample questions offer an idea of how subject/verb agreement is examined on the TOEFL test.

Q. Upon <u>reaching</u> the destination, a number of personnel <u>is</u> expected <u>to change</u>
         A   **B**   **C**

    their reservations and <u>proceed</u> to Hawaii.
                          D

The answer is **B**, *is*. *A number of* must be followed by a plural verb, *are*. The first part of the sentence is not part of the subject.

Q. The students, <u>when</u> confronted with evidence <u>of cheating</u> <u>on</u> the final exam,
              A   **B**   **C**

    <u>was</u> extremely defensive.
    D

The answer is **D**, *was*. If you eliminate the language between the commas, it is easy to see that the subject of the sentence is *The students* so the verb should be plural (*were*).

Q. John Edwards, <u>the</u> first of <u>many</u> black students <u>to attend</u> this law school,
                   A   **B**   **C**

    <u>have</u> been elected a circuit judge.
    D

The answer is **D**, *have*. The clause between the commas is a reduced relative clause. It has the same meaning as *who was the first of many . . . .* The subject of the sentence is *John Edwards,* and the verb should be *has*.

Q. The small town, <u>which was</u> protected <u>by</u> a cliff to the north, a river to the
                  A   **B**

    south, and a large <u>forest</u> to the east, <u>were</u> the best choice for the fort.
                 C   **D**

The answer is **D**, *were*. A relative clause appears between commas. (Notice that the relative clause could have been reduced by omitting the words *which was* and beginning the clause with *protected*.) The subject of the sentence is *The small town*, and the verb must be singular (*was*).

Q. The truck driver, on the open road <u>in</u> the middle of the night, <u>were</u> trying to

                                     A   B

<u>find</u> a station <u>on</u> the radio to help her stay awake.

  C   D

The answer is **B,** *were.* The prepositional phrase between commas should be ignored. The subject is *The truck driver*, and the verb should be singular, *was.*

Sentences with Two or More Verbs

The TOEFL test contains questions that require you to recognize misused verb endings in sentences that contain more than one verb.

Combining Verb Tenses

When a sentence has more than one verb or verb phrase, the tense of the different verbs must make sense together. Sometimes that means they will be the same tense (indicating that things are happening at the same time). Sometimes the tenses need to vary within the sentence. If the actions in the sentence are happening at different times, the verbs will indicate which happens first and which happens second.

Present time verb structures include the following:

- Verb in present tense with stative verbs
- Verb in present progressive
- *Will, can,* or *may* + verb in simple form
- Verb in present perfect

The present progressive tense and simple present tense can be used together to describe two *simultaneous* actions (actions occurring at the same time).

> Edward *thinks* that Sheila *is feeling* better.

If the simple present tense is used in the main clause and the present perfect tense in the dependent clause, that means the action in the dependent clause took place at *an indefinite time before* the action in the main clause.

> He *tells* us that he *has been* to the mountains before.
> We *know* that you *have been* here before.

Past time verb structures include the following:

- Verb in simple past tense
- Verb in past progressive
- *Would, could,* or *might* + verb in simple form
- Verb in past perfect (usually used with a past tense verb in the other clause)

Some sentences contain verbs in both the present and the past tense. If the past tense appears in a dependent clause, that indicates an action took place before the action described in the main clause.

> They *think* he *was* here yesterday.

The simple past tense can be used for both verbs in a sentence, as in the following example.

> I *gave* the book to Sarah when she *visited* yesterday.

In other sentences, the simple past tense and the past progressive tense can be used together.

> Ralph *went* to the Daytona International Speedway while he *was staying* in town.

> Edward *said* that he *was feeling* better.

The past perfect tense in the dependent clause shows that the action occurred *before* the action of the main clause.

> We *hoped* that he *had arrived* before us.
> They *thought* that he *had been* there already.

The modals *will*, *can,* and *may* are present tense modals and thus are frequently used with present time verbs when occurring at the same time as the main verb, whereas the modals *would, could* and *might* are frequently used with past time verbs.

> He *says* that he *will purchase* a new house.
> He *said* that he *would look* for a job the following week.
> Mary *said* that she *could* stay for a while.

Following are typical TOEFL test questions that require you to identify incorrect use of verb tense.

Q. The University of Kentucky <u>has held</u> this prestigious title until 1989, when <u>it</u>
                               A   **B**

was <u>granted</u> <u>to</u> the University of Georgia.
    C   **D**

The answer is **A,** *has held*. Because the sentence gives a specific ending time of the action (*until 1989*), the action is in the past only and does not continue into the present. Also, the verb *was* in the other clause indicates that the sentence is in the past. Therefore, the simple past tense (*held*) must be used.

Q. As soon as George had <u>entered</u> the room, he <u>realizes</u> that he had <u>made</u> <u>a</u>
                            A   **B**   **C** **D**

mistake.

The answer is **B**, *realizes*. The past perfect structures in the other clauses indicate that present tense cannot be used. The correct answer is *realized*.

Q. The boy stopped <u>crying</u> when <u>he</u> realized <u>his</u> parents <u>will</u> arrive shortly.
                       A   B   C   D

The answer is **D**, *will*. The other verbs in the sentence are past, so *will* must be in the past, also *(would)*.

Q. George <u>was among</u> the <u>few</u> students who are going to be <u>chosen</u> to lead the
              A   B   C
commencement <u>exercise</u>.
               D

The answer is **A**, *was among*. The verb must be present, *is*, to match the time sequence of the other clause.

Q. It is <u>normal</u> for students to <u>be</u> nervous when <u>they</u> <u>were</u> preparing for a new
              A   B   C   D
school year.

The answer is **D**, *were*. The sentence is speaking of a custom, which is stated with a present tense verb, *is*. Thus, answer D should be *are*.

Hope and *Wish*

The words *hope* and *wish* have similar meanings, but special rules apply to the use of *wish* in a sentence that has two or more verb phrases.

If the verb *hope* appears in a sentence with two or more verbs, the other verb(s) can be in any tense (as long as the tense is logical). The following examples illustrate this fact.

> Bob *hopes* that he *will get* the job. (future tense)
>
> She *hopes* that her mother *is* comfortable in her new house. (present tense)
>
> The teacher *hopes* that he *did not forget* to make copies of the exam. (past tense)

If the verb *wish* appears in a sentence with two or more verbs, the other verb(s) cannot be in the present tense. The tense of the other verb(s) must be one step further in the past than the tense of *wish*. Also, *was* can never appear as the other verb form in the sentence, because the idea conveyed is contrary to fact (like an unreal condition).

> She *wishes* that the book *were* interesting.

Wishes is present tense, and *were* is past tense. This means that the book is not interesting.

> She *wishes* that her parents *had arrived* last night.

Wishes is present tense, and *had arrived* is past tense. This means that her parents did not arrive last night.

Subjunctive Sentences

In sentences with two or more verbs, if certain verbs appear first, then the other verb(s) must appear in simple form. A subjunctive sentence indicates that one person or group requires another person or group to take an action. The word *that* must always appear in subjunctive sentences. (If it is omitted, the infinitive form of the verb can be used with some of the verbs, but then the sentence is not in subjunctive form.)

> We *urge that* he take immediate action. (subjunctive)
>
> We *urge* him *to take* immediate action. (infinitive)

Verbs that use the subjunctive include:

advise	demand	prefer	require
ask	insist	propose	stipulate
command	move	recommend	suggest
decree	order	request	urge

The construction for a subjunctive sentence is as follows: Subject one + verb that uses the subjunctive + *that* + subject two + verb in simple form + remainder of sentence.

> The doctor *suggested that* the patient *lose* weight.
>
> The judge *insisted that* the jury *return* to deliberate further.
>
> She intends to *move that* the group *adjourn*.

The simple form of the verb is also used after certain expressions beginning with *it*. The adjectives that signal the need for the simple form of the verb include the following:

advised	mandatory	proposed	suggested
imperative	necessary	recommended	urgent
important	obligatory	required	

The construction of this type of sentence is as follows: *It* + a form of *be* in any tense + adjective that requires the subjunctive + *that* + subject + verb in simple form + remainder of sentence.

> *It has been suggested that* we *change* the location of the meeting.
>
> *It is important that* you *arrive* immediately.

Verbs Used as Complements

Often the complement of a verb is another verb. The main verb may control the type of verb structure used in the complement, or an adjective may control it. Some verbs regularly appear with prepositions, and that structure itself directs the structure of the other verb.

Verbs Complementing Verbs

This section reviews verbs that take other verbs as their complements. The verb functioning as the complement may appear in the infinitive form (*to* + verb) or in the gerund form (verb+*ing*), depending upon the verb that it follows.

The following verbs are *always* followed by the infinitive when they are followed by a verb acting as a complement.

agree	expect	need	strive
attempt	fail	offer	tend
claim	forget	plan	want
decide	hesitate	prepare	wish
demand	hope	pretend	
desire	intend	refuse	
determine	learn	seem	

> The board *decided to schedule* another meeting.
>
> Congress *will attempt to increase* the estate tax exemption.

The following verbs are always followed by a gerund when they are followed by a verb acting as a complement.

admit	deny	practice	resume
appreciate	enjoy	quit	risk
avoid	finish	recall	suggest
can't help	mind	report	
consider	miss	resent	
delay	postpone	resist	

> John *admitted sneaking* out of class.
>
> The officers should not *risk climbing* the ladder.

Verbs that are followed by an infinitive or gerund acting as a complement are made negative by adding the negative particle *not* before the infinitive or gerund.

> Tracy *determined not to look* for a job.
>
> We *regretted not preparing* for the test.

The following verbs can be followed by either the infinitive or the gerund as a complement with no change in meaning.

begin	forget	love	remember
continue	hate	prefer	start
dread	like	regret	stop

> He *started to study* Spanish. He *started studying* Spanish.
>
> Jill *hates to* drive at night. Jill *hates driving* at night.

The verbs *stop, remember,* and *forget* can also be followed by either an infinitive or gerund, but their meaning changes depending on their location.

> She remembered *to contact* the man. (She did not forget to contact him.)
>
> She remembered *contacting* the man. (She had a recollection of contacting him.)
>
> He had been playing football, but he stopped *to study*. (He discontinued playing football in order to study.)
>
> He stopped *studying* when she arrived. (He was studying, but he discontinued studying.)

Verbs Following Prepositions

When a verb + preposition, an adjective + preposition, a noun + preposition, or a preposition alone is followed by a verb, the verb will appear as a gerund (verb+*ing*). Following is a list of commonly used verbs + prepositions that would be followed by gerunds:

approve of	give up	put off	think about
count on	insist on	rely on	think of
depend on	keep on	succeed in	worry about

> We don't *approve of* his *choosing* to attend that college.

Note that when there is a noun or pronoun before a gerund, it is in the possessive form, such as *his*.

Although I have not provided a list of adjectives or nouns that commonly use prepositions, the rule is the same: If a verb appears after the preposition, it should be in the gerund form.

Verbs Following Adjectives

The following adjectives are generally followed by the infinitive form of a verb:

anxious	difficult	important	strange
common	eager	normal	unusual
dangerous	easy	pleased	usual

It is *unusual to see* the sun at this time of day.

It is *important to study* every day.

Q. The police officer attempted to <u>learning</u> <u>the</u> <u>suspect's</u> <u>identity</u>.
                                            A   B   C   D

The answer is **A.** *Learning* is incorrect because the infinitive is formed with *to* + verb in simple form, *to learn.*

Q. The children were eager <u>seeing</u> their father <u>after</u> his <u>long</u> absence from the
                              A   B   C

house because he <u>had been working</u> in another country.
                        D

The answer is **A,** *seeing.* After *eager,* the correct form of the verb is the infinitive, *to see.*

Q. The young boy had spent hours <u>working</u> on the airplane model, but <u>finally</u> he
                                      A   B

gave up <u>to try</u> and decided <u>to go</u> outside and play.
              C   D

The answer is **C,** *to try.* After the verb plus preposition, *gave up,* the gerund (verb+*ing*) must be used, *trying.*

Q. Although <u>her</u> friends tried <u>to convince</u> her <u>to apply</u> for the job at the factory,
                 A   B   C

Christine resisted <u>to make</u> an application.
                        D

The answer is **D,** *to make.* The other infinitives in the sentence in answers B and C are correct, but answer D is not because after *resist* a gerund is needed, *making.*

Verbs Used as Adjectives

The present or past participle form of a verb can sometimes be used as an adjective. That is, some adjectives come from root words where there is a noun, a verb, and an adjective form for the same word. Others do not.

Swim, for example, can be used as a verb but not an adjective in the simple verb form. If you need to use it as an adjective, you have to use the verb+*ing* form, *swimming.*

The children like to _swim_.
　　　　　　　　　verb

The children are in the _swimming_ pool.
　　　　　　　　　　　adjective

The word *consent* is either a noun or a verb and has an adjective form, *consensual*, as well. Depending on the meaning, either *consensual* or *consenting* can serve as an adjective.

We need your parents' _consent_ before you can attend the outing.
　　　　　　　　　　noun

Do you think your parents will _consent_ to your going on the outing?
　　　　　　　　　　　　　　　verb

A mortgage is a _consensual_ agreement placing a lien on a piece of property.
　　　　　　　　adjective

Only students with _consenting_ parents can go on the outing.
　　　　　　　　adjective

The present participle (verb+*ing*) is used as an adjective when the noun it modifies performs or is responsible for an action. The verb is usually intransitive (meaning it takes no object), and the verb form of the sentence appears in the progressive.

The woman heard a *crying baby*. (The baby *was crying*.)

The man was awakened by a *barking dog*. (The dog *was barking*.)

The past participle appears as an adjective when the noun it modifies is the receiver of the action. The sentence is generally structured in the passive voice.

The *sorted mail* was delivered. (The mail *had been sorted*.)

Frozen food must be kept in the freezer. (The food *had been frozen*.)

Some verbs, such as *interest, bore, excite,* and *frighten,* may appear as adjectives in either the present participle or past participle form, but they have different meanings in each form. The verb+*ing* form is used when the noun causes the action, and the verb+*ed* form is used when it receives the action.

The *boring professor* caused the students to yawn.

The *bored students* yawned while listening to the *boring professor*.

The child saw a *frightening movie*.

The *frightened child* asked for his mother.

Nouns Used as Adjectives

Nouns can also function as adjectives when they appear before other nouns. For example, we can talk about a *wool* coat, a *gold* watch, and a *history* teacher. The first noun of the combination functions as an adjective describing the second noun. The nouns that function as adjectives are always singular, even when they modify plural nouns. This is true because adjectives do not show number.

Combinations of number words and nouns functioning as adjectives are hyphenated.

He took a course that lasted *five weeks*. (*Weeks* functions as a noun in this sentence.)

He took a *five-week* course. (*Five-week* functions as an adjective in this sentence.)

That student wrote a thesis that was *eighty pages* long.

That student wrote an *eighty-page* thesis.

Structure Quiz 4

Directions: This section measures your ability to recognize language appropriate for standard written English. The first type of question consists of incomplete sentences, with a blank showing where information is to be filled in. Choose the word or phrase that most correctly completes the sentence. The second type of question consists of sentences with four underlined words or phrases. Choose the one word or phrase that is incorrect in standard written English. Mark correct answer on this page or write it on a separate piece of paper.

1. <u>As</u> the result of <u>regularly</u> inspections, the restaurants in this county <u>have</u>
   A   B   C
   improved their sanitation <u>practices</u>.
                             D

2. Erosion is a <u>seriousness</u> problem <u>along</u> the beaches <u>whenever</u> <u>strong</u> storms
                 A   B   C   D
   enter from the sea.

3. The man was in _____ health that the family began to consider whether he could continue to live in his home.

   A. such bad

   B. so bad

   C. such worse

   D. so badly

4. The owner of the sailboat <u>did</u> not <u>accurately</u> <u>calculate</u> the <u>high</u> of the bridge.
                       A   B   C   D

5. Although this car <u>appears</u> <u>to be</u> manufactured by a <u>different</u> company, it has
                     A   B   C
the same body style, size, and <u>perform</u> as that one.
                                 D

6. The environmental damage caused by the oil spill will likely last

_____.

    A. to severals year

    B. for several years

    C. severally years

    D. year several

7. The engineer <u>drew</u> the blueprints and <u>delivered</u> <u>it</u> <u>to</u> the architect.
                    A   B   C D

8. The researcher mixed the <u>two</u> ingredients, poured the <u>mixture</u> into a petri
                                A   B
dish, <u>draw</u> out a <u>measured</u> amount, and carefully applied it to another dish.
       C   D

9. The actress, having worked for many hours without interruption,

_____ it difficult to remember her lines.

    A. find

    B. was finding

    C. was found

    D. were finding

10. The boat rose and fell <u>slow</u> <u>as</u> the huge sea <u>swells</u> <u>moved</u> towards shore.
                              A B   C   D

11. This is the <u>first</u> time Janet has <u>taken</u> <u>so difficult</u> class, but she plans to
               A   B   C
<u>complete</u> it.
   D

12. The woman wished she _____ such drastic action when the stock
market seemed volatile.

    A. had not taken

    B. did not taken

    C. not take

    D. no had taken

Answers and Explanations for Structure Quiz 4

1. **B:** *regularly.* It modifies a noun and therefore must be an adjective, *regular.*

2. **A:** *seriousness.* It should be an adjective because it is modifying the noun *problem.* But the *–ness* suffix indicates that it is a noun.

3. **A:** *such bad.* The rule is *such* + adjective + non-count noun.

4. **D:** *high. High* is an adjective *(a high bridge).* The noun is *height.*

5. **D:** *perform. Perform* is a verb. The parallel structure consists of a list of nouns, *style, size, and performance.*

6. **B:** *for several years. Several* is an adjective so it cannot be plural.

7. **C:** *It.* The antecedent of the pronoun is *blueprints* so the pronoun should be *them.*

8. **C:** *draw.* This is a parallel structure question. All the verbs in the sentence are in the past tense, so *draw* must be *drew.*

9. **B:** *was finding.* The subject is *actress,* which is singular. It is an active sentence so the only possible choice is past progressive.

10. **A:** *slow.* It must be an adverb because it modifies the verbs *rose* and *fell.* The adverb form is *slowly.*

11. **C:** *so difficult.* The order is *so* + adjective + *a* + singular noun *(so difficult a class)* or *such* + *a* + adjective + singular noun *(such a difficult class).*

12. **A:** *had not taken.* The past perfect is formed by *had* + verb in past participle.

Word Choice

The Word Choice type of question in the Structure section tests your knowledge of idiomatic expressions, your understanding of when to use certain prepositions with certain words, your recognition of problem words that are easily confused, and similar matters.

Idiomatic Expressions

There are many, many idiomatic expressions in English. An *idiomatic expression* is a combination of words that have a particular meaning when used together that may not be an exact translation of the individual words. It does little good to study lists of idiomatic expressions. You learn them by reading and listening to English as much as possible, paying particular attention to new expressions that you encounter.

For example, the expression *check out* means to inspect something or to remove something that is registered (like from a library). These definitions have nothing to do with the meaning of the word *check* or the word *out*. Therefore, *check out* is considered an idiomatic expression.

A TOEFL test question might look like the following:

> **Q.** Languages such for French are known as romance languages.
>   A   B   C   D

The answer is **B.** *For* is incorrect because the correct idiomatic expression is *such as.*

> **Q.** She was unable to figure on the mathematical formula.
>   A   B   C   D

The answer is **C.** The idiomatic expression that would make sense in this sentence is *figure out.*

> **Q.** Redwood trees are among the tallest in world.
>   A   B   C   D

The answer is **D,** because the correct idiomatic expression is *in the world.*

Completing a Construction

In addition to idiomatic expressions, the English language also has many common sentence constructions. This means that when you see certain words or phrases in a sentence, you know that other words or phrases should also appear in that sentence. Again, common constructions are best learned by experiencing English through reading and listening, not by memorizing lists.

A typical TOEFL test question on this subject might look like this:

> **Q.** Professor Benton has more experience in this type of procedure from
>   A   B   C   D
>
> Professor Edwards.

The answer is **D,** because *from* does not complete the sentence construction here. The common construction is *more* + adjective . . . *than*, so *than* should appear instead of *from.*

Not Only . . . But Also

The expression *not only . . . but also* means "in addition to." (Other constructions and phrases, such as *both . . . and* and *as well as,* have the same meaning.) When you see a sentence with this expression, keep in mind that the words following the two separate phrases, *not only* and *but also,* must be the same part of speech. If

129

not only is followed by an adjective, then *but also* must be followed by an adjective as well. If the parts of speech are different, then the sentence construction is flawed. Also, if the expression itself appears in any altered form, such as *not only . . . and,* then the construction is incorrect.

> **A typical sentence construction using the expression *not only . . . but also* looks like the following: Subject + verb + *not only* + {noun/adjective/adverb/prepositional phrase} + *but also* + {noun/adjective/adverb/prepositional phrase}.**

James is not only *artistic* but also *scholarly*.
               adjective   adjective

Note that scholarly looks like an adverb because it ends in *–ly,* but it is not.

Sharon writes not only *short stories* but also *poetry*.
                noun   noun

He works not only *diligently* but also *quietly*.
             adverb   adverb

This bus stops not only *in large cities* but also *in small towns*.
            prepositional phrase   prepositional phrase

TOEFL test questions might look like this:

Q. <u>She</u> <u>is</u> <u>studying</u> not only chemistry <u>and</u> botany.
   A   B   C   D

The answer is **D,** because *and* does not correctly complete the sentence construction. *And* should be replaced by *but also*.

Q. He <u>enjoyed</u> <u>not only</u> riding his bike <u>but also</u> <u>the scenery</u>.
      A   B   C   D

The answer is **D.** The phrase *not only* is followed by a verb, *riding.* Therefore, the second phrase in this construction, *but also,* must also be followed by a verb. *The scenery* is a noun phrase, so it is incorrect. It would be correct to say *viewing the scenery*.

Count and Non-Count Nouns

Some word choice questions on the TOEFL test require you to be able to distinguish between count nouns and non-count nouns. The word *count* means "countable." If a noun is countable, you can count individual items of that noun; you can say "one _____ , two _____ , three _____" followed by the noun in the plural form (except with *one*). If a noun is not countable, you cannot logically put a number before it or make it plural.

For example, *desk* is countable because you can say "one desk, two desks, three desks." (Note that you use the singular form of the noun when you count only one, and you use the plural form of the noun when you count more than one.) However, *sand* is not countable because you cannot say "one sand, two sands, three sands." You can say "some sand," but *some* is not a specific number.

Examples of other non-count nouns include *news, food, air, meat,* and *money.* Abstract concepts such as *information, sophistication, mathematics,* and *geography* are also non-countable, as are other words ending in *-sion, -tion, -ics,* or *-aphy.*

The following determiners can be used only with count nouns: *a, an, one, two, three, number of, these, those, few, fewer,* **and** *many*.

The following determiners can be used only with non-count nouns: *little, less, amount of,* **and** *much*.

There is too *much sugar* in this coffee. (*Sugar* is not countable.)

There are too *many students* in this room. (*Students* are countable.)

Some non-count nouns are measured or contained in units that are countable. For example, *coffee* is a non-count noun (although in spoken English you may sometimes hear people use it as though it is countable). But while *coffee* itself cannot be counted, containers that hold coffee can be counted. Therefore, it is correct to refer to *one cup of coffee, two cups of coffee,* and so on.

Likewise, *money* is not countable but *dollars* are. You cannot say "one money, two moneys." You can say "one dollar, two dollars."

Definite and Indefinite Articles

An article or determiner often precedes a noun. If there is an adjective describing the noun, the article precedes the adjective as well. Word choice questions on the TOEFL test sometimes require you to distinguish when a definite article (*the*) should be used and when an indefinite article (*a* or *an*) should be used.

***The* is used to designate specific or known items, as opposed to general items.**

Edwin has to go to *the* class this morning.

This means that Edwin has to go to a specific class this morning and the speaker and the listener know which one.

The woman in the corner will be the speaker.

This sentence refers to a specific woman by describing her.

> **A** and **an** are used to designate a general item as opposed to a specific item, or to designate that the item has not been mentioned previously.

Note: A and *an* appear only before singular count nouns, while *the* can appear before both singular and plural count nouns.

> A teacher must be dedicated to his students.

The sentence refers to teachers in general, not one specific teacher.

> Edwin has to go to *a* class this morning.

This sentence does not indicate which specific class Edwin must attend.

TOEFL test questions might appear like the following:

> **Q.** This <u>building</u> is <u>an</u> oldest <u>building</u> <u>in</u> town.
>   A   B   C   D

The answer is **B**, because *an* is not correct. The use of the superlative *oldest* indicates that the article *the* would make sense instead.

> **Q.** One of <u>a</u> most difficult problems we <u>confront</u> is <u>determining</u> how to <u>present</u>
>   A   B   C   D
>
> a new topic to an unreceptive audience.

The answer is **A**. The determiner *the* must be used with *one of*.

> **Q.** Although <u>not</u> widely <u>sold</u>, that book is considered to be <u>best</u> book on <u>the</u> subject.
>   A   B   C   D

The answer is **C**. The sentence should read *the best*. Use the specific determiner, *the*, with superlatives. The superlative means it is the ultimate one, so it is specific.

> **Q.** Everybody should consider pursuing <u>the</u> hobby, whether it is a thought-
>   A
>
> intensive <u>one</u> like collecting coins or a <u>physical</u> exercise like working in <u>a</u>
>   B   C   D
>
> garden.

The answer is **A**. *The* should be *a* because it is obviously an indefinite concept. We do not know which hobby is being considered.

Another, Other, and *Others*

The same rules that apply to determiners (articles) apply to the word *other.*

Another is used when the indefinite article *a* would make sense. In other words, it is used with a singular noun not previously mentioned or not known by the listener. It can be used only with a count noun, because it means one.

The other is used when the definite article *the* would make sense, that is with a specific singular or plural count noun or a non-count noun already mentioned or known to the listener.

Other is used for plural count nouns or non-count nouns.

Others or *the others* actually act as pronouns, replacing plural nouns.

> Jane was tired of working for the same company, so she started looking for *another* job.
>
> Jane had been offered two jobs, one from her former employer, and *the other* from a new company.
>
> Jane has been offered a job, but she still wishes to pursue *other* choices.

The other and *another* can serve as either adjectives or pronouns, depending on whether they modify a noun or replace a noun.

> I do not want these books. I need the <u>other</u> books.
>
> adjective
>
> I do not want these books. I need the <u>others</u>.
>
> pronoun

Comparisons and Comparatives

Another word choice type of question requires you to know how comparative sentences are generally structured. A *comparison* indicates the degree of difference or similarity between two things.

Equal Comparisons

An equal comparison indicates that two nouns or noun phrases are (or are not) exactly the same.

> A sentence that creates a positive comparison will contain the structure *as* + {adjective/adverb} + *as* + remainder of sentence.

This picture is *as* <u>old</u> *as* that.

adjective

Grisham writes *as* <u>well</u> *as* any modern writer.

adverb

To make the phrase negative, add *not* before the construction. Sometimes *so* is substituted for *as* before the adjective or adverb in negative comparisons.

A sentence that creates a negative comparison will contain the structure *not* {*as/so*} + {adjective/adverb} + *as* + remainder of sentence.

Jeff is *not as athletic as* James.

Jeff is *not so athletic as* James.

When a comparison is made between two people and a pronoun is used to represent one of them, the subject form of the pronoun should be used after the final *as*. (Keep in mind that in conversational English, many people use the object form of the pronoun after *as,* which is incorrect.)

Peter is as tall as *I*.

You are as old as *she*.

Unequal Comparisons

Some sentences compare things that are not equal. In these sentences, the comparisons may be created by adding *-er* to an adjective or adverb and following that word with *than*. Another way to create the comparison is to use *more* or *less* before the adjective or adverb, which is still followed by *than*. In general, it is more common to use *more* and *less* when creating a comparative form from an adverb; this is also the most common form when an adjective is more than one or two syllables. The TOEFL test will probably not test the difference between these two choices.

John's grades are <u>*higher*</u> than his sister's.

adjective

He studies <u>*more frequently*</u> than she does.

adverb

This year's exhibit is <u>*less impressive*</u> than last year's.

adjective

Unequal comparisons can be further intensified by adding *much* or *far* before the comparative form.

This house is *far more expensive than* the others we have seen.

This book is *much less interesting than* the one I read last month.

Double Comparatives

Double comparative sentences contain two comparative constructions, one at the beginning of the sentence and one at the beginning of the second clause.

The sooner we finish the project, *the sooner* we can start the next one.

The more he ate, *the hungrier* he became.

Superlatives

Most descriptive adjectives and adverbs have three forms: the positive, the comparative, and the superlative.

Positive	Comparative	Superlative
smart	smarter	smartest
interesting	{more/less} interesting	{most/least} interesting
cautiously	{more/less} cautiously	{most/least} cautiously

The *positive* is the basic adjective or adverb. It simply describes a noun or verb. The *comparative* describes a greater or lesser degree of difference between two subjects. If there are only two items being compared, technically the comparative, not the superlative, should be used, although the TOEFL test will probably not require you to make the distinction.

This game is *more dangerous than* that one.

Robert worked *more diligently than* Bob.

That child behaves *the most carelessly* of all.

The *superlative* compares three or more items, one of which is superior or inferior to the others.

This is the *most powerful* car of the three.

This house is the *least expensive* of all.

Adverbs are generally formed with *more* or *less*, rather than with *-er.*

Problem Items

No Sooner

If the expression *no sooner* appears at the beginning of a sentence, an auxiliary appears immediately after it, and the word *than* introduces the second clause.

No sooner had the rain started *than* it stopped.

This means the rain stopped as soon as it started.

Despite/In Spite of

The word *despite* and the expression *in spite of* mean the same thing, but the former cannot be used with *of* and the latter must appear with all three words.

> *Despite* his lack of training, he is very knowledgeable.
>
> *In spite of* his lack of training, he is very knowledgeable.

The words *although*, *even though* and *though* mean the same as *despite* and *in spite of*, but they are used differently because they cannot be followed by a noun or noun phrase alone. Each must be followed by a clause.

> *Although <u>he lacks training</u>*, he is very knowledgeable.
>   clause

Rise/Raise

Rise and *raise* have similar meanings but are frequently confused with each other. *Rise* is an *intransitive verb* (meaning it cannot have a complement), and *raise* is a *transitive verb* (meaning it requires a complement).

Rise means "get up," "move upwards (without outside assistance)," or "increase." The tenses of this verb are *rise, rose, risen,* and *rising*.

> The tide *rises* at the inlet several hours before it *rises* further inland.
>
> As the ambassador entered the room, the delegates *rose*.
>
> When interest rates *rise*, stock values frequently fall.

Raise means "lift" or "elevate" an object or "increase" something. The tenses of this verb are *raise, raised, raised,* and *raising*.

> You must raise <u>*your grades*</u> if you hope to be awarded the scholarship.
>   complement
>
> This company has entered into a contract to attempt to raise <u>*the remains*</u> of
>   complement
> the sunken ship.

Lie/Lay

Much like *rise* and *raise*, *lie* and *lay* are often confused.

The first source of confusion is that there are two completely different verbs spelled *lie* in the English language. One verb means to say something that is not true. That is not the verb I refer to in this section.

The verb *lie* that is often confused with *lay* means to "rest," "repose," or "be situated in a place." It is often followed by the preposition *down*. *Lie* does not take a complement (because it is intransitive). The tenses of this verb are *lie, lay, lain,* and *lying*.

The old dog is *lying* in the sun.

The nurse asked the patient to *lie* on the table.

Lay means to "place somebody or something on a surface." This verb must have a complement (because it is transitive). The tenses of this verb are *lay, laid, laid,* and *laying*.

She *laid* the baby in the crib.

The man *had laid* the documents on the table before he sat down.

Sit/Set

Sit and *set* are easily confused as well.

Sit means to "take a seat." Like *lie*, it is also often used with the preposition *down*. It is intransitive, so it does not take a complement. The tenses of this verb are *sit, sat, sat,* and *sitting*.

After swimming, Bob *sat* on the beach to dry off.

They *have sat* in the same position for two hours.

Set means to "put somebody or something on a surface or in a place." *Set* is often interchangeable with *lay* or *put* except in certain idiomatic expressions like *set the table*. It is transitive, so it must take an object.

The man *set* the computer on the table.

Melinda *is setting* the forms in the trays.

Prepositions

The Structure section of the exam frequently tests your knowledge of prepositions, sometimes in terms of their general use and sometimes as part of idiomatic expressions. The following chart shows how prepositions are used.

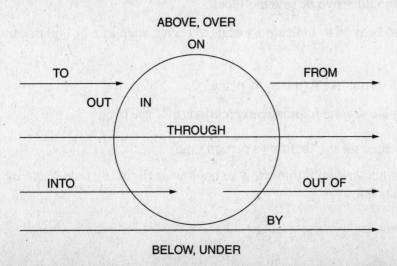

During

This preposition sometimes gets confused with *since* and *for*. *During* is usually followed by a noun indicating time. It indicates duration of time.

During our vacation, we visited many relatives across the country.
During the summer, we do not have to study.

From

From is the opposite of *to*, as shown in the previous figure.

Jorge traveled *from* Columbia.

This means the opposite of "Jose traveled *to* Columbia."

From can be used to mean "beginning," but it must be followed by an ending time as well.

Maria worked on the project *from* 7 o'clock until midnight.

The idiomatic expression *from time to time* means the same as "occasionally."

She works on her novel *from time to time*.

By

By means "near" or "next to."

They passed *by* the store.

By may also be used to describe who performed an action in a passive sentence.

The play was performed *by* the original New York cast.

By followed by a specific time means "before" that time.

You should arrive *by* seven o'clock.

By can also be used to indicate a means of travel, such as a bus, plane, train, or ship.

She does not like to travel *by* plane.

Following are several idiomatic expressions that use *by:*

- *By then* means "before (a certain time)."

    Do not wait until tomorrow to book your flight. *By then*, there may be no seats left.

- *By way of* indicates a stop on a route.

  She flew to Vancouver *by way of* Minneapolis and Seattle.

- *By far* means "considerably."

  This book is *by far* the worst he has written.

In

In means the opposite of *out*. It indicates a constant state, as opposed to *into*, which shows movement from the outside to the inside.

The meeting will be held *in* the gym.

In is generally used to indicate that something is inside a room, building, town, city, country, state, or any other enclosed place or place with geographical boundaries.

The coat is *in* the closet.

She lives *in* Florida.

In can be followed by a general time, such as a month, year, decade, or *the past* or *the future*. (Use *on* when indicating that something happens on a very specific date.)

The next class will begin *in* January.

I hope to learn how to speak French *in the future*.

In can also be followed by a general time of day, such as the morning, the afternoon, or the evening.

I need to see you *in* the afternoon.

Following are several idiomatic expressions that use *in:*

- *In time* means "occurring before a deadline."

  She arrived *in time* to catch the plane. (This has a slightly different meaning than *on time.)*

- *In place of* means "instead of."

  Heather will sing *in place of* Yolanda.

- *In the way* means "obstructing."

  He could not drive down the narrow street because a car was *in the way*.

- *Once in a while* means "occasionally."

  Once in a while, she likes to backpack in the wilderness.

139

- *In the middle* means "located an equal distance from two sides."

  The players met *in the middle* of the court for the coin toss.

- *In case* means "if."

  He wants to buy more insurance so his family will be protected *in case* he dies.

Into

Into is used to show the action of moving from the outside to the inside (while *in* is used to show that something or somebody is already inside).

The candidate waved and shook hands as he walked *into* the room.

Out

Out is the opposite of *in*. However, *in* and *out* are not always used in the same way. For example, "The man is *in* the room" means the same as "The man is *inside* the room." The opposite of this sentence is "The man is *outside* the room." It would not be correct to say "The man is *out* the room."

Out is frequently used in idiomatic expressions and is often used in conjunction with the preposition *of*.

Out of can sometimes be used as the opposite of *into*.

She walked *into* the library.
She walked *out of* the library.

Out of plus a noun indicates a lack of something.

Peter's car stalled because it was *out of* gas.

Following are idiomatic expressions that use *out of*:

- *Out of town* means away from home.

  Patricia is *out of town*.

- *Out of date* means not current.

  This telephone book is *out of date*.

- *Out of work* means unemployed.

  Mike is currently *out of work*.

- *Out of the question* means not reasonable.

  The proposal is *out of the question*.

- *Out of order* means not functioning.

  This pay phone is *out of order*.

On

On is the opposite of *off*, but again the conversion is not exact. *On* and *off* are exact opposites when we discuss whether something such as an electrical appliance is running.

> The light is *on*. The dishwasher is *on*.
>
> The light is *off*. The dishwasher is *off*.

However, we do not use *on* and *off* as opposites when we discuss whether something is sitting on a surface. "The book is *on* the table" is correct. "The book is *off* the table" is not a standard English sentence. In this case, you would say that "The book is *not on* the table."

On can be followed by the name of a day of the week or by a specific date. While we say that "The meeting will be held *in* March," when we get to a specific day or date we say that "The meeting will be *on* March 29th."

> The next class will be *on* Monday.
>
> Classes resume *on* January 23rd.

On can also be followed by a means of transportation, such as a bus, a plane, or a train. The difference between *on* and *by* in this situation is that *on* generally indicates that someone is currently using that transportation whereas *by* is more general. Also, *on* requires an article (*a* or *the*) in this circumstance while *by* does not.

> Jill likes to travel *by train*.
>
> Jill is *on the train*.

On plus the name of a street indicates the location of something.

> The hotel is *on* Concord Avenue.

If the exact address were stated, the preposition *at* would be used.

> The hotel is *at* 433 Concord Avenue.

On can be followed by the floor of a building.

> Patty works *on* the 77th floor.

Idiomatic expressions that use *on* include the following:

- *On time* means punctual. This phrase is more specific than *in time*.

  The plane arrived *on time*.

- *On the corner* means at the intersection of two streets.

  His office is *on the corner* of Granada and Pearl Drive.

- *On the sidewalk*.

  Florence was standing *on the sidewalk*.

- *On the way* means between two places. (This has a very different meaning than *in the way*.)

  Ocala is *on the way* to Gainesville when traveling from Daytona Beach.

- *On the right* or *on the left* means to the right side or to the left side of something.

  The museum is *on the left* side of the street.

- *On television* or *on the radio* means a show or transmission sent via television or radio.

  She heard about the accident *on the radio*.

- *On the telephone* means the transmittal of a call by telephone.

  The teenagers seem to be constantly *on the telephone*.

- *On the whole* means "in general."

  On the whole, the space program has been successful.

- *On the other hand* means "however" and is used to show contrast between two thoughts.

  Mr. Miller is a good coach. *On the other hand,* the assistant is rude and arrogant.

At

At is used to indicate a general location and is less specific than *in*.

Jane is *at* the office.

This sentence does not describe specifically in which room or part of the office she is located.

At can also be followed by a specific address or a specific time.

> Ritsuko lives *at* 105 East 24th Place.
> The movie begins *at* 7:30.

The phrases *at home, at school,* and *at work* are common in standard English.

> John will be *at work* until 5:30.
> Julie should be *at home* now.

Idiomatic expressions that contain *at* include the following:

- *At night* means "during the night." (*In* is used with other times of day, such as *in the morning* and *in the afternoon*.)

  She always has to work *at night*.

- *At least* means "at a minimum."

  The plane tickets will cost *at least* as much as the hotel.

- *At once* means "immediately."

  The woman dialed 911 *at once* when she realized the boy was in trouble.

- *At times* means "occasionally."

  At times, Barbara has considered returning to work.

- *At first* means "initially."

  At first, the company was not given serious consideration.

Under

Under means "below."

> The book is *under* the table.

This would suggest that the book is on the floor; it is not touching the table. *Below* could be used instead of *under* in this sentence.

Idiomatic expressions that contain *under* include the following:

- *Under the influence* means "under the control of somebody or something."

  Martin was arrested for driving *under the influence* of alcohol.

  The woman believes that she is *under the influence* of a magic spell.

- *Under the weather* means "ill."

  Sharon did not attend the meeting because she was *under the weather.*

- *Underweight* is the opposite of *overweight.* It means "too thin."

  Her health problems stem from her being so *underweight.*

Through

Through indicates that something begins outside an object, enters the object, and exits the object.

We traveled *through* Indianapolis on the way to Fort Wayne.

Structure Quiz 5

Directions: This section measures your ability to recognize language appropriate for standard written English. The first type of question consists of incomplete sentences, with a blank showing where information is to be filled in. Choose the word or phrase that most correctly completes the sentence. The second type of question consists of sentences with four underlined words or phrases. Choose the one word or phrase that is incorrect in standard written English. Mark your answers on this page or on a separate piece of paper.

1. The course Bernard signed up <u>for</u> <u>lasts</u> longer <u>from</u> the <u>one</u> Michelle is taking.
                    A   B   C   D

2. Bill took not only a French class _____ a Japanese class.

   A. but also

   B. and

   C. too

   D. but too

3. The waves on the beach on the west coast of Florida are not as high _____ those on the east coast.

   A. as

   B. than

   C. that

   D. so

4. The new computer chip is <u>the</u> smallest one <u>than</u> has ever <u>been</u> <u>developed</u>.
                                 A   B   C   D

5. The farther he <u>ran</u>, the more <u>exhaustion</u> he became, <u>until</u> he could not <u>continue</u>.
                     A   B   C   D

6. No sooner had Janice arrived at the office _____ she contacted her sister.

    A. the later

    B. that

    C. as

    D. than

7. The farmers <u>tried</u> to <u>rise</u> corn, <u>but</u> the birds and insects <u>destroyed</u> it.
                 A   B   C   D

8. The hills <u>lie</u> to the north of town, <u>raising</u> to the foot of a rocky mountain, and
             A   B

a shallow stream runs <u>along</u> the <u>eastern</u> border of the town.
                   C   D

9. _____ , these students are among the best prepared who have been through this university.

    A. At the whole

    B. On the whole

    C. In the general

    D. In generally

10. The children became ill after taking medicine that was _____ date.

    A. off the

    B. outside

    C. out of

    D. over

11. The exam <u>to become</u> a lawyer is <u>on</u> far the <u>most</u> difficult he <u>has</u> taken.
              A   B   C   D

12. One of the two students is studying to be a doctor, but _____ wants to be a musician.

    A. other

    B. others

    C. another

    D. the other

Answers and Explanations for Structure Quiz 5

1. **C:** *from*. The correct expression is *longer than*. Notice that the sentence also has another idiomatic expression: *sign up for*.

2. **A:** *but also*. The expression is *not only . . . but also;* this means the same thing as *both . . . and*.

3. **A:** *as*. The equal comparison is made using *as* + adjective + *as*.

4. **B:** *than*. A comparative is made using adjective +-er+ *than*. The superlative cannot appear with *than* because it is not being compared to anything. In this case, the word should be *that* because it is introducing another clause.

5. **B:** *exhaustion*. The expression is created by using the comparative . . . comparative: *the farther . . . the more exhausted. Exhaustion* is a noun.

6. **D:** *than*. The expression is *no sooner . . . than*.

7. **B:** *rise*. Use *raise* + complement because it is transitive.

8. **B:** *raising*. The word *raise* is transitive, so it requires a complement. This context means it *rises* on its own; it does not *raise* something. So the correct word would be *rising*. Notice that *lie* is correct because it is properly used as an intransitive verb.

9. **B:** *On the whole*. This expression means the same as *in general*.

10. **C:** *out of*. The correct expression is *out of date*.

11. **B:** *on*. The correct expression is *by far*, which means that the exam is much harder than any others.

12. **D:** *the other*. The sentence states that there are two, so the article should be specific.

Missing and Extra Words

The TOEFL test will frequently test your ability to notice that a word is missing or that an extra word appears.

Missing Subjects

As I stated at the beginning of this chapter, a subject is required in every standard English sentence. Do not be confused by distracting words or phrases that are not the actual subject of the sentence.

Q. In spite of Chuck's <u>numerous</u> daily meetings, <u>always</u> finds the time
                          A   B

    <u>to organize</u> his schedule and <u>stay</u> on top of all the issues.
       C   D

The answer is **B**, *always*, because there should be a subject before it. The first phrase in the sentence is a distracter. There must be a subject after the introductory phrase, and it must be either *Chuck* or *he*.

Missing Articles

An article (*a, an,* or *the*) is sometimes required in a sentence. You must be able to ascertain whether a required article has been omitted in a test question. Frequently the article *an* will be omitted from an idiomatic expression or *the* will be omitted from a superlative. Sometimes other clues in the sentence will indicate that an article is required.

Q. Even <u>when graduate</u> of a <u>reputable</u> business school has the proper
            A   B

    credentials, he or she may have <u>difficulty</u> finding a job due to <u>lack</u> of
                                      C   D

    practical experience.

The answer is **A**, *when graduate*. The sentence is clearly referring to an indefinite person, so the indefinite article, *a*, is required.

Q. <u>View</u> <u>from</u> the mountain <u>was</u> <u>breathtaking</u>.
   A   B   C   D

The answer is **A**, *View*. The context of the sentence makes the specific article, *the*, necessary.

Missing Conjugated Verbs

Every clause, whether dependent or independent, must have a conjugated verb. This means that a clause cannot have only a simple form of a verb, an infinitive, or a participle in place of a conjugated verb. It also cannot have only the auxiliary without the main verb.

Q. The <u>problems</u> encountered <u>while</u> developing the prototype of the new
            A   **B**

product line <u>proving</u> insurmountable, so the developers determined the
          C

product would have been unreliable and <u>excessively</u> expensive.
                                  D

The answer is **C,** *proving*. The sentence requires a conjugated verb. The word *encountered* is a past participle from a reduced relative clause in the passive voice, "that were encountered." The word *developing* also is not a conjugated verb. It could not be a conjugated verb without an auxiliary. It is a reduced clause from "while they were developing." The answer *proving* is incorrect because it must be the conjugated verb. *Prove* is a verb and would make sense in the past tense, *proved*.

Q. This company, although <u>having</u> made <u>considerable</u> progress in recent years,
                       A   **B**

still <u>to suffer</u> from a <u>lack</u> of focus and positive momentum.
     C   **D**

The answer is **C,** *to suffer*. It is an infinitive form, and the sentence lacks a conjugated verb. *Having* in this sentence is a participle and *lack*, which is sometimes used as a verb, is functioning as a noun in this sentence. If *to suffer* were replaced with *is suffering*, the sentence would make sense.

Extra Articles

Just as a question might omit a necessary article or use the wrong one, a TOEFL test question might add an article when it is not logical to do so. Often, this type of question will involve an idiomatic expression.

Q. This is <u>the</u> <u>largest</u> breed of <u>the</u> horse <u>found</u> in this country.
         A **B**   **C**   **D**

The answer is **C,** *the*. The expression *breed of horse* is general, so there should be no article within it. As for answer A, a superlative is always one, so it requires the specific article, *the*.

Extra Nouns and Pronouns

Some TOEFL test questions add nouns or pronouns where they are not necessary.

Q. This is the <u>only</u> course that <u>it</u> is available for seniors <u>this</u> semester.
  A   B   C   D

The answer is **C**, *it*. The pronoun *it* is incorrect here because the relative pronoun *that* replaces the noun or pronoun in this sentence structure. If *it* is removed, the sentence is correct.

Q. Ernest Hemingway <u>he</u> <u>wrote</u> *The Old Man and the Sea,* in addition <u>to</u> a
                        A   B   C
  number of <u>other</u> works.
            D

The answer is **A**. The pronoun *he* is incorrect because it appears immediately behind the noun and is not necessary.

Structure Quiz 6

Directions: This section measures your ability to recognize language appropriate for standard written English. The first type of question consists of incomplete sentences, with a blank showing where information is to be filled in. Choose the word or phrase that most correctly completes the sentence. The second type of question consists of sentences with four underlined words or phrases. Choose the one word or phrase that is incorrect in standard written English. Mark your answers on this page or on a separate piece of paper.

1. To give an effective speech, _____ is the delivery that is most important.

    A. it

    B. which

    C. and

    D. there

2. The actress, having <u>been</u> chosen to play the lead role, <u>deciding</u> to try <u>out</u> <u>for</u>
                          A   B   C   D
  other parts.

3. The moon's <u>gravitational</u> field is responsible for <u>the</u> tides, and <u>its</u> location
                  A   B   C
  affects how high and how <u>low tide</u> is from time to time.
                            D

4. Even though the school is struggling as _____ lack of funds, it is expected to continue to operate, due to the immense popularity among the local residents.

   A. the result of a

   B. result a

   C. result

   D. result of

5. One of Cuba's <u>major</u> sources <u>of</u> income <u>is</u> raising <u>the</u> sugar.
                      A   B   C   D

6. A brilliant presenter, _____ used to draw a tremendous crowd, but now the amount of money he is charging is considered too high.

   A. always

   B. he

   C. be

   D. he was

7. In spite of the antagonistic display by their opponents' supporters, _____ city commissioners tried to keep reason and calm at the forefront.

   A. the three incumbent

   B. a three incumbent

   C. three incumbently

   D. the incumbent three

8. Modern outboard boat <u>engines</u> frequently are sold <u>with pump</u> that
                            A   B

   <u>automatically</u> mixes oil <u>with</u> gasoline.
       C   D

9. Whether there should be more control over handguns _____ long been a topic of debate in the United States.

   A. having

   B. has

   C. is

   D. have

10. Having been found guilty of theft, _____ to find work in his chosen field as an accountant.

    A. was difficult for Henry Jones

    B. Henry Jones found it difficult

    C. found Henry Jones difficult

    D. it was found by Henry Jones difficult

11. Henry Flagler <u>was</u> the railroad baron who <u>he</u> also developed <u>a</u> number of
    A B C
    magnificent hotels and <u>other</u> fabulous structures.
    D

12. This course is one of _____ few English courses offered by the college each month.

    A. the

    B. only

    C. mostly

    D. almost

Answers and Explanations for Structure Quiz 6

1. **A:** *it.* A subject of the second clause is required because the *that* clause is the main clause. The sentence, as corrected, means the same as, "To give an effective speech, delivery is the most important thing."

2. **B:** *deciding.* The sentence requires a conjugated verb, *decided.*

3. **D:** *low tide.* The context is definite, so the definite article *the* is necessary: *how low the tide is.*

4. **A:** *the result of a.* This is an idiomatic expression.

5. **D:** *the.* Sugar is being used as a general statement, meaning all sugar.

6. **B:** *he.* He used to means he was accustomed to doing something in the past. *He was used to* would have to be following by a verb+*ing.*

7. **A:** *the three incumbent.* The article *the* is necessary because it is specific and makes sense with the ordinal number *three. Incumbent* is an adjective because it modifies *commissioners,* which in this case is also modified by *city.*

8. **B:** *with pump.* It would make sense to say *with a pump.*

9. **B:** *has.* The sentence requires a conjugated verb, so *having* makes no sense. It is not passive, so *is* makes no sense. The subject is *whether,* so the verb must be singular.

10. **B:** *Henry Jones found it difficult.* The second clause needs a clause beginning with a subject. Because the sentence begins with a participle, *having,* the subject of the second clause must be the same person or thing as the subject of the original sentence.

11. **B:** *he.* After the relative pronoun *who*, it is not correct to have another pronoun. The word should be omitted.

12. **A:** *the.* The expression is *one of the*. The answer *only* would have been correct if it had been followed by *a (only a few)*.

In this chapter, you get an overview of what to expect when you take the Reading section of the TOEFL test. I cover the various items tested in the Reading section and provide sample questions that help you understand what you'll encounter on test day.

As I indicated in Part II, the Reading section consists of several reading passages that are each followed by a series of questions. In general, you will encounter the following four types of questions in the Reading section:

- **General.** You will be asked to identify the main idea of a passage or to indicate what an appropriate title for the passage would be.

- **Details.** You will be asked questions about particular details explained in the passage.

- **Vocabulary.** Vocabulary questions test your understanding of particular words within the passage.

- **Referents.** Referent questions test your ability to identify antecedents of pronouns used in the passage.

When you read a passage on the TOEFL test, first skim the entire passage, paying attention to the first sentences of each paragraph, in order to grasp the main idea. Then read the passage completely and move on to the questions. The reading passage appears on the computer screen while you look at the questions. The Reading section isn't computer adaptive, so you can return to prior questions if necessary. The computer program will not allow you to read the questions until you have viewed the entire reading passage.

Identifying Main Ideas and Purpose

Prepare yourself for Reading section questions that ask for the main idea, a good title, or what you can infer from the reading passage. Keep in mind that questions asking for the main idea of a passage or a good title for the passage are essentially the same question. You must determine the overall meaning of the entire passage and not be tricked into identifying some specific detail.

The main idea is just what it says: the principal thought that the passage conveys. The main idea is the one major concept that pervades the entire passage. Look at the entire passage and watch for the topic that is discussed in every paragraph. Don't be confused by a detail or even a subtopic. The answer to the questions asking you to identify the main idea will be very general.

Sometimes the TOEFL test asks you to identify the author's purpose in presenting an idea in the passage. These questions ask you to identify why the author gave the information. When you encounter a question about purpose, ask yourself what the writer was trying to accomplish. What positive effect does the information in the passage provide?

Studying the Details

As you read, concentrate on the main idea and don't dwell on the details. You will be able to return to the passage and reread sections that deal with specific details. Generally, questions are asked in order of how information is presented in the passage, so you should be able to skim back through the reading and find the details you need. Questions on details require a strong understanding of vocabulary, because frequently different words will be used in the question than are used in the passage.

Some detail questions will ask you to identify the correct drawing, picture, graph, or other depiction that explains something that was covered in the reading. You may also be asked to match or organize items to show your understanding of the passage.

Testing Your Vocabulary

On previous versions of the TOEFL test, vocabulary was tested independently, out of context. Now, vocabulary is tested in context, which means that you have the context of the entire reading passage to assist you in determining the meaning of a specific word.

A strong knowledge of vocabulary is important for scoring well on the Reading section not only because you have to answer individual vocabulary questions, but also because you can use your vocabulary knowledge to answer other questions. In the Reading section, you need to understand the vocabulary words or be able to figure out their meaning from other techniques.

Remember: The best way to improve your reading and vocabulary is to read as much as and as many different types of material as possible. Read newspapers, magazines, books, and whatever else you can. Pay attention to the types of things that the TOEFL test will ask.

Studying lists of vocabulary words as you prepare for the TOEFL test doesn't make sense, because there are simply too many words to learn. If you're unfamiliar with a word that you find in a reading passage, try to determine its meaning from the context. To help you do so, the following sections offer an overview of commonly used prefixes, suffixes, and roots. With a working knowledge of these elements of English vocabulary, you increase your chances of determining the meaning of words that are unfamiliar to you.

Prefixes

A *prefix* is a short string of letters (usually only one syllable long) affixed to the beginning of a word in order to change its meaning. For example, the prefix *pre-* means "comes before." When *pre-* is attached to the root *-fix,* which means "attach," you can determine that a *prefix* is a group of letters attached to the front of a word. Following are some of the most commonly used prefixes and examples that will help you to identify them.

a- or ab-

The prefix *a-* or *ab-* means "away from," "from," or "not."

> The men *averted* their eyes from the accident.
> Meaning: The men turned their eyes *away* from the accident. (See *–vert* in the "Roots" section later in the chapter.)

> The man's skin growth was *abnormal.*
> Meaning: The man's skin growth was *not* normal.

> The women *abducted* the young boy.
> Meaning: The women led the boy *away,* meaning she kidnapped him.

> Sheila was *absent* yesterday.
> Meaning: Sheila was *not* present yesterday.

> It is *atypical.*
> Meaning: It is *not* typical.

a- or an-

The prefix *a-* can have another meaning, which is the same as the meaning of the prefix *an-*. As the following examples show, this prefix means "without."

> It is *amorphous.*
> Meaning: It is *without* shape.

> It is *anhydrous.*
> Meaning: It is *without* water.

> He is *amoral.*
> Meaning: He is *without* morals.

It is *aseptic*.

Meaning: It is *without* disease-causing microorganisms.

ad-

The prefix *ad-* means "to" or "toward." When this prefix is attached to a root that starts with certain letters — *d, f, g, l, m, q, r, s,* and *t* — the *d* drops out and the first letter of the root is repeated. For example, when ad- is added to the root -fix, the resulting word is affix (rather than adfix); the d drops out and the letter f is repeated. Verbs that contain this prefix are often followed by the preposition *to* (even though the word *to* is part of the definition of *ad-*).

The university *admitted* Bill.

Meaning: The university granted Bill entrance *to* the university.

The glue has dried and will not *adhere* to the surface.

Meaning: The glue has dried and will not stick *to* the surface.

She has found it easy to *adapt* to her new situation.

Meaning: She has found it easy to fit well *to* her new situation.

She used tape to *affix* the picture to the wall.

Meaning: She used tape to attach or fix the picture *to* the wall.

ante-

The prefix *ante-* means "before."

This room is called the *anteroom*.

Meaning: This room comes *before* another room.

It is from the *antediluvian* period.

Meaning: It is from the period *before* the flood.

This is from the *antebellum* period.

Meaning: This is from the period *before* the war.

anti- or ant-

The prefix *anti-* or *ant-* means "opposite" or "counteracting."

Michelle drank the *antacid*.

Meaning: Michelle drank the substance to *counteract* acid.

They haven't found a suitable *antibody*.

Meaning: They haven't found a suitable substance to *counteract* the harmful one.

The plane was shot down by an *antiaircraft* weapon.

Meaning: The plane was shot down by a weapon that *counters* aircraft.

This is the *antithesis* of that.

Meaning: This is the exact *opposite* of that.

They say that Mary is *antisocial*.

Meaning: They say that Mary is the *opposite* of social; she is not sociable.

bi-

The prefix *bi-* means "two."

James fell off his *bicycle*.

Meaning: James fell off his *two-wheeled* cycle.

He is serving on the *bipartisan* committee.

Meaning: He is serving on the committee consisting of *two* political parties.

The legislature is *bicameral*.

Meaning: The legislature has *two* chambers.

He used the *binoculars* to see the distant figures.

Meaning: He used the optical device for *two* eyes to see the distant figures.

We need to complete the *biweekly* bulletin.

Meaning: We need to complete the bulletin that comes out every *two* weeks.

circum-

The prefix *circum-* means "around" or "on all sides."

The *circumference* of the circle is two inches.

Meaning: The length of the boundary *around* the circle is two inches.

Please stop trying to evade the issue with *circumlocution*.

Meaning: Please stop trying to evade the issue by speaking *around* what you mean.

Everybody please *circumscribe* the correct answer on your paper.

Meaning: Everybody please draw a circle *around* the correct answer on your paper.

They *circumnavigated* the globe.

Meaning: They sailed *around* the globe.

con-

The prefix *con-* means "together" or "with." When *con-* precedes a root that starts with the letters *l* or *r,* the *n* becomes *l* or *r,* respectively. When *con-* precedes a root that starts with the letters *p, m,* or *b,* the *n* becomes *m.*

The men *conspired* to overthrow the government.

Meaning: The men plotted *together* to overthrow the government.

Michelle and Susan *conferred* about the proper procedure.

Meaning: Michelle and Susan discussed the proper procedure *together.*

They *corresponded* by videotape while he was away.

Meaning: They communicated *with* each other by videotape while he was away.

The materials were very *compact.*

Meaning: The materials were very well packed *together.*

contra-

Contra- means "against," "opposing," or "opposite."

Helen *contradicted* Ellen's testimony.

Meaning: Helen's testimony was *opposite* Ellen's.

He described a *contrary* view of the situation.

Meaning: He described an *opposing* view of the situation.

The students *contravened* the rules.

Meaning: The students acted in *opposition* to the rules.

The two men had *contrasting* views on the issue.

Meaning: The two men held *opposing* views on the issue.

de-

The prefix *de-* means "from" or "down."

The soldier was *demoted* for improper behavior.

Meaning: The soldier's rank was lowered, or brought *down*, for improper behavior. (*Demoted* is the opposite of *promoted.*)

She *deducted* forty dollars from the total cost of the coat.

Meaning: She subtracted (marked *down*) forty dollars from the total cost of the coat.

They *debarked* the ship peacefully.

Meaning: They came *down from* the ship peacefully.

The dead plants began to *decay*.

Meaning: The dead plants began to break *down* to basic parts.

dis-

Dis- means "apart" or "away."

The boys *dissected* the frog.

Meaning: The boys took the frog *apart*.

She *dissented* from the majority opinion.

Meaning: She voted *apart* from the majority opinion.

The employer *dismissed* the staff member.

Meaning: The employer sent the staff member *away*.

The materials *dissipated*.

Meaning: The materials separated or moved *away* from each other.

He is a *dissident*.

Meaning: His ideas are *apart* from those of the majority.

dys-

The prefix *dys-* means "bad," "faulty," "difficulty," or "illness."

He was suffering from *dysentery*.

Meaning: He was suffering from an *illness* of the large intestine.

Joe has *dyslexia*.

Meaning: Joe has *difficulty* reading.

The doctor has treated Jane for *dysphasia*.

Meaning: The doctor has treated Jane for *difficulty* in swallowing.

Many children in that country have died from *dystrophy*.

Meaning: Many children in that country have died from *bad* nutrition or *illness* caused by lack of proper nutrition.

eu-

The prefix *eu-* means "good" or "well." It's the opposite of the prefix *dys-*.

Tim gave a beautiful *eulogy* about Glenn.

Meaning: Tim gave a beautiful statement about the *good* things Glenn has done.

He tried to think of an appropriate *euphemism* to lessen the impact of his words.

Meaning: He tried to think of an appropriate *good* substitute expression to lessen the impact of his words.

The doctor says his dyspepsia has been replaced by *eupepsia*.

Meaning: The doctor says his dyspepsia has been replaced by *good* digestion.

This instrument provides a *euphonious* sound.

Meaning: This instrument provides *good*, or pleasing, sound.

ex-

The prefix *ex-* means "out," "out of," or "from."

He *emitted* a low sound. (The *x* is deleted before the *m*.)

Meaning: He sent *out* a low sound.

They *expelled* the unruly students.

Meaning: They drove *out*, or removed, the unruly students from the institution.

The doctor asked him to *exhale* slowly.

Meaning: The doctor asked him to breathe *out* slowly.

That organ *excretes* waste.
Meaning: That organ sends *out* waste.

They *exculpated* him.
Meaning: They showed that he was *without* blame.

in-

Before *l, m,* or *r,* the *n* of this prefix becomes the same as the first consonant of the word.

The prefix *in-* has two meanings. The first meaning is "not."

Jim knew his actions were *illegal*.
Meaning: Jim knew his actions were *not* legal.

The amount of poisonous gas was *insignificant*.
Meaning: The amount of poisonous gas was *not* significant.

He suffered from an *irregular* heartbeat.
Meaning: He suffered from a heartbeat that was *not* regular.

Bruce's actions were *immoral*.
Meaning: Bruce's actions were *not* moral.

The council's decision was *impossible* to understand.
Meaning: The council's decision was *not* possible to understand, or comprehend.

The second meaning of the prefix *in-* is "in," "into," or "on."

The doctor *injected* him with an antibiotic.
Meaning: The doctor forced an antibiotic *into* his body with a syringe.

This country *imports* a large amount of grain from overseas.
Meaning: This country *brings in* a large amount of grain from overseas.
(*Import* is the opposite of *export*.)

They need to *illuminate* the field better.
Meaning: They need to put more light *on* the field.

She tried to *introduce* a new topic.
Meaning: She tried to bring a new topic *into* the discussion.

inter-

The prefix *inter-* means "between."

The new *interstate* highway is wonderful.
Meaning: The new highway *between* two or more states is wonderful.

His major is really *interdisciplinary*.
Meaning: His major is *between* two or more disciplines.

Larry tried to talk to Heidi during the *intermission*.
Meaning: Larry tried to talk to Heidi during the period *between* acts.

The *interlineal* comments were difficult to decipher.
Meaning: The comments written *between* the lines were difficult to decipher.

intro-

The prefix *intro-* means "into."

The chemical was *introduced* to the solution through a tube.
Meaning: The chemical was placed *into* the solution through a tube.

She is suffering because she is very *introverted*.
Meaning: She is suffering because she is not outgoing (not extroverted); she focuses her attention *into* herself rather than onto other people.

per-

The prefix *per-* means "through."

The substance can *permeate* only this type of blotting paper.
Meaning: The substance can pass *through* only this type of blotting paper.

This is a *perennial* process.
Meaning: This is a process that lasts *through* the year.

The pieces of broken glass *perforated* the canvas.
Meaning: The pieces of broken glass passed *through* the canvas.

He *persisted* in attempting to convince his employers to use more technology and fewer people.
Meaning: He followed *through* in attempting to convince his employers to use more technology and fewer people.

post-

The prefix *post-* means "after."

This *postwar* era brought the realization that the victory was not as meaningful as previously believed.

Meaning: The era *after* the war brought the realization that the victory was not as meaningful as previously believed.

Maria *postponed* the party.

Meaning: Maria rescheduled the party *after* the originally scheduled time.

It's not proper to add a *postscript* in this type of letter.

Meaning: It's not proper to add a short paragraph *after* the body of this type of letter.

George and Helen signed a *postnuptial* agreement.

Meaning: George and Helen signed an agreement *after* they were married.

pre-

The prefix *pre-* means "before" or "prior."

She says that she had a *premonition* that he was not going to arrive today.

Meaning: She says that she had a *prior* warning that he was not going to arrive today.

Harry and Mary signed a *prenuptial* agreement.

Meaning: Harry and Mary signed an agreement *before* they were married.

The students took a *pretest* the first day of the course.

Meaning: The students took a test *before* the course to determine their knowledge at that time.

The doctors hope that with this vaccine, they'll be able to *prevent* her from getting the disease her mother has.

Meaning: The doctors hope that with this vaccine, they'll be able to take *prior* action to avoid her getting the disease that her mother has.

Bob read the *preview* but not the actual homework that he was assigned.

Meaning: Bob read the short description *before* the chapter but not the actual homework that he was assigned.

pro-

The prefix *pro-* means "forward."

The man's body was *propelled* through the air by the force of the explosion.

Meaning: The man's body was driven *forward* through the air by the force of the explosion.

The boys are *progressing* slowly on their bike ride through the state.

Meaning: The boys are moving *forward* slowly on their bike ride through the state.

The Dean says that Professor Borglum is entitled to a *promotion*.

Meaning: The Dean says that Professor Borglum is entitled to be moved *forward* (advanced).

re-

The prefix *re-* means "again" or "back."

The paramedics *revived* the surfer after pulling him from the rough water.

Meaning: The paramedics made the surfer alive *again* (brought him back to life) after pulling him from the rough water.

Her *retort* was devastating.

Meaning: Her sharp answer *back* (reply) was devastating.

Gary has not completely *recovered* from his injuries.

Meaning: Gary has not completely become well *again* (been rehabilitated) from his injuries.

These materials can be *recycled*.

Meaning: These materials can be processed *again* (reprocessed).

She *reverted* to her previous attitude.

Meaning: She went *back* (returned) to her previous attitude.

retro-

Retro- means "backward" or "back."

This statute is intended to apply *retroactively*.
Meaning: This statute is intended to apply *backward* in time.

In *retrospect*, I probably should've asked for a jury trial.
Meaning: Looking *back* to the past, I probably should've asked for a jury trial.

The range of motion in *retroflexion* has improved.
Meaning: The range of motion in bending *backward* has improved.

sub-

The prefix *sub-* means "under."

The town council decided to build a *subterranean* hurricane shelter.
Meaning: The town decided to build an *under*ground hurricane shelter.

The *submarine* rose suddenly to the surface.
Meaning: The vessel that travels *under*water rose suddenly to the surface.

He needs to improve the way he treats *subordinates*.
Meaning: He needs to improve the way he treats people whose positions are *under* his position.

Without the landlord's permission, a *sublease* is not permitted by your agreement.
Meaning: Without the landlord's permission, a lease *under* another lease is not permitted by your agreement.

Prefix Practice Exercise

Choose the correct prefix that, when added to the root, gives the meaning indicated. Write your answer on the line provided.

Sample

> **Q.** de-
>
>   dis-
>
>   sub-
>
>   contra-
>
> *Meaning of whole word:* below water
>
> This _____marine plant life has suffered because of the drought.

The answer is *sub-*. Write the prefix *sub-* on the line preceding *marine* to form the word *submarine*.

1. ab-

    un-

    extra-

    bi-

Meaning of whole word:
not normal

Because of the child's _____normal behavior, he was referred to a psychiatrist.

2. ad-

    a-

    anti-

    circum-

Meaning of whole word: stick

This material will _____here to that one without glue.

3. ante-

    sub-

    ad-

    post-

Meaning of whole word:
underground

The mole is a _____terranean animal that destroys lawns.

4. anti-

    sub-

    ad-

    ante-

Meaning of whole word: next to last

The _____penultimate meeting of the legislators was the most fruitful one.

5. bi-

    semi-

    contra-

    post-

Meaning of whole word: every other month

The _____monthly newsletter was sent to press yesterday.

6. ex-

    per-

    con-

    contra-

Meaning of whole word: say the opposite of

I would appreciate it if you would not _____dict me in front of the children.

7. dys-

    dis-

    pre-

    post-

Meaning of whole word: take apart

The children said it was disgusting to _____sect a dead frog.

8. dis-

    contra-

    ex-

    dys-

Meaning of whole word: bad digestion

His bouts with _____pepsia caused his doctor to order tests in an attempt to locate the problem.

9. dis-

    anti-

    contra-

    a-

Meaning of whole word: not typical

The result obtained from this batch of tests is _____typical; therefore, we must reconfigure the plan.

10. ante-

    af-

    de-

    dys-

Meaning of whole word: attach

To make this word, you must _____fix the prefix to the root.

11. eu-

    dys-

    ad-

    per-

Meaning of whole word: pleasing expression, expression that sounds better

It angered Peggy to hear the funeral director use a _____phemism to refer to the dreaded disease that killed her husband.

12. ad-

    contra-

    ex-

    eu-

Meaning of whole word: removed blame from, found guilty

Harry sued the police for false arrest after the court system _____culpated him in the criminal prosecution.

13. pre-

    post-

    anti-

    re-

Meaning of whole word: before marriage

The marriage was called off because John and Becky could not agree on the terms of the _____nuptial agreement.

14. con-

    anti-

    contra-

    dis-

Meaning of whole word: plot together

She believes that Helen and Sue will _____spire against you if you don't change your proposal.

15. con-

    ad-

    bi-

    circum-

Meaning of whole word: distance around

This is not the correct formula for calculating the _____ference of a circle.

16. ant-

    contra-

    pro-

    ad-

Meaning of whole word: counteracting acid

Susan felt much better after drinking an _____acid formula.

17. anti-

    a-

    bi-

    contra-

Meaning of whole word: two party

The two political groups became enraged at each other and came to no conclusion in the _____partisan session.

18. ante-

    contra-

    post-

    anti-

Meaning of whole word: opposite

What you are proposing is the _____thesis of what I've been trying to accomplish for many months.

19. pro-

de-

dys-

anti-

Meaning of whole word: bring down, reduce rank of

There is a feeling that they are going to _____mote the colonel because of his questionable actions.

20. de-

dys-

in-

ante-

Meaning of whole word: reduce, bring down

If you don't _____crease the speed soon, you may not be able to stop in time.

21. a-

re-

pro-

sub-

Meaning of whole word: without disease-causing microorganisms

The _____septic condition of the operating room must be maintained at all times.

22. re-

retro-

pro-

anti-

Meaning of whole word: applied backward in time

Lisa quit her job because her employers refused to make her raise _____active.

23. post-

re-

inter-

eu-

Meaning of whole word: become healthy again, be rehabilitated

Patty would like to return to work, but she must wait another two weeks to _____cover completely from her illness.

24. re-

pro-

in-

inter-

Meaning of whole word: moving forward

We have made a great deal of _____gress in combating this disease.

25. pro-

in-

inter-

per-

Meaning of whole word: pass through

When a rib breaks like that, there is an added danger that it will _____forate an organ.

Answers

1. *ab*normal
2. *ad*here
3. *sub*terranean
4. *ante*penultimate
5. *bi*monthly
6. *contra*dict
7. *dis*sect
8. *dys*pepsia
9. *a*typical

10. *af*fix
11. *eu*phemism
12. *ex*culpated
13. *pre*nuptial
14. *con*spire
15. *circum*ference
16. *ant*acid
17. *bi*partisan
18. *anti*thesis

19. *de*mote
20. *de*crease
21. *a*septic
22. *retro*active
23. *re*cover
24. *pro*gress
25. *per*forate

Roots

A *root* is a base to which you can attach prefixes or suffixes. Like prefixes and suffixes, roots come from Latin, Greek, or other language origins. An understanding of certain roots can help you recognize the meaning of words that you may not otherwise know.

-cide-

The root *-cide-* is used in nouns that derive from the verb "kill."

Joseph committed *fratricide*.
Meaning: Joseph *killed* his brother.

This cleaning product contains a strong *germicide*.
Meaning: This cleaning product contains a strong substance that *kills* germs.

Pesticides can be very dangerous for humans.
Meaning: Substances that *kill* pests can be very dangerous for humans.

Charles was contemplating *suicide*.
Meaning: Charles was contemplating *killing* himself.

That man was found guilty of *homicide*.
Meaning: That man was found guilty of *killing* a person.

-corp-

The root -*corp*- means "body" or "bodily."

We're removing our child from that school because we don't believe in *corporal* punishment.

Meaning: We're removing our child from that school because we don't believe in *bodily* punishment.

The children found a *corpse* under the bridge.

Meaning: The children found a dead *body* under the bridge.

The *corpus* of the book is finished.

Meaning: The *body* of the book is finished.

This information must be *incorporated* into the main text.

Meaning: This information must be put into the *body* of the main text.

-cred-

The root -*cred*- means "believe."

I find it very difficult to give *credence* to his statements.

Meaning: I find it very difficult to *believe* his statements.

Sarah is very *credulous*.

Meaning: Sarah is too ready to *believe* (easy to deceive).

I need to see your *credentials*.

Meaning: I need to see the documents that make it so people can *believe* your identity.

It was an *incredible* performance.

Meaning: It was an *unbelievable* (unbelievably good) performance.

-cur-, -curr-, or -curs-

The roots -*cur*-, -*curr*, or -*curs*- mean "run."

His *precursor* was well liked by all.

Meaning: His fore*runner* (the person who came before him) was well liked by all.

He gave the script a *cursory* glance before tossing it aside.

Meaning: He *ran* his eyes over the script hastily before tossing it aside.

The children are learning to write *cursive*.

Meaning: The children are learning to write *running*, or flowing, handwriting.

The criminal was given *concurrent* sentences in prison.

Meaning: The criminal was given prison sentences that *ran* together.

-duc- or -duct-

The roots *-duc-* or *-duct-* mean "lead," "conduct," "bring," or "draw."

You can *deduce* from the evidence that he was murdered.

Meaning: You can be *led* to the conclusion from the evidence that he was murdered.

This room is always warm because the air-conditioning *duct* is too small.

Meaning: This room is always warm because the tube that *leads* the cool air here from the air conditioner is too small.

They tried to *induce* him to give up smoking.

Meaning: They tried to *lead* (convince) him to give up smoking.

Listening to a loud radio while reading is not *conducive* to good study habits.

Meaning: Listening to a loud radio while reading does not *lead* to good study habits.

-fid-

The root *-fid-* means "faith" or "trust."

As the trustee, you have *fiduciary* responsibilities.

Meaning: As the trustee, you have responsibilities of being *faith*ful and *trust*worthy.

His *infidelity* resulted in his divorce.

Meaning: His un*faith*fulness resulted in his divorce.

Her *confidence* in herself causes others to feel at ease.

Meaning: Her *faith* or *trust* in herself causes others to feel at ease.

Jane has always been Helen's *confidant*.

Meaning: Jane has always been the one that Helen could *trust* with personal matters.

-ject-

The root *-ject-* means to "throw" or "transfer."

Don's request for an extension was *rejected*.

Meaning: Don's request for an extension was refused (*thrown* back at him).

The horse was *injected* with a painkiller.

Meaning: The horse had painkiller introduced (*transferred* or *thrown* in) with a syringe.

"But what about her?" he *interjected*.

Meaning: "But what about her?" he interposed (*threw* into the conversation).

-mor- or *-mort-*

The roots *-mor-* or *-mort-* mean "death," "dead," or "dying."

This church believes in *immortality*.

Meaning: This church believes in eternal life (no *death*).

Angel is studying to become a *mortician*.

Meaning: Angel is studying to become a person who takes care of *dead* bodies.

The environmentalists have struggled for years to save the *moribund* lake.

Meaning: The environmentalists have struggled for years to save the *dying* lake.

George was *mortified* by the memory of his first dance.

Meaning: George felt extreme shame (wanted to *die*) when he thought of his first dance.

-omni-

The root *-omni-* means "all," "many," or "every."

This legislation came from an *omnibus* bill.

Meaning: This legislation came from a bill that covered *many* different subjects.

We shouldn't let this committee become *omnipotent*.

Meaning: We shouldn't let this committee become *all* powerful.

A mortal cannot be *omniscient*.

Meaning: A mortal cannot be *all* knowing.

That animal is *omnivorous*.

Meaning: That animal eats *every*thing.

-ped-

The root *-ped-* means "foot."

The *centipede* crawled slowly up the leaf.

Meaning: The hundred-*footed* animal crawled slowly up the leaf.

We shouldn't *impede* her progress.

Meaning: We shouldn't hinder (stop the *feet* of) her progress.

The *pedestrian* was hit by a car.

Meaning: The person on *foot* was hit by a car.

The bicycle's *pedal* is stuck.

Meaning: The bicycle's lever operated by a *foot* is stuck.

-rupt-

The root *-rupt-* means "break" or "burst." Make sure that you distinguish *-rupt-* from *-fract-* when discussing the body. You fracture something hard, like a bone, and rupture something soft, like an organ.

The sewer pipes *ruptured*.

Meaning: The sewer pipes *burst*.

His skin *erupted* in a rash.

Meaning: His skin *broke* out in a rash.

The angry man *disrupted* the meeting.

Meaning: The angry man *broke* up the meeting.

Do not *interrupt* me.

Meaning: Do not *break* into my conversation.

-secut- or -sequ-

The root -*secut*- or -*sequ*- means "follow."

We'll be meeting on five *consecutive* Saturdays.

Meaning: We'll be meeting on five Saturdays *following* each other (in a row).

He suffered serious *consequences* for his carelessness with his client's money.

Meaning: His carelessness with his client's money was *followed* by serious misfortune for him.

I am sure a *sequel* to this movie will come out next year.

Meaning: I am sure this movie will be *followed* with a continuation.

It's not enough to plan. You must *execute* those plans.

Meaning: It's not enough to plan. You must *follow* through with those plans.

-string- or -strict-

The roots -*string*- or -*strict*- mean "bind," "close," or "tight."

He underwent surgery to correct a *stricture* in the urethral canal.

Meaning: He underwent surgery to correct a place in his urethral canal that had partially *closed* or become too *tight*.

His probation office *restricted* his activities greatly.

Meaning: His probation officer placed *tight* controls on his activities.

The boa *constrictor* is a family pet.

Meaning: The snake known for squeezing its prey *tightly* is a family pet.

The professor made very *stringent* rules about the written work of her students.

Meaning: The professor made very *tight* (strict) rules about the written work of her students.

-tact-, -tang-, -tig-, or -ting-

The roots -*tact*-, -*tang*-, -*tig*-, and -*ting*- mean "touch."

I need to *contact* Professor Byrd.

Meaning: I need to get in *touch* with Professor Byrd.

He had to pay quite a bit of money in *intangible* tax last week.

Meaning: He had to pay quite a bit of money in tax on items that you can't *touch* (stocks, mortgages, and bonds) last week.

The two properties are *contiguous*.

Meaning: The two properties are *touching* each other.

His *tactile* sense was damaged in the fire.

Meaning: His sense of *touch* was damaged in the fire.

-vict- or -vinc-

The roots -*vict*- and -*vinc*- mean "conquer," "prevail," "use authority," or "overcome."

Sally *convinced* her employers to change the overtime rule.

Meaning: Sally *prevailed* in an argument with her employers to change the overtime rule.

The sheriff *evicted* the tenants because they hadn't paid their rent.

Meaning: The sheriff *used authority* to remove the tenants because they hadn't paid their rent.

The politician was *convicted* of accepting a bribe from a contractor.

Meaning: The politician was *conquered* in a trial for accepting a bribe from a contractor.

The *victor* shook hands with his opponent.

Meaning: The one who *prevailed* (won) shook hands with his opponent.

-viv-

The root -*viv*- means "life," "live," "lively," or "alive."

The lifeguard *revived* the child he pulled from the pool.

Meaning: The lifeguard brought the child back to *life* after pulling him from the pool.

The eagles have *survived* in Acadia National Park because parts of the park have been closed to protect them.

Meaning: The eagles have continued to *live* in Acadia National Park because parts of the park have been closed to protect them.

Jonathan has a *vivid* personality.

Meaning: Jonathan has a personality that is *lively*, or full of *life*.

-vor- or *-vour-*

The roots *-vor-* and *-vour-* mean "eat."

This animal is *carnivorous*.

Meaning: This animal *eats* meat.

That animal is *herbivorous*.

Meaning: That animal *eats* plants.

That animal is an *insectivore*.

Meaning: That animal *eats* insects.

The homeless man *devoured* everything on his plate.

Meaning: The homeless man *ate* everything on his plate ravenously.

Michael is a big boy for his age and has a *voracious* appetite.

Meaning: Michael is a big boy for his age and *eats* a lot.

Root Practice Exercise

Choose the correct root that, when added to the remainder of the word, gives the meaning indicated. Write your answer choice on the line provided.

Sample

> **Q.** -cide-
>
>   -corp-
>
>   -duct-
>
>   -ject-
>
> *Meaning of root:* to kill (noun variation)
>
> *Meaning of whole word: killing one's brother*
>
> Scott was arrested for fratri_____.

Write the root *cide* on the line after *fratri* to form the word *fratricide*.

1. -corp-

   -grad-

   -tact-

   -ject-

Meaning of root: throw

Meaning of whole word: throw a comment into conversation

If she inter_____s one more time, I will leave.

2. -mor-

   -grat-

   -corp-

   -cred-

Meaning of root: thank

Meaning of whole word: money to thank, tip

Jennifer left a large tip because she didn't realize that the menu said the _____uity was included.

3. -fract-

   -rupt-

   -secut-

   -ped-

Meaning of root: break

Meaning of whole word: burst

He's in intensive care, not because of the broken bones, but because of a _____ured spleen.

4. -corp-

   -cred-

   -ped-

   -vict-

Meaning of root: believe

Meaning of whole word: belief

Julie gives no _____ence to anything Becky says.

5. -cred-

   -curs-

   -fract-

   -duct-

Meaning of root: run

Meaning of whole word: running style

Michelle finds it difficult to read _____ive writing.

6. -duc-

   -cur-

   -flect-

   -rupt-

Meaning of root: lead

Meaning of whole word: lead, cause

The mediator attempted to elicit information to in_____e the parties to settle.

7. -corp-

   -cred-

   -grat-

   -fid-

Meaning of root: trust

Meaning of whole word: relationship of faith or trust

Rob was suspended from practicing law because of a breach of _____uciary responsibility.

8. -mort-

   -ped-

   -secut-

   -viv-

Meaning of root: death

Meaning of whole word: not subject to death, not able to die

Sometimes teenagers seem to believe they are im_____al.

9. -string-

   -tact-

   -vict-

   -rupt-

Meaning of root: conquer

Meaning of whole word: remove from property

Ms. Rodgers retrieved the order from the court clerk so the sheriff could e_____ the tenants quickly.

10. -rupt-

   -ject-

   -gress-

   -flect-

Meaning of root: bent

Meaning of whole word: bent aside

Light is often de_____ed by light colors and absorbed by dark colors, making dark materials hotter than light materials.

11. -fract-

   -flect-

   -rupt-

   -secut-

Meaning of root: break

Meaning of whole word: broken

Doctors can't put a cast on a _____ured rib; the only way to hold it together while it heals is to apply a tight wrap around the entire torso.

12. -ped-

   -gress-

   -tact-

   -secut-

Meaning of root: follow

Meaning of whole word: following each other

The board members were upset that Mary missed three con_____ive meetings.

13. -tang-

-strict-

-gress-

-grat-

Meaning of root: touch

Meaning of whole words: something you can touch; something you can't touch

A corporation has to pay _____ible tax on personal property it owns and in_____ible tax on stocks, notes, and other paper obligations.

14. -viv-

-mort-

-ject-

-vor-

Meaning of root: eat

Meaning of whole word: meat eating

Some dinosaurs were carni_____ous.

15. -viv-

-vor-

-secut-

-cred-

Meaning of root: live

Meaning of whole word: lively, full of life

Mr. Pinder is a talented author whose _____id imagination brings the characters to life.

16. -mor-

-omni-

-vict-

-viv-

Meaning of root: every

Meaning of whole word: all powerful

A proper government carefully follows a series of checks and balances so that no person or group can become _____potent.

17. -viv-

-ped-

-mor-

-fid-

Meaning of root: foot

Meaning of whole word: person on foot

Anne was charged with careless driving when she struck a _____estrian while driving too fast.

18. -cred-

-fid-

-corp-

-viv-

Meaning of root: body

Meaning of whole word: embodiment of an organization

Mr. Padgett said that the articles of in_____oration could be filed the day after they were signed.

19. -frag-

-grat-

-viv-

-mort-

Meaning of root: break

Meaning of whole word: easy to break, not strong

Her health is very _____ile at this time.

20. -gress-

-grad-

-cred-

-secut-

Meaning of root: step

Meaning of whole word: one step at a time, little by little

Richard _____ually improved in his anatomy course.

Answers

1. inter*jects*	**8.** im*mort*al	**15.** *viv*id
2. *grat*uity	**9.** e*vict*	**16.** *omni*potent
3. *rupt*ured	**10.** de*flect*ed	**17.** *pede*strian
4. *cred*ence	**11.** *fract*ured	**18.** in*corp*oration
5. *curs*ive	**12.** con*secut*ive	**19.** *frag*ile
6. in*duce*	**13.** *tang*ible; in*tang*ible	**20.** *grad*ually
7. *fid*uciary	**14.** carni*vor*ous	

Suffixes

A *suffix* is a group of letters attached at the end of a word. Usually, suffixes indicate the word's part of speech. For example, a suffix may indicate that the word is a noun, adjective, or adverb, and it may indicate the verb tense, aspect, or person. I cover verb tenses, aspects, and forms in the "Structure Section" chapter.

Normally, the TOEFL test Reading section does not use incorrect parts of speech in the answer choices. For example, if the word being tested is a noun, all the answer choices are also nouns. Therefore, you normally can't use your knowledge of suffixes to eliminate answer choices without understanding the word. However, understanding suffixes can be very useful in order to recognize that a word is related to another that you know.

If there are words or roots in this section that you don't know, look them up in a dictionary. In fact, you can often understand three or more words from learning one root. The purpose of this section is to assist you in recognizing these suffixes, not in forming words. (That is why I haven't explained in detail how the suffix is affixed to the root.)

A suffix often tells whether the word is a noun, verb, or other form. The following table offers an example of how suffixes work.

Root	+Suffix	= Part of speech
imagin-	-e	imagine (verb)
imagin-	-ation	imagination (noun)
imagin-	-ary	imaginary (adjective)
imagin-	-ative	imaginative (adjective)
imaginative	-ly	imaginatively (adverb)

Noun Endings

The following endings normally indicate that the word is a noun: *-sion, -tion, -ition, -ation, -ance, -ence, -or, -er, -hood, -ship, -ty, -ity, -cy, -ment, -ness, -ism,* and *-ist*.

All of these suffixes are added to the root of verbs except *-ship* and *-hood*, which are added to nouns, and *-ness* and *-ty*, which are added to adjectives.

Suffix (Noun Ending)	Root + Suffix = Noun
-ion, -sion, -tion	action, explosion, invention
-ation, -ition	communication, composition
-ance, -ence	insurance, correspondence
-or, -er	professor, computer
-hood	neighborhood, childhood
-ship	friendship, membership
-ty, -ity, -cy	loyalty, reality, complacency
-ment	judgment, argument
-ness	stubbornness, happiness
-ism, -ist	capitalism, capitalist

Occasionally, *-ant* or *-ent* can indicate a noun, although they normally indicate an adjective and *-ance* and *-ence* indicate the related noun. Examples of *-ant* and *-ent* as noun suffixes are *confidant* and *correspondent*.

Following is a list of suffixes from the previous table that often apply to a person.

Suffix	Person
-or	instructor
-er	teacher
-ist	biologist

Following are suffixes from the same table that often apply to an intangible thing (an abstract concept).

Suffix	Concept
-ion, -sion, -tion	concentration
-ance	radiance
-ence	competence
-ty, -ity, -cy	legality
-ness	stubbornness
-ism	communism

Verb Endings

The endings -en and -ize normally indicate that the word is a verb.

The suffixes -en and -ize are normally added to nouns or adjectives to make verbs.

Root	+ Suffix	= Verb
haste (noun)	-en	hasten
standard (noun or adjective)	-ize	standardize

Other examples of verbs created by -en are awaken, harden, flatten, shorten, heighten, enlighten, weaken, hearten, darken, and strengthen.

Examples of verbs created by -ize are authorize, legalize, criticize, rationalize, intellectualize, symbolize, neutralize, centralize, summarize, emphasize, visualize, mobilize, categorize, stabilize, economize, and terrorize.

Adjective Endings

The following endings normally indicate that the word is an adjective: -less, -ful, -al, -ous, -ious, -eous, -ed, -en (past participle), -ive, -able, and -ible.

You normally add all the previous suffixes to nouns, except *-able, -ible,* and *-ive,* which you add to verbs.

Suffix (Adjective Ending)	Root + Suffix = Adjective
-less	hopeless, thoughtless
-ful	hopeful, thoughtful
-al	original, functional
-ous, -ious, -eous	gaseous, dangerous
-ed, -en (past participle)	cooked, broken, beaten
-ive	aggressive, attractive
-able, -ible	agreeable, digestible

Adverb Endings

The suffix *-ly* added to an adjective usually forms an adverb.

For example, *intelligent* plus *-ly* equals *intelligently.* Other examples of adverbs formed this way include absolutely, independently, delightfully, politely, greatly, silently, nicely, centrally, resolutely, falsely, brightly, meaningfully, definitely, and randomly.

Note: There are some exceptions to this rule. *Hard* and *fast* can be used as both adjectives and adverbs, while *hardly* is an adverb that means "barely." Both *friendly* and *lively* look like they should be adverbs, but they are actually adjectives.

Related Verbs, Nouns, and Adjectives

Following are lists of verbs, nouns, and adjectives that have the same roots (and sometimes prefixes) but different suffixes. If you don't know the meaning of the words, look them up in your dictionary. When you look up one of the words in a row, you should be able to determine the meaning of the other two words by recognizing the words' parts of speech from their suffixes.

In these lists, you may recognize prefixes or roots from the previous sections of this chapter that will help you determine each word's meaning.

In the following table, each noun is made by adding *-tion* or *-sion* to the root.

Verb	Noun	Adjective
apprehend	apprehension	apprehensive
assert	assertion	assertive
communicate	communication	communicative

Verb	Noun	Adjective
conclude	conclusion	conclusive
constitute	constitution	constitutional
construct	construction	constructive
contradict	contradiction	contradictory
contribute	contribution	contributory
create	creation	creative
demonstrate	demonstration	demonstrative
dominate	domination	dominant
exclude	exclusion	exclusive
expand	expansion	expansive
impress	impression	impressive
institute	institution	institutional
isolate	isolation	isolated
predict	prediction	predictable
project	projection	projected
reject	rejection	rejected
repress	repression	repressive
restrict	restriction	restrictive
select	selection	selective
suppress	suppression	suppressive

In the following table, each noun is formed by adding -*ance* to the root.

Verb	Noun	Adjective
assist	assistance	assisted
assure	assurance	assured
comply	compliance	compliant
defy	defiance	defiant
ignore	ignorance	ignorant
signify	significance	significant

In the following table, the noun is created by adding *-ence* to the root.

Verb	Noun	Adjective
adhere	adherence	adherent
cohere	coherence	coherent
emerge	emergence	emergent
excel	excellence	excellent
infer	inference	inferential
insist	insistence	insistent
persist	persistence	persistent
precede	precedence	preceding

Suffix Practice Exercise

Indicate whether the following word is a noun, verb, adjective, or adverb. (Place a check in the correct column.) Don't worry about the definitions of the words. Set a timer for two minutes so that you move quickly and don't dwell on the words' meanings. After you finish, look up any word that you don't know.

Word	Noun	Verb	Adjective	Adverb
1. communication	_____	_____	_____	_____
2. bashful	_____	_____	_____	_____
3. forcefully	_____	_____	_____	_____
4. intelligent	_____	_____	_____	_____
5. diligence	_____	_____	_____	_____
6. adherent	_____	_____	_____	_____
7. cohesive	_____	_____	_____	_____
8. persistence	_____	_____	_____	_____
9. significant	_____	_____	_____	_____
10. inference	_____	_____	_____	_____
11. hypothesize	_____	_____	_____	_____
12. ruthless	_____	_____	_____	_____
13. hypothecation	_____	_____	_____	_____
14. dimly	_____	_____	_____	_____
15. extension	_____	_____	_____	_____
16. mechanism	_____	_____	_____	_____

Word	Noun	Verb	Adjective	Adverb
17. machinist	___	___	___	___
18. happiness	___	___	___	___
19. horticultural	___	___	___	___
20. veracity	___	___	___	___
21. neighborhood	___	___	___	___
22. fellowship	___	___	___	___
23. author	___	___	___	___
24. understandable	___	___	___	___
25. courageous	___	___	___	___

Answers

1. noun
2. adjective
3. adverb
4. adjective
5. noun
6. noun or adjective
7. adjective
8. noun
9. adjective

10. noun
11. verb
12. adjective
13. noun
14. adverb
15. noun
16. noun
17. noun
18. noun

19. adjective
20. noun
21. noun
22. noun
23. noun (occasionally used as a verb)
24. adjective
25. adjective

Combining Your Vocabulary Skills

When answering vocabulary questions (or answering detail questions that require a strong understanding of vocabulary), use your abilities in the following order:

- **Knowledge of a word:** If you know what the word in question means, great.

- **Knowledge of prefixes, suffixes, and roots:** If you don't know what the word in question means, try to figure it out from your knowledge of prefixes, suffixes, and roots.

- **Knowledge of grammar:** If you don't know the word and can't figure out its meaning from its prefix, suffix, or root, try to determine which part of speech it is — a noun, verb, adjective, adverb, and so on.

- **Context:** If you still can't determine the word's meaning, try to define it based on how it is used in the context of the paragraph.

Determining Meaning from Prefixes, Suffixes, and Roots

> Her idea of _____ing was to sit with a book open watching television and talking with friends.

Here, part of the word in question is omitted, so your knowledge of the word itself wouldn't help. This word has a suffix, *-ing,* which means that it's part of a verb structure, but there isn't an auxiliary verb (a form of *have, be,* or *do*). Therefore, you know that the word must be acting as a gerund, which is a noun.

Even if you have no idea what the word in question means, you should be able to grasp from the context that the sentence is about studying or something similar. The missing word in this case could be <u>studying</u> or <u>reading</u>. The TOEFL test will give you only one possible answer choice that is correct, unless the question specifically indicates that two answer choices are right.

> The ultimate result of non-payment for vehicles and similar assets is <u>repossession</u>.

Suppose that you don't know the word *repossession.* Your knowledge of prefixes, suffixes, and roots should prove helpful in this situation. *Re-* means "again," *-possess-* means "to hold" or "to own," and *-sion* is a suffix that indicates the word is an abstract noun. Therefore, the word indicates the act of possessing again or again taking control of the asset. If you still aren't sure about the word, look at its context. If someone doesn't pay for something, what is the obvious result?

Determining Meaning from Context

To determine the meaning of a word or a detail of the reading passage from context, use the techniques described below.

Look for a Nearby Definition

The definition of an unusual word may be contained within or near the sentence through the use of an appositive, reduced relative clause, or other grammatical structure. The following examples show how various sentence structures can be used to define a word.

> Probate, *the court-monitored administration of the estate of a deceased person,* is costly, so many people try to take steps to avoid it.
>
> Probate, *which is the court-monitored administration of the estate of a deceased person,* is costly, so many people try to take steps to avoid it.
>
> Probate, *or the court-monitored administration of the estate of a deceased person,* is costly, so many people try to take steps to avoid it.

The court-monitored administration of the estate of a deceased person, known as probate, *is costly, so many people take steps to try to avoid it.*

The court-monitored administration of the estate of a deceased person, which is known as probate, *is costly, so many people take steps to try to avoid it.*

The court-monitored administration of the estate of a deceased person, which is called probate, *is costly, so many people take steps to try to avoid it.*

Defining through Opposites

The sentence can also give you the word's definition by describing the opposite of the word, such as in the following examples.

A child's feeling of well being depends upon familial harmony, *not discord.*

The sentence indicates that harmony and discord are opposite because one leads to the child's feeling of well being and the other does not.

Living in a situation where discord reigns, *unlike living in a harmonious environment,* causes children to be nervous and lack self-confidence.

This sentence also shows that discord is not harmonious by the use of the word *unlike.*

Vocabulary Practice Exercise

Now that you have increased your understanding of prefixes, roots, and suffixes, you should feel more confident in your ability to understand the meaning of vocabulary words, even if you haven't encountered them during your studies.
The format of the following practice exercise is not what you'll encounter on the actual TOEFL exam. To get a feeling for what you'll find on the test, be sure to take the practice tests later in the book. However, this exercise will help you to put into practice the information you learned in the previous section.

Directions: In questions 1 through 30, there is one underlined word or phrase in each sentence and four answer choices marked A, B, C, and D. Select the one answer choice that best maintains the meaning of the original sentence if you use it in place of the word or phrase that is underlined.

1. The presentation by Dr. Dineen was very <u>illuminating</u>.

   A. bright

   B. enlightening

   C. disheartening

   D. boring

2. The <u>postnuptial</u> agreement was prepared by the attorney but never signed before George's death.

   A. trust

   B. before marriage

   C. divorce

   D. after marriage

3. The <u>precursor</u> to his work was a trilogy about the three male characters in their youths.

   A. author

   B. criticism

   C. predecessor

   D. sequel

4. The <u>adhesive</u> qualities of this new substance far surpass those of all others of its type.

   A. cohesive

   B. dissolving

   C. disintegrating

   D. damaging

5. Efforts to <u>revive</u> the large mammal were fruitless.

   A. induce

   B. eliminate

   C. resuscitate

   D. move

6. An Alzheimer patient's <u>incomprehensible</u> ramblings will frequently upset family members, who may take the statements personally.

   A. rude

   B. personal

   C. loud

   D. unintelligible

7. Educators have made great strides in recent years in combating the <u>ignorance</u> of the nation's young about AIDS.

   A. unawareness

   B. fearlessness

   C. arrogance

   D. indoctrination

8. The use of colorful and complicated arrangements of <u>perennial</u> plants in borders, as opposed to beds, stems from the grand gardens of the Victorian and Edwardian times.

   A. beautiful

   B. enduring

   C. short

   D. fast-growing

9. Only <u>aggressive</u> species of small animal life are likely to survive in the rough waters near shallow coral reefs.

   A. marine

   B. strong

   C. a few

   D. passive

10. A common cause of <u>dysentery</u> is the use of untreated water in the preparation of foods, which is quite common in certain underdeveloped countries.

    A. displeasure

    B. malnutrition

    C. eupepsia

    D. bowel infection

11. A defense attorney's role is not only to achieve <u>exculpation</u> for his or her client, but also to reduce the risk of lengthy incarceration.

    A. dishonor

    B. acquittal

    C. mortification

    D. elation

12. <u>Submarine</u> terrain is much like the terrain we know, with valleys, mountains, ridges, and even volcanoes.

   A. Battleship

   B. Rough

   C. Desert

   D. Underwater

13. Vultures will wait and watch patiently for a <u>moribund</u> animal to pass away.

   A. disheveled

   B. dying

   C. gregarious

   D. valiant

14. <u>Dissection</u> is a requirement of many high school and college biology classes, but many students do not find it enjoyable.

   A. The study of frogs

   B. Anatomization

   C. Oral speech

   D. Division

15. The purpose of environmental water retention areas is to slow down the <u>permeation</u> of water into the soil in order to reduce harmful chemicals reaching the groundwater and waterways.

   A. dissipation

   B. fermentation

   C. infiltration

   D. evaporation

16. Some marine animals don't have fins that move but <u>propel</u> themselves by moving their tails and bodies from side to side.

   A. advance

   B. protect

   C. disguise

   D. submerge

17. The symptoms caused by ingestion of a harmful chemical must be <u>counteracted</u> within minutes in order to avoid permanent damage to the kidneys and other vital organs.

   A. alleviated

   B. increased

   C. distributed

   D. summed up

18. New materials for gauze that doesn't <u>adhere</u> to a wound have recently been developed.

   A. infect

   B. injure

   C. stick

   D. allow air

19. Many companies apply raises <u>retroactively</u> to the employee's anniversary date if the performance review isn't completed at the correct time.

   A. dating back

   B. in the future

   C. compounding

   D. currently

20. An employer must be very careful in dealing with <u>subordinates</u> and documenting their files in order to avoid complaints.

    A. coordinators

    B. employees

    C. bosses

    D. outside help

21. <u>Strictures</u> of vessels that take blood to and from the heart can be treated by a new dilation technique called balloon angioplasty.

    A. Perforations

    B. Expansions

    C. Explosions

    D. Closures

22. Chicken pox results in an <u>eruption</u> on the skin and can leave permanent marks on the skin in some cases.

    A. rash

    B. hole

    C. erosion

    D. division

23. Film producers now have the ability to reproduce <u>vivid</u> colors as the result of new technology.

    A. angry

    B. drab

    C. brilliant

    D. conflicting

24. Predators <u>devour</u> their prey with no hesitation or compassion.

    A. eat

    B. torture

    C. play with

    D. attack

25. Internal bleeding is often hard to detect and usually is the result of a <u>perforation</u> in some organ.

    A. puncture

    B. malfunction

    C. diminishment

    D. deformity

26. When divers venture to great depths under the sea, they carry a variety of equipment, including strong lights to <u>permeate</u> the dark water.

    A. electrify

    B. pass through

    C. detect

    D. enhance

27. Many countries and tourist areas have tourist bureaus that <u>disseminate</u> free information about lodging, restaurants, and recreational areas.

    A. distribute

    B. sell

    C. collect

    D. categorize

28. Emissaries sent to meet with kidnappers often are seen as the enemy and may well find their own lives in danger.

A. Journalists

B. Professors

C. Refugees

D. Messengers

29. It's incomprehensible to a nonaddict that an illicit drug can control the life of a young abuser.

A. obvious

B. understandable

C. imperative

D. unfathomable

30. Salt has been used for centuries as a method of preserving foods.

A. displaying

B. cooking

C. conserving

D. seasoning

Answers

1. B	11. B	21. D
2. D	12. D	22. A
3. C	13. B	23. C
4. A	14. B	24. A
5. C	15. C	25. A
6. D	16. A	26. B
7. A	17. A	27. A
8. B	18. C	28. D
9. B	19. A	29. D
10. D	20. B	30. C

Locating Referents

A *referent* is the noun or noun phrase to which a pronoun refers, and it's a common item on the TOEFL test. Sometimes the antecedent is contained in the same sentence as the pronoun, and sometimes it's contained in a previous sentence. Following are examples of this type of question.

> The antibiotic has long been used for fighting serious infection, but <u>it</u> is virtually ineffective against the simple virus.

The word *it* refers to *antibiotic*. *Antibiotic* is the subject of the first clause, and *it* is the subject of the second clause.

> Physicians have long used the antibiotic for fighting serious infection, but <u>it</u> is virtually ineffective against the simple virus.

The word *it* again refers to *antibiotic*. It cannot refer to *Physicians,* because *it* is singular and *Physicians* is plural. *Antibiotic* is the only singular noun in the first clause.

> Physicians have long used antibiotics for fighting serious infection, but <u>they</u> are virtually ineffective against the simple virus.

In this example, *antibiotic* has been changed to the plural *antibiotics*. As a result, it may be more difficult to discern the referent of *they*. But given the context of the sentence, the referent of *they* is *antibiotics,* not *Physicians.*

> Physicians have long used the antibiotic for fighting serious infection, but <u>they</u> acknowledge that it's virtually ineffective against the simple virus.

In this example, the pronoun *they* refers to the *Physicians,* because *they* is the subject of the verb *acknowledge*.

> A number of stockholders have abandoned this company as the result of poor publicity, but <u>some</u> stick with it no matter what.

Some in this sentence refers to some *stockholders*. Consider the verb that falls after *some;* it's clear that *stick* must refer to people, and *stockholders* are the only people mentioned in the sentence.

> The government has argued that this company is a monopoly and must be divided into two separate companies, with a restriction against the founders' owning stock in more than <u>one</u>.

One in this sentence refers to one *company*. The passage talks about two companies and then uses the word *one*.

> The government has argued that this company is a monopoly and must be divided into two separate companies. The documents it has filed also suggest a restriction against the founders' owning stock in more than <u>one</u>.

In this example, even though the antecedent is in a prior sentence, it's clear that the word *one* again refers to *company*.

Practice Reading Exercise

Time: 32 Minutes

23 Questions

Directions: This section measures your ability to read and understand written English similar to that which one may expect in a college or university setting. Read each passage and answer the questions based on what is stated or implied in the passage. Circle or mark the correct answer in the book or write it on a separate piece of paper.

Passage One

Cholera, a highly <u>infectious</u> disease, has resulted in millions of deaths time after time over centuries. It is caused by the bacterium *Vibrio cholerae,* first isolated by Robert Koch in 1883.

The organism enters the body through the digestive tract when contaminated food or water is ingested. The bacteria multiply in the digestive tract and establish infection. As they die, they release a potent toxin that leads to severe diarrhea and vomiting. This results in extreme dehydration, muscle cramps, kidney failure, collapse, and sometimes death. If the disease is treated promptly, death is less likely.

In many countries, a common source of the organism is raw or poorly cooked seafood taken from contaminated waters. The disease is especially <u>prevalent</u> after a natural disaster or other destruction that results in a <u>lack</u> of fresh water. Sewer systems fail, and waste travels into rivers or streams; piped water is not available so people must take their drinking and cooking water from rivers or streams. Because people frequently develop communities along waterways, the disease can be spread easily from one community to the next community downstream, resulting in serious <u>epidemics</u>.

1. The word *infectious* in the first sentence is closest in meaning to

   A. communicable.

   B. severe.

   C. isolated.

   D. common.

2. According to the passage, cholera is caused by

   A. a virus.

   B. a bacterium.

   C. kidney failure.

   D. dehydration.

3. All of the following are probable causes of infection except

   A. eating food cooked with contaminated water.

   B. eating undercooked seafood.

   C. eating overcooked pork.

   D. eating raw oysters.

4. What is the logical order of the events leading to the illness?

   A. Sanitary system fails, so fresh water is unavailable; disaster occurs; people drink the water; contaminated water flows into waterways.

   B. Disaster occurs; sanitary system fails, so fresh water is unavailable; people drink the water; contaminated water flows into waterways.

   C. Disaster occurs; contaminated water flows into waterways; sanitary system fails, so fresh water is unavailable; people drink the water.

   D. Contaminated water flows into waterways; disaster occurs; sanitary system fails, so fresh water is unavailable; people drink the water.

5. According to the passage, what is a symptom of the infection?

   A. Release of a toxin by the bacteria

   B. Regurgitation

   C. Overeating

   D. Epidemics

6. Which of the following would be an appropriate title for this passage ?

   A. Dysentery and Its Effects

   B. Water Purification Systems and Their Importance

   C. Results of War and Natural Disasters

   D. The Causes and Effects of Cholera

7. The word *prevalent* in the third paragraph is closest in meaning to

   A. dangerous.

   B. commonplace.

   C. unusual.

   D. organized.

8. The word *lack* in the third paragraph is closest in meaning to

   A. contamination.

   B. multitude.

   C. shortage.

   D. well.

9. According to the passage, cholera

   A. is easily passed from one person to another.

   B. is not a real threat.

   C. is no more dangerous than the common cold.

   D. cannot be passed from one to another by casual contact.

10. What can you infer from the passage?

   A. Careful cooking and hygiene practices can reduce the chance of getting the disease.

   B. Water mixed with other substances will not pass the disease.

   C. The respiratory system is the most common area of entrance.

   D. Kidney disease is the most common cause of the illness.

11. Mark the area in the passage where the author states that waterfront communities may be susceptible to the illness from other communities upstream.

12. The word *epidemics* at the end of the passage is closest in meaning to

   A. studies.

   B. vaccines.

   C. bacteria.

   D. plagues.

Passage Two

The <u>ubiquitous</u> bar code, developed more than twenty years ago, is not a <u>stagnant</u> product. On the contrary, the technology has been improved so that it can be used more efficiently. Much less expensive than a computer chip, the bar code can hold more information than it has in the past by adding a second dimension to the structure.

The bar code consists of a series of parallel vertical bars or lines of two different <u>widths</u>, although sometimes four widths are used, printed in black on a white background. Barcodes are used for entering data into a computer system. The bars represent the binary digits 0 and 1, just like basic computer language, and sequences of these digits can indicate the numbers from 0 to 9, which can then be read by an optical laser scanner and processed by a digital computer. Arabic numbers appear below the code.

The <u>traditional</u> bar code has been used to monitor skiers at ski lifts and to determine price and perform inventory control on groceries, drugs, medical supplies, manufactured parts, and library books to name a few. The bar code used on grocery products, introduced in the 1970s, is called a universal product code (or UPC) and assigns each type of food or grocery product a unique code. The five digits on the left are assigned to a particular manufacturer or maker and the five digits on the right are used by that manufacturer to identify a specific type or make of product. Traditional single dimension bar codes are not readily customizable because there is little extra space.

The two-dimensional bar code, with an information density of 1,100 bytes, allows a <u>considerably</u> greater amount of information to be coded than does the traditional bar code, including customized information. It also has built-in redundancy, meaning that the identical information is duplicated on the same code. Therefore, if the code is damaged, it can still be read. The technology even allows pictures or text to be contained within the code, as well as barcode encryption. The new technology dramatically reduces the errors of the single dimensional bar code and reduces the enormous costs that some companies have reported in the past.

13. The word *ubiquitous* in the first sentence is closest in meaning to

   A. outdated.

   B. ever-present.

   C. new.

   D. complicated.

14. The word *stagnant* in the first sentence is closest in meaning to

   A. ever-changing.

   B. useful.

   C. stale.

   D. useless.

15. The author implies that the bar code

    A. has only recently become popular.

    B. will never change.

    C. is not useful.

    D. has existed in one-dimensional form for years.

16. The author's main purpose is to describe

    A. the current technology and newest innovation of bar codes.

    B. problems with the bar code.

    C. the UPC used in grocery stores.

    D. why the bar code is no longer viable.

17. Where in the final paragraph could the following sentence be logically placed?

Thus, the manufacturer is able to add additional information on the bar code that it finds useful for its own tracking purposes.

The two-dimensional bar code, with an information density of 1,100 bytes, allows a considerably greater amount of information to be coded than does the traditional bar code, including customized information. (**A**) It also has built-in redundancy, meaning that the identical information is duplicated on the same code. (**B**) Therefore, if the code is damaged, it can still be read. (**C**) The technology even allows pictures or text to be contained within the code, as well as barcode encryption. (**D**) The new technology dramatically reduces the errors of the single dimensional bar code and reduces the enormous costs that some companies have reported in the past.

18. Which of the following can be a UPC symbol?

    A. A code with five digits on the left, five on the right, two different widths, and one number under each

    B. A code with six digits on the left, four on the right, two different widths, and one roman numeral under each

    C. A code with five digits on the left, five digits on the right, five or six different widths, and one number under each

    D. A code with five digits on the left, five digits on the right, reverse form (white text on black background), and no numbers under

19. A *UPC* is a type of

    A. computer program.

    B. bar code.

    C. grocery item.

    D. scanner.

20. The word *widths* in the second paragraph refers to

    A. its size.

    B. its direction.

    C. its location.

    D. its content.

21. The word *traditional* in the third paragraph is closest in meaning to

    A. conventional.

    B. new.

    C. logical.

    D. technological.

22. In the past, a common use of the bar code was

    A. to encrypt pictures.

    B. to keep track of products stocked and sold.

    C. to act as a computer.

    D. to hide text.

23. The word *considerably* in the final paragraph is closest in meaning to

    A. slightly.

    B. technologically.

    C. interestingly.

    D. far.

Answers and Explanations to Practice Reading Exercise

1. A. *Infectious* means *communicable,* or easy to pass along to others. The passage makes it clear that one person can pass the disease on to another. Notice the word "infect", which means to transmit an illness, and the suffix indicates this is an adjective.

2. B. The second sentence of the first paragraph specifically states that cholera is caused by *a bacterium.*

3. C. The second paragraph indicates that contaminated food and water carry the organism and that certain raw or poorly cooked foods cause infection. However, nothing indicates that food cooked too much (overcooked) causes cholera.

4. C. The order of events leading to the illness are: Disaster occurs; contaminated water flows into waterways; sanitary system fails and fresh water becomes unavailable; and people drink the water.

5. B. Regurgitation, which means the same as vomiting.

6. D. "The Causes and Effects of Cholera" is the most general description of the passage. The entire passage is about cholera. Dysentery, in the first answer choice, is another illness that causes some of the same symptoms. Contaminated water is a cause of the disease, but the second choice is not a good title for the passage. The third answer choice relates to only a portion of the topic. Although war and natural disaster may cause cholera, the passage is about the disease, not the cause.

7. B. The context of the sentence leads you to understand that *prevalent* means very common.

8. C. *Shortage* is nearest in meaning to *lack.* Both words mean "to be without."

9. A. Cholera is easily passed from one person to another.

10. A. Careful cooking and hygiene practices can reduce the chance of getting the disease.

11. *Because people frequently develop communities along waterways, the disease can be spread easily from one community to the next community downstream, resulting in serious epidemics.*

12. D. The sentence states that the *epidemics* have resulted in millions of deaths, so it's clear that epidemic is not a positive thing, which helps you eliminate the first two answer choices. *Bacteria* makes no sense because it means that cholera "has been responsible for" bacteria.

13. **B.** *Ubiquitous* means "omni-present" or "existing everywhere."

14. **C.** The word *stagnant* means *stale*, "out-of-date," or "not changing." This passage states that the bar code concept is still being changed.

15. **D.** The passage indicates that the bar code has been used in various ways since the '70s.

16. **A.** The passage covers both a review of existing technology and the new two-dimensional code.

17. **A.** *The two-dimensional bar code, with an information density of 1,100 bytes, allows a considerably greater amount of information to be coded than the traditional bar code, including customized information. Thus, the manufacturer is able to add additional information on the bar code that it finds useful for its own tracking purposes. It also has built-in redundancy, meaning that the identical information is duplicated on the same code. Therefore, if the code is damaged, it can still be read. The technology even allows pictures or text to be contained within the code, as well as barcode encryption. The new technology dramatically reduces the errors of the single dimensional bar code and reduces the enormous costs that some companies have reported in the past.*

18. **A.** The reading states that the code consists of horizontal lines, black print on a white background, with two and sometimes four different widths, and Arabic numerals underneath.

19. **B.** The passage states: *The bar code used on grocery products, introduced in the 1970s, is called a universal product code (or UPC), and assigns each type of food or grocery product a unique code.*

20. **A.** *Width* is the noun related to the noun *wide*. It describes the size from left to right.

21. **A.** *Traditional* refers to a long-standing tradition or convention.

22. **B.** Keeping track of products stocked and sold means the same thing as inventory control. The other uses mentioned are potential uses of the new two-dimensional bar code.

23. **D.** In this context, *considerably* means "far" or "much."

As I explain in Part II of this book, the Writing section score makes up half of your Structure score. In this chapter, I explain how the TOEFL essay is graded. Understanding how an essay is scored can help you determine how to tackle this section of the test.

Each essay question can receive a score between 0 and 6, with 0 being the lowest and 6 being the highest. Essay scoring is based on a checklist much like the one below. This checklist is adapted from the Writing Scoring Guide contained in the TOEFL test Information Bulletin.

How well

- does the essay address the topic?

- is the essay organized?

- does the essay provide appropriate details to support the thesis?

- does the essay display proper use of language?

- does the essay show variety and use of words?

In other words, to create a successful essay, you need to do the following:

- Write about the topic.

- Organize it.

- Give details.

- Use correct grammar.

- Use correct and varied vocabulary.

A separate score is given for each of these five aspects of your essay. Each separate score can range from 0 to 6, in half-point increments. All five scores are then averaged in order to determine the overall score for your essay. For example, you might receive a score like the following:

Addressing the topic	5.5
Organization	4
Details	2.5
Grammar	5
Vocabulary	3.5
Average	20.5 / 5 = 4.1

Writing about the essay topic is fairly easy to do: Simply answer the question. Don't get carried away trying to use impressive vocabulary or display grammatical abilities and not end up addressing the question.

Use the scratch paper provided at the administration of the TOEFL test to outline your essay topic. You can use any kind of outline technique to organize your thoughts, but don't skip this part. Proper organization translates into a fifth of your writing score.

The particular position that you choose to take on the topic is not important. There isn't a right or wrong answer on this section of the test. However, make sure that you can justify your position with details or examples.

If you use a traditional outline form before you write your essay, it should look something like this:

1. Introduction

2. Major Topic

    a. Detail

    b. Detail

3. Major Topic

    a. Detail

    b. Detail

4. Major Topic

    a. Detail

    b. Detail

5. Conclusion

As the outline shows, try to supply at least two (preferably three) supporting details for each major topic.

Don't try to use grammar that you don't know well. Just make sure that the grammar that you use is correct. Likewise, don't try to use vocabulary that you don't know well. Use only vocabulary that is correct in the context.

Practice Exercise

Directions: This section measures your ability to write in standard English, including your ability to organize ideas and support your thoughts with sufficient examples and evidence. Address the following topic by writing an essay in 30 minutes. You may make notes on a separate piece of paper. Type or hand-write the essay.

> It has recently been announced that a large multi-purpose store, similar to those that offer a great number of different items and are open all the time, will be built near your neighborhood. Do you support or oppose this plan? Why? Use specific reasons and details to support your answer.

First, create a major outline, such as the following. You may initially include items that you will later eliminate.

1. Introduction

2. Convenience for neighborhood

3. 24-hour shopping

4. More products

5. More jobs

6. Eliminate eyesores

7. Conclusion

Next, go back and work on the details. If you can't provide sufficient details for a topic, eliminate the topic or merge it into another. For example:

1. Introduction

2. Convenience for neighborhood

    a.   Close to home, whereas other stores are farther away

    b.   More products and several classes of products in one place (groceries, electronics, automotive, clothing, and so on)

    c.   Late-night shopping

3. More jobs

    a.   Increased number of jobs for older persons

    b.   Increased number of jobs for students

4. Eliminate eyesores

    a.   The property is currently vacant and unsafe

    b.   The owners don't keep up on weed and garbage cleanup

5. Conclusion

From this type of outline, you can successfully organize a logical, effective essay:

I support the idea of building a new large multi-purpose store near my neighborhood. It will provide convenience to me and my neighbors and additional jobs, as well as eliminating unattractive areas of the neighborhood.

Having such a store near our neighborhood will provide convenience. Currently we have to travel in one direction for a grocery store, another direction for clothing stores, and several other places for other types of stores. All of these stores are at least several miles from our neighborhood. We will have much less travel time to this one store. Because this store combines a number of different product classes, we can avoid going to different stores for everything we want to buy. We will be able to buy our groceries, clothing, electronic items and other products all at one time. And we will also have the added convenience of shopping at any hour of the day when we are too busy to shop during normal hours.

At the present time, there are students who would like to work after class, but there are not sufficient jobs available. In addition, there are retired people in our neighborhood who would like to supplement their meager income with some light work. A multi-purpose store like the one that is proposed for our neighborhood will provide a number of different job opportunities for these two classes of people as well as others in the community who need full-time jobs. This benefits the overall economic base of the community.

Now, there are two abandoned homes, one occupied home with junk cars and another with debris in the yard, and several overgrown vacant lots on the property where this store will be built. There is nothing beneficial about any of these properties. They contribute to rodent and insect growth, contain hiding places for criminals, and are dangerous for our young children. Replacing these lots with the contemplated store will eliminate these dangers.

Allowing this store to be built will be much more convenient for the people in my neighborhood than our current situation. Because it will provide additional jobs and clean up eyesores in the neighborhood, it has many benefits, and we should all support it.

The above essay certainly is not of the highest quality if you compare it to ones prepared for a writing class. But for purposes of the TOEFL test, in which you have a short time to create an essay and no opportunity to research issues, it will likely obtain a high score because it answers the question adequately. The introductory and conclusion paragraphs summarize the three major topics. Each major topic contains two or three subtopics or examples, and there are no major grammar, vocabulary, or spelling errors.

Sample Essay Topics

The following writing topics are *not* identical to those provided in the TOEFL Bulletin, but they are similar in format. If you wish to write an essay to send to my grading service or another service, use one of these essay topics or a topic from the TOEFL Bulletin.

Almost all sample questions in the TOEFL Bulletin end with the sentence "Use specific reasons and examples to support your answer." I've omitted that sentence from the following topics.

1. A significant effort and significant expense are spent on space travel and research, including sending unmanned spacecraft to faraway planets. Do you agree or disagree with this practice? Why?

2. Some people believe that the public should be able to keep guns for protection. Others believe that guns should be illegal. Give your opinion on the issue.

3. Some students prefer to attend a large university, while others prefer to attend a smaller one. Indicate your opinion of the best choice.

4. Many young people have the opportunity to participate in organized sporting events. The more organized the event, the greater the cost. Do you believe that organized sports are important to young people? Why or why not?

5. What is one of the most important decisions that a teenager will have to make? Why is it so important?

6. Do you agree or disagree with the statement "haste makes waste"?

7. Do you believe that the increasing use of computers and the Internet is beneficial to society or not?

8. What improvement would you make to the city where you live to make it a better place, or in the alternative, why does it require no improvement?

9. Do you believe that home ownership is a goal that is important to many people?

10. Do you believe that people work better when they have sufficient free time?

PART IV

PUTTING IT ALL TOGETHER: PRACTICE TESTS

Listening Section

Time: 45 Minutes

35 Questions

To work through the Listening section of the practice test, you need to use the first audio CD that is included in this book. Starting with Track 2 of the CD, you will hear people having brief conversations. At the end of each conversation, you will hear a question that you must answer based on your understanding of what the speaker(s) said. Each question is printed below, along with answer choices. Mark your answer choices as you go along. The CD track numbers that you need to listen to are indicated throughout the section.

After you have completed this practice test and checked your answers, turn to the appendix of this book. The conversations that you heard on the CD are transcribed there. If you had any difficulty understanding what a speaker was saying, listen to the CD again, this time reading what is being said at the same time you listen to it. Do not turn to the appendix until you have worked through this practice test at least once by just listening to the CD.

Part A

Directions: In this part, you will hear short conversations between two people. After the conversation, a question will be asked. Choose the answer that most accurately answers the question based on what is stated or implied by the speakers. Mark the answer in your book or on a separate piece of paper.

CD A, Track 2

1. What does the woman mean?

   A. She is tired of trying to get into the university.

   B. She has already entered a university.

   C. She took a job instead of going to college.

   D. She has continued to try to find a university that will accept her.

2. What will the woman probably do?

   A. Study linguistics

   B. Contact Professor Stafford

   C. Take Professor Stafford's class

   D. Decide later

GO ON TO THE NEXT PAGE

3. What does the woman suggest that the man do?

A. Consider another computer with a well-known brand name

B. Research and reconsider

C. Buy a slower computer

D. Purchase the computer she first suggested

4. What does the man mean?

A. He will not build the fence.

B. He believes he can build the fence without waiting.

C. He will apply again.

D. He will join the committee.

5. What is the woman's problem?

A. She wants to sign up for trigonometry, but there is no room.

B. She is unhappy with what her advisor suggested.

C. She hates trigonometry.

D. She is failing trigonometry.

6. What does the man mean?

A. The computer is used by many people.

B. The computer she is considering has fallen out of favor.

C. The price of the computer has been reduced.

D. The computer is out of service.

7. What does the man mean?

A. He has not exercised and his body shows it.

B. He has been exercising while traveling.

C. He does not want to exercise anymore.

D. He is not able to exercise because he does not feel well.

8. What are the speakers talking about?

A. The dangers of extreme temperatures

B. Ancient Egyptian burial processes

C. Preserved human remains

D. A program that the man found unconvincing

9. What does the woman mean?

A. She believes the salesman paid no attention to her.

B. She needed the man's advice.

C. She has never bought such a complicated car.

D. She has never bought a car before.

10. What is the woman probably doing?

A. Filling a prescription

B. Renewing her driver's license

C. Having her eyes examined by an optometrist

D. Obtaining a driver's license for the first time

11. What had the woman assumed about the man?

   A. That he wants to leave his house before he sells it.

   B. That he can't find anybody to buy his house.

   C. That he cannot stay in his house for a while after he sells it.

   D. That he already closed on his house.

12. What is the woman's problem?

   A. She lost her job.

   B. She does not have money for her trip.

   C. She can't accept the new job because it conflicts with her trip.

   D. She got a new job, so she can't go on her trip.

13. What do the speakers imply about Celine Dion?

   A. They do not care for her music.

   B. She is going to take some time off.

   C. Her husband is a singer too.

   D. They think she should give more concerts.

14. What does the man mean?

   A. He is sorry that they upgraded the software because it caused another problem.

   B. He believes one should always be on the cutting edge of technology.

   C. He believes that there is no connection between his new program and his problem.

   D. He does not believe in computers.

15. What will the man probably do?

   A. Sit back down

   B. Put the encyclopedia away

   C. Get several books for the woman

   D. Put one book on the shelf and get an encyclopedia

Part B

Directions: In this part, you will hear several conversations and talks. You will hear each conversation or talk only once, and then you will hear several questions. Answer the questions based on what is stated or implied by the speakers. Choose the best of the answer choices provided. Mark the answer in your book or on a separate piece of paper.

GO ON TO THE NEXT PAGE

CD A, Track 3

16. What are the speakers discussing?

   A. Financial assistance for older people

   B. The woman's grandmother and how to handle a progressive illness

   C. Assisted living facilities

   D. The benefits of elder law

17. Why does the lawyer require a meeting with the grandmother?

   A. To assess her mental capacity

   B. To show her assisted living facilities

   C. To convince her she needs help

   D. To explain elder law to her

18. What did the woman describe as an example of the grandmother's failing capacity?

   A. She is often angry and combative.

   B. She does not recognize her granddaughter.

   C. She does not understand anything about her assets.

   D. She forgets things, like when to turn off the stove.

19. Which of the following is not an example of Elder Law?

   A. Estate planning

   B. Bankruptcy

   C. Financial assistance

   D. Elder abuse

20. According to the man, a power of attorney will do which *two* of the following?

   A. Place a person in a nursing home

   B. Provide money

   C. Give the agent authority to sign documents

   D. Assign the right to make decisions

21. What does the man suggest for the grandmother's safety?

   A. Stop allowing her to cook

   B. Sign her up for a day-care program

   C. Place her into a nursing home immediately

   D. Initiate a guardianship

22. What does the man imply?

   A. The grandmother can sign a power of attorney if she is incapacitated.

   B. Only older people should sign powers of attorney.

   C. The grandmother does not need to sign a "durable" power of attorney.

   D. A guardianship will be required if the grandmother has lost her capacity.

CD A, Track 4

23. According to the speaker, what is a biennial?

    A. A plant able to fertilize seeds without another plant

    B. A member of the cabbage family

    C. A plant that grows over a two-year period, alternating between producing plants and seeds

    D. A plant that cannot withstand cold temperatures

24. According to the speaker, where was cabbage originally found?

    A. All over the world

    B. In France and England

    C. In Europe, the Americas, and Asia

    D. In Asia

25. According to the speaker, what is the main difference between the types of cabbage mentioned?

    A. Taste

    B. Method of cultivation

    C. Appearance

    D. Ability to withstand cold

26. According to the speaker, which of the following is not a characteristic of all cabbage types?

    A. Loose leaves and soft heads

    B. Biennial growing season

    C. Being grown successfully in many parts of the world

    D. Small seeds

27. Which type of plant does the speaker say was discussed previously?

    A. Kale and collard greens

    B. Brussels sprouts

    C. Broccoli

    D. Cauliflower

CD A, Track 5

28. How does the man describe the physical features of the camera?

    A. Large and bulky

    B. Lightweight and compact

    C. Heavy

    D. Complicated to operate

29. What is the talk mainly about?

    A. New types of cameras

    B. New video cameras

    C. Thermal cameras

    D. Archeology

GO ON TO THE NEXT PAGE

30. Regarding the Civil War prison camp site that was studied, what does the man imply that the researchers learned?

   A. The prisoners were not mistreated.

   B. The prisoners were not treated well.

   C. More prisoners were killed than they had thought.

   D. Most prisoners died of malnutrition and exposure.

31. What does the man say about the culture that existed in the year 1200 AD?

   A. The people died in a huge battle.

   B. The people died of disease.

   C. The site lies beneath the site of the war.

   D. The site is not as deep in the ground as the Civil War battlefield.

32. Which of the following was not stated as an example of uses of the technology?

   A. Finding something under snow

   B. Viewing something at night

   C. Finding leaks

   D. Locating distant planets

CD A, Track 6

33. What had the woman assumed?

   A. That she would be in a new building

   B. That her deposit would be returned

   C. That the unit air conditioner would cool well

   D. That she would be in one of the original buildings

34. What does the woman indicate is the biggest problem with the old dormitory?

   A. It costs too much.

   B. The utilities are charged separately.

   C. The air conditioning is insufficient.

   D. It's too cold.

35. What does the woman give as an example of the temperature problem?

   A. Bananas ripen too quickly.

   B. Her plants are wilting.

   C. She can't sleep at night.

   D. Her food spoils.

Structure Section

Time: 18 Minutes

23 Questions

Directions: This section measures your ability to recognize language appropriate for standard written English. One type of question consists of incomplete sentences, with a blank showing where information is to be filled in. Choose the word or phrase that most correctly completes the sentence. A second type of question consists of sentences with four underlined words or phrases. For each sentence, choose the one underlined word or phrase that is incorrect in standard written English. Mark the answer in your book or on a separate piece of paper.

1. Although a number of voters <u>has cast</u>
                            A

   their ballots in the city election,

   <u>the supervisor</u> of elections <u>temporarily</u>
     B   **C**

   ended the election because <u>of</u> a
                            D

   malfunction in the voting mechanism.

2. Neither Professor Johnson nor any other faculty member _____ to apply for the dean's position.

   A. intend

   B. intends

   C. are intending

   D. has intend

3. While this is not <u>the most popular</u>
                            A

   course offered at the university, just like

   many <u>others</u> classes that <u>have</u> low
        B   **C**

   attendance in spite of their <u>importance</u>,
                              D

   at least several classes are always

   available.

4. E. Coli has proven to be _____ most dangerous bacteria that can be acquired from food and water, even in developed countries.

   A. one of the

   B. one of

   C. one

   D. of one

5. The death toll would _____ much higher if immediate action had not been taken.

   A. probably being

   B. probably be

   C. probably been

   D. be probable

6. For years, <u>this</u> varsity athletes
               A

   <u>have been known</u> throughout the
          B

   country <u>for</u> their <u>tremendous</u> abilities.
          C   **D**

Section 2 Structure

GO ON TO THE NEXT PAGE

7. A fire in the _____ building could be a problem for firefighters.

   A. ninety-story-tall

   B. ninety-tall-story

   C. ninety-stories-tall

   D. ninety stories

8. The company had been <u>operate</u> in an
                    A
old warehouse since <u>its</u> inception, when
             B
it built a <u>huge</u>, <u>efficient</u>, and modern
         C   **D**
office building.

9. Their office consisted of three rooms, _____ was used as a conference room.

   A. larger of which

   B. the largest of which

   C. the largest of them

   D. largest

10. Before <u>administering</u> the exam, the
            A
proctor <u>required</u> that the students take
        B
their seats and <u>removing</u> all items from
           C
<u>their</u> workplaces.
 D

11. In the past six months, the company has already received twice _____ in gross revenues as it earned in the entire preceding year.

   A. as much

   B. more

   C. as many

   D. as more

12. Some people enjoy <u>preparing</u> <u>their</u> own
                A   **B**
meals <u>while</u> <u>another</u> would rather eat
      C   **D**
out regularly.

13. _____ better, the team would have been able to defeat the opponent.

   A. If it prepares

   B. If prepares

   C. Preparing

   D. Had it prepared

14. <u>The</u> news of the decision <u>to</u> invade with
   A   **B**
armed forces <u>were</u> not well <u>received</u> by
         C   **D**
the citizens.

15. Nobody knows why _____ postponed until next week.

   A. the meeting

   B. was the meeting

   C. did the meeting

   D. the meeting was

16. Air traffic controllers must <u>use</u> <u>a</u> form
                   A **B**
of communication that is <u>universal</u>
                   C
understood because a pilot's
<u>understanding</u> of instructions is critical.
 D

17. The curriculum at the public school is as good _____ of any private school.

   A. or better than

   B. as or better that

   C. as or better than that

   D. as or better than those

18. Hurricanes hardly <u>never</u> <u>reach</u> the east
            A   B
coast of Florida, but some <u>that have</u>
                      C
were <u>extremely</u> hazardous.
      D

19. Children raised <u>in</u> foster homes
             A
<u>requirement</u> special attention to
   B
<u>overcome</u> the feelings <u>of</u> abandonment
   C   D
and isolation.

20. Being a private university, _____ a well-organized charitable giving program in order to offer a sufficient number of quality courses and activities.

   A. development of

   B. it developed

   C. develop

   D. developing

21. <u>With</u> so many <u>choices</u> of wireless
   A   B
technology available, it is often
<u>difficulty</u> to <u>determine</u> which offers the
   C   D
best value and quality.

22. <u>Entering</u> the country <u>in</u> car may <u>cause</u>
   A   B   C
<u>different</u> treatment by customs officials
   D
than entering by way of mass
transportation.

23. The greater the number of bacteria attacking the system, _____.

   A. the sooner treatment must be begun

   B. sooner must begin treatment

   C. begin treatment as soon as possible

   D. must begin treatment sooner

Section **2** Structure

Reading Section

Time: 75 Minutes

47 Questions

Directions: This section measures your ability to read and understand written English similar to that which one may expect in a college or university setting. Read each passage and answer the questions based on what is stated or implied in the passage. Circle or mark the correct answer in the book or write it on a separate piece of paper.

Passage 1

Even a muddy pond contributes to the ecosystem that affects the environment. A <u>vernal</u> or springtime pool is only a few feet deep and lasts only from March until mid-summer but <u>yields</u> a considerable number of <u>diverse</u> life forms. Like all of nature, there are predators and victims, and a particular living being may be one or the other, depending on <u>its</u> age and characteristics. One may find masses of spotted salamander eggs floating just under the surface of the pond, left behind by adults who entered the pond early in the season before predators arrived. Other amphibians and reptiles return to the <u>recurrent</u> pond year after year to reproduce, as their ancestors have done for years.

Various forms of algae grow well in the <u>murky</u> water, if there is sufficient sunlight. <u>They</u> in turn produce and transmit oxygen to the salamander embryos and other young that are not yet able to survive outside of water. Diving beetles feast on eggs and larvae deposited in the pond by the salamanders and other amphibians that have called it home. Tadpoles are born in the late spring and feed on the algae. The pond also invites wood frogs staking their territory and courting potential mates, calling as loud as quacking ducks.

By the end of the short season, the pond dries to spongy mud and then dries further, becoming covered with leaves and debris, until the following spring when the process repeats itself.

1. The word *vernal* in the second sentence means most nearly the same as

   A. springtime.

   B. pool.

   C. deep.

   D. transitory.

2. What is the author's purpose stated in the first sentence: *Even a muddy pond contributes to the ecosystem that affects the environment*?

   A. To explain that a vernal pool is very muddy

   B. To describe how the vernal pool fits into the larger environmental picture

   C. To explain that mud is important to the environment

   D. To show how algae grows

3. The word *yields* in the third sentence means most nearly the same as

   A. produces.

   B. contributes to.

   C. kills.

   D. harms.

4. The word *diverse* in the third sentence means most nearly the same as

   A. distinct.

   B. living.

   C. numerous.

   D. primitive.

5. The word *its* in the fifth sentence refers to

   A. predator.

   B. pond.

   C. living being.

   D. nature.

6. Which sentence in the first paragraph indicates that a young life form might be prey to an older life form?

   A. A vernal or springtime pool is only a few feet deep and lasts only from March until midsummer but yields a considerable number of diverse life forms.

   B. Like all of nature, there are predators and victims, and a particular living being may be one or the other, depending on its age and characteristics.

   C. One may find masses of spotted salamander eggs floating just under the surface of the pond, left behind by adults who entered the pond early in the season before predators arrived.

   D. Other amphibians and reptiles return to the recurrent pond year after year to reproduce, as their ancestors have done for years.

7. Which sentence in the first paragraph indicates that life forms continue to act in the same way as the same life forms did previously?

   A. A vernal or springtime pool is only a few feet deep and lasts only from March until midsummer but yields a considerable number of diverse life forms.

   B. Like all of nature, there are predators and victims, and a particular living being may be one or the other, depending on its age and characteristics.

   C. One may find masses of spotted salamander eggs floating just under the surface of the pond, left behind by adults who entered the pond early in the season before predators arrived.

   D. Other amphibians and reptiles return to the recurrent pond year after year to reproduce, as their ancestors have done for years.

8. The word *murky* in the first sentence of the second paragraph means most nearly the same as

   A. clear.

   B. cloudy.

   C. cold.

   D. life-producing.

Section 3 Reading

GO ON TO THE NEXT PAGE

9. The word *they* in the second sentence of paragraph two refers to

  A. salamander embryos.

  B. young.

  C. forms of algae.

  D. sunlight.

10. Which of the following does the author imply in the first two sentences of paragraph two?

  A. The life forms in the pool live in water their entire lives.

  B. Some of the life forms live in water first and later on land.

  C. The life forms found in the pool do not require oxygen to live.

  D. Algae is strictly a food source.

11. The word *recurrent* in the last sentence of paragraph one means most nearly the same as

  A. moving.

  B. recurring.

  C. stagnant.

  D. warm.

Passage 2

Scientists have experimented with a new procedure for <u>alleviating</u> the damage caused by strokes. Strokes are frequently caused by a blood clot lodging in the tree of arteries in the head, choking the flow of blood. Some brain cells die as a direct result of the stroke, but others also die over several hours because the proteins spilling out of the first cells that die trigger a chemical chain reaction that kills the neighboring cells.

The current method of reducing the amount of damage is to give a clot dissolver, known as TPA, as soon as possible. But generally TPA is not given to the patient until he or she reaches the hospital, and it still does not immediately stop the damage.

The new technology, still in the research stage, involves chilling the area or the entire patient. It is already known that when an organ is cooled, damage is slowed. This is why sometimes a person who has fallen into an icy pond is not significantly harmed after being warmed up again. The biggest issue is the method of cooling. It is not feasible to chill the head alone. Doctors have chilled the entire body by wrapping the patient in cold materials, but extreme <u>shivering</u> was a problem.

The new idea is to cool the patient from the inside out. Several companies are studying the use of cold-tipped catheters, inserted into the artery in the groin and threaded up to the inferior vena cava, which is a large vein that supplies blood to the abdomen. The catheter is expected to cool the blood that flows over it, thus allowing cooler blood to reach the area of the stroke damage.

It is not expected that the cooling will be <u>substantial</u>, but even a slight decrease in temperature is thought to be helpful. In effect, the patient is given a kind of forced hypothermia. And doctors believe it is important to keep the patient awake so that they can converse with the patient in order to ascertain mental condition.

Studies continue to determine the most effective and least damaging means of cooling the patient in order to reduce this damage.

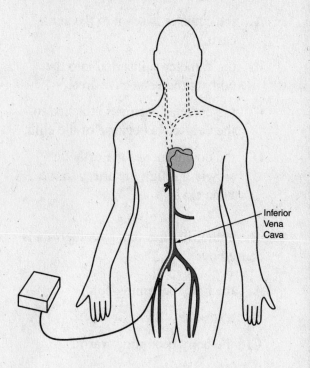

Inferior
Vena
Cava

12. The word *alleviating* in the first sentence is closest in meaning to

A. reducing.

B. devastating.

C. causing.

D. increasing.

13. According to the passage, the method of chilling from the inside out is being considered for all of the following reasons except

A. it is not possible to chill the head alone.

B. chilling from the inside out avoids shaking.

C. cold dissolves blood clots.

D. drugs are not helpful in stopping the chain reaction.

14. According to the passage, what causes a stroke?

A. A blood clot sticking in an area of the brain

B. Low blood flow

C. Hot blood

D. A patient choking on food

15. The word *shivering* in the last sentence of the third paragraph is closest in meaning to

A. shaking.

B. delirious.

C. sick.

D. dying.

16. According to the passage, all of the following are true except that

A. some cells die immediately when a person has a stroke, and others die later.

B. cells die only as a direct result of the stroke.

C. the protein from dead cells kills other cells.

D. TPA is effective in removing blood clots.

17. What is the passage mainly about?

A. Causes and effects of strokes

B. New pharmaceutical methods for reducing stroke damage that are being researched

C. A new method of cooling the body to reduce stroke damage that is being researched

D. The dangers of cooling the body

GO ON TO THE NEXT PAGE

Section **3** Reading

18. The word *substantial* in the fifth paragraph is closest in meaning to

   A. considerable.

   B. slight.

   C. unsubstantiated.

   D. effective.

19. In the passage, the author implies that

   A. the internal chilling process has not been proven yet.

   B. drug therapy properly addresses all the problems of stroke victims.

   C. chilling the head alone is viable.

   D. nothing is likely to reduce the chain reaction problem.

20. The author describes a person falling into cold water in order to

   A. evoke sympathy.

   B. show that cooling a body does not necessarily harm it.

   C. show how one who falls into cold water could also benefit from the internal chilling research.

   D. describe the warming process.

21. The author implies that

   A. the catheter is moved all the way to the brain.

   B. the artery in the leg connects directly to the brain.

   C. the artery in the leg connects to the vena cava.

   D. the goal is to chill the brain directly with the catheter.

22. When the author states that the catheter is *threaded* to the vena cava, the author means that

   A. the catheter is sewn to the vena cava.

   B. the catheter is inserted into the body at the vena cava area.

   C. the catheter becomes attached to the vena cava because of the cold.

   D. the doctor moves the catheter slowly through the artery to the vena cava.

23. The author implies that hypothermia is caused by

   A. the body becoming cold.

   B. a stroke.

   C. the body becoming warm.

   D. drugs.

24. According to the passage, doctors prefer to keep the patient awake in order to

   A. monitor vital signs with equipment.

   B. watch the patient.

   C. talk to the patient.

   D. find out if the procedure is painful.

Passage 3

Bees, classified into over 10,000 <u>species</u>, are insects found in almost every part of the world except the northernmost and southernmost regions. One commonly known species is the honeybee, the only bee that produces honey and wax. Humans use the wax in making candles, lipsticks, and other products, and they use the honey as a food. While gathering the nectar and pollen with <u>which</u> they make honey, bees are <u>simultaneously</u> helping to fertilize the flowers on which they land. Many fruits and vegetables would not survive if bees did not carry the pollen from blossom to blossom.

Bees live in a structured environment and social structure within a hive, which is a nest with storage space for the honey. The different types of bees each perform a unique function. The worker bee carries nectar to the hive in a special stomach called a honey stomach. Other workers make beeswax and shape it into a honeycomb, which is a waterproof mass of six-sided compartments, or cells. The queen lays eggs in completed cells. As the workers build more cells, the queen lays more eggs.

All workers, like the queen, are female, but the workers are smaller than the queen. The male honeybees are called drones; they do no work and cannot sting. They are developed from unfertilized eggs, and their only job is to impregnate a queen. The queen must be fertilized in order to lay worker eggs. During the season when less honey is available and the drone is of no further use, the workers block the drones from eating the honey so that they will starve to death.

25. Which of the following is the best title for this reading?

   A. The Many Species of Bees

   B. The Useless Drone

   C. The Honeybee — Its Characteristics and Usefulness

   D. Making Honey

26. The word *species* in the first sentence is closest in meaning to

   A. mates.

   B. varieties.

   C. killers.

   D. enemies.

27. The word *which* in the fourth sentence refers to

   A. fertilizer.

   B. flowers.

   C. honey.

   D. bees.

28. The word *simultaneously* in the fourth sentence is closest in meaning to

   A. stubbornly.

   B. concurrently.

   C. skillfully.

   D. diligently.

Section **3** Reading

GO ON TO THE NEXT PAGE

29. According to the passage, a *hive* is

    A. a type of honey.

    B. a nest.

    C. a type of bee.

    D. a storage space.

30. According to the passage, the drone

    A. collects less honey than workers.

    B. mates with the queen and has no other purpose.

    C. comes from eggs fertilized by other drones.

    D. can be male or female.

31. The author implies that

    A. bees are unnecessary in the food chain.

    B. drones are completely dispensable.

    C. the queen can be a worker.

    D. drones are never females.

32. According to the passage, honey is carried to the hive in a honey stomach by the

    A. queens.

    B. drones.

    C. males.

    D. workers.

33. In what way does the reading imply that bees are useful in nature?

    A. They pollinate fruit and vegetable plants.

    B. They make marvelous creations from wax.

    C. They kill the dangerous drones.

    D. They create storage spaces.

34. All of the following are characteristic of a honeycomb except

    A. it contains hexagonal sections.

    B. it is made of honey.

    C. it is made of wax.

    D. it is impermeable.

35. The passage implies that bees can be found in each of the following parts of the world except

    A. Africa.

    B. China.

    C. Europe.

    D. Antarctica.

36. It can be inferred from the reading that beeswax is

    A. absorbent.

    B. pliable.

    C. complex in structure.

    D. sweet.

Passage 4

Diabetes Mellitus is a disorder of carbohydrate metabolism resulting from insufficient production of insulin or reduced sensitivity to insulin. A polypeptide hormone, insulin is synthesized in the pancreas and is necessary for normal utilization of glucose by most cells in the body. People with diabetes suffer an inhibition in the normal ability of body cells to use glucose, which results in increased blood sugar levels. As more glucose accumulates in the blood, excess levels of sugar are <u>excreted</u> in the urine.

There are two varieties of the disease, Type 1 and Type 2. The two types were <u>previously</u> designated by Roman numerals, but now Arabic numerals are used; for example, Type II is now known as Type 2. Type 1 was formerly referred to as juvenile onset diabetes, but it can occur at any age. In Type 1 diabetes, insulin is not secreted by the pancreas, so <u>it</u> must be injected. This type of diabetes is most often seen in people whose parents, siblings, or other close relatives are affected by the disease.

Type 2, representing 90 percent of all diabetes, used to be called adult onset diabetes, but it can also occur at any age. It results from <u>sluggish</u> pancreatic insulin secretion and tissue resistance to secreted insulin, which is complicated by subtle changes in the secretion of insulin by the beta cells. It is generally controlled by dietary restriction. People who are at risk for this type include: women who have delivered a baby of 9 pounds or more or have been diagnosed with gestational diabetes; people over 45 years of age, particularly those of African-American, Asian-American, Hispanic, Native American, or Pacific Islander heritage; those who have a history of diabetes in the family; those who are <u>obese</u>; and those with high blood pressure, a high triglyceride level, or high blood sugar.

A person affected with diabetes may have no symptoms at all. Or, he or she may experience one or more of the following common symptoms: fatigue; increased urination and thirst; hunger; blurred vision; weight loss; repeated infections of the skin, genitals, or feet; or itching and dizziness. The diagnosis is reached by testing the blood sugar. If the blood sugar is over 126 milligrams per deciliter (mg/dl) after an 8-hour overnight fast, or over 200 mg/dl at other times of the day, the patient is diagnosed as having the disease.

Diabetes is a formidable illness that can result in serious complications, including heart attack, blindness, kidney failure, and loss of circulation to the lower extremities (feet and legs). This loss of circulation can lead to amputation of the affected areas. Prior to the isolation of insulin in the 1920s, rapid death was common among diabetes sufferers. Now, the illness can be managed and those affected can lead a long, fairly normal life with proper medical attention and proper attention to personal care. Patients should follow nutrition plans designed to help them reach and maintain normal body weight and to limit their intake of carbohydrates and fats. They should also exercise regularly, which enhances the movement of glucose into muscle cells and inhibits the increase in glucose in the blood.

37. Insulin is

    A. a hormone.

    B. a drug.

    C. a disease.

    D. an organ.

Section **3** Reading

GO ON TO THE NEXT PAGE

38. The word *excreted* in the last sentence of paragraph one means most nearly the same as

   A. eliminated.

   B. ingested.

   C. utilized.

   D. inserted.

39. The word *previously* in the second paragraph means most nearly the same as

   A. occur.

   B. formerly.

   C. designated.

   D. used.

40. The word *it* in the fourth sentence of paragraph two refers to

   A. insulin.

   B. Type 1 diabetes.

   C. Type 2 diabetes.

   D. pancreas.

41. According to the passage, insulin is produced

   A. in the pancreas.

   B. in tissue.

   C. in hormones.

   D. in glucose.

42. The word *sluggish* in the third paragraph means most nearly the same as

   A. accelerated.

   B. excreted.

   C. normal.

   D. slow.

43. The word *obese* in the last sentence of paragraph three means most nearly the same as

   A. severely overweight.

   B. diabetic.

   C. suffering from high blood pressure.

   D. active.

44. What is a suitable title for this passage?

   A. Treatment of Diabetes

   B. An Overview of Diabetes

   C. Juvenile Diabetes — a Killer

   D. How to Diagnose Diabetes

45. The author distinguishes between Type 1 and Type 2 diabetes to describe how

   A. one affects only juveniles and the other affects only adults.

   B. the symptoms and treatment are different.

   C. the two types are extremely similar to each other.

   D. the understanding of the disease has improved over time.

46. All of the following are correct except that

    A. Type 2 diabetes is much more common than Type 1.

    B. both types of diabetes are hereditary to some extent.

    C. Type 2 results from a lack of secretion of insulin.

    D. diabetes is treatable.

47. It can be inferred from the passage that

    A. amputation is the most common treatment for diabetes.

    B. Type 1 sufferers are generally not overweight.

    C. the symptoms of diabetes are always severe.

    D. too much insulin is secreted in Type 1 diabetes.

Writing Section

Time: 30 Minutes

1 Question

Directions: This section measures your ability to write in English, including your ability to organize ideas, create an essay in standard written English, and support the thoughts with sufficient examples and evidence. Write an essay in 30 minutes. You may make notes on a separate piece of paper, and then type or handwrite the essay.

What change would you make to your high school to make it a more appealing place for students? Use specific reasons and examples to support your choice.

PRACTICE TEST 2

Listening Section

Time: 40 Minutes

29 Questions

To work through the Listening section of the practice test, you need to use the first audio CD that is included in this book. Starting with Track 7 of the CD, you will hear people having brief conversations. At the end of each conversation, you will hear a question that you must answer based on your understanding of what the speaker(s) said. Each question is printed below, along with answer choices. Mark your answer choices as you go along. The CD track numbers that you need to listen to are indicated throughout the section.

After you have completed this practice test and checked your answers, turn to the appendix of this book. The conversations that you heard on the CD are transcribed there. If you had any difficulty understanding what a speaker was saying, listen to the CD again, this time reading what is being said at the same time you listen to it. Do not turn to the appendix until you have worked through this practice test at least once by just listening to the CD.

Part A

Directions: In this part, you will hear short conversations between two people. After the conversation, a question will be asked. Choose the answer that most accurately answers the question based on what is stated or implied by the speakers. Mark the answer in your book or on a separate piece of paper.

CD A, Track 7

1. What does the woman say about the project?

   A. They must cancel it.

   B. An error was probably made in figuring the employee cost.

   C. A complete report must be provided of the estimated costs.

   D. They have to determine the cost.

2. What does the man say about his ability to attend the conference?

   A. He could not attend.

   B. His boss paid his way.

   C. He thought it wasn't worth the money.

   D. He went even though his boss did not pay.

3. What does the man imply?

    A. He thinks somebody broke the machine and kept quiet about it.

    B. He thinks the machine has been repaired.

    C. There are insects in the machine.

    D. He damaged the machine.

4. What does the man mean?

    A. The administrator chose to postpone the announcement.

    B. The administrator spoke the previous day.

    C. The administrator changed the procedure.

    D. An announcement about the new administrator was made the previous day.

5. What is the man probably going to do?

    A. Drop Ms. Nelson's class

    B. Change to Ms. Nelson's class

    C. Complain to the administration

    D. Move from Ms. Nelson's class

6. What does the man mean?

    A. He was totally satisfied with his experience at the exhibit.

    B. He did not like the exhibit.

    C. He felt it took too long.

    D. He wanted to see more than he was able to see.

7. What does the woman say about the paramedics?

    A. They were very late arriving.

    B. They ran into the house the moment they arrived.

    C. They did not seem to know what to do.

    D. They were unable to locate the house.

8. What does the man suggest the woman do?

    A. Eat dinner at his house

    B. Eat dinner and then go to the library with him

    C. Go out to eat and leave him at the library

    D. Go to the library with him and then eat dinner

9. What does the woman say about going on the cruise?

    A. She hopes to go.

    B. She still may be able to go.

    C. She is planning to go.

    D. She is unable to go.

10. What does the woman imply about Nancy?

    A. She has unlimited energy.

    B. She is too ill to continue working so hard.

    C. She has put her illness behind her and can begin again.

    D. She is not actually sick.

GO ON TO THE NEXT PAGE

11. What does the man imply about Professor Winger?

    A. He is too strict.

    B. He is requiring extra projects that the students were not expecting.

    C. He will not allow the students to rewrite their papers.

    D. He lost the students' papers.

12. What does the woman ask the man to do?

    A. Signify where in the manual she can find the procedure

    B. Advise her if she makes an error

    C. Leave her alone

    D. Point to the correct answer

13. What will the man probably do?

    A. Go to see a doctor

    B. Get some medical books in the library

    C. Wait to see if he feels better

    D. Leave the motel and go home

14. What does the woman mean?

    A. She formerly lived on 34th Street.

    B. She lives on 34th Street.

    C. She is very accustomed to her apartment.

    D. She is temporarily living on 34th Street.

15. What does the man suggest that the woman do?

    A. Wait for his call

    B. Call him when she is awake

    C. Sleep all afternoon

    D. Stay awake

Part B

Directions: In this part, you will hear several conversations and talks. You will hear each conversation or talk only once, and then you will hear several questions. Answer the questions based on what is stated or implied by the speakers. Choose the best of the answer choices provided. Mark the answer in your book or on a separate piece of paper.

CD A, Track 8

16. What are the speakers talking about?

    A. A difficult book

    B. A computer program

    C. A mathematics problem

    D. A composition

17. What does the woman advise the man to do?

    A. Read the book.

    B. Write the procedure.

    C. Try harder.

    D. Give up.

18. What is the man likely to do the next time he has a computer problem?

    A. Take notes.

    B. Ask the woman again.

    C. Get the manual.

    D. Experiment.

19. Is the man probably going to be able to repeat the procedure that the woman showed him?

    A. No, because he wasn't paying attention.

    B. Yes, because he wrote down the procedure.

    C. Yes, because the woman will remember.

    D. No, because they couldn't figure it out the first time.

CD A, Track 9

20. According to the speaker, which of the following is true about Stephen Crane?

    A. He lived a long life.

    B. He died before the age of 30.

    C. He was a 20th century author.

    D. He wrote nothing significant.

21. What does the speaker imply that Crane did?

    A. He lived dangerously.

    B. He never experienced what he wrote about.

    C. He was afraid of everything.

    D. He wrote in the abstract.

22. According to the speaker, how did Crane write?

    A. He wrote with realism only.

    B. He wrote only one story about life at sea.

    C. He wrote about the sea before he experienced it and then again afterwards.

    D. He never wrote about anything he did not experience.

23. How does the speaker contrast "The Open Boat" and *The Red Badge of Courage*?

    A. One was written while Crane was young and the other when he was much older.

    B. One was written from experience and the other was not.

    C. One contained symbolism and the other did not.

    D. One was highly acclaimed and the other was not.

GO ON TO THE NEXT PAGE

CD A, Track 10

24. What does the speaker say about the similarity of termites to ants?

   A. Termites are more closely related to ants than they are to wasps.

   B. Termites are actually white ants.

   C. Termites are quite different from ants, but their social structure is similar.

   D. Termites have no similarity to bees.

25. According to the speaker, which types of termites are the most destructive to man-made structures?

   A. Termites that are native to an area

   B. Termites that eat only man-made wood structures

   C. Termites that have been transplanted to an area

   D. White termites

26. Which of the following items does the author imply that termites will *not* be transported in?

   A. Wooden furniture

   B. Pottery

   C. Plants

   D. Logs

27. Which of the following would the speaker probably say?

   A. Termites are of no use whatsoever to mankind.

   B. Termites can be beneficial to the ecological system.

   C. Subterranean termites are harder to control than dry-wood termites.

   D. Only dry-wood termites are ever useful.

28. According to the speaker, in what way are subterranean termites distinct from dry-wood termites?

   A. Subterranean termites enter only from the soil.

   B. Dry-wood termites destroy wood faster.

   C. Dry-wood termites are easier to prevent.

   D. There is no useful method of controlling subterranean termites prior to infestation.

29. The speaker implies that dry-wood termites are most effectively treated using what method?

   A. Pretreating the soil

   B. Treating the entire structure by tenting

   C. Spraying insecticide into the soil

   D. Spot treating

Structure Section

Time: 20 Minutes

25 Questions

Directions: This section measures your ability to recognize language appropriate for standard written English. One type of question consists of incomplete sentences, with a blank showing where information is to be filled in. Choose the word or phrase that most correctly completes the sentence. A second type of question consists of sentences with four underlined words or phrases. For each sentence, choose the one underlined word or phrase that is incorrect in standard written English. Mark the answer in your book or on a separate piece of paper.

1. A congressional committee has been appointed to study a new procedure _____ to eliminate some costly expenditures.

    A. that is expected

    B. what is expected

    C. which expects

    D. that expected

2. Some professors enjoy <u>writing</u> articles
            A
    and <u>performing</u> research, while <u>anothers</u>
            B   C
    would be more content <u>to devote</u> all
                                    D
    their time to teaching.

3. Some people send job applications even when they are reasonably happy in their jobs, _____ improving their position.

    A. with hoping to

    B. hoping that

    C. with hopes of

    D. hoping to

4. Swimming is a beneficial exercise, _____ aerobic activity and uses a number of muscle groups.

    A. not only because it provides

    B. because it both provides

    C. for provision

    D. as result of providing

5. Tests have <u>been</u> performed to determine
                    A
    <u>whether</u> <u>studying</u> TOEFL questions will
        B   C
    help students <u>rise</u> their test scores.
                        D

6. The professor instructed the students _____ the essay without preparing an outline first.

    A. to not write

    B. not to write

    C. do not write

    D. to no write

GO ON TO THE NEXT PAGE

7. It is not clear when _____, although there are many different theories.

   A. dinosaurs becoming extinct

   B. dinosaurs extinction

   C. dinosaurs became extinct

   D. did dinosaurs become extinct

8. The professor decided <u>to allow</u> the
   A
   students to <u>take</u> the examination a
   B
   <u>second</u> time <u>because</u> the low scores.
     C   D

9. If the driver's own car _____ damaged, the favorite probably would have won the race.

   A. had not been

   B. not

   C. no had been

   D. has no be

10. <u>Having</u> withdrawn from the race, the
    A
    candidate decided <u>supporting</u> his
    B
    opponent <u>despite</u> the opponent's
    C
    representing the <u>other</u> political party.
    D

11. The soldiers were unable to determine where _____.

    A. the jeep had been left

    B. had been leave the jeep

    C. had the jeep been left

    D. had the jeep left

12. The manager was angry because somebody _____.

    A. had allowed the photographers to enter the building

    B. had let the photographers to enter the building

    C. permitting the photographers enter the building

    D. the photographers let into the building

13. The committee members resented _____ of the meeting.

    A. the president that he did not tell them

    B. the president not to inform them

    C. the president's not informing them

    D. that the president had failed informing themselves

14. _____ did Arthur realize that there was danger.

    A. Upon entering the store

    B. When he entered the store

    C. After he had entered the store

    D. Only after entering the store

15. The congressman, accompanied <u>by</u>
                                   A

    secret service agents and aides, <u>are</u>
                                     B

    preparing <u>to enter</u> the convention hall
              C

    <u>within the next</u> few minutes.
         D

16. <u>Because</u> the <u>torrential</u> rains that <u>had</u>
       A   B

    <u>devastated</u> the area, the governor sent
       C

    the National Guard <u>to assist in</u> the
                      D

    clean-up operation.

17. Lack <u>of sanitation</u> in restaurants <u>are</u> a
          A   B

    major <u>cause of</u> disease <u>in some areas of</u>
          C   D

    the country.

18. <u>Had the committee members</u> considered
            A

    the alternatives <u>more carefully</u>, they
               B

    would have realized that the <u>second was</u>
                           C

    better <u>as the first</u>.
         D

19. Malnutrition <u>is a major</u> cause of
             A

    death <u>in those countries</u> where the
           B

    cultivation of rice <u>have</u> been impeded
               C

    <u>by recurrent drought</u>.
        D

20. The decision <u>to withdraw</u> <u>all support</u>
            A   B

    from the activities of the athletes

    <u>are causing</u> an uproar <u>among</u> the
       C   D

    athletes' fans.

21. <u>Underutilized</u> species of fish <u>has been</u>
       A   B

    proposed <u>as</u> a solution <u>to the famine</u> in
          C   D

    many underdeveloped countries.

22. <u>Because</u> the residents <u>had worked</u> so
       A   B

    <u>diligent</u> <u>to renovate</u> the old building, the
      C   D

    manager had a party.

23. John's wisdom teeth <u>were troubling</u>
                     A

    him, so he went to a dental surgeon

    <u>to see</u> <u>about</u> having <u>them pull</u>.
      B   C   D

24. Hardly _____ the office when he

    realized that he had forgotten his wallet.

    A. he had entered

    B. had entered

    C. entered

    D. had he entered

25. Suzy <u>had</u> better <u>to change</u> her study
         A   B

    habits if she <u>hopes to be</u> admitted
              C

    <u>to a good university</u>.
        D

Section **2** Structure

Reading Section

Time: 75 Minutes

48 Questions

Directions: This section measures your ability to read and understand written English similar to that which one may expect in a college or university setting. Read each passage and answer the questions based on what is stated or implied in the passage. Circle or mark the correct answer in the book or write it on a separate piece of paper.

Passage 1

Hummingbirds are small, often brightly colored birds of the family Trochilidae that live exclusively in the Americas. About 12 species are found in North America, but only the ruby-throated hummingbird breeds in eastern North America and is found from Nova Scotia to Florida. The greatest variety and number of species are found in South America. Another hummingbird species is found from southeastern Alaska to northern California.

Many hummingbirds are <u>minute</u>. But even the giant hummingbird found in western South America, <u>which</u> is the largest known hummingbird, is only about 8 inches long and weighs about two-thirds of an ounce. The smallest species, the bee hummingbird of Cuba and the Isle of Pines, measures slightly more than 5.5 centimeters and weighs about two grams.

Hummingbirds' bodies are compact, with strong muscles. They have wings shaped like blades. Unlike the wings of other birds, hummingbird wings connect to the body only at the shoulder joint, which allows them to fly not only forward but also straight up and down, sideways, and backward. Because of their unusual wings, hummingbirds can also hover in front of flowers so they can suck nectar and find insects. The hummingbird's <u>bill</u>, adapted for securing nectar from certain types of flowers, is usually rather long and always slender, and it is curved slightly downward in many species.

The hummingbird's body feathers are <u>sparse</u> and more like scales than feathers. The unique character of the feathers produces brilliant and iridescent colors, resulting from the refraction of light by the feathers. Pigmentation of other feathers also contributes to the unique color and look. Male and female hummingbirds look alike in some species but different in most species; males of most species are extremely colorful.

The rate at which a hummingbird beats its wings does not vary, regardless of whether it is flying forward, flying in another direction, or merely hovering. But the rate does vary with the size of the bird — the larger the bird, the lower the rate, ranging from 80 beats per second for the smallest species to 10 times per second for larger species. Researchers have not yet been able to record the speed of the wings of the bee hummingbird but imagine that they beat even faster.

Most hummingbirds, especially the smaller species, emit scratchy, twittering, or squeaky sounds. The wings, and sometimes the tail feathers, often produce humming, hissing, or popping sounds, which apparently function much as do the songs of other birds.

1. According to the passage, where are hummingbirds found?

   A. Throughout the world

   B. In South America only

   C. In North America only

   D. In North and South America

2. The author indicates that the ruby-throated hummingbird is found

   A. throughout North America.

   B. in California.

   C. in South America.

   D. in the eastern part of North America.

3. The word *minute* in the second paragraph is closest in meaning to

   A. extremely tiny.

   B. extremely fast.

   C. unique.

   D. organized.

4. The word *which* in the second paragraph refers to

   A. western South America.

   B. the giant hummingbird.

   C. all hummingbirds.

   D. Florida hummingbirds.

5. What does the author imply about the rate hummingbirds' wings beat?

   A. Although the bee hummingbird is the smallest, its wings don't beat the fastest.

   B. The hummingbird's wings beat faster when it is sucking nectar than when it is just flying.

   C. The rate is not much different than that of other birds of its size.

   D. The speed at which a bee hummingbird's wings beat is not actually known.

6. The author indicates that a hummingbird's wings are different from those of other birds because

   A. they attach to the body at one point only.

   B. they attach to the body at more points than other birds.

   C. they attach and detach from the body.

   D. they are controlled by a different section of the brain.

7. The author implies that the hummingbird's unique wing structure makes it similar to what type of vehicle?

   A. A helicopter

   B. A sea plane

   C. A jet airplane

   D. A rocket

Section 3 Reading

GO ON TO THE NEXT PAGE

8. The word *bill* in the third paragraph is closest in meaning to

   A. beak.

   B. body.

   C. tail.

   D. wing.

9. The word *sparse* in the fourth paragraph is closest in meaning to

   A. meager.

   B. thick.

   C. fishlike.

   D. unique.

10. According to the passage, what causes the unique color and look of hummingbirds?

   A. The color of the feathers

   B. The structure of the feathers as well as pigmentation

   C. The rapidity of flight

   D. The pigmentation of the body

11. The author indicates that hummingbirds emit noise from their

   A. wing and possibly tail movement.

   B. unique vocal chords.

   C. song only.

   D. wing movement only.

Passage 2

The term *lichen* refers to any of over 20,000 species of thallophytic plants that consist of a symbiotic association of algae and fungi, plural for alga and fungus. Previously, lichens were classified as single organisms until scientists had the benefit of microscopes, at which time they discovered the association between algae and fungi. Thus, the lichen itself is not an organism, but the morphological and biochemical product of the association. Neither a fungus nor an alga alone can produce a lichen.

The intimate symbiotic relationship between these two living components of a lichen is said to be *mutualistic,* meaning that both organisms benefit from the relationship. It is not certain when fungi and algae came together to form lichens for the first time, but it certainly occurred after the mature development of the separate components.

It appears that the fungus actually gains more benefit from the relationship than does the alga. Algae form simple carbohydrates that, when excreted, are absorbed by fungi cells and transformed into a different carbohydrate. Algae also produce vitamins that the fungi need. Yet, fungi also contribute to the symbiosis by absorbing water vapor from the air and providing shade for the algae, which are more sensitive to light.

Lichens grow relatively slowly, and it is uncertain how they propagate. Most botanists agree that reproduction is vegetative because portions of an existing lichen break off and fall away to begin a new organism nearby.

Lichens are hardy organisms, being found in hostile environments where few other organisms can survive. Humans have used lichens as food and as sources of medicine and dye. The presence of lichens is a sign that the atmosphere is pure. Lichens help reduce erosion by stabilizing soil. They also are a major source of food for the caribou and reindeer that live in the extreme north.

12. Which of the following is true about the association of the lichen?

   A. The association is more beneficial to the alga.

   B. The association is solely of benefit to the fungus.

   C. The association is merely a joint living arrangement, with neither organism receiving any benefit from the other.

   D. The association is beneficial to each organism, although it provides more benefit to the fungus.

13. The word *previously* in the first paragraph is closest in meaning to

   A. currently.

   B. formerly.

   C. believed.

   D. no longer.

14. Prior to the invention of microscopes, what did scientists believe about lichens?

   A. The entire plant was an alga.

   B. The entire plant was a fungus.

   C. A lichen constituted a single plant.

   D. The fungus was the catalyst of the association.

15. The word *intimate* in the second paragraph is closest in meaning to

   A. distant.

   B. parasitic.

   C. close.

   D. unusual.

16. The author uses the word *mutualistic* in paragraph two to describe

   A. the fungus' benefits from the association.

   B. the harmful effects of the relationship.

   C. the joint benefit each organism receives from the relationship.

   D. the alga's benefits from the association.

17. The author implies that

   A. neither plant requires carbohydrates to survive.

   B. the fungus manufactures carbohydrates on its own.

   C. the alga receives carbohydrates from the fungus.

   D. the fungus uses the carbohydrates manufactured by the alga.

18. The author states that the relationship between the words *fungus/fungi* and *alga/algae* is

   A. singular/plural.

   B. compound/complex.

   C. symbiotic/disassociated.

   D. mutual/separate.

19. The author implies that vegetative reproduction means

   A. vegetables combine with other vegetables.

   B. reproduction occurs using vegetative plant growth.

   C. new organisms are grown from pieces of existing organisms.

   D. propagation occurs slowly.

Section 3 Reading

GO ON TO THE NEXT PAGE

20. The author states that

   A. fungi are more sensitive to light than algae.

   B. neither plant is sensitive to light.

   C. neither plant individually can thrive in sunlight.

   D. algae are more sensitive to light than fungi.

21. The word *nearby* at the end of paragraph four is closest in meaning to

   A. almost.

   B. completely.

   C. connected.

   D. close.

22. The word *hardy* at the beginning of the last paragraph is closest in meaning to

   A. tender.

   B. ubiquitous.

   C. scarce.

   D. strong.

23. The word *hostile* in the last paragraph is closest in meaning to

   A. unusual.

   B. dry.

   C. harsh.

   D. complex.

24. The author indicates that lichens are beneficial because they

   A. purify the air.

   B. reduce fungi.

   C. destroy algae.

   D. reduce soil erosion.

Passage 3

Collecting coins can be a good investment, but it requires the study of popularity, availability, and grading techniques. Some coins are more desirable than others, their popularity being affected by the artists' talent, the subject of the design, the material from which the coin is made, and the time period when the coin was created. Availability is just as critical. Providing the coin is otherwise interesting or pleasing to the eye, the number of coins minted and available on the market seems to have a direct relationship to the popularity.

The ability to grade coins is perhaps the most important requirement of a collector. A coin that is popular and scarce, which would normally make it valuable, may be worth much less or nothing at all if it has a low grade. Grading is standardized, and one can buy books and take courses on how to do it.

Grades are given letter designations as well as numbers. The letters represent general levels of the grade, while the numbers are more detailed. For example, there are 11 number grades within the letter grade for a mint state coin. A mint state coin is uncirculated, which means it has never been used in commerce. It is in the condition that it left the mint, the place where a coin is created. The mint state letter designation is *MS,* and the numbers range from 60 through 70. An absolutely perfect coin is MS-70. It takes much training and a good eye to tell the difference between coins in this range. The things one considers include whether the coin has contact marks, which are marks obtained when coins bounce against each other in a coin bag; hairlines, which are marks appearing on the face of the coin from the minting process; luster, which is the natural coloration; and eye appeal. For example, an MS-70 is said to have no contact marks, no hairlines, very attractive and fully original <u>luster</u>, and outstanding eye appeal, while an MS-60 may have heavy contact marks, noticeable hairlines, impaired luster, and poor eye appeal.

Below the mint state coin, the letter designation and number have the same meaning. That is, there are generally no numbers within the range of letters. But there are categories:

- **Coins that are About Uncirculated:** Very Choice About Uncirculated, known as AU-58; Choice About Uncirculated, known as AU-55; and About Uncirculated, known as AU-50.

- **Coins that are Fine:** Choice Extremely Fine, known as EF-45; Extremely Fine, known as EF-40; Choice Very Fine, known as VF-30; Very Fine, known as VF-20; and Fine, known as F-12.

- **Coins that are Good:** Very Good, known as VG-8; Good, known as G-4; and About Good, known as AG-3.

Thus, a circulated coin can have a number designation between 3 and 58, with only the numbers shown above available. That is, one cannot have a coin with a grade of 6, for example. It is either G-4 or VG-8. It is possible for a coin labeled G-4 or even AG-3 to be extremely valuable, but generally it will be a coin that is almost unavailable in higher grades. Books and publications monitor the coin market regularly, just like the stock market is monitored, and they describe a coin's type, date, and grade, assigning a price to every one unless that grade would have no value.

In general, coin collectors loathe cleaned coins, so artificial cleaning by adding any chemical will detract greatly from a coin's value. A true coin collector will say the dirt in the creases is a positive attribute and much preferable to a cleaned coin.

25. A good title for this passage would be

   A. The Financial Benefits of Coin Collecting.

   B. How Popularity and Availability Affect Coin Value.

   C. Coin Grading — One of the Most Important Skills in Coin Collecting.

   D. How to Grade Coins — A Detailed Study.

26. The word *talent* in the second sentence is closest in meaning to

   A. ability.

   B. pay.

   C. source.

   D. money.

27. The author describes a coin's popularity as involving all the following except

   A. grade.

   B. how well the artist created the work.

   C. the depiction on the coin.

   D. the coin's material.

GO ON TO THE NEXT PAGE

Section **3** Reading

241

28. The word *scarce* in the second paragraph is closest in meaning to

   A. popular.

   B. old.

   C. rare.

   D. valuable.

29. The author implies that availability is primarily related to

   A. the popularity of a coin.

   B. the material used to create a coin.

   C. the age of a coin.

   D. the number of coins of a given type and date that they were minted.

30. The author implies that the most important feature of a coin is its

   A. grade.

   B. date.

   C. artist.

   D. depiction.

31. Organize the following according to grade from the highest to the lowest.

   A. AU-58

   B. MS-60

   C. AG-3

   D. VF-20

32. The one grading category that has the most numbered grades within it is

   A. Good.

   B. Mint State.

   C. Fine.

   D. About Uncirculated.

33. According to the author, the phrase *contact marks* means

   A. marks on a coin caused by banging from other coins.

   B. defects in the minting process.

   C. connections among coin dealers.

   D. defects caused by cleaning.

34. The word *luster* in the third paragraph is closest in meaning to

   A. value.

   B. sheen.

   C. marked.

   D. material.

35. According to the passage, a Mint State coin with which of the following characteristics would be graded the highest?

   A. One small contact mark, full luster, good eye appeal, and no hairlines

   B. One large hairline, diminished luster, good eye appeal, and no contact marks

   C. A small contact mark, a small hairline, foggy luster, and fair eye appeal

   D. No contact marks, luster affected by cleaning, average eye appeal, and no hairlines

36. All of the following grades would be possible except

   A. MS-64.

   B. AU-56.

   C. VF-30.

   D. AG-3.

37. The author implies that

   A. a low-grade coin never has value.

   B. the only difference between an MS-60 and an AU-58 may be that the AU-58 has been in circulation.

   C. cleaning a coin can increase its value.

   D. one must be a professional in order to obtain information on coin value.

Passage 4

Hepatitis C is an illness, unknown until recently, that has been discovered in many individuals. It has been called an epidemic, yet unlike most illnesses with that designation, it is not easily transmitted. It is accurately referred to as epidemic in that so many people have been discovered with the illness, but it is different in that these people have actually carried the virus for many years. It is only transmitted by direct blood-to-blood contact; casual contact and even sexual contact are not believed to transmit the illness. Hepatitis means an inflammation or infection of the liver. Hepatitis C is generally chronic, as opposed to acute. This means that it continues to affect the patient and is not known to have a sudden <u>onset</u> or recovery.

The <u>great</u> majority of people infected with the illness either had a blood transfusion before the time that the disease was recognized in donated blood, or experimented with injecting illegal drugs when they were young. Many victims are educated, financially successful males between the ages of 40 and 50 who experimented with intravenous drugs as teenagers. There are frequently no symptoms, so the illness is discovered through <u>routine</u> blood tests. Most commonly, people learn <u>they</u> have the illness when they apply for life insurance or donate blood. The blood test reveals elevated liver enzymes, which could be caused by any form of hepatitis, by abuse of alcohol, or by other causes. Another test is then performed, and the result is learned.

Because the illness produces no symptoms, it of itself does not affect the victim's life, at least at first. But the constant infection in the liver can eventually lead to cirrhosis of the liver, which is scarring and death of portions of the liver. The cirrhosis in turn can lead to liver cancer and, ultimately, death. Severe cases can be reversed with a liver transplant. Yet, because the virus may exist in the body for more than 20 years before being discovered, after reviewing the condition of the liver, doctors often suggest waiting and periodically checking the condition rather than performing radical treatment procedures. The liver's condition is determined by a biopsy, in which a device is inserted into the liver and <u>its</u> condition is viewed. If there is little or no cirrhosis, it is more likely that treatment will be postponed.

Treatment frequently causes more discomfort than the illness itself. It consists of some form of chemotherapy. Currently, the most frequent treatment is a combination therapy, with one drug injected three times a week and another taken orally, costing hundreds of dollars a week. The therapy causes the patient to have symptoms similar to influenza, and some patients suffer more than others.

GO ON TO THE NEXT PAGE

Section **3** Reading

Unfortunately, many patients do not respond, or do not respond completely to the therapy. There is no alternative therapy at this time for non-responders, although researchers are continually trying to find a cure.

38. The author implies that

    A. physicians have been treating patients for hepatitis C for over 20 years.

    B. other forms of hepatitis were known before the hepatitis C strain was discovered.

    C. hepatitis C is generally seen as an acute illness.

    D. hepatitis C is easily transmitted through any type of contact.

39. The word *onset* at the end of paragraph one is closest in meaning to

    A. illness.

    B. termination.

    C. inception.

    D. treatment.

40. The best title for this passage would be

    A. Treatment Choices for Hepatitis C.

    B. The History of Different Forms of Hepatitis.

    C. Hepatitis C — Its Characteristics and Treatment.

    D. The Causes and Symptoms of Hepatitis C.

41. The word *great* at the beginning of paragraph two is closest in meaning to

    A. vast.

    B. magnificent.

    C. small.

    D. important.

42. The word *routine* in paragraph two is closest in meaning to

    A. standard.

    B. elevated.

    C. required.

    D. complex.

43. The word *they* in paragraph two refers to

    A. symptoms.

    B. illness.

    C. enzymes.

    D. people.

44. The author implies that

    A. patients usually learn of the illness because they have severe symptoms.

    B. liver transplants are a very common form of treatment.

    C. many people with hepatitis C were not addicts but simply experimented with illegal drugs.

    D. people are still in danger of acquiring the illness from blood transfusions.

45. The author indicates that a biopsy is performed in order to

   A. prepare for a liver transplant.

   B. determine whether one has the virus.

   C. learn the degree of damage to the liver.

   D. decide which form of drug to prescribe.

46. The author implies that hepatitis C

   A. attacks rapidly.

   B. does not affect many people.

   C. only rarely results in liver cancer.

   D. attacks the central nervous system.

47. The author states that people sometimes choose not to take treatment for hepatitis C for all of the following reasons except

   A. the medicine must be taken intravenously.

   B. the treatment does not work for everybody.

   C. often the level of illness is not severe.

   D. the side effects of the medicine are sometimes worse than the symptoms of the illness.

48. The word *its* in the third paragraph refers to

   A. device.

   B. liver.

   C. biopsy.

   D. doctor.

Section 3 Reading

STOP

245

Writing Section

Time: 30 Minutes

1 Question

Directions: This section measures your ability to write in English, including your ability to organize ideas, create an essay in standard written English, and support the thoughts with sufficient examples and evidence. Write an essay in 30 minutes. You may make notes on a separate piece of paper, and then type or handwrite the essay.

Do you believe that a person should seek a college degree or higher education? Use specific reasons and examples to support your position.

Listening Section

Time: 47 Minutes

37 Questions

To work through the Listening section of the practice test, you need to use the first audio CD that is included in this book. Starting with Track 11 of the CD, you will hear people having brief conversations. At the end of each conversation, you will hear a question that you must answer based on your understanding of what the speaker(s) said. Each question is printed below, along with answer choices. Mark your answer choices as you go along. The CD track numbers that you need to listen to are indicated throughout the section.

After you have completed this practice test and checked your answers, turn to the appendix of this book. The conversations that you heard on the CD are transcribed there. If you had any difficulty understanding what a speaker was saying, listen to the CD again, this time reading what is being said at the same time you listen to it. Do not turn to the appendix until you have worked through this practice test at least once by just listening to the CD.

Part A

Directions: In this part, you will hear short conversations between two people. After the conversation, a question will be asked. Choose the answer that most accurately answers the question based on what is stated or implied by the speakers. Mark the answer in your book or on a separate piece of paper.

CD A, Track 11

1. What do the speakers assume about Adam?

   A. He already left the meeting.
   B. He is lost.
   C. He does not intend to come to the meeting.
   D. He is already in the room.

2. What is the woman's problem?

   A. She is unable to teach her class.
   B. She must go to a speech therapist.
   C. She has never taught speech before and wants to be reassigned.
   D. She dislikes teaching.

GO ON TO THE NEXT PAGE

3. What is the man's problem?

   A. The fund-raising event was canceled.

   B. He expected more people to attend the event.

   C. He had to pay too much money.

   D. He is angry at the woman because she did not attend.

4. What is the man probably going to do?

   A. Buy a new car

   B. Take his car in for repair.

   C. Drive the woman to class.

   D. Take a bus.

5. What is the man's problem?

   A. He studied too much.

   B. He lost his book.

   C. He did not prepare adequately for the test.

   D. He is tired because he spent too much time studying.

6. What does the man say about the job interview?

   A. He wishes he had presented himself better.

   B. He thinks he might get the job although he did not speak well.

   C. He did not like the job offer.

   D. He believes the interview went very well.

7. What does the woman mean?

   A. She had to work so she did not go to Seattle.

   B. She has a new job in Seattle.

   C. She does not like to fly.

   D. She plans to go to Seattle after work.

8. What does the woman mean?

   A. Brenda is sorry she chose the textbook.

   B. Another teacher chose the textbook.

   C. Brenda replaced the textbook.

   D. Brenda does not mind the textbook.

9. What do the speakers imply about Ms. Murphy?

   A. She is not talented as a speaker.

   B. She is a prolific writer.

   C. She speaks well but does not write well.

   D. She is giving an important talk on writing.

10. What did the man assume about Scott?

    A. That he would definitely travel to France

    B. That he had turned down the scholarship absolutely

    C. That he would travel to France in the spring

    D. That he lost the papers

11. What does the man mean?

    A. He bought the house.

    B. He is still trying to buy the house.

    C. He chose not to purchase the house.

    D. He was unable to buy the house.

12. What does the woman say about Jim?

    A. He is at his family's beach house.

    B. His sister says that he uses the beach house too much.

    C. His sister says that he does not use the beach house enough.

    D. He is angry at his sister, so he does not want to see her at the beach house.

13. What is the woman's problem?

    A. She has no time to relax.

    B. She is disappointed that the man never helps.

    C. She arrived too soon.

    D. She wasn't expecting the baby at this time.

14. What had the man assumed about the woman?

    A. That she would remain in town

    B. That she was moving away

    C. That she was skipping exams

    D. That she had quit her job

15. What does the man imply?

    A. Susan accidentally started the fire.

    B. Susan's father was injured in the fire.

    C. Susan is ashamed of what happened.

    D. Only Susan's father's room was damaged.

Part B

Directions: In this part, you will hear several conversations and talks. You will hear each conversation or talk only once, and then you will hear several questions. Answer the questions based on what is stated or implied by the speakers. Choose the best of the answer choices provided. Mark the answer in your book or on a separate piece of paper.

CD A, Track 12

16. What had the woman assumed about the man's current living arrangements?

    A. That he had sold his house

    B. That he was happy with his living arrangements

    C. That he had already moved

    D. That he was unhappy with his apartment

17. What does the man say about the location he prefers?

    A. He likes to live in the country.

    B. He is trying to find a place close to work and school.

    C. He will accept a place close to either work or school.

    D. Distance is not important to him.

GO ON TO THE NEXT PAGE

18. How does the man react to the suggestion made by the woman?

   A. He thinks it is too far away from everything.

   B. He thinks it is close to conveniences.

   C. He is disappointed that there is no swimming pool.

   D. He thinks the rent is outrageous.

19. What does the woman offer to do for the man?

   A. Share the apartment with him

   B. Contact her friend to inquire about it

   C. Take him to see houses

   D. Talk to an apartment broker

CD A, Track 13

20. What is the discussion mainly about?

   A. Similarities between reflux disease and heart attacks

   B. Diagnosis, symptoms, and treatment of reflux disease

   C. Problems of eating a fatty diet

   D. The relationship between the stomach and the heart

21. How does the woman describe the sphincter?

   A. As a disease

   B. As a useless body part

   C. As a necessary protective mechanism

   D. As the cause of problems

22. According to the woman, when does acid reflux occur?

   A. When eating

   B. When the sphincter opens when it shouldn't

   C. When talking

   D. When the sphincter is stuck closed

23. According to the woman, why does the reflux cause the burning sensation?

   A. The stomach contains strong chemicals.

   B. Food cannot travel down easily when there is an attack.

   C. The esophagus constricts.

   D. The sphincter hits the wall of the esophagus.

24. According to the woman, what results from metaplastic changes?

   A. Burning

   B. Hiatal hernia

   C. Acid reflux disease

   D. Cancer

25. How does the woman describe a hiatal hernia?

   A. As reflux disease

   B. As a cause of reflux disease

   C. As the result of reflux disease

   D. As a cancer of the esophagus

26. According to the woman, what are two reasons a patient may want to control his or her diet?

    A. Diet can affect how and when the sphincter acts up.

    B. One should always avoid spicy foods.

    C. Fatty foods make reflux more likely.

    D. If one eats little, the sphincter does not have to work so hard.

27. Which of the following is *not* a suggested course of action to treat reflux disease?

    A. Repair the sphincter.

    B. Watch diet.

    C. Take medication.

    D. Ignore the problem.

CD A, Track 14

28. What is the man talking about?

    A. An ancient tool

    B. An old book

    C. Ancient artwork

    D. Fossilized bones

29. What had scientists believed before these tools were found?

    A. That Africans were more advanced than Middle Easterners

    B. That Middle Easterners were more advanced than Africans

    C. That the Chinese were more advanced than both Middle Easterners and Africans

    D. That Africans and Middle Easterners were more advanced than anybody else

30. How does the speaker describe the comparison between the new tools and the tools found previously?

    A. They are quite similar.

    B. They are quite different.

    C. The tools were used for different purposes.

    D. The designs are similar, but the materials are different.

GO ON TO THE NEXT PAGE

CD A, Track 15

31. What does the speaker imply about Hawthorne's success as a writer?

   A. He was financially and professionally successful from the outset.

   B. He never achieved success in his own eyes.

   C. He often struggled, but he did enjoy professional success eventually.

   D. He made money as a writer but was not well respected.

32. How does the speaker describe Hawthorne's scholastic abilities?

   A. He did not enjoy school but he did enjoy learning on his own.

   B. He was an honors student.

   C. He enjoyed school.

   D. He did not like reading materials of any sort.

33. How does the speaker describe Hawthorne's early home life?

   A. His family was wealthy.

   B. His parents were financially successful.

   C. His mother was outgoing.

   D. His father died when he was young, and his mother was a recluse.

34. What does the speaker imply that Hawthorne did during his reclusive years?

   A. He never left the room.

   B. He stayed in a room with his mother.

   C. He read and wrote quite a bit, but he also got out from time to time.

   D. He did not actually write anything during the 12-year period.

35. According to the speaker, what was Hawthorne's reaction to his first published work, which was self-published?

   A. He praised it often.

   B. He was thrilled with the amount of money he made from it.

   C. He destroyed copies of it because it was a failure.

   D. He was disappointed that it was not well respected.

36. What does the speaker imply about Hawthorne's financial success?

   A. He never achieved financial independence.

   B. He became extremely rich.

   C. He disdained riches.

   D. He lived on his family's wealth.

37. What does the speaker indicate happened to *The Scarlet Letter* during Hawthorne's lifetime?

   A. Some unscrupulous publishers printed it without Hawthorne's permission.

   B. It sold so well that Hawthorne became financially successful.

   C. It bankrupted Hawthorne.

   D. It made Hawthorne extremely popular.

Structure Section

Time: 20 Minutes

25 Questions

Directions: This section measures your ability to recognize language appropriate for standard written English. One type of question consists of incomplete sentences, with a blank showing where information is to be filled in. Choose the word or phrase that most correctly completes the sentence. A second type of question consists of sentences with four underlined words or phrases. For each sentence, choose the one underlined word or phrase that is incorrect in standard written English. Mark the answer in your book or on a separate piece of paper.

1. Overeating, in addition to lack of
   A
   attention to nutrition, are said to be the
                          B   C
   major cause of obesity in the United
            D
   States.

2. Once the employees had begun receiving financial information on the company, _____ income.

   A. they diligently assisted in reducing costs and increasing

   B. it made the employees more eager to assist in reduce costs and increase

   C. diligently they assist to reduce costs and increase

   D. with extreme diligence helped lower costs and increase

3. Because the students showed they had
   A
   read the materials so thorough, the
   B   C
   instructor decided not to administer an
                           D
   exam.

4. The plumber attempted to loosen the nut with regular pliers but then decided he needed to retrieve his toolbox in order to use _____.

   A. another pliers

   B. others pliers

   C. the others ones

   D. another pair

5. Judy decided to wait until after she
                A
   had taken her exams before having her
   B   C
   wisdom teeth pull.
                D

6. The committee has met and _____.

   A. have approve the budget

   B. budget was approved

   C. its approval of the budget

   D. approved the budget

7. Hardly the plane had landed when
   A
   Adam realized that he had left the file
          B   C
   that he needed at his office.
              D

GO ON TO THE NEXT PAGE

8. After Michelle had taken control of the Accounts Receivable department, the financial situation improved dramatically; her fiscal and management capabilities _____ to the success.

   A. should contribute

   B. should have contributed

   C. must have contributed

   D. must contribute

9. The consultant said management had

better <u>to formalize</u> <u>its</u> employment
        A   B

policies and procedures in order to

<u>avoid</u> <u>adverse</u> employment claims in the
 C   D
future.

10. Having been presented the financial aspects of the proposed agreement, _____.

   A. legal terms were addressed by the board members

   B. the board members turned their attention to the legal terms

   C. they were begun to discuss legal terms

   D. a discussion of the legal terms by the board members

11. The <u>author</u> has <u>not rarely</u> written
      A   B
<u>anything</u> that was not <u>a</u> best-seller.
 C   D

12. Rafael will not be able to attend class tomorrow because _____ an interview with the immigration officials.

   A. he must to attend

   B. he will be attending

   C. of he must attend

   D. he will have attending

13. <u>The</u> Dean of the College of Education
   A

has <u>already to decide</u> whether <u>to permit</u>
      B   C

the meeting to be <u>held</u> on campus.
           D

14. The faculty of the university is not expected to approve the collective bargaining proposal, and _____.

   A. the administration either

   B. neither is the administration

   C. neither the administration

   D. the administration is not neither

15. The professor had <u>already</u> completed
            A

calculation <u>of</u> the final grades and
       B

<u>had submit</u> them to the office when
 C

Elizabeth <u>delivered</u> her paper.
        D

16. The chairman requested that _____.

   A. a committee appointed to study the problem thoroughly

   B. a committee be appointed to make thoroughly review of the problem

   C. thoroughly review the problem by a committee

   D. a committee be appointed to review the problem thoroughly

17. Several cars <u>plunged</u> <u>into</u> the water
             A   B
    when the pier <u>was striking</u> by a barge
              C
    that separated <u>from</u> its tugboat.
              D

18. Internet companies rely heavily on income from on-line purchases, but _____.

    A. traditional companies as well

    B. traditional companies too

    C. also traditional companies

    D. so do traditional companies

19. The company had difficulty distributing _____ so that they could meet production quotas.

    A. sufficiently number of parts in a timely manner to its manufacturers

    B. a sufficient number of parts to its manufacturers in a timely manner

    C. to its manufacturers in a timely manner a sufficient number of parts

    D. in a timely manner to its manufacturers a sufficient number of parts

20. The new prospect for the team has great
    <u>height</u> and agility, but the coaches do
     A
    not believe he moves <u>enough quickly</u> to
                 B
    play in the <u>position</u> that they need to fill.
     C   D

21. So <u>much</u> people applied <u>for</u> service
      A   B
    <u>from</u> the new company that it found it
     C
    <u>impossible</u> to meet the demand.
      D

22. The company sustained an angry reaction from its employees after announcing how _____ to reduce operating costs.

    A. it planned

    B. planned

    C. did it plan

    D. was planned

23. The meeting is <u>being</u> held <u>in</u> the <u>fifth</u>
              A   B   C
    floor of the convention center, but there
    <u>are</u> functions on every floor.
     D

24. Professor Anderson wrote _____, which is expected to be published in the next few months.

    A. a new textbook last year

    B. last year a new textbook

    C. in last year a new textbook

    D. during last year a new textbook

25. The tube worm, _____ stationary plant-like creature that lives at the bottom of the deep sea, can live for hundreds of years.

    A. is a

    B. it is a

    C. a

    D. that is a

Reading Section

Time: 72 Minutes

45 Questions

Directions: This section measures your ability to read and understand written English similar to that which one may expect in a college or university setting. Read each passage and answer the questions based on what is stated or implied in the passage. Circle or mark the correct answer in the book or write it on a separate piece of paper.

Passage 1

Sometimes people worry about the germs that they come into contact with daily. In fact, most people would be surprised to learn just how many microbes actually inhabit a human's body at any given time, in addition to the larger visitors that come around occasionally. Such natural species that regularly come into contact with our bodies include mites, lice, yeast, and fungus, just to name a few. We are, in fact, an ecosystem much like a rain forest is to the natural flora and fauna that call it home.

Lice, or nits, are particularly horrible to even think about. To learn that one's child has been found in school with head lice can cause trauma and shame. People think that having lice is a symptom of being unclean, although one can be infected by contact with somebody else who has them. Although lice are not that common in general circles, children can easily acquire them just because of their close contact with other children at school or play. Some large cities host high-priced nit pickers who make a living removing head lice from children.

Mites on the human body are much more common, and cleanliness does not eliminate the chance of having them. They are also microscopic, so they are invisible to the naked eye. There are a number of different species of mites, two of which have the human face as their natural habitat, particularly the skin of the forehead. Others are very content among human hair, living among the follicles of the eyelashes, eyebrows, and scalp hair.

Not all such inhabitants are harmful. In fact, even the annoying mite lives on dead skin cells, actually doing us a favor by removing them. The dreaded dust mite, for example, blamed for causing allergies, removes dead skin from bed coverings. And harmless bacteria often keep potentially harmful bacteria from being able to survive. So people should not try to eliminate mites from their bodies, although some have tried. Some sufferers of obsessive/compulsive disorder have scrubbed themselves raw trying to eliminate all scavengers from their bodies, only to damage their skin, and all to no avail.

Certain types of yeast also regularly live on the human body, sometimes causing annoyances. One common type lives on the oil produced in the skin of the face or scalp, causing a condition known as pityriasis versicolor, which is a scaling and discoloration of the skin.

Ailments such as athlete's foot are caused by a fungus that grows in warm, moist conditions. To avoid them or avoid a recurrence, patients are encouraged keep their feet dry and cool, which of course may not be easy, depending on one's work or personal habits. Ringworm is also a fungus acquired by contact with keratin-rich soil in many parts of the world.

Besides the tiny inhabitants, we are also regularly harassed by insects that feed off of our bodies, like mosquitoes, ticks, and fleas, which sometimes deposit harmful illnesses at the same time they probe the skin for the blood on which they live. Mosquitoes have been known to cause malaria and yellow fever as well as encephalitis. Fleas have transmitted bubonic plague, and ticks have caused lime disease.

Just like a river, an ocean, a rain forest, or any other ecological wonder in which numerous species survive, feeding upon other inhabitants, our bodies are natural providers of nutrition and life for various small and microscopic species.

1. The word *inhabit* in the second sentence is closest in meaning to

   A. escape.
   B. live in.
   C. feed on.
   D. abuse.

2. The author's main point is

   A. to describe the dangerous ailments that can result from insects and microbes.
   B. to describe how the human body is host to a number of different harmful and harmless inhabitants and visitors.

   C. to warn people about the dangers of being attacked by small life forms.
   D. to describe how to rid oneself of bacteria and insects.

3. The author infers that lice and mites are different in that

   A. mites are totally unavoidable, while lice may be avoidable.
   B. lice are not harmful, but mites are.
   C. mites live only on the skin, and lice live only in the hair.
   D. mites are treatable, and lice are not.

4. The word *shame* in the second paragraph is closest in meaning to

   A. embarrassment.
   B. anger.
   C. disbelief.
   D. contentment.

5. The word *their* in the second paragraph refers to

   A. lice's.
   B. children's.
   C. circles'.
   D. schools'.

Section 3 Reading

GO ON TO THE NEXT PAGE

6. Where, in the third paragraph, could the following sentence be inserted logically?

In fact, one mite is generally about one-fourth the size of a period on a page of text.

Mites on the human body are much more common, and cleanliness does not eliminate the chance of having them. **(A)** They are also microscopic, so they are invisible to the naked eye. **(B)** There are a number of different species of mites, two of which have the human face as their natural habitat, particularly the skin of the forehead. **(C)** Others are very content among human hair, living among the follicles of the eyelashes, eyebrows, and scalp hair. **(D)**

7. The word *others* in the third paragraph refers to

A. foreheads.

B. follicles.

C. habitats.

D. mite species.

8. The author indicates that lice are also known as

A. nits.

B. microbes.

C. yeast.

D. ticks.

9. The author indicates that a nit picker is

A. somebody who is afraid of mites.

B. somebody who removes lice professionally.

C. a doctor who treats patients for infection.

D. somebody who has been bitten by a tick.

10. The author infers that

A. being host to insects and microbes is unwise.

B. being host to insects and microbes is inevitable.

C. one can avoid infestation by microbes.

D. insects are the cause of microbial infestation.

11. What does the author mean by the statement *Not all such inhabitants are harmful* at the beginning of the fourth paragraph?

A. Mites are the same as yeast.

B. Mites actually are beneficial because they remove dead skin particles from the body and habitat.

C. Some mites eat other harmful mites.

D. The diseases mites carry do not pass to humans.

Passage 2

Sinkholes may <u>occur</u> slowly and be completely harmless or may quickly cause <u>devastating</u> damage. It is interesting that sinkholes may be caused by two opposite conditions — extreme drought or too much rain.

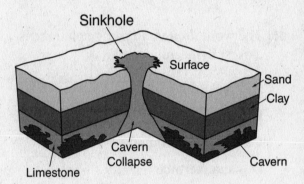

Sinkhole
Surface
Sand
Clay
Cavern
Collapse
Cavern
Limestone

As depicted in the drawing, under the sandy surface soil is a layer of clay and then a layer of limestone. Sinkholes generally occur only in areas where the geology has this composition. Within the limestone areas are pockets of water and air. When the underground aquifer is full of ground water, the pockets are generally filled with water and perhaps air above the water. But when there is too much rain or not enough rain, the caverns may become unstable. When there is too much, the cavern walls can be broken through because of excess pressure, and when there is too little, the cavern walls can collapse because there is not enough internal pressure to withstand the weight from above. When that occurs, the cavern collapses, and the sandy soil close to the surface seeps or pours into the cavern. The speed of the collapse and amount of damage depends on the size of the collapsing cavern.

In <u>drought</u> conditions, sinkholes become more common over time. They may harmlessly appear in a lawn and then stop.

Sometimes, small sinkholes recur or continue to eat soil for years without causing any damage. But at other times they open in the middle of streets, surprising drivers and swallowing cars, or in residential areas, swallowing houses. Sinkholes are not <u>discriminating</u>. They have <u>swallowed</u> small inexpensive homes, as well as huge homes worth millions of dollars. It is very rare for people to be hurt when it occurs, because it usually occurs over some length of time and is noisy as the ground becomes unstable.

Sinkholes have also swallowed lakes. There are areas in Florida where 40 or more homes had been built around a beautiful lake. One day, the entire lake disappeared because the cavern beneath the ground opened. Instead of sand being above the cavern, there was water, which flowed into the cavern, leaving behind dead and dying fish and plants and docks that led to nowhere. In one neighborhood, the neighbors managed to plug the hole in the lake with a huge block of concrete, and rain eventually filled the lake. But their efforts were to no avail because several years later the lake disappeared again.

Sinkholes are a natural phenomenon caused in particular geological areas by particular events. Unfortunately, even knowing the cause and having time to plan, it is not possible to stop a sinkhole.

12. The word *occur* in the first sentence is closest in meaning to

A. happen.

B. leak.

C. stop.

D. cause.

GO ON TO THE NEXT PAGE

Section **3** Reading

13. The word *devastating* in the first sentence is closest in meaning to

    A. overwhelming.

    B. quick.

    C. slow.

    D. unpleasant.

14. A good title for this passage would be

    A. Where did the Water Go? How Lakes Disappear.

    B. The Causes and Effects of Sinkholes.

    C. The Dangers of Living Above Limestone.

    D. How to Avoid Sinkhole Damage.

15. The author states that sinkholes can be caused by

    A. too much precipitation or not enough precipitation.

    B. too little rain or unstable sandy soil.

    C. too much rain or certain types of limestone.

    D. water filling limestone caverns or air filling limestone caverns.

16. The author implies that sinkholes

    A. can occur anywhere.

    B. only occur where there are limestone caverns below the surface.

    C. can be prevented.

    D. occur very rapidly and without notice.

17. The author indicates that the layers of material in soil from the top down are

    A. surface, limestone, clay, and sand.

    B. surface, clay, sand, and limestone.

    C. surface, limestone, sand, and clay.

    D. surface, sand, clay, and limestone.

18. The word *drought* in paragraph three is closest in meaning to

    A. lack of liquid.

    B. overabundance of liquid.

    C. seeping of liquid.

    D. summertime.

19. The word *discriminating* in the third paragraph is closest in meaning to

    A. discerning.

    B. unusual.

    C. dangerous.

    D. automatic.

20. The word *swallowed* in paragraph three is closest in meaning to

    A. filled.

    B. consumed.

    C. formed in.

    D. damaged.

21. According to the passage, caverns are normally filled with

    A. air and water.

    B. water and sand.

    C. limestone and air.

    D. sand and clay.

22. An example of a harmless sinkhole would be

    A. one that opens in a yard and never expands.

    B. one that opens in a city street so long as nobody is injured or killed.

    C. one that opens under a house.

    D. one that eliminates a lake.

23. According to the passage, how successful was the attempt to replace a lake by plugging the hole?

    A. Unknown. It has not yet been completed.

    B. Completely successful over the long term.

    C. Initially successful, but later it failed.

    D. Not successful at all.

Passage 3

It was previously believed that dinosaurs were cold-blooded creatures, like reptiles. However, a recent discovery has led researchers to believe <u>they</u> may have been warm-blooded. The fossilized remains of a 66 million-year-old dinosaur's heart were discovered and examined by x-ray. The basis for the analysis that they were warm-blooded is the number of chambers in the heart as well as the existence of a single aorta.

Most reptiles have three chambers in their hearts, although some do have four. But those that have four chambers, such as the crocodile, have two arteries to mix the oxygen-heavy blood with oxygen-lean blood. Reptiles are cold-blooded, meaning that they are dependent on the environment for body heat. Yet the fossilized heart had four chambers in the heart as well as a single aorta. The single aorta means that the oxygen-rich blood was completely separated from the oxygen-poor blood and sent through the aorta to all parts of the body.

Mammals, on the other hand, are warm-blooded, meaning that they <u>generate</u> their own body heat and are thus more tolerant of temperature extremes. Birds and mammals, because they are warm blooded, move more swiftly and have greater physical endurance than reptiles.

Scientists believe that the evidence now points to the idea that all dinosaurs were actually warm-blooded. Ironically, the particular dinosaur in which the discovery was made was a Tescelosaurus, which translates to *"marvelous lizard."* A lizard, of course, is a reptile.

24. The word *they* in the second sentence refers to

    A. researchers.

    B. discoveries.

    C. reptiles.

    D. dinosaurs.

25. According to the author, what theory was previously held and now is being questioned?

    A. That dinosaurs were warm-blooded

    B. That dinosaurs had four-chambered hearts

    C. That dinosaurs were swifter and stronger than reptiles

    D. That dinosaurs were cold-blooded

Section **3** Reading

GO ON TO THE NEXT PAGE

26. What is the basis of the researchers' new theory?

    A. They performed mathematical calculations and determined that dinosaurs must have had four-chambered hearts.

    B. They found a fossil of an entire dinosaur and reviewed the arteries and veins flowing from and to the heart.

    C. They found a fossil of a dinosaur's heart and discovered it had four chambers and one aorta.

    D. They viewed a fossil of a dinosaur's heart and discovered that it had two aortas.

27. The author implies that reptiles

    A. have four-chambered hearts.

    B. have one aorta.

    C. are cold-blooded.

    D. are faster and have more endurance than mammals.

28. The word *generate* in paragraph three is closest in meaning to

    A. produce.

    B. lose.

    C. use.

    D. tolerate.

29. The author implies that birds

    A. move faster and have greater endurance than reptiles.

    B. move slower and have less endurance than reptiles.

    C. move faster and have greater endurance than dinosaurs.

    D. move slower and have less endurance than dinosaurs.

30. What does the author imply by the sentence:

Ironically, the particular dinosaur in which the discovery was made was a Tescelosaurus, which translates to "marvelous lizard."

    A. It is paradoxical that the dinosaur's name includes the word *lizard,* because now scientists believe it is not a lizard.

    B. It is unusual that the creature would have a name with the suffix of a dinosaur.

    C. It is surprising that the fossilized heart was discovered.

    D. It should have been realized long ago that dinosaurs were warm-blooded.

Passage 4

Many people suffer from an <u>ailment</u> of the gallbladder, <u>which</u> occurs when stones form within the organ. The gallbladder is a small sac in the upper-right section of the abdomen, beneath the liver and near the pancreas. Its function is to store bile, which is produced by the liver to help digest fat and absorb vitamins and minerals. Bile consists mainly of water, cholesterol, lipids (fats), <u>bile salts</u>, which are natural detergents that break up fat, and <u>bilirubin</u>, which is a pigment that gives bile its greenish-yellow color.

Gallstones form when the cholesterol and the bilirubin form crystals, which then <u>fuse</u> in the gallbladder to form the stones. They range in size from tiny specks the size of grains of sand to stones as large as golf balls, although most are quite small. Sometimes the crystals accumulate but do not form stones. But even then, they form a <u>sludge</u> that causes indigestion and discomfort, which is not as serious as the symptoms that stones cause.

The great majority of gallstones are made of cholesterol, but some consist of bile pigment. The former are produced when the bile is too rich in cholesterol or the gallbladder is not functioning properly, and they generally occur in people within the risk factors.

Gallstones can <u>irritate</u> the lining of the gallbladder, causing chronic inflammation and infection, resulting in pain in the abdominal area. An acute gallstone attack occurs when the gallbladder contracts while squeezing its bile through the cystic duct, and one or more stones lodge in the duct. The muscles in the duct wall then contract in an attempt to <u>dislodge</u> the stone, causing severe pain. If they are not dislodged, the bile backs up into the liver and eventually the bloodstream.

Risk groups include people who are overweight; people who fast habitually or are on long-term extremely low-calorie diets; pregnant women; people with diabetes; females between the ages of 20 and 60; native American men or Pima Indian women of Arizona; and Mexican-American men or women. As anybody ages, the chance of gallstones increases, with 10 percent of all men and 20 percent of women having gallstones by age 60.

Gallstones are diagnosed with an ultrasound, which is a device that transmits sound waves into the body and returns a <u>depiction</u> of the organ. Even patients with gallstones generally do not need treatment unless the stones are causing chronic symptoms. Large stones can be crushed through a procedure called shock wave lithotripsy, but the fragments then must exit the body, which can be uncomfortable. The most common treatment is to remove the gallbladder entirely. The body gets along quite well with no gallbladder because <u>it</u> is simply a storage area. The manufacture of bile in the liver goes on just the same, although there is no bile present in the event it is needed quickly. For that reason, patients are urged to avoid excessively fatty foods.

31. The word *ailment* in the first sentence is closest in meaning to

   A. organ.

   B. disorder.

   C. enlargement.

   D. loss.

32. The word *which* in the first sentence refers to

   A. people.

   B. ailment.

   C. suffer.

   D. stone

GO ON TO THE NEXT PAGE

33. The author implies in the first paragraph that *sludge* is similar to

   A. stones.

   B. mud.

   C. liquid.

   D. medicine.

34. The word *fuse* in the second paragraph is closest in meaning to

   A. crystallize.

   B. join.

   C. separate.

   D. collapse.

35. The author implies in the first paragraph that *bile salts* are similar to

   A. soap.

   B. oil.

   C. fat.

   D. stones.

36. The author implies in the first paragraph that *bilirubin* is similar to

   A. paint.

   B. bile.

   C. soap.

   D. cholesterol.

37. The author indicates that crystals of cholesterol and bilirubin that do not fuse cause

   A. severe pain.

   B. indigestion.

   C. chronic attacks.

   D. crystallization.

38. The author states that most gallstones are caused by

   A. cholesterol-rich bile or a malfunctioning gallbladder.

   B. overabundance of bile pigment.

   C. sludge.

   D. eating fatty foods.

39. The word *irritate* in the fourth paragraph is closest in meaning to

   A. affect.

   B. inflame.

   C. treat.

   D. result.

40. The word *dislodge* in the fourth paragraph is closest in meaning to

   A. treat.

   B. displace.

   C. expand.

   D. entrench.

41. The author implies that most severe attacks occur when a stone becomes stuck in the

   A. gallbladder.

   B. cystic duct.

   C. sludge.

   D. liver.

42. One common cause of gallstones is

   A. excessive dieting.

   B. eating too many vegetables.

   C. excessive eating.

   D. eating too much fruit.

43. All of the following people are potentially at high risk of getting gallstones except

   A. a woman who is pregnant.

   B. a man of Pima Indian descent.

   C. a person over 55.

   D. a Mexican-American woman.

44. The word *depiction* in the last paragraph is closest in meaning to

   A. illustration.

   B. diagnosis.

   C. wave.

   D. stone.

45. The word *it* in the last paragraph refers to

   A. body.

   B. gallbladder.

   C. stone.

   D. treatment.

Writing Section

Time: 30 Minutes

1 Question

Directions: This section measures your ability to write in English, including your ability to organize ideas, create an essay in standard written English, and support the thoughts with sufficient examples and evidence. Write an essay in 30 minutes. You may make notes on a separate piece of paper, and then type or handwrite the essay.

Do you agree or disagree with the following statement: *All work and no play makes Jack a dull boy*? Use specific reasons and examples to support your position.

PRACTICE TEST 4

Listening Section

Time: 50 Minutes

40 Questions

To work through the Listening section of the practice test, you need to use the second audio CD that is included in this book. Starting with Track 1 of the CD, you will hear people having brief conversations. At the end of each conversation, you will hear a question that you must answer based on your understanding of what the speaker(s) said. Each question is printed below, along with answer choices. Mark your answer choices as you go along. The CD track numbers that you need to listen to are indicated throughout the section.

After you have completed this practice test and checked your answers, turn to the appendix of this book. The conversations that you heard on the CD are transcribed there. If you had any difficulty understanding what a speaker was saying, listen to the CD again, this time reading what is being said at the same time you listen to it. Do not turn to the appendix until you have worked through this practice test at least once by just listening to the CD.

Part A

Directions: In this part, you will hear short conversations between two people. After the conversation, a question will be asked. Choose the answer that most accurately answers the question based on what is stated or implied by the speakers. Mark the answer in your book or on a separate piece of paper.

CD B, Track 1

1. What does the woman imply is the best course of treatment?

   A. Discontinue all medicine.

   B. Have a new blood test right away.

   C. Have a blood test every two weeks.

   D. Try new medicine and then have a blood test.

2. What do the speakers imply about the new Greek restaurant?

   A. They don't like it.

   B. They have both eaten there.

   C. They hear it is almost as good as a former restaurant.

   D. They have never had a good Greek restaurant in their area.

3. What does the woman say about taking the certification exam?

    A. She thinks she should take it, but it's too time-consuming.

    B. She doesn't think she is smart enough to pass it.

    C. She already took it and failed.

    D. She does not believe it will benefit her career.

4. What does the man imply about what happened on the highway?

    A. He was not afraid.

    B. Nothing really happened. The accident was just a rumor.

    C. He was not driving the car at the time of the accident.

    D. He was extremely frightened.

5. What does the man say about Jose?

    A. He is sick.

    B. He did not wish to attend the function.

    C. He came to the party, but the man did not see him.

    D. He is in jail in another city.

6. According to the woman, why is Roberto considering changing schools?

    A. His father believes a well-known school is better.

    B. Roberto wants a school farther away from home.

    C. Roberto would prefer a smaller school.

    D. His father wants him to make better grades.

7. What do the speakers imply about the procedure the students will view?

    A. It's very interesting.

    B. It's not pleasant.

    C. It's hard work.

    D. The paper will be hard to write.

8. What does the woman imply about Allan's leaving the meeting?

    A. He had a prior engagement.

    B. He was not at the meeting at all.

    C. He was unhappy with the presentation.

    D. The leader made him leave.

9. What do the speakers mean?

    A. Neither Helen nor the man could find the books.

    B. Helen found the books on the Internet.

    C. The man found the books for Helen.

    D. Helen found the books for the man.

10. What does the woman mean?

    A. The jury probably will not make a decision today.

    B. The jury has already made a decision.

    C. The jury is voting right now.

    D. The jury will likely make a decision tonight.

GO ON TO THE NEXT PAGE

11. What do the speakers imply about Bill and the stock market?

   A. Bill has been studying the stock market lately.

   B. Bill never believes anything he reads about stocks.

   C. Bill made a bad decision about a stock purchase.

   D. Bill has made an enormous amount of money in the stock market.

12. What do the speakers say about what happened to Stephen?

   A. He lost his job.

   B. He quit his job.

   C. He was killed in an accident.

   D. He was injured severely in an accident.

13. What is the woman's problem?

   A. She needs more sleep.

   B. She is sleeping a lot but feels exhausted.

   C. She has been having bad dreams.

   D. She is having trouble sleeping at night.

14. What do the speakers say about their opinions of the receptionist?

   A. She eats too much at her desk.

   B. She writes messages that contain incorrect information.

   C. She refuses to write down phone numbers.

   D. She is rude to callers.

15. What does the man say about interviewing with the new company?

   A. He absolutely will not interview with the company.

   B. He will interview if he is invited.

   C. He already took a job with his old company.

   D. He already interviewed with them.

Part B

Directions: In this part, you will hear several conversations and talks. You will hear each conversation or talk only once, and then you will hear several questions. Answer the questions based on what is stated or implied by the speakers. Choose the best of the answer choices provided. Mark the answer in your book or on a separate piece of paper.

CD B, Track 2

16. What does the woman indicate about the next process in the case?

   A. The judge may send them to an arbitrator.

   B. The judge will require mediation.

   C. The judge will set a trial date.

   D. The judge will give them an option, and the woman suggests mediation.

17. What had the man assumed about mediation?

- **A.** That it is very useful
- **B.** That it involves an arbitrator
- **C.** That the court can be convinced to allow a trial
- **D.** That it will cost too much money

18. How does the man apparently feel about the opposing parties in this matter?

- **A.** He feels that the opponents are entrenched in an incorrect position.
- **B.** He feels that an arbitrator could convince them.
- **C.** He feels that mediation is a great idea.
- **D.** He feels that the opposing party is being too sensitive.

19. How does the woman appear to feel about mediation?

- **A.** That it is a waste of time
- **B.** That the court should be talked out of it

- **C.** That arbitration is better
- **D.** That it often produces positive results

20. What does the man indicate that the woman previously advised him to do?

- **A.** To try mediation
- **B.** To resist mediation
- **C.** To settle the case
- **D.** To try arbitration

21. What does the woman state about the mediation procedure?

- **A.** The mediator will listen to the evidence and render a decision.
- **B.** The mediator will separate the parties and carry settlement offers from one to the other.
- **C.** The mediator will push the parties like an exercise coach.
- **D.** The mediator will listen to evidence and then contact the judge.

CD B, Track 3

22. How long does the man indicate that Claire Nelson has been interested in carcinogens?

- **A.** She recently became interested.
- **B.** She has been researching carcinogens for years.

- **C.** She started research long ago but then put it off until just recently.
- **D.** She performed research long ago but only obtained access to equipment when she met the Nobel Prize winners.

GO ON TO THE NEXT PAGE

23. What does the man indicate is the nature of her research?

   A. She studies whether microwave ovens cause radiation to migrate into food.

   B. She studies whether olive oil is a carcinogen.

   C. She studies whether carcinogens in plastic wrap can get into food when heated in microwave ovens.

   D. She studies whether microwave ovens cause cancer.

24. How did the man learn about Claire Nelson?

   A. He is a scientist.

   B. He read her scientific journal.

   C. He read about her in a newspaper.

   D. He assisted her in acquiring equipment.

25. How old is Claire Nelson at the time of the discussion?

   A. In seventh grade

   B. Seven years old

   C. A senior in college

   D. Eighteen years old

26. What is the woman's impression of Claire Nelson?

   A. She is lucky, and she is not a hard worker.

   B. She is very resolute.

   C. She took advantage of the government unnecessarily.

   D. She is not very intelligent.

CD B, Track 4

27. What does the woman imply that she just finished talking about before she began this topic?

   A. A will

   B. Handling things for an incapacitated person

   C. Guardianships

   D. Advanced directives

28. How is a power of attorney different from a will?

   A. The woman suggests never using the same person for both.

   B. A will is executed, while a power of attorney is not.

   C. A will is only activated upon death.

   D. A power of attorney has more detailed instruction than a will.

29. What does the woman indicate that a designee can do with a durable financial power of attorney?

   A. Access accounts and property while the grantor is alive

   B. Become the grantor's guardian

   C. Direct that life-prolonging procedures be withheld or withdrawn

   D. Administer the will

30. Why does the woman say that a durable power of attorney is the form to use?

A. It is still effective after death.

B. It remains valid in the case of incapacity.

C. It has stronger language.

D. It includes the right to terminate life support.

31. How does the man initially react to the suggestion of a power of attorney?

A. He is hesitant.

B. He is angry.

C. He is obstinate.

D. He is ready.

32. Which of the following would probably not be a use of an advance directive?

A. To disconnect a ventilator on a dying 95-year-old man

B. To remove food and hydration from a person who is in a permanent vegetative condition

C. To write checks for medical care

D. To discontinue chemotherapy and other medicines on a 46-year-old man with terminal cancer

33. How does the man appear to feel about advance directives?

A. Hesitant

B. Ready

C. Afraid

D. Confused

CD B, Track 5

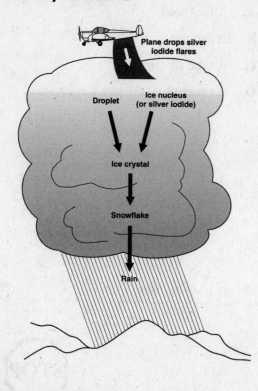

34. What does the woman say has led to a new interest in cloud seeding?

A. The fact that the process is easy and inexpensive

B. Scientific studies that have proven its success

C. Extended periods of drought

D. The need for agricultural advances

35. Does the man indicate that he has heard of cloud seeding before?

A. No, it is totally new to him.

B. Yes, he heard of it some years ago.

C. Yes, he just read an article about it recently for the first time.

D. Yes, he has studied it extensively at the university.

GO ON TO THE NEXT PAGE

36. Why isn't cloud seeding used to combat dry conditions?

  A. It is not known to be effective.

  B. It definitely works but is far too expensive.

  C. The dry conditions are not that serious.

  D. It is not scientifically proven to be effective.

37. What does the man imply should be done?

  A. He thinks they should use it anyway.

  B. He thinks they should postpone use until it is proven to work.

  C. He thinks they should continue to research.

  D. He thinks they should give it up for good.

38. What is the correct order of the process of seeding a cloud?

  A. Ice crystals develop, iodides merge with water droplets, snow and rain develop, and iodides are deposited.

  B. Snow and rain develop, iodides are deposited, ice crystals develop, and iodides merge with water droplets.

  C. Iodides are deposited, iodides merge with water droplets, ice crystals develop, and snow and rain develop.

  D. Iodides merge with water droplets, ice crystals develop, snow and rain develop, and iodides are deposited.

39. According to the speaker, into what is the iodide deposited?

  A. Hurricane clouds

  B. Light wispy Cirrus clouds, which do not normally become storm clouds

  C. Large convective clouds, which are precursors to storm clouds

  D. Clouds that are full of condensation

40. According to the woman, what is a nuclei?

  A. A foothold

  B. A droplet

  C. A type of cloud

  D. A process

Structure Section

Time: 20 Minutes

25 Questions

Directions: This section measures your ability to recognize language appropriate for standard written English. One type of question consists of incomplete sentences, with a blank showing where information is to be filled in. Choose the word or phrase that most correctly completes the sentence. A second type of question consists of sentences with four underlined words or phrases. For each sentence, choose the one underlined word or phrase that is incorrect in standard written English. Mark the answer in your book or on a separate piece of paper.

1. The gymnasium facilities of this public school are _____ those of the finest private school in the county.

   A. second after

   B. second only to

   C. first except for

   D. second place from

2. An orangutan escaped <u>from</u> the zoo and
   A
   <u>was foraged</u> food <u>in</u> a <u>residential</u>
   B   C   D
   neighborhood.

3. The more the horse tried to free itself from the restraint, _____.

   A. the tighter it became

   B. it became tighter

   C. the horse could not escape

   D. it was unable to move

4. The school officials <u>are</u> considering a
   A
   comprehensive <u>planning</u> to <u>alleviate</u> the
   B   C
   problem of <u>overcrowding</u> in the
   D
   dormitories.

5. _____, that runner is likely to be the first one chosen.

   A. Due to her agility and speed

   B. Because of she is agile and fast

   C. Because agile and rapid

   D. Because her agility and speed

6. Spanish is the only course that <u>it</u> is not
   A
   <u>offered</u> in the summer term, but there
   B
   are <u>several</u> classes <u>offered</u> in the fall.
   C   D

7. It was not until the students were seated _____ the proctor realized he had the wrong test booklets.

   A. that

   B. when

   C. as soon as

   D. and

8. Sarah was <u>not best</u> speaker in the class,
   A
   but <u>her</u> personality and <u>ability</u> to convey
   B   C
   her feelings helped her become the most
   <u>requested</u>.
   D

GO ON TO THE NEXT PAGE

9. As a result of the additional rain with so much flooding already having occurred, residents were seeking shelter _____ than in previous years.

  A. in more numbers

  B. more numerously

  C. greater in numbers

  D. in greater numbers

10. The issues learned <u>during</u> the early
            A
<u>stages</u> of the project <u>causing</u> the
   B   C
researchers to initiate <u>additional</u>
                          D
research.

11. The company president wrote an e-mail and planned to send _____ as soon as the vote was complete.

  A. to all directors the message

  B. the message by all directors

  C. message to all directors

  D. the message to all directors

12. Only <u>when black</u> bear has <u>been</u> spotted
          A   B
by the forest rangers <u>will</u> this portion of
                       C
the park be <u>closed</u> down.
             D

13. As the result of Diane's illness and the effects of the medication, _____ to curtail her work and public speaking activities.

  A. has

  B. had

  C. she has had

  D. she will had

14. Television <u>news</u> producers are
                   A
sometimes <u>accuse</u> of sensationalism,
            B
but <u>it</u> appears that is <u>what</u> the public
     C   D
desires.

15. The man displayed his anger when he discovered that the laundry machine was _____ order.

  A. out

  B. out of

  C. no on

  D. outside

16. The workers <u>attempted</u> to <u>free</u> the cat
                     A   B
<u>from</u> the trap, but several obstacles
 C
were <u>in way</u>.
      D

17. In spite of the fact that the Olympic athletes are not permitted to compete for compensation, some of them _____ the past and will again in the future.

  A. so did in

  B. compete in

  C. in

  D. did so in

18. Not only could the younger people

<u>completed</u> all the work <u>quickly</u> and
 A   B
accurately, but the retired workers <u>could</u>
                                     C
<u>also</u>.
 D

19. <u>Allen's not</u> having <u>finished</u> his thesis
A   B
did not <u>discourage</u> him from applying
         C
for <u>other</u> degree program.
     D

20. To master the art of fiction writing
_____ discipline and practice, as
well as studying the works of other
great authors.

     A. require

     B. requires

     C. requiring

     D. that requires

21. That investors in the stock market

<u>enjoys</u> increases and suffer <u>declines</u> is
A   B
simply a fact of the financial market,

and a smart investor is not too excited

about the <u>former</u> or <u>crestfallen</u> about the
         C   D
latter.

22. Because it is impossible for rescuers to
dig through much of the rubble, the
number of people affected by the
devastating earthquake _____ yet
been determined with certainty.

     A. have not

     B. has not

     C. not

     D. only

23. <u>Having</u> been found guilty of
A
racketeering, even though he was never

<u>proven</u> guilty of many crimes he was
B
<u>believe</u> to <u>have</u> committed, the mobster
C   D
was sentenced to a number of years in

prison.

24. Had Jorge <u>be</u> able to <u>complete</u> his thesis
           A   B
instead of <u>returning</u> to work, he would
              C
<u>have</u> graduated a year ago.
D

25. Heather Friedman, _____ at
many school functions and other
community events, is destined for fame
and fortune if she receives the right
backing and is discovered by the right
people.

     A. who has sung

     B. has sung

     C. sung

     D. sang

Section **2** Structure

Reading Section

Time: 75 Minutes

45 Questions

Directions: This section measures your ability to read and understand written English similar to that which one may expect in a college or university setting. Read each passage and answer the questions based on what is stated or implied in the passage. Circle or mark the correct answer in the book or write it on a separate piece of paper.

Passage 1

Tube worms live <u>anchored</u> to the sea floor, 1,700 feet below the ocean surface, near natural spring vents that <u>spew forth</u> water from the earth. They live off geothermal energy instead of sunlight. There are two species of the tube worm family, with very different lengths of life and growth rates, but similarities as well.

The slow-growing tube worms are known to live as long as 250 years, making them the longest-living sea invertebrates known. This species lives near cold sea-floor seeps and may not grow at all from one year to the next. Even when they do grow, it is generally from a half an inch to four inches per year. In spite of their slow growth, due to their long lives, they can reach nine feet before they die, although they are thinner than the hot-water worms.

The seeps under the slow-growing tube worms are rich with oily materials. The environment in which they live is slow and peaceful, stable and low-energy. The cold-water seeps and the tube worms that reside there may live hundreds or thousands of years.

In <u>stark</u> contrast, the fast-growing tube worms live a quick and short life, growing rapidly. They attach themselves near hot steaming vents that force water into the sea, growing about two and a half feet a year, and up to eight feet <u>overall</u>. They live by absorbing sulfur compounds metabolized by bacteria in a symbiotic relationship.

The hot water vents spew forth <u>scalding</u> water filled with hydrogen sulfide, which the tiny bacteria living in the worms' tissues consume. These tube worms live a rapid life, with none of the relaxing characteristics of the cold-water tube worms.

1. The word *anchored* in the first sentence is closest in meaning to

   A. affixed.

   B. contentedly.

   C. feeding.

   D. above.

2. The expression *spew forth* in the first sentence is closest in meaning to

   A. inhale.

   B. discharge.

   C. control.

   D. eliminate.

3. The author implies that a *vent* and a *seep* are

   A. the same.

   B. different in that a *vent* involves rapid discharge while a *seep* involves slow discharge.

   C. different in that a *vent* involves discharge while a *seep* involves intake.

   D. different in that a *vent* involves slow discharge while a *seep* involves rapid discharge.

4. The passage indicates that the two types of tube worms discussed are

   A. from totally different families.

   B. different in that one is not a true tube worm at all.

   C. from the same family but different species.

   D. from the same species and only differ because of habitat.

5. The author states that the cold-water tube worm

   A. grows slower than the hot-water tube worm.

   B. grows faster than the hot-water tube worm.

   C. does not grow as high as the hot-water tube worm.

   D. does not live as long as the hot-water tube worm.

6. The word *stark* in the fourth paragraph is closest in meaning to

   A. complete.

   B. somewhat.

   C. comparative.

   D. interesting.

7. The word *overall* in the fourth paragraph is closest in meaning to

   A. lifetime.

   B. annually.

   C. generally.

   D. rapidly.

8. The word *scalding* in the last paragraph is closest in meaning to

   A. hydrogen-filled.

   B. bacteria-filled.

   C. boiling.

   D. rapidly spewing.

9. The author indicates that the ingredients in the water that comes from the two types of vents are

   A. different only because the heat of the hot vents destroys the oil as it spews forth.

   B. different in that one contains bacteria and the other contains oily materials.

   C. the same.

   D. different in that one contains oily materials and the other contains hydrogen sulfide.

Section **3** Reading

GO ON TO THE NEXT PAGE

Passage 2

A new procedure has been developed to treat aneurysms, particularly those that occur near the brain stem, where surgery is dangerous.

Aneurysms are blood sacs formed by enlargement of the weakened wall of arteries or veins. They are dangerous and thus must generally be removed before they cause considerable damage. If one ruptures, it can cause strokes or fatal hemorrhaging, the latter of which occurs in 50 percent of all patients. Before rupturing, an aneurysm frequently shows no sign or symptom that it exists. Brain aneurysms occur in approximately 5 percent of the population. Most patients are between 40 and 65 years old, with hemorrhages most prevalent in those between 50 and 54.

The new procedure involves inserting a soft, flexible micro-catheter through the femoral artery in the groin area and snaking it up through blood vessels to the brain. Inside the catheter is a small, coiled wire, which can be extruded after it reaches its destination. After the coil is outside the catheter, a low voltage electrical current is applied, and the coil detaches at a preset solder point. Additional coils are snaked through the catheter and also detached at the site, creating a basket, or metal framework, which causes the blood to clot around it. The micro-catheter is withdrawn, the clot remains, and the healed aneurysm no longer is exposed to the stress that can cause another rupture.

The procedure lasts two hours, which is half as long as invasive surgery, and recovery time is generally limited to a few days instead of a few weeks. The procedure was discovered in the 1990s, was approved by the U.S. Food and Drug Administration in 1995, and is available in various hospitals where there are advanced neurology departments and specialists trained in the procedure. Many lives have been saved by use of the procedure, because the alternative would have been to watch and wait rather than risk the hazards of surgery.

10. The author implies that the procedure described is useful for

    A. all aneurysms.

    B. aneurysms that occur anywhere in the brain.

    C. aneurysms that occur near the brain stem only.

    D. aneurysms that occur near large blood vessels.

11. The word *They* in the first paragraph refers to

    A. aneurysms.

    B. brain stems.

    C. surgeries.

    D. procedures.

12. The word *considerable* in the first paragraph is closest in meaning to

    A. slight.

    B. kind.

    C. significant.

    D. recurring.

13. The word *one* in the first paragraph refers to

    A. brain stem.

    B. aneurysm.

    C. procedure.

    D. surgery.

14. The word *snaking* in the second paragraph is closest in meaning to

   A. meandering.

   B. extruding.

   C. living.

   D. damaging.

15. The word *withdrawn* in the second paragraph is closest in meaning to

   A. removed.

   B. too large.

   C. charged.

   D. inserted.

16. An aneurysm is most similar to

   A. an ulcer.

   B. a hernia.

   C. a heart attack.

   D. cancer.

17. The author indicates that half of the patients who have a brain aneurysm could also have

   A. a stroke.

   B. a seizure.

   C. a heart attack.

   D. hemorrhaging that results in death.

18. The author indicates that the point of creating a basket near the aneurysm is to

   A. catch the aneurysm when it breaks off.

   B. serve as a base for a blood clot to form.

   C. dissolve the aneurysm.

   D. provide a means of studying the aneurysm.

19. The author indicates that the femoral artery is

   A. small.

   B. in the upper thigh.

   C. in the brain.

   D. connected to the brain.

20. The author states that the electrical charge is applied in order to

   A. stimulate the brain.

   B. stimulate the aneurysm.

   C. dissolve the aneurysm.

   D. separate the coil from the wire.

21. The author implies that the wire breaks off

   A. randomly.

   B. by being cut with an additional tool.

   C. at a predetermined and prepared location on the wire.

   D. inside the micro-catheter.

22. According to the passage, traditional surgical techniques take

   A. longer and require more recuperation time than the new procedure.

   B. longer but require less recuperation time than the new procedure.

   C. less time and require less recuperation time than the new procedure.

   D. less time but require longer recuperation time than the new procedure.

GO ON TO THE NEXT PAGE

Section 3 Reading

23. The author implies that the new procedure

    A. can be performed at any hospital.

    B. is performed only at hospitals containing the required equipment and certified doctors.

    C. is performed by certified doctors but requires no special equipment.

    D. is performed by any surgeon using special equipment.

Passage 3

Scientists have discovered the bones of what may be the largest meat-eating dinosaur ever to walk the earth. The discovery was made by a team of researchers from Argentina and North America in Patagonia, a desert on the eastern slopes of the Andes in South America. Besides the interesting fact that the dinosaur was huge and horrifying, it is even more astounding that the bones of a number of the dinosaurs were found together. This discovery challenges the prior theory that the biggest meat-eaters lived as loners and instead indicates that they may have lived and hunted in packs. The Tyrannosaurus Rex lived in North America and was believed to hunt and live alone.

The newly discovered meat-eater appears to be related to the Giganotosaurus family, being as closely related to it as a fox would be to a dog. It is actually not of the same family at all as the Tyrannosaurus Rex, being as different from it as a cat is from a dog.

The fossilized remains indicate that the animals lived about 100 million years ago. With needle-shaped noses and razor sharp teeth, they were larger than the Tyrannosaurus Rex, although their legs were slightly shorter, and their jaws were designed to be better able to dissect their prey quickly and precisely.

24. The author states that the newly discovered dinosaur remains are evidence that it was the largest

    A. dinosaur ever.

    B. carnivorous dinosaur.

    C. herbivorous dinosaur.

    D. South American dinosaur.

25. The word *Besides* in the first paragraph is closest in meaning to

    A. in spite of.

    B. in addition to.

    C. although.

    D. mostly.

26. The word *horrifying* in the first paragraph is closest in meaning to

    A. frightening.

    B. large.

    C. fast.

    D. interesting.

27. The word *astounding* in the first paragraph is closest in meaning to

    A. terrifying.

    B. pleasing.

    C. displeasing.

    D. surprising.

28. The author implies that the most interesting fact about the find is that this dinosaur

    A. lived and hunted with others.

    B. had a powerful jaw and sharp teeth.

    C. was found in the Andes.

    D. was larger than Tyrannosaurus Rex.

29. The passage indicates that prior to this discovery scientists believed that

- **A.** meat-eating dinosaurs lived alone.
- **B.** there were no meat-eating dinosaurs in the Andes.
- **C.** Tyrannosaurus Rex lived in the Andes.
- **D.** meat-eating dinosaurs were small in stature.

30. The word *it* in the second paragraph refers to

- **A.** newly discovered meat-eater.
- **B.** relationship.
- **C.** Giganotosaurus.
- **D.** dog.

31. The author states that the newly discovered meat-eating dinosaur is

- **A.** closely related to Tyrannosaurus Rex.
- **B.** not closely related to Tyrannosaurus Rex.
- **C.** not closely related to Giganotosaurus.
- **D.** closely related to the large cat family.

32. The word *dissect* in the last sentence is closest in meaning to

- **A.** dismember.
- **B.** swallow.
- **C.** chew.
- **D.** escape.

33. The word *prey* in the last sentence of the passage is closest in meaning to

- **A.** victim.
- **B.** enemy.
- **C.** dinosaurs.
- **D.** attacker.

Passage 4

Scientists have developed a new bionic computer chip that can be <u>mated</u> with human cells to combat disease. The tiny device, smaller and thinner than a <u>strand</u> of hair, combines a healthy human cell with an electronic circuitry chip. Doctors can control the activity of the cell by controlling the chip with a computer.

It has long been established that cell membranes become permeable when exposed to electrical impulses. Researchers have conducted genetic research for years with a trial-and-error process of <u>bombarding</u> cells with electricity in an attempt to introduce foreign substances such as new drug treatments or genetic material. They were unable to apply a particular level of voltage for a particular purpose. With the new invention, the computer sends electrical impulses to the chip, which <u>triggers</u> the cell's membrane pores to open and activate the cell in order to correct diseased tissues. It permits physicians to open a cell's pores with control.

Researchers hope that <u>eventually</u> <u>they</u> will be able to develop more advanced chips whereby they can choose a particular voltage to activate <u>particular</u> tissues, whether they be muscle, bone, brain, or <u>others</u>. They believe that they will be able to implant multiple chips into a person to deal with one problem or more than one problem.

GO ON TO THE NEXT PAGE

Section **3** Reading

34. The word *mated* in the first sentence is closest in meaning to

   A. avoided.

   B. combined.

   C. introduced.

   D. developed.

35. The word *strand* in the second sentence is closest in meaning to

   A. type.

   B. thread.

   C. chip.

   D. color.

36. The author implies that scientists are excited about the new technology because

   A. it is less expensive than current techniques.

   B. it allows them to be able to shock cells for the first time.

   C. it is more precise than previous techniques.

   D. it is possible to kill cancer with a single jolt.

37. The author states that scientists previously were aware that

   A. they could control cells with a separate computer.

   B. electronic impulses could affect cells.

   C. electric charges could harm a person.

   D. cells interact with each other through electrical charges.

38. The word *bombarding* in the second paragraph is closest in meaning to

   A. barraging.

   B. influencing.

   C. receiving.

   D. testing.

39. The author implies that up to now, the point of applying electric impulse to cells was to

   A. kill them.

   B. open their walls to introduce medication.

   C. stop growth.

   D. combine cells.

40. The word *triggers* in the second paragraph is closest in meaning to

   A. damages.

   B. causes.

   C. shoots.

   D. assists.

41. The word *eventually* in the third paragraph is closest in meaning to

   A. finally.

   B. in the future.

   C. possibly.

   D. especially.

42. The word *they* in the first sentence of the third paragraph refers to

    A. researchers.

    B. chips.

    C. voltages.

    D. tissues.

43. The word *particular* in the third paragraph is closest in meaning to

    A. huge.

    B. slight.

    C. specific.

    D. controlled.

44. The word *others* in the third paragraph refers to other

    A. researchers.

    B. chips.

    C. voltages.

    D. tissues.

45. The author indicates that it is expected doctors will be able to

    A. place one large chip in a person to control multiple problems.

    B. place more than one chip in a single person.

    C. place a chip directly inside a cell.

    D. place a chip inside a strand of hair.

Writing Section

Time: 30 Minutes

1 Question

Directions: This section measures your ability to write in English, including your ability to organize ideas, create an essay in standard written English, and support the thoughts with sufficient examples and evidence. Write an essay in 30 minutes. You may make notes on a separate piece of paper, and then type or handwrite the essay.

Do you agree or disagree with the following statement: *Don't leave until tomorrow what you can do today*? Use specific reasons and examples to support your stance.

Listening Section

Time: 45 Minutes

37 Questions

To work through the Listening section of the practice test, you need to use the second audio CD that is included in this book. Starting with Track 6 of the CD, you will hear people having brief conversations. At the end of each conversation, you will hear a question that you must answer based on your understanding of what the speaker(s) said. Each question is printed below, along with answer choices. Mark your answer choices as you go along. The CD track numbers that you need to listen to are indicated throughout the section.

After you have completed this practice test and checked your answers, turn to the appendix of this book. The conversations that you heard on the CD are transcribed there. If you had any difficulty understanding what a speaker was saying, listen to the CD again, this time reading what is being said at the same time you listen to it. Do not turn to the appendix until you have worked through this practice test at least once by just listening to the CD.

Part A

Directions: In this part, you will hear short conversations between two people. After the conversation, a question will be asked. Choose the answer that most accurately answers the question based on what is stated or implied by the speakers. Mark the answer in your book or on a separate piece of paper.

CD B, Track 6

1. What do the speakers think of the two movies they are discussing?

   A. They did not care for either movie.

   B. They think they have seen both movies previously.

   C. They liked the Clooney movie so much that they would see it again.

   D. Both are probably action movies.

2. What does the woman say about Ellen's plans?

   A. Ellen is likely to seek a degree in English.

   B. Ellen has already been accepted into the linguistics program.

   C. Ellen has already received her doctorate.

   D. Ellen does not intend to go to graduate school of any sort.

3. What do the speakers say about Josh and Michael?

    A. Michael is taller now.

    B. Josh is taller now.

    C. Michael and Josh are currently equal in height.

    D. Michael has stopped growing, but Josh has not.

4. What does the man imply about his lack of study for the test?

    A. He is not participating in a study group this time.

    B. His study group has not kept up with its studies.

    C. He has been studying quite a bit, but he cannot grasp the concepts.

    D. He does not believe the professor uses fair questions.

5. What does the man seem to think about the lot they are discussing?

    A. It's the worst choice available.

    B. They should buy it immediately before somebody else does.

    C. It's probably the best choice available.

    D. All the lots are equal in usable space.

6. What does the woman say about her cottage?

    A. She has been working hard at renovating it.

    B. She is not able to go there much because of her work.

    C. She does not enjoy going there as much as she used to.

    D. She has been visiting it quite regularly but is getting tired of it.

7. What does the woman say about Michelle?

    A. She chose the University of Miami over the University of North Florida.

    B. She is changing schools because she wants to be farther from home.

    C. She will probably attend the University of North Florida.

    D. She had never actually applied at the University of Miami.

8. What do the speakers imply about the new employee?

    A. The new employee is lazy.

    B. The new employee is on a lunch break.

    C. The new employee is extremely helpful.

    D. The new employee is able to do her work efficiently while reading.

GO ON TO THE NEXT PAGE

9. What are the speakers thinking of doing?

   A. Taking a replacement test

   B. Writing a paper

   C. Changing classes

   D. Taking an essay test instead of a multiple choice test

10. What do the speakers say that the man did?

   A. Dropped out of school

   B. Quit one class for another

   C. Decided to take a more advanced math class

   D. Decided to take the honors level of geometry

11. What does the woman say about the races?

   A. She has not attended lately.

   B. She has never been to the races.

   C. She regularly attends the races.

   D. She is hoping to go to the races soon.

12. What had the man assumed?

   A. That Nadia was going to work instead of Allison

   B. That Allison was going to work for Nadia

   C. That Allison was going to work instead of trying to get the day off

   D. That Allison found a job for Nadia

13. According to the woman, why hasn't the man seen Christopher?

   A. Christopher was late because he stopped somewhere on the way.

   B. Christopher has been attending, but the man has missed him.

   C. Christopher has quit attending.

   D. Christopher did not attend because of the rain.

14. What does the woman imply about the man?

   A. He needs help but will not admit it.

   B. He can easily handle the project himself.

   C. He is very handy.

   D. He should help the woman.

15. What does the woman suggest that the man do?

   A. Give up

   B. Keep trying

   C. Look at the book

   D. Call the help desk

Part B

Directions: In this part, you will hear several conversations and talks. You will hear each conversation or talk only once, and then you will hear several questions. Answer the questions based on what is stated or implied by the speakers. Choose the best of the answer choices provided. Mark the answer in your book or on a separate piece of paper.

CD B, Track 7

16. What does the woman say about the health of coral reefs since 1998?

  A. It has declined since 1998.

  B. It has improved somewhat since 1998.

  C. It was improving but now is declining again.

  D. It has improved so much that work has been discontinued.

17. According to the woman, which of the following is not a reason why coral reefs are important?

  A. Healthy coral reefs cause the ocean water to be healthy.

  B. Coral reefs provide protection for the shore.

  C. Coral reefs are home to fish and other sea animals.

  D. Coral reefs have some benefits for human health.

18. What does the speaker describe as a major cause of coral reef death?

  A. Contaminants, such as bleach, in the water

  B. The death of sea life

  C. Higher temperatures

  D. Overabundance of algae

19. What does the speaker describe as the relationship between coral and algae?

  A. Algae cannibalize coral.

  B. Algae are required for coral's health.

  C. Algae cause bleaching.

  D. Algae and coral rarely coexist.

20. What has been done to improve the health of coral reefs?

  A. The government has tried a complicated procedure for cooling ocean water.

  B. The government has spent money for research, education, and monitoring reefs.

  C. Nothing.

  D. The coral reefs' health has improved with no assistance.

GO ON TO THE NEXT PAGE

CD B, Track 8

21. Where is the man living currently?

    A. In an apartment complex

    B. In a hotel

    C. At a friend's house

    D. He just arrived today and does not have a place to sleep yet.

22. Who does the woman imply is eligible for help by her office?

    A. Any student of the university

    B. Only students of the intensive English program

    C. Anybody at all

    D. Only people with scholarships

23. How does the woman seem to know the man is in the intensive English program?

    A. She looked at his identification card.

    B. She looked on a roster.

    C. It was not relevant.

    D. She took his word for it.

24. What size apartment does the man say he needs?

    A. The size does not matter to him.

    B. He needs a place with two bedrooms.

    C. He just wants to share a place with other students.

    D. He needs a very large apartment.

25. What does the man seem to think is the most important difference between the two apartments the woman discusses?

    A. Proximity to the university

    B. Benefits that his wife and child would enjoy

    C. Cost

    D. Size

26. What does the woman imply is the biggest drawback of the less expensive apartment?

    A. Lack of air conditioning

    B. Distance from the university

    C. Cost

    D. Lack of laundry facilities close by

CD B, Track 9

27. Why does the speaker indicate that the digestive system is the best place for the new technology?

    A. Because using the endoscope in that system is more painful than in other systems

    B. Because there is a natural flow, facilitated by the body itself

    C. Because the digestive juices will not dissolve the capsule

    D. Because there is more incidence of illness in the digestive system than in other areas

28. For which of the following items would the capsule not be helpful?

    A. Locating a tumor in the bowel

    B. Locating pre-cancer cells in the esophagus

    C. Obtaining tissue for a biopsy

    D. Viewing abnormalities in the stomach lining

29. What is the main reason that some scientists believe the capsule would be helpful?

    A. The endoscope is uncomfortable.

    B. The endoscope does not have as many unique benefits as the capsule will.

    C. The endoscope is more expensive to operate.

    D. The endoscope is outdated.

30. Which of the following does the speaker imply would not be part of the capsule?

    A. A camera

    B. Lights

    C. A transmitter

    D. A scalpel

31. Which of the following does the speaker imply is true?

    A. The capsule is an advance in science along the same lines as digital and wireless technology.

    B. The capsule will be easy to control as it moves through the body.

    C. Scientists generally believe that this technology will replace endoscopes in a few years.

    D. The capsule will dissolve before it reaches the end.

GO ON TO THE NEXT PAGE

CD B, Track 10

32. What appears to be the woman's level of knowledge of Canavan Disease?

A. She is quite familiar with it.

B. She has studied it in the past.

C. She has no prior knowledge of it.

D. She knows that she is a carrier.

33. According to the man, which of the following is possibly a carrier of the illness?

A. Somebody of Ashkenazi Jewish descent

B. Somebody whose parents are both of Ashkenazi Jewish descent

C. Somebody with any Jewish background

D. A person whose mother was Jewish

34. How does the man indicate that the disease affects the body?

A. The disease causes the brain to grow rapidly.

B. The disease causes a protective material to disappear.

C. The disease results from too much of an enzyme.

D. The disease results from one problematic gene.

35. Why does the man want to know the woman's cultural background?

A. If her background is not the same as her husband's, then there is no chance they could pass on the disease.

B. Women from other Jewish backgrounds can carry the disease.

C. The woman would have to undergo a different type of test.

D. The woman is the primary carrier.

36. What is the woman's demeanor at the end of the discussion?

A. Angry

B. Disgusted

C. Resigned

D. Mistrustful

37. What does the gene on Chromosome 17 do?

A. Synthesizes the enzyme

B. Destroys the enzyme

C. Destroys white matter

D. Creates white matter

Structure Section

Time: 20 Minutes

25 Questions

Directions: This section measures your ability to recognize language appropriate for standard written English. One type of question consists of incomplete sentences, with a blank showing where information is to be filled in. Choose the word or phrase that most correctly completes the sentence. A second type of question consists of sentences with four underlined words or phrases. For each sentence, choose the one underlined word or phrase that is incorrect in standard written English. Mark the answer in your book or on a separate piece of paper.

1. After the data <u>has received</u> and
             A

   reviewed, the finance department

   <u>employees</u> should <u>be</u> able <u>to determine</u>
     B   **C**   **D**

   the best course of action.

2. The Board of Directors determined, after having tried to enter several related business arenas, _____ concentrate on its core business.

   A. that the company should

   B. should

   C. that

   D. company should

3. <u>Owning</u> a home, the dream of many, <u>an</u>
     A   **B**

   unattainable goal for many young

   people (particularly unmarried mothers)

   without <u>aid</u> from governmental and
         C

   non-profit <u>sources</u>.
           D

4. That fast foods frequently contain a considerable amount of fat _____ well-known, but many people still find it difficult to avoid them due to their work schedules.

A. is

B. quite

C. be

D. being

5. After the jury <u>had</u> determined liability,
               A

   its <u>next</u> task was <u>to decide</u> how much
     B   **C**

   money <u>should it</u> assess as damages.
          D

6. This application must be rejected because it should _____ submitted prior to the commencement of classes for the term.

   A. of been

   B. have been

   C. being

   D. have be

7. If the Board had not reversed <u>its</u>
                           A

   position on the petition <u>to approve</u>
                      B

   the fence, the owner <u>would had</u> to
                  C

   <u>remove</u> it.
    D

GO ON TO THE NEXT PAGE

Section 2 Structure

8. A prolific writer, even when he was
   A   **B**
   teaching a number of classes, Harry
                              C
   Crews never achieving popularity
                     D
   among the masses.

9. Whereas many people visit Internet
   sites where products are sold, a great
   number of them still _____ to
   actually make purchases online.

   A. are hesitant

   B. hesitating

   C. hesitation

   D. being hesitant

10. Attorneys who practice in the area of

    personal injury generally spending
                                 A
    considerably more money on
    B
    advertising in telephone books and on

    television than other types of attorneys.
                      C   **D**

11. Earlier in the year, the researchers
    found _____, which they
    determined is over 6 million years old.

    A. a fossil extremely large

    B. extremely large fossil

    C. a large extremely fossil

    D. an extremely large fossil

12. St. Augustine, Florida, known as oldest
                               A   **B**
    city in the United States, is home to the

    oldest schoolhouse, a fort called
                                   C
    Castillo de San Marcos, and other areas
                                     D
    of historical interest.

13. In spite _____ seen as a
    comfortable and open speaker, Larry
    dislikes public speaking and will do
    almost anything to avoid it.

    A. have been

    B. of being

    C. being

    D. having been

14. The committee voted purchase the land
                        A
    next to the company's existing building,
    B   **C**
    but the resolution was not approved at
                                   D
    the full Board meeting.

15. How long _____ left in the cold
    wilderness is anybody's guess, although
    it appears that they will all be brought
    back to health.

    A. has been the children

    B. have the children

    C. the children have been

    D. the children been

16. Students may buy used books if they
                       A
    had been readily available and correctly
    B   **C**
    priced.
    D

17. Having been stopped by the police for
    running a red light, _____ it was
    not in her best interest to argue since
    she was not wearing her seat belt.

    A. Jane's decision

    B. Jane decided

    C. decided

    D. decision

18. Without a <u>doubt</u>, the best way to do
    A
    well in college <u>to</u> keep up <u>constantly</u>
    B   C
    with the homework, read everything
    that is required, and <u>regularly</u> outline all
    D
    the class notes.

19. The children were warned not
    _____ in the retention pond
    because the water was polluted and a
    large alligator called it home.

    A. swim

    B. swimming

    C. to swim

    D. should swim

20. In the <u>early</u> morning, the hikers broke
    A
    camp and <u>began</u> the long trek <u>towards</u>
    B   C
    home, hoping to <u>before noon arrive</u>.
    D

21. That Ana could handle the job well
    _____ to her friends and
    colleagues, who could not understand
    how the university was still considering
    the other candidate.

    A. obviously

    B. was obvious

    C. obvious

    D. has obviously

22. Though the danger had <u>passed</u>, officials
    A
    were <u>hesitant</u> to allow residents <u>to return</u>
    B   C
    to their homes because they were unsure
    how much damage <u>caused</u> by the high
    D
    winds.

23. The company had a two-tier
    contingency plan in case power was
    lost, first using gas-operated generators,
    and then _____ its distant safe
    operation, where the entire computer
    operation, including all hardware,
    software, and data, was able to be run
    without interruption.

    A. initiation

    B. initiate

    C. initiating

    D. to initiate

24. After having success with individual
    singers and several bands consisting of
    teenage boys, _____ both sing
    and dance, he decided to experiment
    with bands consisting of teenage girls as
    well as a co-ed band.

    A. who could

    B. could

    C. that could

    D. which

25. Bob is certain to be hired for the <u>position</u>
    A
    <u>because</u> at his interview he <u>displayed</u> his
    B   C
    talents in writing, speaking, organizing,
    delegating and <u>to lead</u>.
    D

STOP

293

Section 2 Structure

Reading Section

Time: 75 Minutes

45 Questions

Directions: This section measures your ability to read and understand written English similar to that which one may expect in a college or university setting. Read each passage and answer the questions based on what is stated or implied in the passage. Circle or mark the correct answer in the book or write it on a separate piece of paper.

Passage 1

For a time, the Hubble telescope was the brunt of jokes and subject to the wrath of those who believed the U.S. government had spent too much money on space projects that served no valid purpose. The Hubble was sent into orbit with a satellite by the Space Shuttle Discovery in 1990 amid huge hype and expectation. Yet after it was in position, it simply did not work, because the primary mirror was misshapen. It was not until 1993 that the crew of the Shuttle Endeavor arrived like roadside mechanics, opened the hatch that was installed for the purpose, and replaced the defective mirror with a good one.

Suddenly, all that had originally been expected came true. The Hubble telescope was indeed the "window on the universe," as it had originally been dubbed. When you look deep into space, you are actually looking back through time, because even though light travels at 186,000 miles a second, it requires time to get from one place to another. In fact, it is said that in some cases, the Hubble telescope is looking back eleven billion years to see galaxies already forming. The distant galaxies are speeding away from Earth, some traveling at the speed of light.

Hubble has viewed exploding stars such as the Eta Carinae, which clearly displayed clouds of gas and dust billowing outward from its poles at 1.5 million miles an hour. Prior to Hubble, it was visible from traditional telescopes on earth, but its details were not ascertainable. But now, the evidence of the explosion is obvious. The star still burns five million times brighter than the sun and illuminates clouds from the inside.

Hubble has also provided a close look at black holes, which are described as cosmic drains. Gas and dust swirl around the drain and are slowly sucked in by the incredible gravity. It has also looked into an area that looked empty to the naked eye and, within a region the size of a grain of sand, located layer upon layer of galaxies, with each galaxy consisting of billions of stars.

The Hubble telescope was named after Edwin Hubble, a 1920s astronomer who developed a formula that expresses the proportional relationship of distances between clusters of galaxies and the speeds at which they travel. Astronomers use stars known as Cepheid variables to measure distances in space. These stars dim and brighten from time to time, and they are photographed over time and charted. All the discoveries made by Hubble have allowed astronomers to learn more about the formation of early galaxies.

1. The author states that the Hubble was not always popular because

   A. people were afraid of what might be found.

   B. many people believed space exploration was a waste of time.

   C. it was defective for its first three years in space.

   D. it was more expensive than most space shuttles.

2. The word *brunt* in the first sentence is closest in meaning to

   A. subject.

   B. expense.

   C. contentment.

   D. unhappiness.

3. The word *wrath* in the first sentence is closest in meaning to

   A. interest.

   B. contentment.

   C. fury.

   D. pleasure.

4. The author implies that at the time the Hubble was initially deployed from Earth

   A. there was little attention paid to it.

   B. all attention was focused on the space shuttle, not the Hubble.

   C. there was considerable excitement about the potential uses.

   D. it was already known that the mirror was defective.

5. The word *misshapen* in the first paragraph is closest in meaning to

   A. unusual.

   B. useful.

   C. expected.

   D. distorted.

6. The word *it* in the second sentence of the second paragraph refers to

   A. one.

   B. space.

   C. light.

   D. second.

7. The author implies that the satellite that carries the Hubble was specifically designed so that

   A. the known defective mirror could be replaced in space rather than on Earth.

   B. maintenance could be done by traveling astronauts.

   C. the Hubble could move easily.

   D. the mirror could contract and expand.

8. The author compares the astronauts of the Endeavor to

   A. astronomers.

   B. scientists.

   C. mechanics.

   D. politicians.

Section **3** Reading

GO ON TO THE NEXT PAGE

9. The author states that Edward Hubble

   A. developed the Hubble telescope.

   B. was the first person to use the Hubble telescope.

   C. developed a mathematical formula to measure speed and distances between galaxies.

   D. was a politician who sponsored funding in Congress.

10. The word *dubbed* in the second paragraph is closest in meaning to

    A. detracted.

    B. named.

    C. anticipated.

    D. purchased.

11. The author states that

    A. when viewing a distant galaxy through the Hubbell telescope, you are actually looking back in time.

    B. the new mirror distorts the image.

    C. the view from Hubble is not accurate, but it is interesting.

    D. you cannot discern distance or time with any kind of accuracy.

12. According to the passage, a Cepheid variable is

    A. a star.

    B. a Hubble calculation.

    C. the dimming and brightening of a star.

    D. a mirror.

13. The author indicates that the Eta Carinae was previously viewed from other telescopes, but

    A. its details could not be seen.

    B. its speed and distance were not known.

    C. its location was not known.

    D. it had not been named.

14. The word *billowing* in the third paragraph is closest in meaning to

    A. sitting.

    B. pouring.

    C. exploding.

    D. stopping.

15. The author implies that a black hole is analogous to

    A. water draining in a bathtub.

    B. a galaxy.

    C. a group of stars.

    D. a cloud.

Passage 2

The pain of a migraine headache can virtually disable a person who suffers from <u>it</u>. Millions and millions of people suffer from migraines, although many of them do not even recognize that a migraine is different from a regular headache. A migraine is not at all the same as a normal headache, and it seems to have a very physical cause.

One symptom of a migraine is a precursor, which is a visual aura before an attack. Yet only about a third of patients actually experience that, and it is therefore not a requirement in the diagnosis. Other symptoms include increased pain when a person moves, nausea, and sensitivity to light and sound.

Scientists now believe that migraines are caused, not by abnormal blood vessels as previously believed, but instead by a unique electrical disorder of brain cells. Physicians used to treat migraines with medicine to constrict blood vessels because of the belief that dilated blood vessels were the cause.

The new research has been <u>enhanced</u> by imaging devices that allow scientists to watch patients' brains during an attack. The results show that sufferers have abnormally excitable neurons, or brain nerve cells. Prior to the attack, the neurons suddenly fire off electrical pulses at the back of the brain, which ripple like waves on a lake after a stone hits the water. They ripple across the top and then the back of the brain, ultimately affecting the brain stem where the pain centers are located. The pain then generates possibly from the brain stem itself or from blood vessels inflamed by the rapidly changing blood flow, or perhaps from both.

Scientists have experimented by applying a powerful magnet to stimulate the neurons and discovered that some people's brains react differently than others'. When stimulation was applied to the brains of people who had suffered migraines, they saw the initial aura, and some actually suffered migraines. When the same stimulation was applied to the brains of people who had never suffered migraines, they realized no effect and the neurons showed no change.

Scientists and doctors continue to work on the research in an attempt to find the perfect treatment. It is considered important to treat migraines because it is believed that prolonged untreated attacks could cause physical changes in the brain leading to chronic pain.

16. The word *it* in the first sentence refers to

    A. pain.

    B. migraine.

    C. person.

    D. suffering.

17. The author implies that a migraine

    A. is just a strong headache.

    B. can be treated with regular aspirin.

    C. is caused by the same things that cause a headache.

    D. has a specific scientific cause, unlike a headache.

18. The author indicates that the precursor to a migraine

    A. is a fiction.

    B. happens to all migraine sufferers.

    C. occurs during or after the attack.

    D. is something some sufferers see before an attack.

Section **3** Reading

GO ON TO THE NEXT PAGE

19. The author implies that in the past scientists had thought migraines were caused by

    A. neuron firings.

    B. stress.

    C. constricted blood vessels.

    D. expanded blood vessels.

20. The prior treatment for migraines included medicine that

    A. eliminated any pain.

    B. tightened blood vessels.

    C. eliminated the aura.

    D. eliminated stress.

21. The word *enhanced* in the fourth paragraph is closest in meaning to

    A. hindered.

    B. augmented.

    C. described.

    D. studied.

22. The new research indicates that the neurons in the brain of migraine sufferers

    A. have more electrical charge than those of people who do not suffer migraines.

    B. tend to fire in an unusual pattern when a migraine begins.

    C. do not react.

    D. have no effect on migraines.

23. Scientists have recently learned more about the cause of migraines from

    A. using imaging devices that allow one to watch the neurons.

    B. taking blood tests.

    C. giving patients aspirin and watching for results.

    D. asking patients to describe the symptoms.

24. The author indicates that researchers have determined that

    A. neurons fire suddenly and follow a specific pattern when a migraine is coming.

    B. magnetic fields in the environment cause migraines.

    C. everybody is susceptible to migraines.

    D. they know what stimuli cause the neurons to react.

25. The author describes the firing of the neurons during a migraine as

    A. random.

    B. moving in a specific order along the brain towards the brain stem like ripples of water.

    C. unrelated to the migraine itself.

    D. starting at the brain stem and radiating towards the top of the head.

26. According to the passage, what is the significance of an attack reaching the brain stem?

    A. It is insignificant.

    B. The brain stem is the location of pain centers.

    C. The stem is at the bottom of the brain.

    D. An attack on the brain stem causes migraines.

27. According to the passage, now that scientists know that unusual neurons in certain people are the cause of migraines, they

    A. know all they need to know about the cause of migraines.

    B. have developed medicine to permanently reverse the neurons' charge.

    C. still do not know exactly what causes the pain.

    D. know that the defective neurons reside in the brain stem.

28. Scientists have caused neurons to react by applying

    A. drugs.

    B. a magnetic field.

    C. electric charges.

    D. imaging.

29. The best title for this passage would be what?

    A. Imaging As a Means of Studying Migraines

    B. How Migraines and Headaches are Different

    C. New Evidence of How Migraines Are Formed

    D. New Treatments for Migraines

30. Researchers believe that long-term migraine sufferers

    A. are susceptible to illness.

    B. can suffer physical changes in the brain and be in chronic pain.

    C. are not following instructions about their environment.

    D. can take a migraine medicine and avoid problems in the future.

GO ON TO THE NEXT PAGE

Passage 3

Lightning has been a mystery since early times. People of ancient civilizations believed angry gods threw lightning bolts from the sky. Nobody understood that lightning resulted from electricity until Ben Franklin flew a kite with a key <u>dangling</u> from the string, and it was struck by lightning.

In current times, it is known that lightning has a very scientific cause. Generally, within a storm cloud, friction from water and ice-laden clouds creates a negative charge at the bottom of the cloud. When that charge grows too great for the air to hold it back, it is united with a positive charge from the Earth, creating a channel of electricity that flows between the two points. The charge remains invisible as it moves towards the ground until it meets the charge rising from the ground. Once they meet, a fifty thousand degree current superheats the air around the channel, resulting in an explosion of sound known as thunder. In fact, very recently it has been discovered that occasionally the positive charges appear at the bottom of the cloud, which are then met by negative charges from earth.

Florida leads the nation in lightning deaths. Approximately ten people die each year in Florida from lightning, which surpasses the number of deaths caused by the winds of other weather events such as tornados and hurricanes. Lightning is much harder to forecast than a storm. Forecasters can indicate when a storm is likely to produce lightning, but there is no way to know when or where lightning will actually strike. It is known that it can actually strike up to 25 miles from the center of a storm, which occurs when lightning originates under a cloud but travels horizontally for a time before turning towards earth. Thunder is only heard up to ten miles from where lightning strikes, so it is possible to be struck by lightning without even realizing there is a storm in the area.

Generally, people are injured by lightning when they are in the open, near or in water, or near tall structures like trees. Golfers, swimmers, beach-goers, and outdoor workers are in greatest danger. The greatest number of victims are males, but it is believed that this is because males are more likely to be in the places where lightning strikes. When lightning is about to strike, one feels an odd, tingling sensation, and one's hair stands on end. Of course, there is little chance to do anything about it, because the full blow will occur within a second and be over in a couple of seconds. The victim may be thrown, lose consciousness, be burned, die, or suffer permanent injury. Some people recover completely, but others do not.

31. According to the passage, the first recorded evidence that lightning came from electricity was discovered by

    A. people of ancient civilizations.

    B. Ben Franklin.

    C. researchers from the 1400s.

    D. modern researchers.

32. The word *dangling* in the first paragraph is closest in meaning to

    A. connected.

    B. hanging.

    C. tied.

    D. sewed into.

33. According to the passage, the relationship between the charge in the cloud and that from earth is that

   A. they meet each other in the sky.

   B. they are the same polarity.

   C. the charge from earth travels to the cloud.

   D. the charge from the cloud reaches the ground before they meet.

34. According to the passage, the primary cause of the charge in the storm cloud is

   A. ice build-up.

   B. friction.

   C. unknown.

   D. water.

35. The author implies that as the lightning comes towards earth, but before it strikes,

   A. it can be seen in the sky.

   B. it can turn back.

   C. its approach can be felt by someone about to be struck.

   D. thunder is heard several miles away.

36. The author indicates that thunder is created when

   A. the charge from the earth meets the charge from the cloud.

   B. lightning strikes the ground.

   C. friction occurs in the cloud.

   D. lightning leaves the cloud.

37. The author indicates that lightning can strike far from the center of a storm when

   A. it travels horizontally first.

   B. the storm cloud is large.

   C. lightning has already emanated from the same cloud.

   D. it emanates from a positive charge in the cloud.

Section 3 Reading

GO ON TO THE NEXT PAGE

Passage 4

The strangler fig tree, home to many birds and animals that enjoy the figs as nutrition, is found in the rain forests of Indonesia as well as in a 220,000-acre park known as Gunung Palung National Park on the island of Borneo.

The trees are referred to as *stranglers* because of the way they envelope other trees. Yet, the expression *strangler* is not quite accurate because the fig trees do not actually squeeze the trees on which they piggyback nor do they actually take any nutrients from the host tree. But they may <u>stifle</u> the host tree's growth as the fig tree's roots meet and <u>fuse</u> together, forming rigid rings around the host's trunk and restricting further growth of the supporting tree.

The most interesting aspect of the strangler fig is that it grows from the sky down to the ground. Birds are a major factor in the birth of new fig trees, ingesting the fruit and later dropping the seeds contained in them. Most seeds that are dropped to the ground do nothing, but those that drop into a moist <u>mulch</u> of decayed leaves and mosses that have collected in branches of trees have a chance of survival. They are more likely to receive some sunlight than those that drop all the way to the ground.

After the seeds of the fig trees germinate high in the canopy, their roots descend to form a <u>menacing</u> vise around the trees that support them. Eventually the host tree may begin to die, but it may take many years. Some types of fig trees put down roots so thick that they completely surround the host. In that case, all that is left is a moss-covered <u>scaffold</u> of fig roots.

38. According to the passage, fig trees are referred to as *stranglers* because they

   A. are unknown.

   B. are unusual.

   C. wrap themselves around other trees.

   D. kill wildlife.

39. The author implies that the term *strangler* is not accurate because

   A. while the fig trees may damage the host tree, they do not actually squeeze it.

   B. the host tree actually strangles the fig.

   C. the fig tree does not harm animals.

   D. the fig tree provides nutrition to the host tree.

40. The word *stifle* in the second paragraph is closest in meaning to

   A. assist.

   B. nourish.

   C. suffocate.

   D. live on.

41. The author indicates that the fig trees

   A. grow from seeds dropped to the ground.

   B. grow from the top of a tree down to the ground.

   C. grow from the ground up.

   D. receive nutrients from the host tree.

42. The word *fuse* in the second paragraph is closest in meaning to

    A. combine.

    B. avoid.

    C. cannibalize.

    D. enjoy.

43. The word *mulch* in the third paragraph is closest in meaning to

    A. rock.

    B. compost.

    C. seeds.

    D. moss.

44. The word *menacing* in the final paragraph is closest in meaning to

    A. friendly.

    B. strong.

    C. spiraling.

    D. ominous.

45. The word *scaffold* in the last sentence is closest in meaning to

    A. decay.

    B. framework.

    C. graveyard.

    D. host.

Writing Section

Time: 30 Minutes

1 Question

Directions: This section measures your ability to write in English, including your ability to organize ideas, create an essay in standard written English, and support the thoughts with sufficient examples and evidence. Write an essay in 30 minutes. You may make notes on a separate piece of paper, and then type or handwrite the essay.

What are the skills that a person should have to be a good teacher? Use specific details and examples to support your position.

Listening Section

Time: 48 Minutes

38 Questions

To work through the Listening section of the practice test, you need to use the second audio CD that is included in this book. Starting with Track 11 of the CD, you will hear people having brief conversations. At the end of each conversation, you will hear a question that you must answer based on your understanding of what the speaker(s) said. Each question is printed below, along with answer choices. Mark your answer choices as you go along. The CD track numbers that you need to listen to are indicated throughout the section.

After you have completed this practice test and checked your answers, turn to the appendix of this book. The conversations that you heard on the CD are transcribed there. If you had any difficulty understanding what a speaker was saying, listen to the CD again, this time reading what is being said at the same time you listen to it. Do not turn to the appendix until you have worked through this practice test at least once by just listening to the CD.

Part A

Directions: In this part, you will hear short conversations between two people. After the conversation, a question will be asked. Choose the answer that most accurately answers the question based on what is stated or implied by the speakers. Mark the answer in your book or on a separate piece of paper.

CD B, Track 11

1. Why does the woman say Donna is not present?

   A. She left to make a call.
   B. She had to leave.
   C. She is having a baby.
   D. She will be back quite soon.

2. What does the man mean?

   A. He definitely will go.
   B. He will go in May.
   C. He might go.
   D. He definitely will not go.

3. What does the man mean?

   A.   He is asking whether Jim submitted his application on time.

   B.   He means that Jim submitted his application late.

   C.   He means that Jim was awarded financial aid.

   D.   He means that he submitted his application too early.

4. What does the woman mean?

   A.   She paid the same amount for books this semester as last semester.

   B.   She bought fewer books this semester than last semester.

   C.   She paid more for books this semester than last semester.

   D.   She paid less for books this semester than last semester.

5. What does the man mean?

   A.   They will not be able to complete the project.

   B.   The project is complete.

   C.   They have just begun work on the project.

   D.   If they organize, they will be able to complete the project.

6. What will the woman probably do next?

   A.   Ask the counselor whether her license will be sufficient.

   B.   Leave and not come back.

   C.   Go home and get her student identification.

   D.   Obtain a new identification.

7. What will the woman probably do?

   A.   Talk louder.

   B.   Leave the room.

   C.   Continue talking at the same volume.

   D.   Stop talking.

8. What does the man imply about Susan?

   A.   She is lazy.

   B.   She is very determined.

   C.   She is not actually considering another job.

   D.   She is not very smart.

9. What does the man mean?

   A.   He was not able to purchase the slides.

   B.   He bought new slides.

   C.   He thinks the slides are fine.

   D.   He thought somebody else bought the slides.

10. What does the woman imply about her promotion?

   A.   She is going to be promoted.

   B.   She does not know whether she got the promotion.

   C.   She does not want to be promoted.

   D.   She is not happy about the new job.

11. What do the speakers imply about Professor Roberts?

   A.   He likes perfection.

   B.   He is sloppy.

   C.   He does not care about grammar.

   D.   He can't spell.

12. What does the woman imply about Professor Hall?

   A. He is not flexible.

   B. Schedules are not important to him.

   C. He studies too much.

   D. He cancelled the exam.

13. What does the woman mean?

   A. She thinks the extra rent is reasonable.

   B. She can't afford an increase in rent.

   C. She believes the landlord doesn't keep the property in good repair.

   D. The apartment is worth much more.

14. What does the man imply about Janet?

   A. She is ill.

   B. She will work tomorrow.

   C. She has quit her job.

   D. She cancelled the doctor's appointment.

15. What does the man plan to do?

   A. Take a cruise without his friends.

   B. Forget about the cruise.

   C. Go with other friends on the cruise.

   D. Take a flight instead.

Part B

Directions: In this part, you will hear several conversations and talks. You will hear each conversation or talk only once, and then you will hear several questions. Answer the questions based on what is stated or implied by the speakers. Choose the best of the answer choices provided. Mark the answer in your book or on a separate piece of paper.

CD B, Track 12

16. What does the man say about his family status?

   A. He's single and has three children from his former marriage.

   B. He's married and has three children.

   C. He's married with no children.

   D. He's married and has one child.

17. What does the man say about his assets?

   A. The amount is over $700,000 and owned jointly with his wife or with his wife as beneficiary.

   B. The amount is less than $700,000 and owned jointly with his wife or with his wife as beneficiary.

   C. The amount is less than $700,000, and he owns some assets in his own name without beneficiaries named.

   D. The amount is over $700,000, and he owns some assets in his own name without beneficiaries named.

18. How would you describe the woman's manner of presentation?

    A. Pushy

    B. Open and informing

    C. Gruff

    D. Obstinate

19. What kind of estate planning document does the woman say the man needs?

    A. A joint trust

    B. A tax planning trust

    C. Nothing

    D. A will

20. Which of the following is not a correct description of the difference between a will and a trust?

    A. A trust must have assets transferred while a will does not.

    B. A will is less expensive to create than a trust.

    C. A trust must go through probate while a will does not.

    D. A will costs more after death than a trust.

21. Why does the woman say that the couple will not have to go through probate now if only one of them dies?

    A. Because they do not have a will

    B. Because they have a will

    C. Because they already have a trust

    D. Because they own their assets in a way that allows them to pass to the survivor

22. How does the woman define probate?

    A. Administration of a trust

    B. Administration of a will

    C. Placing assets into a trust

    D. How an estate is handled only if one dies without a will

23. According to the woman, what is the major drawback of probate?

    A. The cost.

    B. Nobody is appointed to carry it out.

    C. It is not suitable for a married couple.

    D. It only happens if there is no will.

24. Does the woman imply that she would suggest the same type of estate planning if the couple were younger?

    A. No, she would be less likely to suggest a trust.

    B. Yes, because it depends on assets, not age.

    C. No, she would suggest a tax-planning trust if they were younger.

    D. No, she would suggest that a younger couple do nothing at all.

GO ON TO THE NEXT PAGE

CD B, Track 13

25. What fact does the speaker state as common knowledge?

   A. Alcoholism is not a disease.

   B. Alcoholism seems to run in families.

   C. Alcoholism is believed to have no chemical basis.

   D. Alcoholism results merely from a lack of willpower.

26. What example does the woman give to indicate that alcoholism is not just sociological?

   A. It runs in families.

   B. It is known to occur in children of alcoholics even when they do not live together.

   C. People are sometimes depressed when they drink.

   D. Not everybody reacts the same to beta-endorphin.

27. What is beta-endorphin, according to the speaker?

   A. An enzyme

   B. A hormone

   C. Morphine

   D. A reaction

28. Which of the following does the speaker imply would not be a true statement about beta-endorphins?

   A. Only some people have the hormone in their bodies.

   B. It naturally causes a reaction when the body encounters severe pain.

   C. It contributes to the feeling one has when one drinks alcohol.

   D. Some people react differently to alcohol because of the way beta-endorphin is released in their bodies.

29. What does the speaker indicate is the difference between a person with alcoholic tendencies and a person without them?

   A. The alcoholic responds more strongly to beta-endorphin release.

   B. An alcoholic can will beta-endorphin to be released without needing to drink.

   C. An alcoholic has no beta-endorphin and must replace it with alcohol.

   D. An alcoholic does not have a reaction to beta-endorphin when drinking.

30. What does the speaker say about family members inheriting the alcoholic trait?

   A. Both parents must carry the trait for it to be inherited.

   B. There is a specific mathematical calculation to determine who will inherit the disease.

   C. Even though it can be inherited, it is not expected to be subject to testing.

   D. It can be inherited but is not inherited by all family members.

31. Does the speaker indicate that everybody with the reaction to beta-endorphin will become alcoholic?

   A. Yes, it is inevitable if one has the trait.

   B. No, only some people with the trait react strongly to alcohol.

   C. No, because they may choose not to drink to excess.

   D. No, if they take the proper medicine.

CD B, Track 14

32. Why is the woman asking the man for help?

   A. She did not understand what the professor discussed in class.

   B. She just wants to talk to the man.

   C. She did not understand what she read before class.

   D. She missed class.

33. What do the speakers say is the difference between a tort and a crime?

   A. There is no difference. A tort is a crime.

   B. A tort is a civil wrong punishable with money damages, and a crime is a criminal act punishable with criminal penalties.

   C. A tort is intentional.

   D. A tort always consists of negligence.

34. According to the man, how long will the class be studying torts?

   A. Only during the class the woman missed

   B. Two days

   C. Two weeks

   D. Two months

35. What does the man imply would happen if the driver drove carefully and the child darted out in front of him?

   A. The driver would be guilty of a crime.

   B. The driver would have committed a tort.

   C. The driver would have done no wrong.

   D. The child would have committed a tort.

GO ON TO THE NEXT PAGE

36. According to the man, is it possible to commit both a crime and a tort?

   A. No, every wrong is one or the other.

   B. A tort can be a crime, but not vice versa.

   C. A wrong can be both a tort and a crime.

   D. If a person goes to jail, he cannot be sued for damages also because that would be double jeopardy.

37. According to the definition read by the woman, which of the following could be a tort?

   A. A man is struck by a car but is not hurt.

   B. A man is injured when he intentionally runs in front of a car with no warning.

   C. A man is walking down the street in the early evening and is killed by a car speeding with no lights on.

   D. Occupants of a home are injured after a car strikes another car, which hits a third car, and its driver has a heart attack and runs into the house.

38. What is the woman probably going to do?

   A. Drop the class

   B. Read in order to prepare for the next class

   C. Miss class again and rely on the man

   D. Talk to the professor

Structure Section

Time: 20 Minutes

25 Questions

Directions: This section measures your ability to recognize language appropriate for standard written English. One type of question consists of incomplete sentences, with a blank showing where information is to be filled in. Choose the word or phrase that most correctly completes the sentence. A second type of question consists of sentences with four underlined words or phrases. For each sentence, choose the one underlined word or phrase that is incorrect in standard written English. Mark the answer in your book or on a separate piece of paper.

1. The Strangler Fig Tree, _____ Borneo, grows from seeds deposited in the top of trees around which the Fig Tree grows.

   A. native to

   B. native from

   C. how native to

   D. is native to

2. Hepatitis C generally <u>occurs</u> 20 to 30
   ^A
   <u>year</u> after one <u>is</u> <u>exposed</u> to the illness.
   ^B   ^C ^D

3. Some types of digital telephones cannot _____ in places where others work fine.

   A. to function

   B. functioned

   C. functioning

   D. function

4. Ricky Martin, _____ of the band Menudo, attained great popularity in the late 1990s.

   A. formerly member

   B. a former member

   C. was a former member

   D. being former member

5. The knee is the <u>recipient</u> of constant
   ^A
   pressure, <u>which</u> causes <u>them</u> <u>to fail</u>
   ^B   ^C   ^D
   often and requires replacement with
   artificial parts.

6. Of all the harmful bacteria that can be acquired from unsanitary food handling, E. Coli is the one _____ the most media attention.

   A. that has gained

   B. it has gained

   C. disease that it has gained

   D. gained it

7. Effective <u>speaking</u> and <u>proficient</u>
   ^A   ^B
   writing <u>is</u> generally <u>seen</u> as
   ^C   ^D
   requirements for a professor to achieve
   tenure.

GO ON TO THE NEXT PAGE

Section 2 Structure

8. _____ of the history of words is called etymology.

   A. Study

   B. The study

   C. Studying

   D. To study.

9. Universities often ignore a student's

   lack of scholastically ability when the
   A   B

   student has great athletic potential in a
                  C

   sport that is important to the school.
       D

10. With great care and skill, _____
    Lasik surgery by peeling back a flap of
    the cornea so that it can be reshaped.

    A. doctor performs

    B. a doctor performs

    C. performance

    D. performing

11. John Steinbeck he wrote down-to-earth
                      A

    accounts of individuals and families
      B   C

    who suffered through the Great
             D
    Depression.

12. The possibility of being sued is
    _____ of construction companies.

    A. often the greatest fear

    B. often the fear greatest

    C. the greatest often fear

    D. the often greatest fear

13. Numismatics, the study of coins, can be

    very rewarding once a person becomes
         A   B

    familiar with determining the date and
     C

    type of a coin, as well as grade it.
                    D

14. By analyzing high pressure systems,
    fronts, and other influences, weather
    forecasters can determine the direction
    towards which _____ to travel.

    A. a storm is expected

    B. is expected a storm

    C. is a storm expected

    D. an expected storm

15. Listening to recorded books while
              A

    driving is a means of utilize time
            B   C

    wisely.
    D

16. *The Old Man and the Sea,* a novel
    about an old fisherman's harrowing
    adventure catching a huge fish, is one
    of Ernest Hemingway's _____
    books.

    A. most famous

    B. the most famous

    C. are most famous

    D. and most famous

17. The passionate and exhuberant display
                   A

    of the orchestra conductor moving
    B   C

    several members of the audience to
                   D

    tears.

18. The Internet has lived up to expectations expressed years ago, in _____ the way the public researches, practices business, and communicates.

  A. changing

  B. to change

  C. change of

  D. changed

19. <u>In</u> 1947, Jackie Robinson became <u>a</u> first
   A   B
Black American <u>to play</u> <u>major</u> league
         C   D
baseball.

20. _____ a successful rock star, a singer must have stage presence and charisma in addition to mere musical talent.

  A. To become

  B. Becomes

  C. In order becoming

  D. For becoming

21. <u>As</u> a company grows <u>in</u> size, it is
  A   B
important to maintain <u>communicate</u>
                  C
<u>among</u> the various departments.
 D

22. After hurricane Floyd brushed by the East Florida Coast, emergency management agencies, _____ with each other and the Hurricane Center, coordinated efforts for evacuation of citizens.

  A. working

  B. works

  C. is working

  D. has worked

23. Research <u>involving</u> animals <u>is useful</u>
           A   B
<u>when</u> researchers developing medicines
 C
<u>to combat</u> illnesses of both animals and
   D
people.

24. To give an effective speech, _____ is the delivery that is most important.

  A. it

  B. which

  C. and

  D. there

25. The Internet has dramatically affected _____ people communicate.

  A. the way

  B. is the way

  C. that the way

  D. which way do

Section **2** Structure

STOP

Reading Section

Time: 72 Minutes

45 Questions

Directions: This section measures your ability to read and understand written English similar to that which one may expect in a college or university setting. Read each passage and answer the questions based on what is stated or implied in the passage. Circle or mark the correct answer in the book or write it on a separate piece of paper.

Passage 1

The process for making a coin is quite complicated, and many types of errors can be made during the procedure. Coin collectors study the errors because they can dramatically affect the value of a coin. That is, some kinds of errors are considered interesting and add value to a collected coin. Some errors will affect only one or a few coins, while others will affect all coins made at a given time. While the word *error* is generally a negative concept, it can be a positive concept to a coin collector because it makes the coin interesting and more valuable, unlike damage to the coin after it is in circulation or the cleaning of a coin, both of which detract from its value.

After an artist creates the drawing that will appear on a coin, a die is made in plastic or plaster from the drawing. The die is a mirror image of the coin. Where there is a raised area on the coin, there is a depressed area on the die, and vice versa. The die is then transferred to a metal pattern in order to create a master die. The dies, one for the front of the coin and one for the back, are placed in a coin press. The metal in the coin comes from a large metal piece called a planchet, which is used at room temperature rather than melted. A feed mechanism passes planchets through the coin press. The two dies, surrounded by collars, strike the planchet, which causes the softer planchet metal to flow into all the design cavities of the die up to the collars, resulting in the flat or reeded edge of the coin.

Sometimes errors take place on the planchet itself. Normally, because the strip of planchet material is used on only one or a few coins, an error on the planchet will only affect one or a few coins. The types of errors possible on the planchet include: an improper mixture of the alloy used to make the planchet; damaged, defective or incomplete planchets; or unstruck planchets. The alloy-mix error occurs when the wrong metals or wrong percentages of metals go into the alloy mix, resulting in discoloration. A defective planchet may be scratched or dented. Specialists can sometimes tell whether the scratch or dent occurred prior to or after the strike, and it might make a difference to a collector. Planchets are cut from strips through a rough punch, like cutting cookies out of dough, so there may be overlaps into already punched areas.

A die error occurs during the creation of the die or by a change or alteration after it is created. Because one die is used on many coins, the error will be reflected on every coin struck by that die. Common errors affecting the die are: errors in engraving; die cracks and die breaks; dents, gouges, and scratches; and the polishing of the die.

The earliest dies were made by hand using engraving tools to cut the design directly into the die. Many errors were made in the dies themselves, and often have no significant value. Sometimes these errors appear as a date on top of another date, known as doubling, or as a ghost or duplicate image. A die crack will result in a raised, irregular line on the coin metal above the normal surface of the coin, while a die break is a raised, irregular area of coin metal above the normal surface of the coin. Scratches, dents, and other marks on the die will transfer to the coin when it is struck.

Another type of error is a striking error, which occurs only when the planchet is actually struck by the dies. This type of error is commonly caused by misaligned or rotated dies, multiple or double strikes, or similar problems. It is important to be sure that the die for the front of the coin is exactly opposite the die of the reverse.

1. The author explains that collectors often view errors in minting coins as

   A. detracting from the coin's value.

   B. not affecting the coin's value.

   C. adding to the coin's value.

   D. causing a coin to be reminted.

2. The author explains that an error on the die will affect

   A. more coins than an error on the planchet.

   B. fewer coins than an error on the planchet.

   C. no coins.

   D. only coins within collars.

3. The word *others* in the first paragraph refers to

   A. kinds of errors.

   B. values.

   C. collectors.

   D. coins.

4. The word *detract* in the first paragraph is closest in meaning to

   A. increase.

   B. reduce.

   C. affect.

   D. have no effect.

5. The author implies that cleaning a coin after it is minted

   A. has no effect on the coin's value.

   B. increases the coin's value.

   C. increases demand for the coin.

   D. decreases the coin's value.

6. The passage states that a die is made of plastic or plaster and a master die is made of

   A. plaster.

   B. plastic.

   C. metal.

   D. lanchet.

GO ON TO THE NEXT PAGE

Section **3** Reading

7. According to the passage, the image on a die is

   A. affected by the color of the planchet.

   B. impossible to see.

   C. identical to the coin's image.

   D. the exact opposite of the coin's image.

8. According to the passage, after the master die is created it is

   A. placed in a coin press.

   B. attached to a planchet.

   C. colored.

   D. transferred to a plaster mold.

9. The author describes a planchet as a

   A. die.

   B. piece of metal that will become the coin.

   C. collar.

   D. coin press.

10. According to the passage, what is true about the planchet when the die strikes it to create a coin?

    A. The planchet has been heated.

    B. The planchet is the same temperature as the room.

    C. The planchet has already been struck.

    D. The planchet has been cooled.

11. The design or flat edge on the rim of the coin is caused by the metal of the planchet flowing against

    A. a collar.

    B. a coin press.

    C. the die.

    D. the mold.

12. According to the passage, an error in the planchet could result in

    A. an identical defect on multiple coins.

    B. no effect on the coin.

    C. breakage of the die.

    D. discoloration of the coin.

13. The author uses the analogy of cutting cookie dough to explain how the

    A. die strike the planchet.

    B. die are made.

    C. planchet is cut from the strip.

    D. planchet is rolled through the machine.

14. A crack in the die will result in

    A. an indentation in the coin.

    B. a raised line on the face of the coin.

    C. no effect on the coin.

    D. a discoloration on the face of the coin.

15. The author implies that errors in the die are often made by

    A. errors in the planchets.

    B. humans.

    C. errors in the collar.

    D. cracks in the planchet.

Passage 2

Tequila is created from one of the hundred species of agave, which was discovered as a source of alcohol by the ancient Aztecs. In the 1500s, it was used to create an alcoholic beverage called octli, which was sour and not tasty. But later, the Spanish used the distillation process to create mezcal. Finally, double-distilling was used with a special type of agave known as *agave azul*, or *blue agave* in English (scientifically known as *agave tequilana weber*), and tequila was born.

Creating tequila is a long, involved process. The plant is 8 to 12 years old before it can be used. The plant itself resembles a huge green aloe plant. To maintain the potency of the agave, the leaves are periodically cut back. Finally, when the plant has reached the proper age and weight, the leaves are cut, and workers known as Jimadors use a special hoe-type tool called a *coa* to remove the huge heart from the ground. The heart is large, brown, hard, and heavy, weighing 80 or more pounds. It is filled with a sweet sap referred to as agua miel, or honey water, which is actually the source of the tequila.

The heavy roots are then carried to trucks on the backs of burrows. At the processing plant, the roots are chopped into quarters with machetes and carried on conveyor belts to huge ovens where they are baked for four days at 120 degrees Celsius. Next, they are placed in a dark room for a day or so, and finally, they are thrown onto a conveyor belt, which runs them through a shredding machine, where they are ground to a pulp. As they are ground, the liquid is released and falls into collectors below. The pulp continues to be run through additional shredders where it is further crushed and manipulated so that all the juice is released. The liquid is sent by a hose to an aluminum vat where yeast is added, and it is kept at a cool temperature for two days. Next, the liquid is transported via another hose to an open vat, where the yeast assists in the natural fermentation process. Then, approximately 10 percent of the liquid continues in the process, and the balance is discarded. The liquid is then sent by hoses to other vats to be distilled twice in order to achieve the desired purity. It is measured and tested at every step. Finally, when it has reached the proper temperature, it is transported by another hose or a tanker truck to the bottling plant. If it will be a select brand, it is placed in oak vats to be aged, which allows the distillate to mellow and affects the color slightly.

In the bottling area, a machine fills the bottles, which are measured by an attendant. The bottles then travel on a conveyor belt to several different workers, one who affixes the large label, another the neck label, another the top, another the tape over the top, and so on. Then workers meticulously clean and polish the bottles and peer through the glass for impurities. Finally, the bottles are boxed and transported for wholesale or retail sale.

16. According to the passage, blue agave is

    A. very rare.

    B. used to make octli.

    C. used to make mezcal.

    D. one of over 100 species of agave.

17. The author implies all of the following except that

    A. the Aztecs used agave for something other than alcohol.

    B. the octli was not distilled.

    C. mezcal was distilled only one time.

    D. tequila was the first product made from agave plants that was distilled twice.

GO ON TO THE NEXT PAGE

Section **3** Reading

18. The author states all of the following about the agave plant except that

    A. the agave plant grows anywhere in the world.

    B. the agave plant is trimmed back from time to time.

    C. the agave plant grows for years before it is ready.

    D. the agave plant has a huge heart or root that contains a sweet liquid.

19. The word *periodically* in the second paragraph is closest in meaning to

    A. occasionally.

    B. annually.

    C. daily.

    D. roughly.

20. The word *sap* in the second paragraph is closest in meaning to

    A. mezcal.

    B. juice.

    C. octli.

    D. tequila.

21. According to the passage, tequila is formed from

    A. the outer protective substance around the heart.

    B. the sweet liquid within the heart.

    C. the sweet liquid within the plant leaves.

    D. the plant leaves themselves.

22. The author indicates that the aloe plant

    A. looks like the agave.

    B. is a member of the same family as the agave.

    C. grows in the same location and conditions as the agave.

    D. has some of the same characteristics as the agave.

23. The word *ground* in the third paragraph is closest in meaning to

    A. shredded.

    B. dirt.

    C. combined.

    D. liquefied.

24. The word *pulp* in the third paragraph is closest in meaning to

    A. mash.

    B. liquid.

    C. large mass.

    D. agave.

25. According to the passage, what is true about the hearts of the agave?

    A. They are light in weight.

    B. They are roasted whole.

    C. They are cut in four pieces before being baked.

    D. They are carried on workers' backs to the plant.

26. After the liquid is removed from the heart of the agave, it is transported from place to place by

   A. truck.

   B. hose.

   C. bucket.

   D. conveyor belt.

27. According to the passage, the last process before the agave hearts are ground up is

   A. baking.

   B. keeping them in a dark room.

   C. transporting the plant.

   D. chopping them by machete.

28. According to the passage, the liquid is transported from vat to vat because

   A. it undergoes a different process in each vat.

   B. it must be kept moving.

   C. the yeast is acting upon it.

   D. it must be run through different temperatures.

29. The author implies all of the following except that

   A. yeast is used to cause fermentation.

   B. all of the agua miel is used in the end product.

   C. the temperature of the final product is important.

   D. many tests and processes are performed to assure purity.

30. In describing the bottling process, the author implies that

   A. the jobs are differentiated, and great care is taken.

   B. machines fill the bottles and apply the labels.

   C. quality control is not important.

   D. much of the final product is rejected.

Passage 3

The Greenland Shark, whose scientific name, *somniosus microcephalus*, means "small-headed sleeper," has <u>eluded</u> study until recently and is unique among sharks of the world. As one might imagine, the water of Arctic Bay is extremely <u>frigid</u>, but the Greenland Shark is perfectly suited for it. The shark itself may appear <u>ghoulish</u>, having large nostrils, gray and <u>blotched</u> skin, a mouth full of sharp teeth, and milky eyes (like those of a dead fish) with something that appears like a <u>tassel</u> hanging from each of <u>them</u>.

Its jaw and teeth look quite similar to those of other sharks, with entire layers of teeth being discarded together and replaced with a new set. The <u>lethargic</u> shark feeds on seals, fish, and <u>carrion</u>, with a power to suck in huge pieces of meat. It is known to grow to at least 20 or more feet and to live for at least 16 years, although there is not much data on the subject.

Curiously, when the flesh of one of these sharks is ingested by any being other than another Greenland Shark, a strong neuro-toxin causes extreme intoxication. Researchers have spotted packs of wild dogs that have eaten a dead Greenland Shark and become so intoxicated that <u>they</u> could not walk. The shark meat can be detoxified by

GO ON TO THE NEXT PAGE

Section **3** Reading

soaking it in salt water for several days, and then there is no adverse effect.

The tassel-like object hanging from the eyes is, in fact, a certain type of parasite called a <u>copepod</u> that regularly attaches itself to the cornea of Greenland Sharks, severely damaging their eyesight. The three-inch invertebrate exhibits two claw-like appendages that hook on to the cornea. A <u>scar</u> is created where the copepod latches on and where it moves back and forth across the eye. This is what results in the milky eyes. Unbelievably, the shark still appears to see through the fogginess and the annoying copepod hanging in front of the cornea, although its sight does not appear to be that important. Naturally, it has a keen sense of smell to make up for the lack of sight.

31. The word *eluded* in the first sentence is closest in meaning to

    A. undergone.

    B. escaped.

    C. met.

    D. fulfilled.

32. The word *frigid* in the second sentence is closest in meaning to

    A. freezing.

    B. deep.

    C. warm.

    D. food-filled.

33. The word *ghoulish* in the first paragraph is closest in meaning to

    A. ghastly.

    B. huge.

    C. gray.

    D. slow.

34. The word *blotched* in the first paragraph is closest in meaning to

    A. dark.

    B. rough.

    C. spotted.

    D. leathery.

35. The word *tassel* in the first paragraph is closest in meaning to

    A. decoration.

    B. amoeba.

    C. eyelid.

    D. tongue.

36. The word *them* in the last sentence of the first paragraph refers to

    A. eyes.

    B. sharks.

    C. mouths.

    D. tassel.

37. The author implies that instead of losing a tooth, the Greenland shark

    A. loses an entire set at once.

    B. retains all its teeth for life.

    C. loses two at a time.

    D. can regenerate a broken tooth like the tail of a lizard.

38. The author implies that due to the extremely cold water,

   A. the shark does not live long.

   B. it has been difficult to observe the shark to any great degree.

   C. the shark hibernates.

   D. the sharks only move around in daylight.

39. The word *lethargic* in the second paragraph is closest in meaning to

   A. sluggish.

   B. energetic.

   C. angry.

   D. violent.

40. The author implies in paragraph two that *carrion* is

   A. dead animal flesh.

   B. a bacteria.

   C. a Greenland Shark.

   D. a tooth.

41. The author indicates that the Greenland Shark's flesh contains

   A. tasty meat.

   B. a material that causes intoxication.

   C. an amoeba.

   D. more fat than that of other sharks.

42. The word *they* in the third paragraph refers to

   A. researchers.

   B. dogs.

   C. sharks.

   D. parasites.

43. The passage indicates in the last paragraph that a *copepod* is

   A. a type of shark.

   B. a type of dog.

   C. a type of parasite.

   D. a researcher.

44. The word *scar* in the last paragraph is closest in meaning to

   A. disfigurement.

   B. cornea.

   C. copepod.

   D. shark.

45. Which **two words** from the last paragraph mean the same as *cloudiness?*

   A. eye

   B. milky

   C. fogginess

   D. copepod

Section 3 Reading

321

Writing Section

Time: 30 Minutes

1 Question

Directions: This section measures your ability to write in English, including your ability to organize ideas, create an essay in standard written English, and support the thoughts with sufficient examples and evidence. Write an essay in 30 minutes. You may make notes on a separate piece of paper, and then type or handwrite the essay.

Do companies have an obligation to their employees to protect their jobs even when businesses merge or are sold? Use specific reasons and examples to support your stance.

Practice Test 1

Listening Section

Part A

1. **D:** *She has continued to try to find a university that will accept her.*

2. **C:** *Take Professor Stafford's class.*

3. **D:** *Purchase the computer she first suggested.*

4. **B:** *He believes he can build the fence without waiting.*

5. **B:** *She is unhappy with what her advisor suggested.*

6. **B:** *The computer she is considering has fallen out of favor.*

7. **A:** *He has not exercised and his body shows it.*

8. **C:** *Preserved human remains.*

9. **A:** *She believes the salesman paid no attention to her.*

10. **B:** *Renewing her driver's license.*

11. **C:** *That he cannot stay in his house for a while after he sells it.*

12. **D:** *She got a new job, so she can't go on her trip.*

13. **B:** *She is going to take some time off.*

14. **A:** *He is sorry they upgraded the software because it caused another problem.*

15. **D:** *Put one book on the shelf and get an encyclopedia.*

Part B

16. **B:** *The woman's grandmother and how to handle a progressive illness.*

17. **A:** *To assess her mental capacity.*

18. **D:** *She forgets things, like when to turn off the stove.*

19. **B:** *Bankruptcy.*

20. **C and D:** *Give the agent authority to sign documents and Assign the right to make decisions.*

21. **B:** *Sign her up for a day-care program.*

22. **D:** *A guardianship will be required if the grandmother has lost her capacity.*

23. **C:** *A plant that grows over a two-year period, alternating between producing plants and seeds.*

24. **B:** *In France and England.*

25. **C:** *Appearance.*

26. **A:** *Loose leaves and soft heads.*

27. **A:** *Kale and collard greens.*

28. **B:** *Lightweight and compact.*

29. **C:** *Thermal cameras.*

30. **A:** *The prisoners were not mistreated.*

31. **C:** *The site lies beneath the site of the war.*

32. **D:** *Locating distant planets.*

33. **A:** *That she would be in a new building.*

34. **C:** *The air conditioning is insufficient.*

35. **A:** *Bananas ripen too quickly.*

Structure Section

1. **A:** *has cast.* The expression *a number of* is a plural concept and is always used with a plural verb, *a number of voters have cast.*

2. **B:** *intends.* The noun after *nor* controls the verb. *Any other faculty member* is a singular idea.

3. **B:** *others. Other* is an adjective in this sentence, modifying the noun *classes.* Therefore, it cannot be plural: *other classes.* You will also notice that the initial clause is dependent, which means that the second clause must have a subject and a verb. In this case, the second clause does have both: *At least several classes are . . . .*

4. **A:** *one of the.* The expression is cardinal number + *of* + *the* + (adjective) + noun: *one of the most dangerous bacteria.*

5. **B:** *probably be.* After the modal *would,* the verb must appear in the simple form. The adverb *probably* must be used instead of the adjective *probable* because it is modifying the verb *would be.*

6. **A:** *this*. The pronoun modifies *varsity athletes,* which is plural. The correct form would be *these*.

7. **A:** *ninety-story-tall*. When a noun is used in an expression like this, the whole expression becomes an adjective. The noun being modified is *building*. The word *story* is singular because it is part of the adjective.

8. **A:** *operate*. Because you are given *had been,* the form is past perfect progressive, so you must use the verb+ing, *operating*. Or it could be viewed as a passive voice sentence, *had been operated*.

9. **B:** *the largest of which*. The relative pronoun *which* refers to *three rooms*. The first answer choice is incorrect because you use a comparative when there are two of something and a superlative when there are three of something in a series. Also, you need a definite article. The other two answers cause the sentence to be incomplete.

10. **C:** *removing*. After the phrase *required that*, which is the subjunctive, the verb must be in the simple form. Here the first verb in the series is in the simple form (*take*), and this verb must also be in the simple form (*remove*).

11. **A:** *as much*. The comparison rule is *as* + adjective + *as*. Here, the second *as* appears later in the sentence. The comparative *more* goes with *than* and cannot be preceded by *as*. *Revenues* looks like a count noun, but it is a non-countable idea, and that is why the preposition *in* precedes the clause it is in.

12. **D:** *another*. The subject is plural, *people*. The pronoun that refers to *people* must also be plural, *others*. Notice that the word *preparing* is correct because it is the object of *enjoy*.

13. **D:** *Had it prepared*. This means the same as *if it had prepared*. The first answer choice is incorrect because the verb cannot be in present tense with a contrary to fact condition, and you know it is contrary to fact because of the verb phrase *would have been*. The second answer choice is incorrect because it has no subject, and the third answer choice is also used for present tense.

14. **C:** *were*. *News* is a non-count noun in American English. The verb form must be *was*.

15. **D:** *the meeting was*. In an embedded question, you reverse the sentence order after the question word. A question would be *Why was the meeting postponed?* But in an embedded question, it is . . . *why the meeting was postponed*. The first answer is not correct because the sentence must be in the passive voice to make sense. A meeting does not act; it receives an action. The third answer is not correct because you cannot have *did*, which is an auxiliary showing tense, with the main verb also showing the tense. The main verb is *postponed,* so it cannot appear with *did*.

16. **C:** *universal*. It must be an adverb, *universally,* because it modifies the adjective *understood*.

17. **C:** *as or better than that.* This combines two phrases, an equal comparison and a comparative. It also tests an illogical comparison idea. Equal comparisons are shown by *as* + adjective + *as*. Comparatives are shown as adjective + *-er* + *than*. Both are present here. You cannot close the idea with either *as* or *than*. They both must appear. Also, the idea of a logical comparison is that you must compare two things of the same type. Here the intention is to compare the *curriculum* in the two types of schools. If you compare the *curriculum* at *public schools* with *private schools*, it is not logical, because you are comparing *curriculum* with *private schools*. You use *that of* as the pronoun for *the curriculum.*

18. **A:** *never.* The word *hardly* is one of the negative concept words that cannot appear with another negative. It would be correct to say *hardly ever.*

19. **B:** *requirement.* The first clause of the sentence contains a reduced relative clause, from a passive structure. The word *raised* is not a conjugated verb. It is the result of the reduction of *children who are raised.* So the noun *requirement* is incorrect because a verb is needed, *require.*

20. **B:** *it developed.* The sentence begins with a participial phrase. The understood subject of the participial phrase is *a private university.* Therefore, it must appear right after the comma, in this case as a pronoun, *it.* Because every sentence must have a conjugated verb and there is no other verb in the sentence, the answer must contain the conjugated verb, *developed.*

21. **C:** *difficulty.* The answer needs to be an adjective (*difficult*), not a noun.

22. **B:** *in.* One can say *in a car, in the car,* or *by car.*

23. **A:** *the sooner treatment must be begun.* A double comparative has the same structure in both clauses.

Reading Section

1. **A:** *springtime.* The sentence states *A vernal or springtime pool. . .,* which indicates that *vernal* and *springtime* mean the same thing.

2. **B:** *To describe how the vernal pool fits into the larger environmental picture.*

3. **A:** *produces.*

4. **A:** *distinct. Diverse* means "different."

5. **C:** *living being.* The sentence states: *Like all of nature, there are predators and victims, and a* particular living being *may be one or the other, depending on its* age and characteristics.

6. **B:** *Like all of nature, there are predators and victims, and a particular living being may be one or the other, depending on its age and characteristics.* This sentence means that something that lives in the pond may sometimes kill older or younger victims and may sometimes be a victim itself.

7. **D:** *Other amphibians and reptiles return to the recurrent pond year after year to reproduce, as their ancestors have done for years.*

8. **B:** *cloudy.* This means the same as "not clear."

9. **C:** *forms of algae.*

10. **B:** *Some of the life forms live in water first and later on land.* The sentence states that the forms of algae produce and transmit oxygen to the salamander embryos and other young *that are not yet able to survive outside of water.* By saying that the embryos and other young are not *yet* able means that at some time they will be able to survive outside of water.

11. **B:** *recurring.*

12. **A:** *reducing.* Generally the word means "avoiding" or "making not necessary." Here, the closest definition is *reducing.*

13. **C:** *cold dissolves blood clots.* Applying cold has certain benefits, but nowhere is it stated that it dissolves the blood clots.

14. **A:** *A blood clot sticking in an area of the brain.*

15. **A:** *shaking.* To shiver is to shake with cold.

16. **B:** *cells die only as a direct result of the stroke.* This is really the opposite of the first answer choice, which is the correct statement.

17. **C:** *A new method of cooling the body to reduce stroke damage that is being researched.* **B** is incorrect because it refers to use of drugs.

18. **A:** *considerable.* Both words mean "to a great degree."

19. **A:** *the internal chilling process has not been proven yet.* The other answer choices are statements made in the reading passage.

20. **B:** *show that cooling a body does not necessarily harm it.*

21. **C:** *the artery in the leg connects to the vena cava.* The passage indicates that the catheter is inserted only to the vena cava.

22. **D:** *the doctor moves the catheter slowly through the artery to the vena cava.* The author explains that the catheter is inserted in the groin area and moved to the vena cava area. *Threaded* just means moved slowly along the vein towards the destination.

23. **A:** *the body becoming cold. Hypothermia* means the condition of the body when exposed to extreme cold.

24. **C:** *talk to the patient.*

25. **C:** *The Honeybee — Its Characteristics and Usefulness.* **A** is too broad and the **B** and **D** too narrow.

26. **B:** *varieties.*

27. **B:** *flowers.*

28. **B:** *concurrently,* which means happening at the same time.

29. **B:** *a nest.* The passage states: *Bees live in a structured environment and social structure within a hive, which is a nest with storage space for the honey.*

30. **B:** *mates with the queen and has no other purpose.* The author states: *The male honeybees are called drones . . . their only job is to impregnate a queen.*

31. **D:** *drones are never females.* Drones impregnate the queen, so they must be male.

32. **D:** *workers.* This is clearly stated in the passage in the sentence: *The worker bee carries nectar to the hive in a special stomach called a honey stomach.*

33. **A:** *They pollinate fruit and vegetable plants.* The reading passage states that when bees carry pollen from one plant to the next, they fertilize the flowers.

34. **B:** *it is made of honey.* The author states the honeycomb is made of wax, has six-sided compartments, and is waterproof.

35. **D:** *Antarctica.* The first sentence of the passage states that bees can be found in every part of the world except the northernmost and southernmost areas.

36. **B:** *pliable.* The passage states that workers make beeswax and *shape it into a honeycomb.* If it can be shaped, it is pliable, or easy to mold.

37. **A:** *a hormone.* The second sentence of paragraph one states: *A polypeptide hormone, insulin is synthesized . . . .* The sentence begins with an appositive, and the phrase following it refers to the same subject.

38. **A:** *eliminated.* This means that sugar leaves the body through the urine.

39. **B:** *formerly. Previously* and *formerly* mean the same thing.

40. **A:** *insulin.*

41. **A:** *in the pancreas.* The passage states that the pancreas is the site of insulin production.

42. **D:** *slow.*

43. **A:** *severely overweight.*

44. **B:** *An Overview of Diabetes.* The other answers are too particular, whereas the article is general in nature.

45. **B:** *the symptoms and treatment are different.* The other answer choices do not show why the author makes a distinction between the two types.

46. **C:** *Type 2 results from a lack of secretion of insulin.* This is not a correct statement because that is the description of Type 1 diabetes. The passage states that Type 2 results from *sluggish . . . insulin secretion,* not a lack of secretion.

47. **B:** *Type 1 sufferers are generally not overweight.* The passage indicates that Type 2 sufferers are often obese, but it does not mention obesity in regard to Type 1 patients.

Writing Section

Have your essay scored by a writing instructor or submit it to my Essay Grading Service, which is described in the "How to Use This Book" section. The scoring criteria appear at the beginning of the "Writing" chapter in Part III.

Practice Test 2

Listening Section

Part A

1. **B:** *An error was probably made in figuring the employee cost.*

2. **B:** *His boss paid his way.*

3. **A:** *He thinks somebody broke the machine and kept quiet about it.*

4. **D:** *An announcement about the new administrator was made the previous day.*

5. **B:** *Change to Ms. Nelson's class.*

6. **D:** *He wanted to see more than he was able to see.*

7. **B:** *They ran into the house the moment they arrived.*

8. **B:** *Eat dinner and then go to the library with him.*

9. **D:** *She is unable to go.*

10. **B:** *She is too ill to continue working so hard.*

11. **B:** *He is requiring extra projects that the students were not expecting.*

12. **B:** *Advise her if she makes an error.*

13. **A:** *Go to see a doctor.*

14. **A:** *She formerly lived on 34th Street.*

15. **B:** *Call him when she is awake.*

Part B

16. **B:** *A computer program.*

17. **B:** *Write the procedure.*

18. **A:** *Take notes.*

19. **B:** *Yes, because he wrote down the procedure.*

20. **B:** *He died before the age of 30.*

21. **A:** *He lived dangerously.*

22. **C:** *He wrote about the sea before he experienced it and then again afterwards.*

23. **B:** *One was written from experience and the other was not.*

24. **C:** *Termites are quite different from ants, but their social structure is similar.*

25. **C:** *Termites that have been transplanted to an area.*

26. **B:** *Pottery.*

27. **B:** *Termites can be beneficial to the ecological system.*

28. **A:** *Subterranean termites enter only from the soil.*

29. **B:** *Treating the entire structure by tenting.*

Structure Section

1. **A:** *that is expected.* The relative pronoun *that* joins the two phrases: *to study a new procedure* and *the new procedure is expected to eliminate.* The expectation must be in the passive voice because the procedure does not expect anything. The form for passive voice is form of *be* + verb in past participle form.

2. **C:** *anothers.* This can never be a word because *others* is the correct pronoun for a plural noun, while the prefix *an-* is used for singular.

3. **C:** *with hopes of.* This is an idiomatic expression. **D** would be correct if the verb *improving* were in the simple form, *improve.*

4. **B:** *because it both provides.* The expression is *both. . . and. . . .* The *both* should appear immediately before the word being compared. In this case there are two verbs, *provides* and *uses.* **A** is incorrect not only because it is missing the *but also,* which is needed to complete the construction, but also because the *not only* is out of place. It would also appear just before the verb. **D** is missing an important word because the expression is *as a result of.*

5. **D:** *rise.* The correct word would be *raise* because it is a transitive verb, meaning it is followed by a direct object, *their test scores.*

6. **B:** *not to write.* The verb *instruct* is followed by the infinitive (*to* + verb in simple form). The negative is formed by adding *not* before the infinitive.

7. **C:** *dinosaurs became extinct.* This is an embedded question, and thus the order is subject + verb, with no auxiliary.

8. **D:** *because.* The expression must be *because of* because it is followed by a noun phrase, *the low scores.*

9. **A:** *had not been.* Use the past perfect construction in past condition.

10. **B:** *supporting. Decide* must be followed by the infinitive, *to support.*

11. **A:** *the jeep had been left.* After the question word in an embedded question, the order is subject + verb.

12. **A:** *had allowed the photographers to enter the building.* **B** is incorrect because *let* is followed by the verb in simple form, not an infinitive. **C** is incorrect because after *because* there must be a clause, and the word *permitting* sets up a phrase, not a clause. **D** is incorrect because the order is incorrect. After the subject of the second clause, *somebody,* must appear the verb, not another noun phrase. Also, documentation is a non-count noun and is not made plural.

13. **C:** *the president's not informing them.* After the verb *resented* there must be a noun phrase or a clause. It would also have been correct to say "resented the president for not informing them of the meeting." Remember that after a verb that requires a gerund in the subordinate clause, any noun must be possessive. *Informing* is a gerund because of *resented.*

14. **D:** *Only after entering the store.* After a limiting word *(only)* introduces a sentence, the order of the subject and verb is altered. That is why this sentence has the auxiliary *did.* **A** would have been correct if the order hadn't been reversed: *Upon entering the store, Arthur realized . . . .*

15. **B:** *are.* The subject of the sentence is *The congressman.* The words in commas after it are parenthetical and do not affect the verb. Thus the verb should be singular, *is.*

16. **A:** *Because.* After *because* a clause must appear. After *because of* a noun phrase must appear. The phrase *the torrential rains that had devastated the area* is a noun phrase, so the sentence should begin with *because of.*

17. **B:** *are.* The subject of the sentence is *lack.* The prepositional phrases *of sanitation* and *in restaurants* are both irrelevant to the determination of the number of the verb. The verb should be *is.*

18. **D:** *as the first.* The comparative is formed with the adjective + *-er* or *more* + adjective ... *than.* So the correct phrase is *than the first.*

19. **C:** *have.* The noun that controls the verb is *cultivation.* It is singular so the verb should be *has.*

20. **C:** *are causing.* The subject that controls the verb is *the decision.* All the other words after that are modifying the noun but do not affect the verb. The correct verb phrase is *is causing.*

21. **B:** *has been.* The subject that controls the verb is *species,* which is plural, so the verb should be *have been.*

22. **C:** *diligent.* This word needs to be an adverb *(diligently)* because it modifies the verb *had worked.*

23. **D:** *them pull.* This is a reduced passive voice structure, combined with a causative verb. The correct phrase would be *having them pulled.*

24. **D:** *had he entered.* After the word *hardly* at the beginning of a sentence, the order is auxiliary + subject + main verb.

25. **B:** *to change.* After *had better,* which means the same as *should* and is used in much the same way, the simple form, *change,* is required.

Reading Section

1. **D:** *In North and South America.* This is explained in the first paragraph.

2. **D:** *in the eastern part of North America.* This is explained in the first paragraph.

3. **A:** *extremely tiny.*

4. **B:** *the giant hummingbird.*

5. **D:** *The speed at which a bee hummingbird's wings beat is not actually known.* The author explains in paragraph five that they have not measured this species yet.

6. **A:** *they attach to the body at one point only.* This is explained in the third paragraph.

7. **A:** *A helicopter.* This is the only aircraft listed that can hover and move in different directions.

8. **A:** *beak.* The bill or beak is the mouth of the bird.

9. **A:** *meager.*

10. **B:** *The structure of the feathers as well as pigmentation.* This is explained in paragraph four.

11. **A:** *wing and possibly tail movement.* This is explained in paragraph four.

12. **D:** *The association is beneficial to each organism, although it provides more benefit to the fungus.* This is indicated in the third paragraph, in which the author states, *It appears that the fungus actually gains more benefit from the relationship than does the alga.*

13. **B:** *formerly.*

14. **C:** *A lichen constituted a single plant.* This is indicated in the first paragraph, in which the author states, *Previously, lichens were classified as single organisms until scientists had the benefit of microscopes . . . .*

15. **C:** *close.*

16. **C:** *the joint benefit each organism receives from the relationship.*

17. **D:** *the fungus uses the carbohydrates manufactured by the alga.* This is indicated in the third paragraph, where the author states, *Algae form simple carbohydrates that, when excreted, are absorbed by fungi cells and transformed into a different carbohydrate.*

18. **A:** *singular/plural.* The author explains in the first paragraph that fungus and alga are singular and fungi and algae are plural forms of the words.

19. **C:** *new organisms are grown from pieces of existing organisms.* This is explained in the fourth paragraph, where the author states, *Most botanists agree that reproduction is vegetative because portions of an existing lichen break off and fall away to begin a new organism nearby.*

20. **D:** *algae are more sensitive to light than fungi.* This is explained in the third paragraph, in which the author states, *Yet, fungi also contribute to the symbiosis by absorbing water vapor from the air and providing shade for the algae, which are more sensitive to light.*

21. **D:** *close.*

22. **D:** *strong.*

23. **C:** *harsh.*

24. **D:** *reduce soil erosion.*

25. **C:** *Coin Grading — One of the Most Important Skills in Coin Collecting.*

26. **A:** *ability.*

27. **A:** *grade.*

28. **C:** *rare.*

29. **D:** *the number of coins of a given type and date that they were minted.*

30. **A:** *grade.* The entire passage indicates this is the most important.

31. **B, A, D, C:** *MS-60; AU-58; VF-20; AG-3.*

32. **B:** *Mint State.* It has 11 numbered grades, from 60 to 70.

33. **A:** *marks on a coin caused by banging from other coins.* This is specifically stated in the third paragraph.

34. **B:** *sheen.*

35. **A:** *One small contact mark, full luster, good eye appeal, and no hairlines.* **B** has a large hairline and reduced luster. **C** has two kinds of marks and defective luster. **D** has been artificially cleaned, which you are told is a negative.

36. **B:** *AU-56.*

37. **B:** *the only difference between an MS-60 and an AU-58 may be that the AU-58 has been in circulation.* The distinction is that MS means Mint State, which also means uncirculated. About Circulated means only slightly circulated.

38. **B:** *other forms of hepatitis were known before the hepatitis C strain was discovered.* The author refers to hepatitis in general, and hepatitis C specifically, implying that there are others.

39. **C:** *inception.*

40. **C:** *Hepatitis C — Its Characteristics and Treatment.*

41. **A:** *vast.* The word in this context is an intensifier, modifying majority.

42. **A:** *standard.*

43. **D:** *people.*

44. **C:** *many people with hepatitis C were not addicts but simply experimented with illegal drugs.*

45. **C:** *learn the degree of damage to the liver.*

46. **C:** *only rarely results in liver cancer.*

47. **A:** *the medicine must be taken intravenously.* It is injected, but not in the vein.

48. **B:** *liver.*

Writing Section

Have your essay scored by a writing instructor or submit it to my Essay Grading Service, which is described in the "How to Use This Book" section. The scoring criteria appear at the beginning of the "Writing" chapter in Part III.

Practice Test 3

Listening Section

Part A

1. **B:** *He is lost.*

2. **A:** *She is unable to teach her class.*

3. **B:** *He expected more people to attend the event.*

4. **B:** *Take his car in for repair.*

5. **C:** *He did not prepare adequately for the test.*

6. **D:** *He believes the interview went very well.*

7. **A:** *She had to work so she did not go to Seattle.*

8. **B:** *Another teacher chose the textbook.*

9. **C:** *She speaks well but does not write well.*

10. **B:** *That he had turned down the scholarship absolutely.*

11. **D:** *He was unable to buy the house.*

12. **B:** *His sister says that he uses the beach house too much.*

13. **A:** *She has no time to relax.*

14. **B:** *That she was moving away.*

15. **B:** *Susan's father was injured in the fire.*

Part B

16. **B:** *That he was happy with his living arrangements.*

17. **C:** *He will accept a place close to either work or school.*

18. **B:** *He thinks it is close to conveniences.*

19. **B:** *Contact her friend to inquire about it.*

20. **B:** *Diagnosis, symptoms, and treatment of reflux disease.*

21. **C:** *As a necessary protective mechanism.*

22. **B:** *When the sphincter opens when it shouldn't.*

23. **A:** *The stomach contains strong chemicals.*

24. **D:** *Cancer.*

25. **B:** *As a cause of reflux disease.*

26. **C and A:** *Fatty foods make reflux more likely; Diet can affect how and when the sphincter acts up.*

27. **D:** *Ignore the problem.*

28. **A:** *An ancient tool.*

29. **D:** *That Africans and Middle Easterners were more advanced than anybody else.*

30. **A:** *They are quite similar.*

31. **C:** *He often struggled, but he did enjoy professional success eventually.*

32. **A:** *He did not enjoy school but he did enjoy learning on his own.*

33. **D:** *His father died when he was young, and his mother was a recluse.*

34. **C:** *He read and wrote quite a bit, but also got out from time to time.*

35. **C:** *He destroyed copies of it because it was a failure.*

36. **A:** *He never achieved financial independence.*

37. **A:** *Some unscrupulous publishers printed it without Hawthorne's permission.*

Structure Section

1. **B:** *are.* The subject is *overeating,* and a gerund as a subject is singular, so the verb should be *is.* Ignore the words between the commas.

2. **A:** *they diligently assisted in reducing costs and increasing.* The pronoun *they* must appear after the comma because *the employees* is the subject of the first clause. The correct order is subject + adverb + verb. Also, after the preposition *in,* verbs must appear in the gerund (verb+*ing*).

3. **C:** *thorough.* The correct word is *thoroughly,* an adverb, because it modifies the verb *had read.*

4. **D:** *another pair.* *Pliers* is a plural noun, so it would have to appear with the adjective *other.* The pronoun *others* replaces the noun, so it cannot appear with a noun. The noun *pair*, as in *pair of pliers,* is singular, and therefore can be used with *another.*

5. **D:** *pull.* This is a passive structure. The dentist pulls the wisdom teeth. The wisdom teeth are *pulled.* Passive voice is formed by using a form of the verb *be* + verb in past participle.

6. **D:** *approved the budget.* The sentence must continue with the same subject and format. The committee met, and *it* approved the budget. It is not correct to turn the second clause around as a passive structure, making the budget the subject. **A** has an incorrect verb structure because *have* cannot be followed by the verb in simple form. **C** would have no conjugated verb in the second clause of the sentence.

7. **A:** *Hardly the plane had.* When a sentence begins with one of the reversed order limiting words like *hardly,* the order is: limiting word + auxiliary + subject + verb. The correct order would be *Hardly had the plane landed.* . . .

8. **C:** *must have contributed.* This question deals with meaning as much as it deals with simple grammar. The present perfect construction with *should* means something much different than the same construction with *must.* *Should have contributed* means the person was supposed to contribute but did not. *Must have contributed* means that one can conclude logically that the person did contribute, which is more in line with the meaning of this sentence.

9. **A:** *to formalize.* The phrase *had better* is just like its alternate, *should,* and must be followed by the simple form of the verb: *had better formalize.*

10. **B:** *the board members turned their attention to the legal terms.* Because the sentence begins with the participial phrase *having been presented,* the subject of that clause must appear after the comma.

11. **B:** *not rarely.* The word *rarely* is negative and cannot be used with *not,* because that causes a double negative.

12. **B:** *he will be attending.* **A** is incorrect because *must* is a modal and must be followed by the simple form of the verb. **C** is incorrect because *because* must be followed by a clause while *because of* is followed by a noun or noun phrase. **D** is incorrect because the perfect construction requires a verb in the past participle as the main verb: *will have attended.*

13. **B:** *already to decide.* This sentence could have a positive or a negative meaning, and the correct answer would depend on which it is. If the sentence stated . . . . *has already decided,* that would be correct and would indicate that the Dean decided before now. The verb form *has decided* is present perfect. Or if the sentence were *has yet to decide* that would be correct and would have a negative meaning. A form of the verb *have* + *yet* + verb in the infinitive (*to* + verb) means that the Dean has not decided yet. It would also be correct as *has not yet decided* or *has not decided yet.*

14. **B:** *neither is the administration.* The structure for *neither* is *neither* + auxiliary verb + subject. **A** and **C** do not have an auxiliary verb at all, and **D** is a double negative — *not neither.*

15. **C:** *had submit.* The past perfect structure is used to indicate that one action occurred before another action. Thus, one clause will be in the past perfect, and the other must be in the simple past. This part of the sentence obviously happened after the other one and the correct verb would be *submitted.* The word *had* can be omitted because it appears with the first verb of the series.

16. **D:** *a committee be appointed to review the problem thoroughly.* After *requested that* or another phrase setting up the subjunctive form, the order is subject + *be* in simple form + verb in the past participle. **A** is incorrect because the verb *appointed* is a conjugated verb, making the committee the subject, whereas the context requires it to be in the passive voice. **B** is incorrect because the verb *make* is awkward and the adverb *thoroughly* does not seem to apply to the correct word, which would have to be a verb, adjective or adverb. **C** would also have a conjugated verb, which doesn't make sense.

17. **C:** *was striking.* The context is passive. The barge struck the pier. Thus the order of the verb phrase is form of *be* + verb in past participle: *was struck.*

18. **D:** *so do traditional companies.* It would also have been correct to say *traditional companies do too* or *traditional companies do as well.*

19. **B:** *a sufficient number of parts to its manufacturers in a timely manner.* The correct order is verb + direct object + *to* + indirect object + modifier of time or place.

20. **B:** *enough quickly.* The order is adjective or adverb + *enough,* or *enough* + noun. Since *quickly* is an adverb, the correct order is *quickly enough.*

21. **A:** *much. People* is a countable noun, and its modifier must be *many.*

22. **A:** *it planned.* In an embedded question, the order is question word + subject + verb.

23. **B:** *in.* The correct preposition for the floor of a building is *on.*

24. **A:** *a new textbook last year.* The correct order is verb + direct object + modifier

25. **C:** *a.* The language between the commas is a reduced relative clause. There must be a complete sentence before and after the commas, which there is: *The tube worm can live for hundreds of years.* The language between commas must have a word making it subordinate, such as: *which is a stationary.* A reduced relative clause is created by omitting the relative pronoun and verb — *which is.*

Reading Section

1. **B:** *live in.*

2. **B:** *to describe how the human body is host to a number of different harmful and harmless inhabitants and visitors.* This is the one answer that is general and does not misstate the author's purpose.

3. **A:** *mites are totally unavoidable, while lice may be avoidable.* In the second and third paragraphs, the passage indicates that one can avoid lice but not mites.

4. **A:** *embarrassment.*

5. **B:** *children's.* Substitute *children's* for the word *their,* and the sentence will make sense.

6. **B:** After the sentence *They are also microscopic, so they are invisible to the naked eye.* This sentence and the one that follows discuss the size of the mite, so it is logical that it would fit in this place.

7. **D:** *mite species.* The previous sentence discusses species of mites, and this sentence is a continuation. Substitute *other species of mites,* and it will make sense.

8. **A:** *nits.* The author states *lice, or nits,* which indicates that they are the same thing.

9. **B:** *somebody who removes lice professionally.*

10. **B:** *being host to insects and microbes is inevitable.* The entire passage indicates that one cannot avoid being host to certain visitors.

11. **B:** *Mites actually are beneficial because they remove dead skin particles from the body and habitat.* This is explained in the fourth paragraph.

12. **A:** *happen.*

13. **A:** *overwhelming.*

14. **B:** *The Causes and Effects of Sinkholes.* This is the only choice that is general enough and does not contain a misstatement.

15. **A:** *too much precipitation or not enough precipitation.* This is explained in the first paragraph.

16. **B:** *only occur where there are limestone caverns below the surface.* This is explained in the second paragraph.

17. **D:** *surface, sand, clay, and limestone.* This is explained in the second paragraph and in the illustration.

18. **A:** *lack of liquid.*

19. **A:** *discerning.*

20. **B:** *consumed.*

21. **A:** *air and water.* This is explained in the second sentence.

22. **A:** *one that opens in a yard and never expands. Harmless* means that it causes no harm.

23. **C:** *Initially successful, but later it failed.* This is explained in the last paragraph, where it indicates that the effort worked for a while.

24. **D:** *dinosaurs.* The noun to which it refers is in the first sentence.

25. **D:** *That dinosaurs were cold-blooded.* The passage begins by stating that a previous belief is no longer believed to be true.

26. **C:** *They found a fossil of a dinosaur's heart and discovered it had four chambers and one aorta.*

27. **C:** *are cold-blooded.* The other answer choices are specifically stated as not being true of reptiles.

28. **A:** *produce.*

29. **A:** *move faster and have greater endurance than reptiles.* This is stated in paragraph three.

30. **A:** *It is paradoxical that the dinosaur's name includes the word* lizard, *because now scientists believe it is not a lizard.*

31. **B:** *disorder.*

32. **B:** *ailment.* If you look back at what could be substituted for *which* in a sentence by itself, this is the logical answer.

33. **B:** *mud.*

34. **B:** *join.*

35. **A:** *soap.* This is explained in the first paragraph, which indicates that bile salts are detergents.

36. **A:** *paint.* This is explained in the first paragraph, where the word *which* indicates that it is defining the word.

37. **B:** *indigestion.* This is explained in the first paragraph.

38. **A:** *cholesterol-rich bile or a malfunctioning gallbladder.*

39. **B:** *inflame.*

40. **B:** *displace.*

41. **B:** *cystic duct.* This is explained in the fourth paragraph.

42. **A:** *excessive dieting.*

43. **B:** *a man of Pima Indian descent.*

44. **A:** *illustration.*

45. **B:** *gallbladder.*

Writing Section

Have your essay scored by a writing instructor or submit it to my Essay Grading Service, which is described in the "How to Use This Book" section. The scoring criteria appear at the beginning of the "Writing" chapter in Part III.

Practice Test 4

Listening Section

Part A

1. **D:** *Try new medicine and then have a blood test.*

2. **C:** *They hear it is almost as good as a former restaurant.*

3. **A:** *She thinks she should take it, but it's too time-consuming.*

4. **D:** *He was extremely frightened.*

5. **A:** *He is sick.*

6. **A:** *His father believes a well known school is better.*

7. **B:** *It's not pleasant.*

8. **A:** *He had a prior engagement.*

9. **A:** *Neither Helen nor the man could find the books.*

10. **A:** *The jury probably will not make a decision today.*

11. **C:** *Bill made a bad decision about a stock purchase.*

12. **A:** *He lost his job.*

13. **B:** *She is sleeping a lot but feels exhausted.*

14. **B:** *She writes messages that contain incorrect information.*

15. **A:** *He absolutely will not interview with the company.*

Part B

16. **B:** *The judge will require mediation.*

17. **B:** *That it involves an arbitrator.*

18. **A:** *He feels that the opponents are entrenched in an incorrect position.*

19. **D:** *That it often produces positive results.*

20. **C:** *To settle the case.*

21. **B:** *The mediator will separate the parties and carry settlement offers from one to the other.*

22. **B:** *She has been researching carcinogens for years.*

23. **C:** *She studies whether carcinogens in plastic wrap can get into food when heated in microwave ovens.*

24. **C:** *He read about her in a newspaper.*

25. **D:** *Eighteen years old.*

26. **B:** *She is very resolute.*

27. **A:** *A will.*

28. **C:** *A will is only activated upon death.*

29. **A:** *Access accounts and property while the grantor is alive.*

30. **B:** *It remains valid in the case of incapacity.*

31. **A:** *He is hesitant.*

32. **C:** *To write checks for medical care.*

33. **B:** *Ready.*

34. **C:** *Extended periods of drought.*

35. **B:** *Yes, he heard of it some years ago.*

36. **A:** *It is not known to be effective.*

37. **A:** *He thinks they should use it anyway.*

38. **C:** *Iodides are deposited, iodides merge with water droplets, ice crystals develop, and snow and rain develop.*

39. **C:** *Large convective clouds, which are precursors to storm clouds.*

40. **A:** *A foothold.*

Structure Section

1. **B:** *second only to.* This is an idiomatic expression.

2. **B:** *was foraged.* The progressive in the active voice would make sense, which would be *was foraging.*

3. **A:** *the tighter it became.* This is a double comparative sentence, and the order is *more* + {adjective or adjective+-*er*} . . . *more* + {adjective or adjective+-*er*}. It means that as one condition increases or changes, the other one does too.

4. **B:** *planning.* This is part of a noun phrase and should be a noun, *plan.*

5. **A:** *Due to her agility and speed.* The choices with *because* misuse grammatical rules. The rule is *because* + clause or *because of* + noun phrase. *Due to* means the same thing and is followed by a noun or noun phrase.

6. **A:** *it.* The relative pronoun *that* replaces the noun, so the pronoun *it* is repetitive and does not belong.

7. **A:** *that.* This is an idiomatic expression, and the order is *not until . . . that.*

8. **A:** *not best.* The superlative structure requires the definite article *the* because it is the one item that meets the definition. It should read *not the best.*

9. **D:** *in greater numbers.* This is an idiomatic expression.

10. **C:** *causing.* The sentence does not have a conjugated verb unless *causing* is changed to *caused.* The word *learned* is a past participle from a reduced relative clause — *that were learned.* So the subject of the sentence is *the issues* and after the relative clause appears the verb, *caused.*

11. **D:** *the message to all directors.* The order is subject + verb + direct object + *to* + indirect object. The other alternative is to omit the *to* and reverse the direct and indirect object — subject + verb + indirect object + direct object

12. **A:** *when black.* The article *a* is missing. Note that the sentence has an unusual structure because it begins with *only when.* For that reason, the word *will* is correct. The last verb structure in the sentence, *be closed down,* is in the passive voice and is correct.

13. **C:** *she has had.* The second clause must have a subject.

14. **B:** *accuse.* The verb is in the passive voice: *are sometimes accused* (*be* + verb in past participle).

15. **B:** *out of.* The idiomatic expression is *out of order,* which means not working.

16. **D:** *in way.* This is an idiomatic expression, *in the way.*

17. **D:** *did so in.* The phrase *did so* stands for *competed.* The first clause of the sentence is dependent, so there must be a conjugated verb in the second clause; in this case, it is an unusual conjugated verb, but it is one. The second answer choice is incorrect because it is in the wrong tense.

18. **A:** *completed.* It is part of a verb phrase with a modal, *could,* so it must be in simple form, *complete.*

19. **D:** *other.* The word *another* must be used with the singular countable noun *program. Other* would be used with noncountable nouns or plural countable nouns. Notice that the initial part of the sentence is correct. It is the same as saying *the fact that Allen had not completed. . . .* The word *Allen's* is possessive because it is followed by a gerund, *having. Completed* is in the past participle as part of that construction.

20. **B:** *requires.* The subject of the sentence is an infinitive, *to master,* and it takes a singular conjugated verb.

21. **A:** *enjoys.* The subject of the sentence is a *that* clause, which is singular, but it contains a plural noun, *investors.* The verb should be *enjoy* to match the plural noun within the clause.

22. **B:** *has not.* The first clause of the sentence is dependent, so the second must have a conjugated verb. The expression *the number of* is a singular concept, and you should not be confused by the plural noun after the preposition *of.*

23. **C:** *believe.* The entire sentence is in the passive voice, and that is why all the main verbs are in the past participle. This verb should be *believed.*

24. **A:** *be.* The verb phrase *had* + subject + verb in past participle means the same as *if* + subject + *had* + verb in past participle, so the correct construction would include *been.*

25. **A:** *who has sung.* This clause is a relative clause and thus requires a relative pronoun.

Reading Section

1. **A:** *affixed.*

2. **B:** *discharge.*

3. **B:** *different in that a* vent *involves rapid discharge while a* seep *involves slow discharge.* The author uses the two words in different contexts.

4. **C:** *from the same family but different species.*

5. **A:** *grows slower than the hot-water tube worm.* See paragraphs two and five, which distinguish between the growth rates of the two worms.

6. **A:** *complete.*

7. **A:** *lifetime.*

8. **C:** *boiling.*

9. **D:** *different in that one contains oily materials and the other contains hydrogen sulfide.*

10. **C:** *aneurysms that occur near the brain stem only.* The first paragraph explains that these aneurysms are dangerous to repair with surgery.

11. **A:** *aneurysms.* The noun is found in the previous sentence, and no other noun in the sentence could make sense.

12. **C:** *significant.*

13. **B:** *aneurysm.* The noun to which *one* refers actually appears two sentences before the reference.

14. **A:** *meandering.* The idea is that it moves slowly and deliberately towards its destination.

15. **A:** *removed.*

16. **B:** *a hernia.*

17. **D:** *hemorrhaging that results in death.* The first paragraph states that this can occur in 50 percent of patients.

18. B: *serve as a base for a blood clot to form.* This is explained in the second paragraph.

19. B: *in the upper thigh.* In the reading, it states that the femoral artery is in the groin area. The word "femoral" is related to femur, which is the thigh bone, and the groin area is where the thigh meets the hip area.

20. D: *separate the coil from the wire.* This is explained in the second paragraph. *After the coil is outside the catheter, a low voltage electrical current is applied, and the coil detaches at a preset solder point.*

21. C: *at a predetermined and prepared location on the wire.* The same sentence that answers question 20 says it is a preset location.

22. A: *longer and require more recuperation time than the new procedure.* This is explained in the last paragraph where it says: *The procedure lasts two hours, which is half as long as invasive surgery, and recovery time is generally limited to a few days instead of a few weeks.*

23. B: *is performed only at hospitals containing the required equipment and certified doctors.* This is also explained in the last paragraph where it says: *. . . is available in various hospitals where there are advanced neurology departments and specialists trained in the procedure.*

24. B: *carnivorous dinosaur.* Carnivorous means the same as meat-eating, which is stated in the first sentence.

25. B: *in addition to.*

26. A: *frightening.*

27. D: *surprising.*

28. A: *lived and hunted with others.* The first paragraph states that it is more astounding that the bones were found with other bones, because that indicates they were not loners.

29. A: *meat-eating dinosaurs lived alone.* The same sentences say that this discovery challenges the prior theory that they were loners.

30. C: *Giganotosaurus.*

31. B: *not closely related to Tyrannosaurus Rex.* The passage states that it is as close to T. Rex as a cat to a dog, which is not close.

32. A: *dismember.*

33. A: *victim.*

34. B: *combined.*

35. B: *thread.*

36. C: *it is more precise than previous techniques.* The passage indicates that they will have control, whereas they previously did not.

37. B: *electronic impulses could affect cells.* The first paragraph indicates that they have known this for a while.

38. **A:** *barraging.*

39. **B:** *open their walls to introduce medication.* The passage states that they have used electrical charges in an attempt to introduce foreign substances such as new drug treatments or genetic material.

40. **B:** *causes.*

41. **B:** *in the future.*

42. **A:** *researchers.* The noun to which *they* refers is in the previous sentence.

43. **C:** *specific.*

44. **D:** *tissues.* The passage indicates that *others* is a pronoun for *other tissues,* because it says: . . . *to activate particular tissues, whether they be muscle, bone, brain, or others.*

45. **B:** *place more than one chip in a single person.* The last sentence of the passage answers this question: *They believe that they will be able to implant multiple chips into a person to deal with one problem or more than one problem.*

Writing Section

Have your essay scored by a writing instructor or submit it to my Essay Grading Service, which is described in the "How to Use This Book" section. The scoring criteria appear at the beginning of the "Writing" chapter in Part III.

Practice Test 5

Listening Section

Part A

1. **B:** *They think they have seen both movies previously.*

2. **A:** *Ellen is likely to seek a degree in English.*

3. **B:** *Josh is taller now.*

4. **A:** *He is not participating in a study group this time.*

5. **C:** *It's probably the best choice available.*

6. **B:** *She is not able to go there much because of her work.*

7. **C:** *She will probably attend the University of North Florida.*

8. **A:** *The new employee is lazy.*

9. **B:** *Writing a paper.*

10. **B:** *Quit one class for another.*

11. **B:** *She has never been to the races.*

12. **A:** *That Nadia was going to work instead of Allison.*

13. **C:** *Christopher has quit attending.*

14. **A:** *He needs help but will not admit it.*

15. **C:** *Look at the book.*

Part B

16. **B:** *It has improved somewhat since 1998.*

17. **A:** *Healthy coral reefs cause the ocean water to be healthy.*

18. **C:** *Higher temperatures.*

19. **B:** *Algae are required for coral's health.*

20. **B:** *The government has spent money for research, education, and monitoring reefs.*

21. **B:** *In a hotel.*

22. **B:** *Only students of the intensive English program.*

23. **A:** *She looked at his identification card.*

24. **B:** *He needs a place with two bedrooms.*

25. **B:** *Benefits that his wife and child would enjoy.*

26. **A:** *Lack of air conditioning.*

27. **B:** *Because there is a natural flow, facilitated by the body itself.*

28. **C:** *Obtaining tissue for a biopsy.*

29. **A:** *The endoscope is uncomfortable.*

30. **D:** *A scalpel.*

31. **A:** *The capsule is an advance in science along the same lines as digital and wireless technology.*

32. **C:** *She has no prior knowledge of it.*

33. **A:** *Somebody of Ashkenazi Jewish descent.*

34. **B:** *The disease causes a protective material to disappear.*

35. **A:** *If her background is not the same as her husband's, then there is no chance they could pass on the disease.*

36. **C:** *Resigned.*

37. **A:** *Synthesizes the enzyme.*

Structure Section

1. **A:** *has received.* The first clause is in the passive voice in the present perfect, which is formed as follows: Subject + form of *have* + *been* + verb in past participle. The verb in this case should be *has been received.*

2. **A:** *that the company should.* The language between commas is parenthetical, so it should be ignored. After the verb *determined*, there should be a clause beginning with *that* plus a subject or with a subject alone. The third answer choice is incorrect because it omits the subject. The fourth answer choice is incorrect because it omits the definite article, *the.*

3. **B:** *an.* The correct sentence would include *is an*, because without *is*, there is no conjugated verb. Disregard the information between commas, and it will be clear that the subject is *owning a home* and the verb must be *is.*

4. **A:** *is.* Without it, there would be no conjugated verb. The entire *that* clause is the subject.

5. **D:** *should it.* This is an embedded question, and the order after the question word is normal sentence order, *it should.*

6. **B:** *have been.* This is a passive voice structure following a modal, and the order is modal + *have* + *been* + verb in past participle, *should have been submitted.*

7. **C:** *would had.* The simple form must always appear immediately after a modal. In this case, since the condition is in the past, the modal structure must be modal + *have* + verb in past participle, *would have had.*

8. **D:** *achieving.* There is no conjugated verb unless it is changed to *achieved.*

9. **A:** *are hesitant.* The first clause is dependent, so the second clause must have a conjugated verb, which this answer has.

10. **A:** *spending.* A conjugated verb is required. The clause beginning with *who* is a restrictive relative clause and should be ignored even though it has no commas around it. The subject is *attorneys,* and the verb should be *spend.*

11. **D:** *an extremely large fossil.* The order is article + (adverb) + adjective + noun.

12. **B:** *as oldest.* The superlative form must appear with a definite article, so the correct use would be *as the oldest.*

13. **B:** *of being.* The expression *in spite of* must appear together, unlike *despite,* which appears alone. After a preposition, the gerund is required.

14. **A:** *voted purchase.* When *vote* is followed by a verb as its complement, the verb must appear in the infinitive, *voted to purchase.*

15. **C:** *the children have been.* After a question word in an embedded question, the order is subject + verb. Note that the main verb in the sentence (which follows the subject *how long* and, therefore, is singular) is the verb *is.*

16. **B:** *had been.* The context of the sentence and the verb of the first clause is present, not past. Because this is a real condition (not unreal), the tense does not go one step further into the past.

17. **B:** *Jane decided.* The first clause is dependent so the second needs a subject and a conjugated verb. The other verb in that clause comes from a reduced *that* clause. *Jane decided (that) it was . . . .*

18. **B:** *to.* There is no conjugated verb in the sentence; instead there is a series of infinitives. The correct sentence would read *is to.*

19. **C:** *to swim.* After *warn,* the infinitive is used.

20. **D:** *before noon arrive.* The verb should not be broken up with the modifier. The modifier appears after verbs and complements. Technically this is a split infinitive, which some grammarians say should never occur, where the *to* and the rest of the verb are separated by something else. The TOEFL test will generally not test something technical like a split infinitive unless it is as awkward as this sentence.

21. **B:** *was obvious.* The sentence begins with a *that* clause and needs a conjugated verb.

22. **D:** *caused.* The clause requires a complete conjugated verb, which is in the past and is passive voice, *had been caused.*

23. **C:** *initiating.* This needs to be parallel with the verb after the word *first.*

24. **A:** *who could.* This is a relative clause.

25. **D:** *to lead.* The verbs are in a series and must be parallel, so *leading* would be correct.

Reading Answers

1. **C:** *it was defective for its first three years in space.* The end of the first paragraph deals with this issue.

2. **A:** *subject.*

3. **C:** *fury.*

4. **C:** *there was considerable excitement about the potential uses.* The first paragraph states that it was sent into space "amid huge hype and expectation."

5. **D:** *distorted.*

6. **C:** *light.*

7. **B:** *maintenance could be done by traveling astronauts.* The passage indicates that the astronauts opened the hatch that was installed for the purpose of repairing the Hubble.

8. **C:** *mechanics.* This is explained at the end of the first paragraph where it is explained that they arrived like roadside mechanics.

9. **C:** *developed a mathematical formula to measure speed and distances between galaxies.* This is explained in the last paragraph.

10. **B:** *named.*

11. **A:** *when viewing a distant galaxy through the Hubbell telescope, you are actually looking back in time.* This is explained in the middle of paragraph 2.

12. **A:** *a star.* In the reading it is stated that *Astronomers use* stars known as *Cepheid variables to measure distances in space."*

13. **A:** *its details could not be seen.* In the third paragraph, the following is stated: *Prior to Hubble, it was visible from traditional telescopes on earth, but its details were not ascertainable.*

14. **B:** *pouring.*

15. **A:** *water draining in a bathtub.* The reading refers to black holes as drains.

16. **B:** *migraine.*

17. **D.** *has a specific scientific cause, unlike a headache.* This is explained in the last sentence of paragraph one.

18. **D:** *is something some sufferers see before an attack.* This is explained in the second paragraph.

19. **D:** *expanded blood vessels.* The third paragraph deals with this issue.

20. **B:** *tightened blood vessels.* This is also explained in the third paragraph.

21. **B:** *augmented.*

22. **B:** *tend to fire in an unusual pattern when a migraine begins.* The firing of the neurons is explained in the fourth paragraph.

23. **A:** *using imaging devices that allow one to watch the neurons.* This is discussed in the fourth paragraph.

24. **A:** *neurons fire suddenly and follow a specific pattern when a migraine is coming.*

25. **B:** *moving in a specific order along the brain towards the brain stem like ripples of water.*

26. **B:** *The brain stem is the location of pain centers.*

27. **C:** *still do not know exactly what causes the pain.* At the end of the fourth paragraph, it is indicated that scientists are not certain how the pain is generated.

28. **B:** *a magnetic field.*

29. **C:** *New Evidence of How Migraines Are Formed.* This title is not too broad or too restrictive and does not contradict anything in the passage.

30. **B:** *can suffer physical changes in the brain and be in chronic pain.* This is explained in the last paragraph.

31. **B:** *Ben Franklin.* This is explained in the first paragraph.

32. **B:** *hanging.*

33. **A:** *they meet each other in the sky.*

34. **B:** *friction.* This is explained in the second paragraph.

35. **C:** *its approach can be felt by someone about to be struck.*

36. **A:** *the charge from the earth meets the charge from the cloud.* The passage indicates that when the two charges meet it results in an explosion of sound known as thunder.

37. **A:** *it travels horizontally first.* This is explained in the third paragraph.

38. **C:** *wrap themselves around other trees.* This is explained in the second paragraph as well as other places.

39. **A:** *while the fig trees may damage the host tree, they do not actually squeeze it.* The second paragraph also explains that while they surround the host tree, they do not really strangle it.

40. **C:** *suffocate.*

41. **B:** *grow from the top of a tree down to the ground.* This is explained in paragraph three.

42. **A:** *combine.*

43. **B:** *compost.*

44. **D:** *ominous.*

45. **B:** *framework.*

Writing Section

Have your essay scored by a writing instructor or submit it to my Essay Grading Service, which is described in the "How to Use This Book" section. The scoring criteria appear at the beginning of the "Writing" chapter in Part III.

Practice Test 6

Listening Section

Part A

1. **B:** *She had to leave.*

2. **C:** *He might go.*

3. **B:** *He means that Jim submitted his application late.*

4. **D:** *She paid less for books this semester than last semester.*

5. **D:** *If they organize, they will be able to complete the project.*

6. **C:** *Go home and get her student identification.*

7. **B:** *Leave the room.*

8. **B:** *She is very determined.*

9. **A:** *He was not able to purchase the slides.*

10. **B:** *She does not know whether she got the promotion.*

11. **A:** *He likes perfection.*

12. **A:** *He is not flexible.*

13. **C:** *She believes the landlord doesn't keep the property in good repair.*

14. **A:** *She is ill.*

15. **A:** *Take a cruise without his friends.*

Part B

16. **B:** *He's married and has three children.*

17. **B:** *The amount is less than $700,000 and owned jointly with his wife or with his wife as beneficiary.*

18. **B:** *Open and informing.*

19. **A:** *A joint trust.*

20. **C:** *A trust must go through probate while a will does not.*

21. **D:** *Because they own their assets in a way that they pass to the survivor.*

22. **B:** *Administration of a will.*

23. **A:** *The cost.*

24. **A:** *No, she would be less likely to suggest a trust.*

25. **B:** *Alcoholism seems to run in families.*

26. **B:** *It is known to occur in children of alcoholics even when they do not live together.*

27. **B:** *A hormone.*

28. **A:** *Only some people have the hormone in their bodies.*

29. **A:** *The alcoholic responds more strongly to beta-endorphin release.*

30. **D:** *It can be inherited but is not inherited by all family members.*

31. **C:** *No, because they may choose not to drink to excess.*

32. **D:** *She missed class.*

33. **B:** *A tort is a civil wrong punishable with money damages, and a crime is a criminal act punishable with criminal penalties.*

34. **C:** *Two weeks.*

35. **C:** *The driver would have done no wrong.*

36. **C:** *A wrong can be both a tort and a crime.*

37. **C:** *A man is walking down the street in the early evening and is killed by a car speeding with no lights on.*

38. **B:** *Read in order to prepare for the next class.*

Structure Section

1. **A:** *native to.* This is a reduced relative clause coming from *which is native to.* The fourth answer choice is incorrect because it contains a conjugated verb, whereas this clause is a dependent clause.

2. **B:** *year.* The modifier indicates that the noun should be plural, *years.*

3. **D:** *function.* Use the simple form after a modal.

4. **B:** *a former member.* This is a reduced relative clause, from *who was a former member.*

5. **C:** *them.* The knee is singular, and so this pronoun should be *it.*

6. **A:** *that has gained.* *One* is a pronoun for one bacterium. The expression is *the one that* + verb.

7. **C:** *is.* The subject is plural so the verb should be *are.*

8. **B:** *The study.* This is the subject of the sentence so the context indicates it should be a noun, and it needs a definite article.

9. **B:** *scholastically.* This word modifies the noun *ability,* so it must be an adjective *(scholastic),* not an adverb.

10. **B:** *a doctor performs.* The first part of the sentence is only a phrase, so this information is the subject and verb of the sentence.

11. **A:** *he wrote.* The pronoun *he* should not appear because it immediately follows the subject and is not part of a dependent clause.

12. **A:** *often the greatest fear.* The order is adverb + adjective + noun.

13. **D:** *grade.* This is a type of parallel structure construction. The verb *(grading)* must be in the same form as *determining.*

14. **A:** *a storm is expected.* This is passive voice.

15. **C:** *utilize.* After a preposition, the gerund of the verb must be used, *utilizing.*

16. **A:** *most famous.* Because the phrase is possessive *(Ernest Hemingway's),* it makes no sense to have a definite article or anything else before the adjective.

17. **C:** *moving.* There must be a conjugated verb in the sentence, *moved.*

18. **A:** *changing*. The gerund must be used after a preposition.

19. **B:** *a*. With the superlative, or a specific one or number, a definite article is required. The definite article is *the*.

20. **A:** *To become*. The sentence requires a subject, and in this case the subject is an infinitive.

21. **C:** *communicate*. This is the object of the verb *maintain* so it must be a noun, *communication*.

22. **A:** *working*. The clause in which this word appears is a dependent clause, so it cannot be a conjugated verb. It is also a reduced relative clause, coming from *who were working*.

23. **C:** *when*. Although there would have been other ways to correct this sentence, the only underlined word that could be changed is *when*. It will be correct if it is changed to *to*.

24. **A:** *it*. The first clause is a dependent clause, so the second must have a subject and a verb; because of the way it is structured, the pseudo subject *it* is required.

25. **A:** *the way*. After a transitive verb (one that takes a direct object), the direct object should appear.

Reading Section

1. **C:** *adding to the coin's value*. In the first paragraph it is explained that coin collectors consider errors interesting and study the type of error, because it can make a coin more valuable.

2. **A:** *more coins than an error on the planchet*. The passage states that the planchet is used only on one or a few coins, while the die is used on numerous coins.

3. **A:** *kinds of errors*. The sentence is: *Some errors will affect only one or a few coins, while others will affect all coins made at a given time*. The word *others* could be *other errors*. *Others* is a pronoun while *other* is an adjective.

4. **B:** *reduce*. To *detract* is to take away, so reduce is the closest choice.

5. **D:** *decreases the coin's value*. At the end of the first paragraph it is explained that cleaning is not good for a coin.

6. **C:** *metal*. This is explained in the second paragraph: *The die is then transferred to a metal pattern in order to create a master die*.

7. **D:** *the exact opposite of the coin's image*. In the second paragraph it states: *The die is a mirror image of the coin*.

8. **A:** *placed in a coin press*. In the second paragraph it states: *The dies, one for the front of the coin and one for the back, are placed in a coin press*.

9. **B:** *piece of metal that will become the coin*. The answer is in the second paragraph where it states: *The metal in the coin comes from a large metal piece called a planchet, which is used at room temperature rather than melted*.

10. **B:** *The planchet is the same temperature as the room.* This is stated in the same sentence shown in the answer for question 9.

11. **A:** *a collar.* At the end of the second paragraph it states that the metal flows up to the collar, which results in the reeded or flat edge on the coin.

12. **D:** *discoloration of the coin.* Choices A and C result from other kinds of errors. The only one that could come from the planchet is D.

13. **C:** *planchet is cut from the strip.* This is stated in the last sentence of the third paragraph.

14. **B:** *a raised line on the face of the coin.* The fifth paragraph states that *A die crack will result in a raised, irregular line on the coin metal above the normal surface of the coin, while a die break is a raised, irregular area of coin metal above the normal surface of the coin.* This, of course, is because the die is the mirror image of the coin.

15. **B:** *humans.* The other answers involve errors that are not in the die.

16. **D:** *one of over 100 species of agave.* This is explained in paragraph one, where it is indicated that neither octli nor mezcal was made with blue agave.

17. **A:** *the Aztecs used agave for something other than alcohol.* The author indicates that octli was not distilled, because distillation is a distinction between it and mezcal; likewise, it is explained that the difference between mezcal and tequila is that the latter is distilled twice. That is also what makes **D** incorrect. **A** is the only item that is not mentioned.

18. **A:** *the agave plant grows anywhere in the world.* This is the only choice that was not mentioned.

19. **A:** *occasionally.*

20. **B:** *juice.*

21. **B:** *the sweet liquid within the heart.* The last two sentences of the second paragraph make this clear.

22. **A:** *looks like the agave.* This is explained in the second paragraph.

23. **A:** *shredded.*

24. **A:** *mash.*

25. **C:** *They are cut in four pieces before being baked.* All three of the other answers are specifically contradicted in the passage.

26. **B:** *hose*

27. **B:** *keeping them in a dark room.* This is explained towards the beginning of the third paragraph.

28. **A:** *it undergoes a different process in each vat.*

29. **B:** *all of the agua miel is used in the end product.* The other answers are true. The reading says that only 10% of the liquid remains in use after processing.

30. **A:** *the jobs are differentiated, and great care is taken.* This is explained in the last paragraph.

31. **B:** *escaped.*

32. **A:** *freezing.* Even if you do not know the word *frigid* you should be able to imagine from the paragraph that it is extremely cold.

33. **A:** *ghastly.* Ghoulish and ghastly both mean frightening or horrible.

34. **C:** *spotted.*

35. **A:** *decoration.* A *tassel* is a decorative item that hangs from something, and may be found on draperies, clothing or other items.

36. **A:** *eyes.* The sentence indicates that a tassel hangs from *each of them*, which refers back to eyes in the previous phrase.

37. **A:** *loses an entire set at once.* This is explained at the beginning of the second paragraph.

38. **B:** *it has been difficult to observe the shark to any great degree.*

39. **A:** *sluggish.*

40. **A:** *dead animal flesh.* Carrion is listed among items the shark eats.

41. **B:** *a material that causes intoxication.* This is explained in paragraph three.

42. **B:** *dogs.* It was the dogs that were too intoxicated to walk.

43. **C:** *a type of parasite.*

44. **A:** *disfigurement.*

45. **B and C:** *milky* and *fogginess.*

Writing Section

Have your essay scored by a writing instructor or submit it to my Essay Grading Service, which is described in the "How to Use This Book" section. The scoring criteria appear at the beginning of the "Writing" chapter in Part III.

SCORING PRACTICE TESTS

For each of the six practice tests, calculate the total correct answers in the Listening, Structure, and Reading sections. Use the tables provided to convert the number of questions you answered correctly in each section into final scores.

Practice Test 1

		Listening, Structure, and Reading Scores			
Listening Number Correct	Listening Score	Structure Number Correct	Structure Score (not including essay)	Reading Number Correct	Reading Score
35	30	23	15	47	30
34	29	22	14	46	29
33	28	21	14	45	28
32	28	20	13	44	28
31	27	19	13	43	27
30	26	18	12	42	26
29	25	17	12	41	26
28	24	16	11	40	25
27	23	15	11	39	24
26	22	14	10	38	23
25	21	13	9	37	22
24	21	12	9	36	21
23	20	11	8	35	20
22	19	10	7	34	19
21	19	9	7	33	19
20	18	8	6	32	18
19	17	7	6	31	18
18	16	6	5	30	17
17	15	5	5	29	16
16	14	4	4	28	16
15	13	3	3	27	15

(continued)

Listening Number Correct	Listening Score	Structure Number Correct	Structure Score (not including essay)	Reading Number Correct	Reading Score
14	13	2	2	26	15
13	12	1	1	25	14
12	11	0	0	24	14
11	10			23	13
10	9			22	13
9	8			21	12
8	7			20	12
7	6			19	11
6	5			18	11
5	4			17	10
4	3			16	10
3	2			15	9
2	1			14	9
1	1			13	8
0	0			12	8
				11	7
				10	6
				9	6
				8	5
				7	5
				6	4
				5	3
				4	3
				3	2
				2	2
				1	1
				0	0

Scoring Your Essay

As explained in the Part III "Writing" chapter, the essay is scored on a scale from 0 to 6 in half-point increments. The score is determined by evaluating each of the following five elements:

1. Does the essay address the topic?

2. Is the essay organized?

3. Does the essay provide appropriate details to support the thesis?

4. Does the essay display proper use of language?

5. Does the essay show variety of structure and use of words?

A separate score is given for each of these five aspects of your essay. Each separate score can range from 0 to 6, in half-point increments. All five scores are then averaged in order to determine the overall score for your essay.

The essay score makes up half of the total Structure section score. This is why the Structure score in the previous chart has 15 points as a maximum. (On test day, when the computer calculates your results immediately after the exam, you can never get higher than a 15 on the Structure section. That number changes when your final test results arrive, because the essay score is added.)

Ask an English-speaking friend or a writing instructor to evaluate your essay. Or, if those options are not available, take advantage of my scoring service, which is explained in "How to Use This Book."

Evaluating Your Essay				
Addresses Topic	Organization	Supporting Details	Proper Language	Variety of Structure and Vocabulary
0	0	0	0	0
.5	.5	.5	.5	.5
1	1	1	1	1
1.5	1.5	1.5	1.5	1.5
2	2	2	2	2
2.5	2.5	2.5	2.5	2.5
3	3	3	3	3
3.5	3.5	3.5	3.5	3.5
4	4	4	4	4
4.5	4.5	4.5	4.5	4.5
5	5	5	5	5
5.5	5.5	5.5	5.5	5.5
6	6	6	6	6

Insert the total score from above (0–30): _____

Divide the total by 5 to get your raw score: _____

Convert your raw score using the following table.

Determining Your Writing Score	
Raw Score	**Converted Score**
6	15
5.5	13
5	11
4.5	10
4	9
3.5	7
3	6
2.5	4
2	3
1.5	2
1	1
.5	.5
0	0

Total Practice Test 1 Score

Section	Converted Score
Listening	_____
Structure	_____
Reading	_____
Writing	_____
TOTAL	_____

Practice Test 2

Listening, Structure, and Reading Scores					
Listening Number Correct	**Listening Score**	**Structure Number Correct**	**Structure Score (not including essay)**	**Reading Number Correct**	**Reading Score**
29	30	25	15	48	30
28	29	24	14	47	29

Listening Number Correct	Listening Score	Structure Number Correct	Structure Score (not including essay)	Reading Number Correct	Reading Score
27	28	23	13	46	29
26	27	22	12	45	28
25	26	21	12	44	28
24	25	20	11	43	27
23	24	19	11	42	26
22	23	18	10	41	26
21	21	17	10	40	25
20	20	16	9	39	24
19	19	15	9	38	23
18	18	14	8	37	22
17	17	13	8	36	21
16	16	12	7	35	20
15	15	11	7	34	19
14	14	10	6	33	19
13	13	9	6	32	18
12	12	8	5	31	18
11	11	7	5	30	17
10	10	6	4	29	16
9	9	5	4	28	16
8	8	4	3	27	15
7	7	3	3	26	15
6	6	2	2	25	14
5	5	1	1	24	14
4	4	0	0	23	13
3	3			22	13
2	2			21	12
1	1			20	12
0	0			19	11
				18	11
				17	10
				16	10

(continued)

361

Listening Number Correct	Listening Score	Structure Number Correct	Structure Score (not including essay)	Reading Number Correct	Reading Score
				15	9
				14	9
				13	8
				12	8
				11	7
				10	6
				9	6
				8	5
				7	5
				6	4
				5	3
				4	3
				3	2
				2	2
				1	1
				0	0

Scoring Your Essay

Evaluating Your Essay				
Addresses Topic	Organization	Supporting Details	Proper Language	Variety of Structure and Vocabulary
0	0	0	0	0
.5	.5	.5	.5	.5
1	1	1	1	1
1.5	1.5	1.5	1.5	1.5
2	2	2	2	2
2.5	2.5	2.5	2.5	2.5
3	3	3	3	3
3.5	3.5	3.5	3.5	3.5
4	4	4	4	4
4.5	4.5	4.5	4.5	4.5

Addresses Topic	Organization	Supporting Details	Proper Language	Variety of Structure and Vocabulary
5	5	5	5	5
5.5	5.5	5.5	5.5	5.5
6	6	6	6	6

Insert the total score for your essay (0–30): _____

Divide the total by 5 to get your raw score: _____

Convert your raw score using the following table.

Determining Your Writing Score	
Raw Score	Converted Score
6	15
5.5	13
5	11
4.5	10
4	9
3.5	7
3	6
2.5	4
2	3
1.5	2
1	1
.5	.5
0	0

Total Practice Test 2 Score

Section	Converted Score
Listening	_____
Structure	_____
Reading	_____
Writing	_____
TOTAL	_____

Practice Test 3

Listening, Structure, and Reading Scores					
Listening Number Correct	Listening Score	Structure Number Correct	Structure Score (not including essay)	Reading Number Correct	Reading Score
37	30	25	15	45	30
36	29	24	14	44	29
35	28	23	13	43	28
34	28	22	12	42	28
33	27	21	12	41	27
32	26	20	11	40	26
31	25	19	11	39	26
30	25	18	10	38	25
29	24	17	10	37	24
28	24	16	9	36	23
27	23	15	9	35	22
26	22	14	8	34	21
25	21	13	8	33	20
24	20	12	7	32	19
23	19	11	7	31	19
22	18	10	6	30	18
21	17	9	6	29	18
20	16	8	5	28	17
19	15	7	5	27	16
18	14	6	4	26	16
17	13	5	4	25	15
16	12	4	3	24	14
15	11	3	3	23	14
14	10	2	2	22	13
13	9	1	1	21	12
12	8	0	0	20	12
11	7			19	11
10	6			18	11
9	5			17	10

Listening Number Correct	Listening Score	Structure Number Correct	Structure Score (not including essay)	Reading Number Correct	Reading Score
8	4			16	10
7	4			15	9
6	3			14	9
5	3			13	8
4	2			12	8
3	2			11	7
2	1			10	7
1	1			9	6
0	0			8	6
				7	5
				6	4
				5	4
				4	3
				3	3
				2	2
				1	1
				0	0

Scoring Your Essay

Evaluating Your Essay				
Addresses Topic	Organization	Supporting Details	Proper Language	Variety of Structure and Vocabulary
0	0	0	0	0
.5	.5	.5	.5	.5
1	1	1	1	1
1.5	1.5	1.5	1.5	1.5
2	2	2	2	2
2.5	2.5	2.5	2.5	2.5
3	3	3	3	3
3.5	3.5	3.5	3.5	3.5

(continued)

Addresses Topic	Organization	Supporting Details	Proper Language	Variety of Structure and Vocabulary
4	4	4	4	4
4.5	4.5	4.5	4.5	4.5
5	5	5	5	5
5.5	5.5	5.5	5.5	5.5
6	6	6	6	6

Insert the total score for your essay (0–30): _____

Divide the total by 5 to get your raw score: _____

Convert your raw score using the following table.

Determining Your Writing Score	
Raw Score	Converted Score
6	15
5.5	13
5	11
4.5	10
4	9
3.5	7
3	6
2.5	4
2	3
1.5	2
1	1
.5	.5
0	0

Total Practice Test 3 Score

Section	Converted Score
Listening	_____
Structure	_____
Reading	_____
Writing	_____
TOTAL	_____

Practice Test 4

Listening, Structure, and Reading Scores					
Listening Number Correct	Listening Score	Structure Number Correct	Structure Score (not including essay)	Reading Number Correct	Reading Score
40	30	25	15	45	30
39	29	24	14	44	29
38	28	23	13	43	28
37	28	22	12	42	28
36	27	21	12	41	27
35	26	20	11	40	26
34	25	19	11	39	26
33	25	18	10	38	25
32	24	17	10	37	24
31	24	16	9	36	23
30	23	15	9	35	22
29	23	14	8	34	21
28	22	13	8	33	20
27	21	12	7	32	19
26	21	11	7	31	19
25	20	10	6	30	18
24	19	9	6	29	18
23	18	8	5	28	17
22	17	7	5	27	16
21	16	6	4	26	16
20	15	5	4	25	15
19	15	4	3	24	14
18	14	3	3	23	14
17	14	2	2	22	13
16	13	1	1	21	12
15	12	0	0	20	12
14	11			19	11

(continued)

Listening Number Correct	Listening Score	Structure Number Correct	Structure Score (not including essay)	Reading Number Correct	Reading Score
13	11			18	11
12	10			17	10
11	10			16	10
10	9			15	9
9	9			14	9
8	8			13	8
7	7			12	8
6	6			11	7
5	5			10	7
4	4			9	6
3	3			8	6
2	2			7	5
1	1			6	4
0	0			5	4
				4	3
				3	3
				2	2
				1	1
				0	0

Scoring Your Essay

Evaluating Your Essay				
Addresses Topic	Organization	Supporting Details	Proper Language	Variety of Structure and Vocabulary
0	0	0	0	0
.5	.5	.5	.5	.5
1	1	1	1	1
1.5	1.5	1.5	1.5	1.5
2	2	2	2	2

Addresses Topic	Organization	Supporting Details	Proper Language	Variety of Structure and Vocabulary
2.5	2.5	2.5	2.5	2.5
3	3	3	3	3
3.5	3.5	3.5	3.5	3.5
4	4	4	4	4
4.5	4.5	4.5	4.5	4.5
5	5	5	5	5
5.5	5.5	5.5	5.5	5.5
6	6	6	6	6

Insert the total score for your essay (0–30): _____

Divide the total by 5 to get your raw score: _____

Convert your raw score using the following table.

Determining Your Writing Score	
Raw Score	Converted Score
6	15
5.5	13
5	11
4.5	10
4	9
3.5	7
3	6
2.5	4
2	3
1.5	2
1	1
.5	.5
0	0

Total Practice Test 4 Score

Section	Converted Score
Listening	_____
Structure	_____
Reading	_____
Writing	_____
TOTAL	_____

Practice Test 5

Listening, Structure, and Reading Scores					
Listening Number Correct	Listening Score	Structure Number Correct	Structure Score (not including essay)	Reading Number Correct	Reading Score
37	30	25	15	45	30
36	29	24	14	44	29
35	28	23	13	43	28
34	28	22	12	42	28
33	27	21	12	41	27
32	26	20	11	40	26
31	25	19	11	39	26
30	25	18	10	38	25
29	24	17	10	37	24
28	24	16	9	36	23
27	23	15	9	35	22
26	22	14	8	34	21
25	21	13	8	33	20
24	20	12	7	32	19
23	19	11	7	31	19
22	18	10	6	30	18
21	17	9	6	29	18
20	16	8	5	28	17
19	15	7	5	27	16

Listening Number Correct	Listening Score	Structure Number Correct	Structure Score (not including essay)	Reading Number Correct	Reading Score
18	14	6	4	26	16
17	13	5	4	25	15
16	12	4	3	24	14
15	11	3	3	23	14
14	10	2	2	22	13
13	9	1	1	21	12
12	8	0	0	20	12
11	7			19	11
10	6			18	11
9	5			17	10
8	4			16	10
7	4			15	9
6	3			14	9
5	3			13	8
4	2			12	8
3	2			11	7
2	1			10	7
1	1			9	6
0	0			8	6
				7	5
				6	4
				5	4
				4	3
				3	3
				2	2
				1	1
				0	0

Scoring Your Essay

Evaluating Your Essay				
Addresses Topic	Organization	Supporting Details	Proper Language	Variety of Structure and Vocabulary
0	0	0	0	0
.5	.5	.5	.5	.5
1	1	1	1	1
1.5	1.5	1.5	1.5	1.5
2	2	2	2	2
2.5	2.5	2.5	2.5	2.5
3	3	3	3	3
3.5	3.5	3.5	3.5	3.5
4	4	4	4	4
4.5	4.5	4.5	4.5	4.5
5	5	5	5	5
5.5	5.5	5.5	5.5	5.5
6	6	6	6	6

Insert the total score for your essay (0–30): _____

Divide the total by 5 to get your raw score: _____

Convert your raw score using the following table.

Determining Your Writing Score	
Raw Score	Converted Score
6	15
5.5	13
5	11
4.5	10
4	9
3.5	7
3	6
2.5	4
2	3

Raw Score	Converted Score
1.5	2
1	1
.5	.5
0	0

Total Practice Test 5 Score

Section	Converted Score
Listening	
Structure	
Reading	
Writing	
TOTAL	

Practice Test 6

Listening, Structure, and Reading Scores					
Listening Number Correct	Listening Score	Structure Number Correct	Structure Score (not including essay)	Reading Number Correct	Reading Score
38	30	25	15	45	30
37	29	24	14	44	29
36	28	23	13	43	28
35	28	22	12	42	28
34	27	21	12	41	27
33	26	20	11	40	26
32	25	19	11	39	26
31	25	18	10	38	25
30	24	17	10	37	24
29	24	16	9	36	23
28	23	15	9	35	22

(continued)

Listening Number Correct	Listening Score	Structure Number Correct	Structure Score (not including essay)	Reading Number Correct	Reading Score
27	22	14	8	34	21
26	21	13	8	33	20
25	20	12	7	32	19
24	19	11	7	31	19
23	18	10	6	30	18
22	17	9	6	29	18
21	17	8	5	28	17
20	16	7	5	27	16
19	15	6	4	26	16
18	14	5	4	25	15
17	13	4	3	24	14
16	13	3	3	23	14
15	12	2	2	22	13
14	11	1	1	21	12
13	10	0	0	20	12
12	10			19	11
11	9			18	11
10	9			17	10
9	8			16	10
8	7			15	9
7	6			14	9
6	5			13	8
5	5			12	8
4	4			11	7
3	3			10	7
2	2			9	6
1	1			8	6
0	0			7	5
				6	4
				5	4

Listening Number Correct	Listening Score	Structure Number Correct	Structure Score (not including essay)	Reading Number Correct	Reading Score
				4	3
				3	3
				2	2
				1	1
				0	0

Scoring Your Essay

Evaluating Your Essay				
Addresses Topic	Organization	Supporting Details	Proper Language	Variety of Structure and Vocabulary
0	0	0	0	0
.5	.5	.5	.5	.5
1	1	1	1	1
1.5	1.5	1.5	1.5	1.5
2	2	2	2	2
2.5	2.5	2.5	2.5	2.5
3	3	3	3	3
3.5	3.5	3.5	3.5	3.5
4	4	4	4	4
4.5	4.5	4.5	4.5	4.5
5	5	5	5	5
5.5	5.5	5.5	5.5	5.5
6	6	6	6	6

Insert the total score for your essay (0–30): _____

Divide the total by 5 to get your raw score: _____

Convert your raw score using the following table.

Determining Your Writing Score	
Raw Score	**Converted Score**
6	15
5.5	13
5	11
4.5	10
4	9
3.5	7
3	6
2.5	4
2	3
1.5	2
1	1
.5	.5
0	0

Total Practice Test 6 Score

Section	Converted Score
Listening	_____
Structure	_____
Reading	_____
Writing	_____
TOTAL	_____

The CDs that come with this book help you to practice for the Listening section of the TOEFL test. The CDs let you hear the conversations and speeches that are included in the Listening section of each practice test, as well as in the section of Part III that provides sample listening questions.

These are audio CDs only; they do not create visual images on your computer screen. In Part IV and in this appendix I have indicated which CD tracks to listen to when taking each practice test. This appendix includes the text of the conversations, speeches, and questions that make up the practice listening exams. While you take the practice exams, do not refer to this appendix. Use it only as a resource if you have trouble understanding what is being said.

Practice Listening Exercise (Part III, "Listening Section")

CD A, Track 1

1. **Woman:** Have you seen the report on changes in the university administration?

   Man: I looked it over briefly, but I didn't have time to study it.

   Woman: I can leave it for you to review later if you'd like.

   Narrator: What does the man say about the report?

2. **Man:** What happened to your car? It didn't have that huge dent yesterday, did it?

   Woman: You wouldn't believe it. It was hit by a school bus. I saw it, but the driver denied it. My paint was on its bumper.

   Man: What are you going to do? The school's insurance should pay for it.

   Narrator: What does the woman say about her car?

3. Man: We're going to have a new teacher in astronomy — Mr. Adams. Know anything about him?

Woman: A graduate student in physics, and quite sure of himself, but he's never taught before.

Man: Oh, great. I guess it's going from bad to worse.

Narrator: What does the woman imply about Mr. Adams?

4. Woman: Did you see Thalía singing last night on Univision? She did the theme song from her new soap. I know you really like to watch her.

Man: No, I would have if I had known about it. When does the new soap start?

Woman: Aha! I knew you couldn't resist.

Narrator: What do the speakers imply about Thalía?

5. Man: If I had only prepared more, I could have done better on the exam.

Woman: I thought you had done well.

Man: Yeah, I did, but not well enough.

Narrator: What does the man imply about the exam?

6. Woman: I wish Jane hadn't heard about the surprise. I tried so hard to carry it off.

Man: She was very grateful anyway. It was a nice thing to do.

Woman: I know, but it would have been even more fun if she hadn't found out.

Narrator: What does the woman imply about Jane?

7. Woman: No sooner had I turned in the paper than I remembered the answer to number 8.

Man: That's not as bad as what I did. I skipped one answer, so I put answers on the wrong line all the way down. By the time I realized it, I didn't have time to fix it.

Woman: Oh, that certainly is worse.

Narrator: What is the man's problem?

8. **Man:** Never have I seen such an interesting documentary. You know, the one about mummies.

Woman: That's an understatement.

Narrator: What do the speakers imply about the documentary?

9. **Woman:** I can't stop thinking about that terrible accident and what those children went through.

Man: Don't remind me.

Narrator: What do the speakers say about the accident?

10. **Man:** I can't figure out how Brenda knew how to fix the car.

Woman: She used to work in a repair shop.

Narrator: What does the woman say about Brenda?

11. **Woman:** I'm not sure how to deal with this. Should I tell the authorities or forget about it?

Man: How could you question it? You know there's no choice.

Woman: You're right. I'll make the call in the morning.

Narrator: What is the woman's problem?

12. **Man:** Wouldn't you rather take a break now? We've been at it for hours.

Woman: I'm beat, too. Let's get something to eat.

Man: We'll be able to concentrate with a little nutrition.

Narrator: What do the speakers mean?

13. **Woman:** Why won't you let Heather find herself? You can't make her decisions forever.

Man: I'm just not ready to let go, to admit that she's an adult now.

Woman: Well she is, and I think she is ready to show it.

Narrator: What does the woman suggest that the man do?

14. **Man:** I need to talk to you. I'm going into the hospital for a few days. You'll need to take over management.

Woman: Oh, I'm sorry. Sure, I'll be happy to help. But I hope you will return as good as ever very soon.

Man: I'm optimistic. But I know you'll take care of things one way or the other.

Narrator: What do the speakers mean?

15. **Man:** Don't bring up the topic we discussed last night while Jeff is here. He doesn't agree with the decision at all.

Woman: I'd like to hear his point of view. The subject isn't closed yet.

Man: You'll be sorry.

Narrator: What does the man mean about Jeff?

Practice Test I

Part A

CD A, Track 2

1. **Man:** I thought you had already been accepted at the university.

Woman: If I had I certainly wouldn't be still submitting applications. But I'm not giving up yet.

Man: There's still plenty of time.

Narrator: What does the woman mean?

2. **Woman:** I haven't been able to decide which class to take. The topics in basic linguistics are interesting, but I don't care for the professor.

Man: Why not take the literature class? Professor Stafford is teaching it.

Woman: Is she really? That's an idea.

Narrator: What will the woman probably do?

3. **Woman:** This computer, which has the most RAM and speed of all the products, also has a good price.

Man: I'm not sure. I don't recognize the brand name.

Woman: It's manufactured by the same company as this one, but it's sold under a different name.

Narrator: What does the woman suggest that the man do?

4. **Man:** I was wondering what happened to the application I submitted to build a fence in my backyard.

Woman: The architectural control committee was disbanded by the board, so there is nobody to approve it. You'll need to wait till the next election.

Man: I think the rules will allow me to consider it approved since it hasn't been disallowed.

Narrator: What does the man mean?

5. **Man:** You don't seem pleased.

Woman: I can't believe my advisor told me to drop trigonometry. I haven't had a chance yet to show that I can do it.

Man: Well, you don't have to do what your advisor says. It's just advice, isn't it?

Narrator: What is the woman's problem?

6. **Woman:** This computer has received good reviews, hasn't it?

   Man: It used to. But lately it's been looked down upon. Service is the issue, I think.

   Woman: That's the most important thing of all.

   Narrator: What does the man mean?

7. **Woman:** I haven't seen you at the gym lately. Are you still working out?

   Man: I've been out of town a lot, and I'm really out of shape.

   Woman: It's not too late to get back into it.

   Narrator: What does the man mean?

8. **Man:** I saw a program last night about mummies found in very cold or very dry areas, like high mountains. It was unbelievable.

   Woman: I thought mummies were created intentionally.

   Man: Me too, but these were created naturally with the protection from the elements caused by the extreme cold or extreme dryness.

   Narrator: What are the speakers talking about?

9. **Woman:** Never before have I been so insulted. I'm not going to buy any car from them.

   Man: What happened? I thought he explained things okay.

   Woman: He paid no attention to me and only looked at you. He thought I couldn't get it.

   Narrator: What does the woman mean?

10. **Man:** Okay, your eyes are fine. Take this form over to that counter and fill it out with the pencil provided.

    Woman: Okay, then what?

Man: Give it to the man at that desk; he'll take your old license and your money.

Narrator: What is the woman probably doing?

11. **Woman:** You haven't had much success trying to convince the buyers to let you stay for a while after closing, have you?

Man: On the contrary, they called last night and agreed to it.

Narrator: What had the woman assumed about the man?

12. **Woman:** I wish I hadn't taken that job. Now I've got to cancel the trip.

Man: Can't you just ask for time off?

Woman: I think that would be frowned upon.

Narrator: What is the woman's problem?

13. **Man:** Celine Dion is taking a hiatus from her career because she wants to spend time with her husband.

Woman: He's quite a bit older than she is, isn't he?

Man: Yes, and I imagine that her concerts took her away from home a lot.

Narrator: What do the speakers imply about Celine Dion?

14. **Man:** We updated our computer billing system last week. Now there's a problem with the system.

Woman: That happened in our office, too. Sometimes I think updating technology is a waste of time.

Man: You take one step forward and two back.

Narrator: What does the man mean?

15. Woman: Please return this book to the shelf while you're up.

Man: Sure. Anything else?

Woman: Well, I could use the volume of Britannica with the letter R.

Narrator: What will the man probably do?

Part B

CD A, Track 3

Narrator: Listen to the following discussion between an attorney and client.

Woman: I hope you can help me with this. I'm not sure what to do. You specialize in elder law, right? What is elder law?

Man: Sure. I am certified by the Bar in that area. It is really a combination of several areas of law, including regular matters like real estate and estate planning, with special issues involving older people. It can also include financial assistance for nursing home residents as well as helping out in the case of abuse.

Woman: Well, uh, my problem involves my grandmother. She has been diagnosed with Alzheimer's. She seems okay right now, at least most of the time. But sometimes she gets really confused. I go to school, and I've been leaving her at home. The other day I came home and she'd put on water for tea and forgotten about it. The pot was completely empty and still on high. I'm worried about her.

Man: Well, is she still aware of who you are? Does she know what she owns?

Woman: Oh, yeah. She, uh, really, her problem is just beginning. Most of the time she's fine. She just forgets. Sometimes she gets a little irritable.

Man: Has she signed a durable power of attorney to you?

Woman: What's that?

Man: A document that assigns power to a person, so the person can make decisions, sign documents, and take care of everything for the incapacitated person. We suggest that everybody sign a durable power of attorney while they are competent. Otherwise, a guardianship would be needed, and it's not a pleasant way to handle things. "Durable" means it'll remain valid even if later she loses her capacity.

Woman: Okay, I'm sure she'll sign one. How do we do that?

Man: We'll make another appointment. Bring her in. I need to talk to her to see that she understands what it is and is willing to sign it. We'll also talk about documents to handle health care decisions. Next, you're going to have to make a decision about what to do with her. You can probably keep her at home for a while, but you need to do something to keep her safe. You may consider a day facility for people with Alzheimer's or dementia. She would be safe during the day there. Eventually, she may need to enter an adult living facility. You just may not be able to keep her if it progresses, and you can't feel guilty about that. There may be a time that such a facility is better for her. But for now, I think it's great that you are taking care of her. She is very lucky.

16. **Narrator:** What are the speakers discussing?

17. **Narrator:** Why does the lawyer require a meeting with the grandmother?

18. **Narrator:** What did the woman describe as an example of the grandmother's failing capacity?

19. **Narrator:** Which of the following is not an example of Elder Law?

20. **Narrator:** According to the man, a power of attorney will do which two of the following?

21. **Narrator:** What does the man suggest for the grandmother's safety?

22. **Narrator:** What does the man imply?

CD A, Track 4

Narrator: Listen to the following talk about cabbage.

Woman: Today, we continue talking about vegetable and fodder plants. We spoke of other types of these, including kale and collards, previously. Today we will review what is normally referred to as cabbage in common conversation.

Cabbage is a common vegetable native to England and northwestern France but now grown in many parts of Europe, Asia, and the American continents. There are three kinds of cabbage, all with the same basic characteristic: The leaves grow very close together, forming a hard, round head. The three types of cabbage are white, savoy, and red. While the white and red cabbages have prominent veins in their leaves, savoy has wrinkled and blistered leaves. All forms of cabbage have succulent leaves covered with a waxy coating. They are low in calories, have little fat, and are an excellent source of ascorbic acid, minerals, and bulk, which helps digestion.

Cabbage seeds are quite small. Farmers normally sow the seeds in rows that are about 36 inches apart. After young plants have sprouted, the rows are thinned to allow a space of 18 to 24 inches between plants.

Cabbage is a biennial, meaning that it grows vegetatively one season, and its flowering and seed production occurs in the second season, after which the plant dies. Cabbage plants grow best in mild to cool climates, although they will tolerate frost and maybe even colder climates. Very hot weather affects the quality of the cabbage and impairs growth.

Please read the materials provided, and then we will discuss brussels sprouts, cauliflower, and broccoli.

23. **Narrator:** According to the speaker, what is a biennial?

24. **Narrator:** According to the speaker, where was cabbage originally found?

25. **Narrator:** According to the speaker, what is the main difference between the types of cabbage mentioned?

26. **Narrator:** According to the speaker, which of the following is not a characteristic of all cabbage types?

27. **Narrator:** Which type of plant does the speaker say was discussed previously?

CD A, Track 5

Narrator: Listen to the following discussion about a new type of camera.

First Man: This camera is special; it does much more than just photograph things. See, it looks normal enough, it's smaller than a regular video camera, and it doesn't weigh much, but you can use it to photograph the unseen. Do you know what I mean by that?

Woman: It photographs through solids.

First Man: That's right, it's a technological breakthrough that can scan objects as deep as 25 feet underground or inside walls. It works much like radar.

Second Man: How does it do that?

First Man: It's thermal. That means it can make distinctions based on the composition of different materials underground. Does that sound useful? Can anybody tell us how this could be used?

Woman: Looking for bodies underground?

First Man: Actually, yes, that is one way it's useful. It's been used to study how soldiers died in the United States Civil War. Thermal archaeology, it's called. Scientists studied a prison camp cemetery where they had always thought that many, many prisoners died of malnutrition and exposure. They found instead that many of the prisoners died of dysentery, not mistreatment, and they found that there were significantly fewer bodies than previously thought.

Woman: It's unbelievable that they could tell all that from a photograph through dirt.

First Man: It is, but the scientists were able to conclude what happened because of this camera. There are many possible uses, and historians should be able to obtain all kinds of information that they couldn't get before.

Second Man: Have they successfully used it on anything else?

First Man: Yes. Archaeologists have obtained information on a bloody Civil War battle in Tennessee in 1862. They have even studied a culture that lived in 1200 A.D. on the same spot as that Civil War battle; they found the culture's remains underneath evidence of the battle. Scientists have also determined the agricultural terrain in Egypt 2000 years ago, and they've found polar bear dens beneath the snow. And the same technology can be used to film night battles, locate leaking water within rock walls, and navigate smoky buildings. It does not replace good old-fashioned digging with a shovel and brush, but it narrows down the area and provides a lot of help.

28. **Narrator:** How does the man describe the physical features of the camera?

29. **Narrator:** What is the talk mainly about?

30. **Narrator:** Regarding the Civil War prison camp site that was studied, what does the man imply that the researchers learned?

31. **Narrator:** What does the man say about the culture that existed in the year 1200 A.D.?

32. **Narrator:** Which of the following was not stated as an example of uses of the technology?

CD A, Track 6

Narrator: Listen to the following discussion between two students.

Woman: I can't stand it. How did I ever end up here in this old dormitory? I was sure I had been approved for the new building.

Man: What do you mean? They switched you?

Woman: Yeah, that's right. I applied for the new dorm. I gave a deposit. They took the deposit. Then I showed up and they said it was never guaranteed that I would get it. It was just a request.

Man: That's annoying. But what's wrong with it? It looks okay.

Woman: The new buildings have central heat and air. These have window units, and they don't work well. It's sweltering in here. Bananas ripen in an hour. I run the air for hours, and it seems to get hotter.

Man: Are you going to do anything about it?

Woman: I filed a complaint, but it seems they don't care. I'm stuck.

33. Narrator: What had the woman assumed?

34. Narrator: What does the woman indicate is the biggest problem with the old dormitory?

35. Narrator: What does the woman give as an example of the temperature problem?

Practice Test 2

Part A

CD A, Track 7

1. Man: We're way over budget on this project.

Woman: Somebody must have miscalculated the cost of the temporary staff.

Narrator: What does the woman say about the project?

2. Woman: I thought you weren't going to be able to attend the seminar.

Man: I wouldn't have if my employer hadn't paid all the expenses.

Narrator: What does the man say about his ability to attend the conference?

3. Man: Who broke the copy machine?

Woman: I don't know. It was jammed when I tried it.

Man: It bugs me when somebody does that and just leaves it that way.

Narrator: What does the man imply?

4. Woman: When was the new administrator chosen?

Man: I'm not sure, but it was announced yesterday late in the afternoon.

Woman: I don't think proper procedure was followed.

Narrator: What does the man mean?

5. Man: I hear Ms. Nelson is an excellent professor.

Woman: She's really good at explaining difficult concepts.

Man: I think I'm going to try to switch sections.

Narrator: What is the man probably going to do?

6. Woman: Did you enjoy the exhibit?

Man: It was okay, but I wish we hadn't been so rushed. I didn't get to spend as much time in some areas as I had hoped.

Woman: We can go back again next week.

Narrator: What does the man mean?

7. Woman: No sooner had the paramedics arrived than they rushed into the house.

Man: Why, what happened?

Woman: I don't really know. The people who live there have a couple of kids and an older relative living with them.

Narrator: What does the woman say about the paramedics?

8. **Man:** I'm thinking of going to the library tonight to get started on the research.

   Woman: I was thinking of doing that, too.

   Man: You want to grab a bite to eat and go together?

   Narrator: What does the man suggest the woman do?

9. **Man:** You're going on the cruise to Nassau, aren't you?

   Woman: I wish I could, but I've got to finish a project.

   Narrator: What does the woman say about going on the cruise?

10. **Woman:** Because of her health problems, I don't think Nancy can keep up this pace.

    Man: She seems to have so much energy.

    Woman: She's pushing too hard, and it's wearing on her.

    Narrator: What does the woman imply about Nancy?

11. **Man:** I don't understand Professor Winger. He's making us do another paper.

    Woman: You just wrote one a week ago, didn't you?

    Man: Yeah, and the way he presented that one, we all thought that was the term paper.

    Narrator: What does the man imply about Professor Winger?

12. **Woman:** If you see me doing this wrong, would you please point it out to me?

    Man: Sure, but you seem to be doing just fine.

    Woman: I keep having trouble with the final calculations.

    Narrator: What does the woman ask the man to do?

13. Man: I don't know what to do. I just feel lousy, but I don't know why.

Woman: Why not go to the clinic and get checked out?

Man: I guess I should.

Narrator: What will the man probably do?

14. Man: You live in the apartments on 34th Street, don't you?

Woman: I used to, but I moved.

Narrator: What does the woman mean?

15. Woman: Please don't call me until noon. I'm not going to get to bed until late.

Man: Why don't you just call me when you wake up?

Woman: Okay, if you'll be home.

Narrator: What does the man suggest that the woman do?

Part B

CD A, Track 8

Narrator: Listen to the following conversation about a computer program.

Man: Can you help me with this computer program? I'm trying to create a report, and I can't figure it out.

Woman: Show me what you've done. Have you written it down?

Man: No, I haven't. But I remember. Let's see, first I clicked reports. Then I chose, uh, I chose budget. Or was it profit and loss?

Woman: Okay, the first thing you need to do is write down what steps you take. That's the only way to either do the same thing or not do the same thing if it's not working.

Man: I know, you're right. Alright, let's try budget. I wrote it down. Okay, click budget comparison. No, budget report.

Woman: We'll start with budget comparison. Let's choose this, and this, and that. Got 'em?

Man: Got 'em.

Woman: What's the date range? Want to choose last month to see?

Man: Yeah, okay, I wrote it down. Wow, that's it! You got it. Why couldn't I do that?

Woman: You know what I'm going to say.

Man: Right, I couldn't have repeated it if I hadn't written it down.

16. **Narrator:** What are the speakers talking about?

17. **Narrator:** What does the woman advise the man to do?

18. **Narrator:** What is the man likely to do the next time he has a computer problem?

19. **Narrator:** Is the man probably going to be able to repeat the procedure that the woman showed him?

CD A, Track 9

Narrator: Listen to the following talk about Steven Crane.

Man: Today, we continue our discussion of nineteenth-century authors. Steven Crane had the great fortune to write two extremely important works before reaching the age of 22. He lived only until age 28 but is as well known and well respected as many more prolific authors with many more years of experience.

Crane is known for his ability to combine realism and symbolism in a unique manner. But it has been said that he wasted his genius by living hard, trying to pack his life with experiences, including too many unhealthy ones. He seemed to believe that he had to experience what he wrote about first-hand. He risked his life by placing himself among bandits in Mexico, artillery fire in Cuba and Greece, and a shipwreck off the coast of Florida.

He described himself as lazy, indicating that he wrote only when he had to. He was driven to write, he said. When the muse hit him, he would rapidly write an entire story or a fragment that he would use with something else in the future. For example, he wrote a story about a sea voyage before he experienced the shipwreck. The story wasn't published at the time, because no magazine would take it. But the realistic story entitled "The Open Boat," which was written about the shipwreck he actually experienced, was considered a masterpiece, and the actual facts were interspersed with brilliant symbolism.

Crane wrote "The Open Boat" to describe his experience after the shipwreck. The realistic account relives the 30-hour search for shore in a 10-foot dinghy after the wreck. The book begins with the sentence, "None of them knew the colour of the sky," describing the point of view of the four men in the boat. The jerky, short sentence structure helped describe the feelings of the men in the boat.

Crane's novel, *The Red Badge of Courage,* was a best seller in the U.S. and England and gave him immediate fame. While "The Open Boat" is a factual account, *The Red Badge of Courage* is fiction. Critics were shocked to learn that Crane was born after the war about which he wrote, because the description is so realistic.

Crane also wrote a series of stories called *The Bowery Tales,* consisting of "Maggie, a Girl of the Streets" and other stories. It is a realistic account of poor people living in misery.

The short stories that you'll read begin with *The Bowery Tales* and end with "The Open Boat." Look for symbolism and realism as well as parallels among the works. We will discuss them in more detail in future classes.

20. **Narrator:** According to the speaker, which of the following is true about Stephen Crane?

21. **Narrator:** What does the speaker imply that Crane did?

22. **Narrator:** According to the speaker, how did Crane write?

23. **Narrator:** How does the speaker contrast "The Open Boat" and *The Red Badge of Courage*?

CD A, Track 10

Narrator: Listen to the following talk about termites

Woman: These are termites: Cellulose-eating social insects in the order *Isoptera.* Sometimes they're referred to as white ants, but they're actually not closely related to ants, which are grouped with bees and wasps in a different order of insects. The social system of termites is very similar to that of ants, but the termite social structure has evolved independently.

There are about 1,900 species of termites, found in many areas of the world, but most commonly in tropical rain forests. Besides the termites that occur naturally in a given area, many species have been transported inadvertently by man from their native habitats to new parts of the world. They are transported in wooden articles such as shipping crates, boat timbers, lumber, and furniture. Dry-wood termites live in small colonies in wood and tolerate long periods of dryness, and thus can survive for a long time in seasoned wood and furniture.

Termites are actually important to the ecology because they help convert plant cellulose into substances that can be recycled into the ecosystem to support new growth. But termites are also very destructive because they feed upon and damage wooden objects and crops. Termites that are transported from other areas are even more dangerous because they're not as able to eat the trees that grow in their new environment. Therefore, they live in and eat man-made wooden structures and crops.

To treat a termite problem, it's important to understand whether the termite is a subterranean or a wood-dwelling species, because treatment methods differ.

Subterranean termites depend on contact with moisture in the soil and generally reach the wood in man-made structures through contact with the ground. The ground below the foundations of new homes is frequently pretreated with an insecticide to prevent entry by these termites. Regular application of the insecticide by injecting it into the soil is helpful. It is also beneficial to use pressure-treated wood, treated concrete foundation blocks, and reinforced concrete foundations. In addition, preventing contact of the wood with the ground and avoiding cracks or other means of entry is important.

Dry-wood termites, on the other hand, nest in the wood and eat it. They are difficult to control because they enter the wood from the air. Some protection can be achieved by using chemically treated wood in building construction, as well as carefully painting and sealing cracks. Once infestation has occurred, tent fumigation is generally necessary to eradicate the pests. However, sometimes it is useful to pour insecticides into small holes drilled into areas of infested wood.

24. **Narrator:** What does the speaker say about the similarity of termites to ants?

25. **Narrator:** According to the speaker, which types of termites are the most destructive to man-made structures?

26. **Narrator:** Which of the following items does the author imply that termites will *not* be transported in?

27. **Narrator:** Which of the following would the speaker probably say?

28. **Narrator:** According to the speaker, in what way are subterranean termites distinct from dry-wood termites?

29. **Narrator:** The speaker implies that dry-wood termites are most effectively treated using what method?

Practice Test 3

Part A

CD A, Track 11

1. **Woman:** I can't imagine what happened to Adam.

   Man: I know. He said he'd be here, but the meeting's already begun. He must be lost.

   Woman: I'm calling him. Maybe he can't find the room.

   Narrator: What do the speakers assume about Adam?

2. **Woman:** I have to go out of town on a family emergency. Can you cover my speech class for me?

   Man: Sure, but I've never taught speech. I'm sure you'll tell me what to do. I hope your emergency works out okay.

   Woman: Thanks. My mother's in the hospital, and I need to arrange for her discharge.

   Narrator: What is the woman's problem?

3. **Woman:** How was the turnout at the fund-raising event?

   Man: Fewer people came than we had expected. It was disappointing, but we made a little money for the organization.

   Woman: I'm sorry I wasn't able to attend. I intended to.

   Narrator: What is the man's problem?

4. Man: I need to have my car repaired, but I can't get around without a car.

Woman: I can give you a ride. I'll take you to drop off your car, to class, and then to pick it up. If it needs to be done, let's just do it.

Man: Thanks a lot. That's really nice of you. I'll call now for an appointment.

Narrator: What is the man probably going to do?

5. Woman: How did you do on the exam?

Man: Not great. I should've studied last night, but I was too tired.

Woman: I'm sure you did fine anyway.

Narrator: What is the man's problem?

6. Woman: Did you have the interview with the computer company? How did it go?

Man: It couldn't have gone better. But they haven't contacted me yet.

Woman: That's great. Good luck.

Narrator: What does the man say about the job interview?

7. Man: I thought you were going to fly to Seattle today. What happened?

Woman: I had planned to, but I couldn't find anybody to work for me.

Narrator: What does the woman mean?

8. Man: Didn't Brenda choose the textbook for the class she is teaching?

Woman: No, the teacher who originally was going to teach the course chose it. Brenda doesn't care for it, but it's not possible to change it.

Man: I'm sure that's annoying.

Narrator: What does the woman mean?

9. **Woman:** Ms. Murphy is a great instructor, isn't she?

   Man: A great instructor, yes. A good writer, not really. And that could cause some problems getting tenure.

   Woman: Is that old idea of "publish or perish" still around? Many times the best teachers are not the best writers.

   Narrator: What do the speakers imply about Ms. Murphy?

10. **Man:** I heard that Scott turned down the scholarship to study in France.

    Woman: He may still go, but he has to resolve a few things first.

    Man: He would lose a great opportunity.

    Narrator: What did the man assume about Scott?

11. **Woman:** You bought a new house recently, didn't you?

    Man: I would have, but I couldn't get the financing I needed.

    Woman: Something better will come along.

    Narrator: What does the man mean?

12. **Man:** I heard that Jim isn't going to his family's beach house this weekend after all.

    Woman: Right. He and his sister are having a problem because she says he uses it more often than she does.

    Man: Family disputes are no fun.

    Narrator: What does the woman say about Jim?

13. **Woman:** No sooner had I sat down than the baby started whimpering again.

    Man: Next time, I'll take care of her. You need to relax a while.

    Narrator: What is the woman's problem?

14. **Man:** I hadn't realized that you were going to stay here after the semester.

   Woman: I wasn't, but I got hired to do some work for the admissions office.

   Man: That's great.

   Narrator: What had the man assumed about the woman?

15. **Woman:** I heard there was a fire at Susan's house. That must be devastating.

   Man: Not only that, her father started it by smoking in bed, and he's in real bad shape.

   Woman: That's a shame. I hope he gets better.

   Narrator: What does the man imply?

Part B

CD A, Track 12

Narrator: Listen to the following conversation about renting an apartment.

Man: I need to find a new apartment, or maybe a house.

Woman: I thought you had a great place already. Why are you moving?

Man: It was a rental house, and the owners sold it. The new owners are going to move in.

Woman: Where do you want to move? Are you planning to get closer to school?

Man: Either that or closer to my job. Right now, it's 20 minutes to both of them.

Woman: I have a friend who's moving out of a two-bedroom apartment on 34th Street, near University Avenue. It's a nice place.

Man: That's great. It's close to the grocery store, restaurants, and everything else. Do you know what it rents for?

Woman: I think about $500 a month, and there's a pool.

Man: That's not bad at all. I'd love to see it.

Woman: I'll call my friend and see if it's still available.

16. Narrator: What had the woman assumed about the man's current living arrangements?

17. Narrator: What does the man say about the location he prefers?

18. Narrator: How does the man react to the suggestion made by the woman?

19. Narrator: What does the woman offer to do for the man?

CD A, Track 13

Narrator: Listen to the following discussion about reflux disease.

Woman: We previously discussed the symptoms of a heart attack. Another condition can cause a very similar feeling, and it's difficult to distinguish from a heart attack. But it has nothing to do with the heart. It's known as gastroesophageal reflux disease. Normally, your lower esophageal sphincter opens only during digestion in order for food to pass down from your esophagus into your stomach. The reflux disease is often caused by the relaxation of the sphincter, which opens it at the wrong time, allowing stomach contents to flow into the esophagus. What do you think is the result?

Man: It burns. That's what causes heartburn, right?

Woman: That's right. The contents, of course, are strong and harmful, because the stomach is full of acid, bile, and pepsin used in digestion. That's fine for the stomach, but not the esophagus. It burns. What causes this problem?

Man: Eating spicy foods?

Woman: Diet certainly can affect it. Eating spicy foods itself does not cause the problem. But cheese, coffee, carbonated beverages, and alcohol are believed to increase the possibility of reflux. Fatty foods relax the sphincter and take longer to digest, thus causing problems. Do you think heartburn is serious?

Man: It's certainly annoying. You can't sleep. But usually it gets better when you take an antacid.

Woman: That's true, but it really is more serious than that when a person has the problem on a recurring basis. The acid does considerable damage to the esophagus over time. The most common such problem is an alteration in the cells in the wall of the esophagus, called metaplastic changes. This causes a type of cancer in the esophagus. Thousands of cases of this cancer are diagnosed each year, and there are many other problems caused by the ailment. What should a person do if he or she is suffering from a reflux problem?

Man: First, I'd say evaluate his diet. Keep a diary of what he eats and when he has a problem.

Woman: Excellent suggestion. Of course, diet isn't always the cause. Reflux can also be caused by a hiatal hernia or other physical defects. Diet can affect the severity of the problem, but controlling it won't help completely. Does anybody know what a hiatal hernia is?

Man: Well, I know that a hernia is a break in the lining of some area of the body, making an organ or tissue go through where it shouldn't. And a hiatus is a break in something or a space between something.

Woman: Yes, a hiatal hernia is a type of hernia in which the stomach itself moves up through a defective sphincter, thus pouring the dangerous acid into the esophagus. So what else should a person do besides change his or her diet?

Man: Get tests. Have one of those scopes where they look inside the esophagus and see what they can see.

Woman: Yes, the doctor must see whether the cause is physical and whether there is already damage. He must assess the total situation. The doctor can then prescribe one of several medications or treatments, or if the physical problem is bad enough, surgically repair the defect. But the thing to do is seek treatment from a qualified physician, and don't wait.

20. **Narrator:** What is the discussion mainly about?

21. **Narrator:** How does the woman describe the sphincter?

22. **Narrator:** According to the woman, when does acid reflux occur?

23. **Narrator:** According to the woman, why does the reflux cause the burning sensation?

24. **Narrator:** According to the woman, what results from metaplastic changes?

25. **Narrator:** How does the woman describe a hiatal hernia?

26. **Narrator:** According to the woman, what are two reasons a patient may want to control his or her diet?

27. **Narrator:** Which of the following is *not* a suggested course of action to treat reflux disease?

CD A, Track 14

Narrator: Listen to the following talk.

Man: This is a tool made of stone. It could be used for digging, cutting, or various other things. Scientists used to believe that the most advanced Stone Age tools were developed in the Middle East and Africa. However, these tools were discovered in China recently, and they're certainly as advanced as those of the other continents, with the same sophisticated shape and consistency of design as the other tools. These tools were found near the Chinese border with Vietnam, and they appear to be about 800,000 years old. It is a particularly interesting discovery, because now scientists know that in spite of slight differences, similar techniques were used over a very great distance.

28. Narrator: What is the man talking about?

29. Narrator: What had scientists believed before these tools were found?

30. Narrator: How does the speaker describe the comparison between the new tools and the tools found previously?

CD A, Track 15

Narrator: Listen to the following talk about Nathaniel Hawthorne.

Woman: Today, we continue discussing American authors of the 1800s. Nathaniel Hawthorne, author of *The Scarlet Letter* and *The House of the Seven Gables*, had an interesting and varied life. At times he enjoyed success, and at times he lived in despair. Hawthorne's father died when he was young, and his family had to move in with relatives. His mother became very reclusive.

Hawthorne didn't care much for formal schooling, but he severely injured his foot when he was 9, causing him to be incapacitated for a long time. While at home, he began reading Shakespeare and other authors. Hawthorne was later sent to a prep school, but he still wasn't a particularly good student. After graduating, he returned to the home where his mother lived in seclusion, and he moved into an upstairs room from which he rarely exited. He said he spent the next 12 years in what he called "this dismal chamber." Actually, some critics say he really didn't spend as much time in seclusion as he led people to believe, and he concocted the idea that he was a hermit-artist. Critics say that he actually went out from time to time and even traveled to various cities. But he did read and write in the room, improving his writing ability considerably, and at the end of the 12 years, he created a great collection of short stories. During that time, he published a book at his own expense, but it was a failure. Later, he destroyed all the books.

Hawthorne continued to write but was unable to find a publisher, and he was often frustrated. He did manage to publish many of his works in magazines. One of his well-known works, *Twice Told Tales,* was published as well. He didn't make enough money from these publications to support a family, so even though he was engaged to marry a woman, they didn't marry for a long time. Hawthorne took various jobs that involved manual labor, and the work made him too tired to write. Finally, after an engagement that lasted many years, Hawthorne got married when he was in his mid-30s. He lost a job, which gave him the time to write his most famous work, *The Scarlet Letter.* Although *The Scarlet Letter* sold well, it was pirated by some publishers, so Hawthorne didn't make much money from it. References he made in *The Scarlet Letter* angered many people from Salem, Massachusetts, so Hawthorne and his wife moved to a new town. In their new town, Hawthorne met Herman Melville, who was writing *Moby Dick,* and he wrote *The House of the Seven Gables.*

31. **Narrator:** What does the speaker imply about Hawthorne's success as a writer?

32. **Narrator:** How does the speaker describe Hawthorne's scholastic abilities?

33. **Narrator:** How does the speaker describe Hawthorne's early home life?

34. **Narrator:** What does the speaker imply that Hawthorne did during his reclusive years?

35. **Narrator:** According to the speaker, what was Hawthorne's reaction to his first published work, which was self-published?

36. **Narrator:** What does the speaker imply about Hawthorne's financial success?

37. **Narrator:** What does the speaker indicate happened to *The Scarlet Letter* during Hawthorne's lifetime?

Practice Test 4

Part A

CD B, Track 1

1. Man: I should have another blood test done, shouldn't I?

Woman: In a couple of weeks.

Man: Okay, should I keep taking these pills in the meantime?

Woman: I'm going to prescribe something else.

Narrator: What does the woman imply is the best course of treatment?

2. Woman: Have you tried the new Greek restaurant downtown?

Man: No, but I hear it's second only to the one that used to be on the hill. What was it called . . . Helena's?

Woman: Yes, I heard the same thing. We have been waiting for a good replacement for Helena's.

Narrator: What do the speakers imply about the new Greek Restaurant?

3. Woman: I was thinking of taking the certification exam again, but I just don't think I can do it. It's too much work.

Man: I wish you wouldn't talk like that. You're so bright that it would be nothing to you. Plus, it would be great for your career.

Woman: Still, I'd have to study and prepare a great deal, and I don't know if I'll have time.

Narrator: What does the woman say about taking the certification exam?

4. Man: I have never been so frightened. I lost control of the car on the wet highway and flew all the way across both lanes of traffic. I was lucky I didn't get hit by traffic or hit one of the trees.

Woman: You are very lucky. That highway is always so busy, and wet roads are very dangerous.

Narrator: What does the man imply about what happened on the highway?

5. Woman: What happened to Jose? I thought he was coming tonight.

Man: He came down with a cold and needed the rest.

Woman: I hope he's back to normal soon.

Narrator: What does the man say about Jose?

6. Man: I thought Roberto was happy at this school, but I hear he's thinking of leaving.

Woman: Yes, his father would rather that he went to a more well-known university. But he's just looking into it at the moment.

Man: It's funny how much importance people put on a school's name.

Narrator: According to the woman, why is Roberto considering changing schools?

7. Woman: Why did the students leave the class early?

Man: Professor Lopez is having them go to a meat packing plant to write a paper on the procedure for making bologna.

Woman: That's not a pretty sight. Do you have any idea what goes into it?

Man: I'd rather not know.

Narrator: What do the speakers imply about the procedure the students will view?

8. Man: Why did Allan leave the meeting so early?

Woman: Because he had to go to an interview.

Man: You'd think he could've rearranged his schedule.

Narrator: What does the woman imply about Allan's leaving the meeting?

9. **Woman:** Helen couldn't find any of the books on the list.

Man: I couldn't either. I'm not sure what to do now.

Woman: Why not search the Internet?

Narrator: What do the speakers mean?

10. **Man:** Has the jury reached a verdict yet?

Woman: Not yet, and they probably won't tonight.

Man: Then I'm coming back in the morning.

Narrator: What does the woman mean?

11. **Man:** I can't believe Bill bought that stock. The company is unknown.

Woman: He usually makes good decisions, but this time he listened to a tip from somebody he didn't even know.

Man: Has he learned his lesson?

Woman: I hope so.

Narrator: What do the speakers imply about Bill and the stock market?

12. **Woman:** Is Stephen here today? I have an appointment with him.

Man: Haven't you heard? They sent a memo this morning saying he was fired on Friday.

Woman: What happened?

Man: They caught him with his hand in the till.

Narrator: What do the speakers say about what happened to Stephen?

13. Woman: The more I sleep the more tired I feel. I don't know what's going on.

Man: You should go to the doctor. Something could be wrong, or maybe it's something simple.

Woman: I guess you're right.

Narrator: What is the woman's problem?

14. Man: I'm fed up with the new receptionist. Not once has she written down a phone number correctly.

Woman: I know, and she has a poor attitude, too.

Narrator: What do the speakers say about their opinions of the receptionist?

15. Woman: Will you interview with the new computer company that moved in downstairs?

Man: Under no circumstances. The CEO used to be with my former company.

Narrator: What does the man say about interviewing with the new company?

Part B

CD B, Track 2

Narrator: Listen to the following discussion about mediation.

Woman: Okay, we need to discuss what's going to happen next. This judge will definitely order mediation before he sets a trial date. Have you ever heard of mediation? Do you have any experience with it?

Man: Yeah. That's where a guy who's like a judge, but not really a judge, makes the decision. Sometimes there are three people together making the decision.

Woman: Actually, I think you're describing arbitration, which is not at all like mediation. Arbitration is more like trying the case in court, and the arbitrator acts like the judge. On the other hand, a mediator is more like a facilitator. He or she doesn't make a decision at all. The mediator listens to the case, points out disadvantages in each party's case, and helps the two parties reach a conclusion.

Man: If we were going to settle out of court, we would have done it by now. They aren't being reasonable. Why should anybody think a mediator is going to talk sense into them?

Woman: Actually, a great number of cases are successfully handled in mediation. It's a very positive process. One thing that will be reviewed during the mediation is the downside of going to trial.

Man: But you've already told me that. You told me that we should settle, but they won't listen to reason. This is a waste of time.

Woman: Regardless, the court demands that we do it, and in good faith. Go in with an open mind and see what happens. You may be surprised. The mediator will suggest or facilitate a settlement offer. Generally, we'll start out together in one room, and then probably be separated. Then, the mediator will probably go back and forth from room to room bringing offers and counteroffers. But the most important difference between this and arbitration is that no decision will be made unless you and the other party make it. The mediator doesn't decide anything, but just tries to help you come to a settlement. If you're not able to settle, we'll move back into the court arena.

16. **Narrator:** What does the woman indicate about the next process in the case?

17. **Narrator:** What had the man assumed about mediation?

18. **Narrator:** How does the man apparently feel about the opposing parties in this matter?

19. **Narrator:** How does the woman appear to feel about mediation?

20. **Narrator:** What does the man indicate that the woman previously advised him to do?

21. **Narrator:** What does the woman state about the mediation procedure?

CD B, Track 3

Narrator: Listen to the following discussion about Claire Nelson.

Man: Claire Nelson was in the seventh grade when she began to wonder whether the carcinogens found in plastic wrap could seep into food when food covered with it was microwaved. She knew that a cancer-causing agent called DEHA is found in many plastic wraps, and she realized that nobody had reported research on the subject previously, so she decided to see what she could find out.

Woman: How'd you hear about this?

Man: I read an article in the paper. She's very well respected in science circles now. She's just 18 and has come a long way in her research, having started the research in earnest when in the tenth grade. She contacted a research organization for help. She managed to get government equipment on which to perform her research. First, she microwaved plastic wrap in virgin olive oil, and she found that the carcinogens and other harmful substances migrated into the oil in substantial amounts.

Woman: She sounds very determined.

Man: She is. She had to travel to the labs several times a week while keeping up with her studies and other activities. She placed well in the national science projects and her studies are published in journals already. She even got to meet a number of Nobel Prize winners recently.

Woman: That's very impressive. It just goes to show that diligence and determination can pay off.

22. **Narrator:** How long does the man indicate that Claire Nelson has been interested in carcinogens?

23. **Narrator:** What does the man indicate is the nature of her research?

24. **Narrator:** How did the man learn about Claire Nelson?

25. **Narrator:** How old is Claire Nelson at the time of the discussion?

26. **Narrator:** What is the woman's impression of Claire Nelson?

CD B, Track 4

Narrator: Listen to the following discussion about power of attorney.

Woman: The next thing we need to talk about is what you would want done and who you would want to handle things for you if you became incapacitated. Everybody should designate somebody they trust in a power of attorney and should sign a health care surrogate designation as well as an advance directive.

Man: Isn't that the same as the executor of my will?

Woman: It may be the same person, but it requires different documents. Your will doesn't come into play until you are dead. We are talking about who handles things for you while you are alive if you can't for yourself. If you do not designate somebody, and something happens to you, the court will appoint a guardian for you, and it may not appoint the same person you would choose. There are actually two types of power of attorney, a financial one and a health care one. The financial power of attorney allows the person you designate to handle all your property, that is your assets. They can access your bank accounts, safe deposit box, and any other account you have, sign a deed to your house, or put a mortgage on it.

Man: Whoa. Why would I want somebody to have that power? Couldn't they wipe me out? Or does it say it's not valid until I am incapacitated?

Woman: In this state, the power of attorney is valid immediately, not when you become incapacitated. But, you designate somebody you trust implicitly, and you don't give up the original document. You will simply advise the person you designate about how to locate the document if something happens to you. And the power of attorney will be a durable form, meaning that it survives mental incapacity. Otherwise, it would expire as soon as we needed it.

Man: I get it.

Woman: Then you are going to designate the same person or a different person to make medical decisions. And, you should consider signing an advance directive, which takes effect if you have an illness or suffer an accident that leaves you in a terminal condition, an end-stage condition, or a persistent vegetative state. If two doctors determine there is no reasonable medical probability you will recover from that condition, the advance directive says that you wish life-prolonging procedures to be withheld or withdrawn.

Man: I definitely want that. I mean, I want to do an advance directive because I don't want to be kept alive artificially if there is no hope for my recovery.

27. **Narrator:** What does the woman imply that she just finished talking about before she began this topic?

28. **Narrator:** How is a power of attorney different from a will?

29. **Narrator:** What does the woman indicate that a designee can do with a durable financial power of attorney?

30. **Narrator:** Why does the woman say that a durable power of attorney is the form to use?

31. **Narrator:** How does the man initially react to the suggestion of a power of attorney?

32. **Narrator:** Which of the following would probably not be a use of an advance directive?

33. **Narrator:** How does the man appear to feel about advance directives?

CD B, Track 5

Narrator: Listen to the following discussion about cloud seeding.

Woman: The lack of rain in Florida has led to a renewed interest in the technology of cloud seeding. Have you heard of it before?

Man: Yes, actually. We used to hear about it back in the '70s and '80s. That's a good point. Why don't they do that?

Woman: Mainly because cloud seeding isn't a proven science. While some scientists believe it works, there is no scientific proof that it does.

Man: So what? It's better than doing nothing, isn't it?

Woman: It's expensive. The research has been very expensive and the act itself is expensive. They aren't willing to take the effort and expense to do something they aren't sure will work. The authorities in Florida don't believe in it.

Man: How is cloud seeding supposed to work, at least according to those who do believe in it?

Woman: Here's a diagram. The concept was created in 1946 by General Electric. An agent, usually silver iodide, is deposited into a convective cloud, which is the type of white fluffy cauliflower-shaped cloud that generally leads to a storm cloud. The agent provides a nuclei, or base, on which tiny water droplets can condense, and once there is enough condensation, the small droplets become larger droplets, then ice crystals, then snowflakes, and ultimately rain.

Man: Don't they use it for agricultural purposes in the Midwest? They think it works.

Woman: They do, but not everybody is convinced.

Man: It sure seems worth it to me to do whatever it takes to stop wildfires.

34. **Narrator:** What does the woman say has led to a new interest in cloud seeding?

35. **Narrator:** Does the man indicate that he has heard of cloud seeding before?

36. **Narrator:** Why isn't cloud seeding used to combat dry conditions?

37. **Narrator:** What does the man imply should be done?

38. **Narrator:** What is the correct order of the process for seeding a cloud?

39. Narrator: According to the speaker, into what is the iodide deposited?

40. Narrator: According to the woman, what is a nuclei?

Practice Test 5

Part A

CD B, Track 6

1. Woman: We've already seen both of these movies, haven't we?

Man: I'm not sure. Who's in the action one?

Woman: Let's see, uh, George Clooney. Oh yeah, we saw it in a hotel. How about this one?

Man: Fine.

Narrator: What do the speakers think of the two movies they are discussing?

2. Man: I think Ellen is going to enter the doctorate program in linguistics.

Woman: Don't be so sure. She's been looking into the English literature program.

Man: Oh, I didn't know that.

Narrator: What does the woman say about Ellen's plans?

3. Woman: I thought Michael was as tall as Josh, but it looks like he's a finger shorter.

Man: They were the same height, but Josh has grown a bit.

Woman: Actually, the doctor says Michael isn't finished yet.

Narrator: What do the speakers say about Josh and Michael?

4. Man: There's no way I'll pass the test. I haven't had a chance to study at all.

Woman: You hardly studied last time, and you did fine.

Man: But that time, I was at least in a study group, so I was exposed to everything.

Narrator: What does the man imply about his lack of study for the test?

5. Man: This is the most favorable of all the lots available.

Woman: Do you think there's room for the building, parking, and water retention?

Man: Probably, but anyway, we would make the contract contingent on your ability to build the building you need.

Narrator: What does the man seem to think about the lot they are discussing?

6. Man: You used to get away to your cottage quite a bit, as I recall. Are you still able to go as often with your new job?

Woman: Seldom. I hope that changes soon, though.

Man: It's a beautiful place, and it's a shame not to be able to relax there.

Narrator: What does the woman say about her cottage?

7. Woman: Michelle is considering attending the University of North Florida in Jacksonville.

Man: Really? I thought she was already registered at the University of Miami.

Woman: That's true, but she decided she didn't want to be so far from home.

Narrator: What does the woman say about Michelle?

8. **Woman:** This is the last straw. I have yet to see that new employee offer to help anybody or do anything but sit there reading her novel.

   Man: I'm glad you realize it. It was bugging me, too.

   Narrator: What do the speakers imply about the new employee?

9. **Woman:** I'm going to start the research to do the optional paper. Professor Adams says he'll throw out one test grade and replace it with the grade for a paper, right?

   Man: Yeah, that's what he said, and I'm going to do it, too.

   Narrator: What are the speakers thinking of doing?

10. **Woman:** I heard you dropped geometry. Is that right?

    Man: I just couldn't follow it. I needed something more basic.

    Narrator: What do the speakers say that the man did?

11. **Man:** You've been to the races before, haven't you?

    Woman: No, not once.

    Man: Oh, I must be thinking of someone else.

    Narrator: What does the woman say about the races?

12. **Man:** Allison, did you get Nadia to work for you on Wednesday?

    Woman: She couldn't, but Dana might be able to.

    Man: I'm sure somebody will be able to cover for you.

    Narrator: What had the man assumed?

13. Man: I haven't seen Christopher at a coin club meeting for a while.

Woman: He stopped coming because he said it was boring.

Man: He used to find it interesting. People sure do change.

Narrator: According to the woman, why hasn't the man seen Christopher?

14. Woman: Why don't you let me help you with that?

Man: I can do it. It's just going to take a little more time.

Woman: I don't know why you're so stubborn.

Narrator: What does the woman imply about the man?

15. Man: I've been trying to figure out this program for hours.

Woman: Why not try reading the manual?

Man: That would be too easy. No, you're right. I guess it's time.

Narrator: What does the woman suggest that the man do?

Part B

CD B, Track 7

Narrator: Listen to the following speech about coral reefs.

Woman: This is a coral reef, which is a very important part of our environment, not just for our personal enjoyment, but for many other reasons as well. Coral reefs have suffered greatly in recent years, but they are making a comeback, thanks in part to a group of volunteers who make it their business to monitor and nurture them.

The United States has 425,000 acres of coral reefs, the majority of which are in Hawaii. Generally, coral grows about one inch a year. Besides providing a habitat for lobsters, fish, and other sea life, coral reefs are important because they are used for bone grafts, for developing pesticides, and for providing natural breakwaters to protect coasts from erosion. They are also a natural source of beauty.

Besides careless treatment by tourists and officials, one major problem for coral reefs is the result of environmental changes. In 1998, El Niño caused the warmest ocean temperatures ever recorded, resulting in the death of necessary algae and, ultimately, the bleaching of the coral itself. The natural color of healthy coral reefs comes from the algae, but the death of the algae bleaches them white. The fact that the damage generally appears closer to the surface is further proof that higher temperatures are the cause of the problem.

Because of the tremendous importance of coral reefs, the U.S. government has funded numerous projects to assist in bringing damaged reefs back to life. We aren't out of the woods yet, but things are looking up for the reefs and the natural inhabitants of them. In 1998, it was determined that 15 percent of the world's reefs were dead, but lately, some have recovered. As the reefs recover, the inhabitants thrive again.

16. **Narrator:** What does the woman say about the health of coral reefs since 1998?

17. **Narrator:** According to the woman, which of the following is not a reason why coral reefs are important?

18. **Narrator:** What does the speaker describe as a major cause of coral reef death?

19. **Narrator:** What does the speaker describe as the relationship between coral and algae?

20. **Narrator:** What has been done to improve the health of coral reefs?

CD B, Track 8

Narrator: Listen to the following conversation about student housing.

Man: Excuse me, I understand that this office helps students with housing. Is that right?

Woman: Are you a student in the intensive English program? May I see your ID card? Um, yes, we can certainly help you. Where are you staying now?

Man: I just arrived yesterday. I'm staying at the hotel across the street.

Woman: Okay, please complete this form. Will you be living alone or do you have a family with you? Or, would you be interested in sharing housing?

Man: Yes, I have a wife and child. They aren't here yet, but they'll be coming as soon as I am settled in. My daughter is 4.

Woman: Okay, so you need a two-bedroom apartment, or would you prefer a house?

Man: An apartment is fine, preferably close to school.

Woman: We have two choices available. This two bedroom is two blocks from campus, but it doesn't have central heat and air. There is a slot in the wall for a unit air conditioner if you want one. It's $500 a month. Then, for $650 a month, there is this one. It's in a modern apartment complex, about 10 minutes from the university by bicycle, but it's closer to shopping, a movie theater, and other things. And the complex has a swimming pool and a Laundromat.

Man: Could I see them both? I'm not sure which I would want at the moment. Sure I'd love to be closer to school, but my wife and daughter would probably like the benefits of the other one.

Woman: Sure. We can go right now if you would like.

21. **Narrator:** Where is the man living currently?

22. **Narrator:** Who does the woman imply is eligible for help by her office?

23. **Narrator:** How does the woman seem to know the man is in the intensive English program?

24. **Narrator:** What size apartment does the man say he needs?

25. **Narrator:** What does the man seem to think is the most important difference between the two apartments the woman discusses?

26. **Narrator:** What does the woman imply is the biggest drawback of the less expensive apartment?

CD B, Track 9

Narrator: Listen to the following talk about medical technology.

Man: Computers, wireless technology, and other innovations have changed our lives in many ways. Someday, intrusive medical procedures may be replaced with new technology. For example, scientists have created a new camera that will remind you of a ride at Epcot Center. They have invented a capsule containing a tiny camera, which is placed within the body and allowed to move through it, gathering information as it goes. The most logical initial use for the camera is in the digestive system, since it has a beginning and an end, and the capsule will move through on its own.

People with health problems in the esophagus, stomach, intestines, and colon currently undergo invasive tests with instruments called endoscopes inserted through the nearest orifice.

Such internal views are necessary when looking for abnormal blood vessels, tumors, ulcers, lymphomas, and abnormalities of the various organ walls through which the endoscope passes. Skeptics point out that endoscopes have become very sophisticated and allow much more control than the capsule allows. For example, a doctor can back up and aim at a particular area with an endoscope, which will not be possible with the capsule. Endoscopes even provide the ability to perform biopsies and other tests as well as surgical procedures, whereas the capsule will not permit that. But for simple viewing, endoscopes are uncomfortable, so this new technology is believed to be a less intrusive choice.

The capsule, no larger than a medicinal capsule, will be swallowed by the patient and will light its way with built-in lights. It will transmit video images in color as it progresses through the body. The video that it records can be up to five hours long and is later downloaded to a computer for viewing.

27. Narrator: Why does the speaker indicate that the digestive system is the best place for the new technology?

28. Narrator: For which of the following items would the capsule not be helpful?

29. Narrator: What is the main reason that some scientists believe the capsule would be helpful?

30. Narrator: Which of the following does the speaker imply would not be part of the capsule?

31. Narrator: Which of the following does the speaker imply is true?

CD B, Track 10

Narrator: Listen to the following conversation about Canavan Disease.

Man: I see that your husband is a Jew from Ashkenazi descent. Has he ever been tested for Canavan Disease?

Woman: What's that?

Man: An inherited, degenerative disease, found most frequently among Jewish families of Ashkenazi descent. Children with the disease are severely disabled, both mentally and physically, and have limited life spans. Generally, they can't sit, crawl, walk, or speak. They have very limited ability to move their hands, to play, or to perform the simplest of tasks. They gradually lose the ability to see and to swallow food. The disease affects the white matter of the brain, causing spongy degeneration. Victims can't generate myelin, the white matter that insulates the nerve cell processes, much like the covering of electrical wires, which is necessary for normal brain function.

Myelin is a substance made up of proteins and lipids. Its function is to protect nerves and allow messages to be sent to and from the brain. The white matter deteriorates because patients have a deficiency in a critical enzyme, which leads to the accumulation of a damaging chemical in the brain. It is not exactly known how this chemical imbalance causes the destruction of myelin.

Woman: I've never heard of anything like this at all. And my husband has never mentioned it.

Man: Do you know your own heritage? You're Jewish too, aren't you?

Woman: Yes, I am. But I don't know any details like my husband does.

Man: The disease is inherited as an autosomal recessive trait. Both of the parents of an affected child are carriers of an altered gene on Chromosome 17, which is responsible for synthesizing the problematic enzyme. A parent who is a carrier is healthy because he or she has one functional copy of the gene, which produces a sufficient amount of the enzyme. A child who receives two altered copies of the gene, one from each parent, is unable to produce any of the enzyme and will develop the symptoms of the disease. So if only your husband is a carrier, there's no problem. Only if both of you are carriers do we have to worry. DNA testing of Ashkenazi Jewish couples can tell whether each parent is a carrier with more than 97 percent certainty. If both parents are carriers, there is a 25 percent chance with each pregnancy that the child will have Canavan Disease.

Woman: Oh, this is terrible. I'm afraid.

Man: I'm sorry. I'm only trying to take precautions. If the two of you were carriers and had children, that would be much more unpleasant, believe me.

Woman: No, I'm sorry. I do appreciate your concern. We'll be happy to participate. Thank you.

32. **Narrator:** What appears to be the woman's level of knowledge of Canavan Disease?

33. **Narrator:** According to the man, which of the following is possibly a carrier of the illness?

34. **Narrator:** How does the man indicate that the disease affects the body?

35. **Narrator:** Why does the man want to know the woman's cultural background?

36. **Narrator:** What is the woman's demeanor at the end of the discussion?

37. **Narrator:** What does the gene on Chromosome 17 do?

Practice Test 6

Part A

CD B, Track 11

1. Man: Where is Donna? I had expected her to be here this morning.

Woman: She was called away due to a family emergency.

Man: When will she be back?

Woman: She didn't say, but I imagine she will call soon.

Narrator: Why does the woman say Donna is not present?

2. Woman: Are you going to the meeting at the library tonight?

Man: I may.

Woman: Well, I'm going. Maybe I'll see you there.

Narrator: What does the man mean?

3. Man: Had Jim submitted his application earlier, he could have gotten financial aid.

Woman: He always puts things off till the last minute.

Narrator: What does the man mean?

4. Woman: I didn't pay as much for my books this semester as I did last semester.

Man: How'd you manage that? Prices are always higher.

Woman: I found a used book outlet. You have to be careful to get the right edition, but I found several and saved quite a bit.

Narrator: What does the woman mean?

5. **Man:** Only by organized teamwork will we be able to finish this entire project on time.

   Woman: I'm game. Who do you want to help?

   Narrator: What does the man mean?

6. **Woman:** The counselor says we should have our student ID. I forgot mine at home.

   Man: Do you have any other identification? Will a driver's license do?

   Woman: No. I guess I'll have to run home and get it.

   Man: If you hurry, you should be back in time.

   Narrator: What will the woman probably do next?

7. **Man:** Excuse me, I hate to bother you, but I can't concentrate when the two of you are talking.

   Woman: Oh, sorry. We didn't realize we were bothering you.

   Man: Maybe you could just whisper.

   Woman: We'll go out to the hallway. Sorry for the interruption.

   Narrator: What will the woman probably do?

8. **Man:** Susan is thinking of getting a job at a computer store.

   Woman: Can she handle that in addition to her other job and classes?

   Man: You know Susan — she wouldn't consider it unless she was sure she could do it.

   Woman: It'll probably enhance her knowledge of computers, too.

   Narrator: What does the man imply about Susan?

9. **Woman:** I thought you were going to order new slides for the lab class.

   Man: I was going to, but the department head didn't approve the purchase.

   Woman: The ones we have are all cloudy and cracked.

   Man: Maybe he'll listen to you.

   Narrator: What does the man mean?

10. **Man:** Hey, that's great news about your promotion.

    Woman: What? You must be thinking of someone else. I haven't heard from them.

    Man: Well, I guess I spoke too soon; I'm sure you're the one they have in mind.

    Woman: That would be great. I wish they would call.

    Narrator: What does the woman imply about her promotion?

11. **Woman:** Did you proofread the essay?

    Man: Yes, and I ran spell check, too.

    Woman: Good, you know Professor Roberts is a stickler for good spelling.

    Man: And impeccable grammar, too.

    Narrator: What do the speakers imply about Professor Roberts?

12. **Man:** Professor Hall will put off the exam till next week, won't he?

    Woman: I'm not so sure. He likes to stick to the schedule.

    Man: Well, I'd better start studying then.

    Woman: Me too.

    Narrator: What does the woman imply about Professor Hall?

13. Woman: What's that notice from the landlord?

Man: The rent is being increased.

Woman: What? I can't believe it. They need to spend some money fixing this place up.

Man: Even so, I'm not sure what we can do about this.

Narrator: What does the woman mean?

14. Man: Janet said she's going to the doctor tomorrow.

Woman: But she has to work tomorrow afternoon, doesn't she?

Man: She had to take the afternoon off for the appointment.

Woman: I hope she's okay.

Narrator: What does the man imply about Janet?

15. Woman: I heard that you and some friends were organizing a cruise to the Caribbean.

Man: It never really got off the ground.

Woman: That's too bad; it sounded like fun.

Man: Yeah, I'm still planning to go, alone if I have to.

Narrator: What does the man plan to do?

Part B

CD B, Track 12

Narrator: Listen to the following conversation about estate planning.

Woman: Okay, if you add up everything you own, what is the total?

Man: About five hundred thousand, if you add the house, life insurance, and retirement account. About three fifty if you leave out the life insurance.

Woman: Do the two of you own everything together now? That is, are all your accounts and your home jointly owned, and is your spouse the beneficiary on retirement funds, life insurance, and things like that?

Man: Yes.

Woman: How old are you? And do you have children to whom you want to give your assets when you pass away?

Man: I'm 55 and she's 52. Yes, we have three children, and they will be our beneficiaries.

Woman: Fine. You have a couple of choices for your estate plan. You don't need a tax-planning trust because your assets fall within the amount that passes free of estate tax. But you may decide to create a joint trust, which has certain advantages for you and your heirs. First, let's talk about how your estate would be handled with a will. A will is inexpensive to create and simple to deal with while you're alive. If one of you dies, the other will most likely not have to do anything with the will, not because you are married, but because of the way you own things. You own your assets in a way that allows them to pass to the survivor, so the fact that you make a will is irrelevant. It's how you hold your assets that matters. But when the surviving spouse dies, probate honors the will.

Man: What's that?

Woman: Probate is the court-monitored administration of your will. By itself, your will has no effect. After your death, it must go through probate to have validity. Some people who try to sell trusts make probate sound like a bad word and make you think that you should avoid its effect at all costs. Yet, probate is a fine way to take care of many estates, and some people go to far too much trouble trying to avoid it, sometimes creating other problems. The major drawback of probate in this state is the cost, which is actually a fee that the attorney and personal representative are permitted to charge. The probate process also takes more time than a trust administration, and it's not as private. That is, if somebody wants details of your estate, they can go to the probate court and see many of the documents involved.

Man: I'm confused. I thought you had a will made to avoid probate.

Woman: That's a common misconception. If you die with a will and your assets are in your name alone, the will is honored through probate. Now let's talk about using a trust instead. The document alone isn't what makes the difference. Think of a trust like a corporation. In a trust, you own your assets as trustee rather than owning them in your own name. When you die, the trust continues, just like a business continues. So the critical part of creating a trust is following through with changing all your bank accounts and everything you own so that the trust owns it. You must own some assets individually, like retirement accounts. We change them by changing beneficiaries or, more likely, contingent beneficiaries.

So when the second spouse dies, the successor trustee who you name in the trust simply steps in and takes over, handling assets and distributing them to the people and on the conditions you state in the trust, without court involvement. There is no delay, my work is minimized, and the document is totally private.

Man: Well then, why in the world wouldn't I want a trust?

Woman: There are three basic drawbacks to the trust: It costs more to create, you must make an extra effort by transferring assets into the trust to make it work, and you must continue to hold everything that way in the future. If you die with any asset not in the trust, we'll have to probate that asset. Of course, if that happens, the probate expense would still be much less than now, because it would be based only on the one or two assets that aren't in your trust, instead of all your assets.

Man: Do you suggest a trust for us?

Woman: The decision is yours. Your assets are within the range where a trust makes financial sense, and your ages are also within that range. If you were still in your 30s or 40s, it would make less sense. Since the heirs are your children, you probably want to pass as much to them as possible without diluting it with expenses. This chart shows the cost of the two routes now versus after you die. If you choose to do the trust, you're paying this much more now, for this much benefit later.

Man: I think it makes sense to do the trust. We'll talk about it and decide soon. Thank you.

16. **Narrator:** What does the man say about his family status?

17. **Narrator:** What does the man say about his assets?

18. **Narrator:** How would you describe the woman's manner of presentation?

19. **Narrator:** What kind of estate planning document does the woman say that the man needs?

20. **Narrator:** Which of the following is not a correct description of the difference between a will and a trust?

21. **Narrator:** Why does the woman say that the couple won't have to go through probate now if only one of them dies?

22. **Narrator:** How does the woman define probate?

23. **Narrator:** According to the woman, what is the major drawback of probate?

24. **Narrator:** Does the woman imply that she would suggest the same type of estate planning if the couple were younger?

CD B, Track 13

Narrator: Listen to the following speech about alcoholism.

Woman: It has long been recognized that those people with a family history of alcoholism are at much higher risk of becoming alcoholics themselves. And it's also known that this isn't just sociological, because it happens even when the children don't grow up in the same home with the alcoholic. Researchers in the United States have located a specific hormone in the brain that can indicate a predisposition for the disease.

Beta-endorphin is a hormone that produces euphoria and acts like morphine. The body produces this hormone to help control pain during childbirth and other physical trauma. The hormone also contributes to the feeling of well being that accompanies intoxication. It's now known that in people with a family history of alcoholism, the response to the beta-endorphin is greater and more prolonged than in those people who aren't apt to abuse alcohol. This hormone reaction is what causes a potential alcoholic to crave alcohol. Researchers also learned that the manner in which the person responds to the hormone can be inherited.

Of course, not everybody in the family of an alcoholic will abuse alcohol. This is because the reaction to the hormone does not affect everybody who is genetically related to the alcoholic. It's believed that with the new knowledge, doctors will soon be able to test a family and determine who is likely to abuse alcohol and who is not.

However, researchers are quick to point out that people who are prone to alcoholism many times do not succumb to the disease simply because they choose not to drink and never get to the point that the inherited trait affects them.

25. Narrator: What fact does the speaker state as common knowledge?

26. Narrator: What example does the woman give to indicate that alcoholism is not just sociological?

27. Narrator: What is beta-endorphin, according to the speaker?

28. Narrator: Which of the following does the speaker not imply would be a true statement about beta-endorphins?

29. Narrator: What does the speaker indicate is the difference between a person with alcoholic tendencies and a person without them?

30. Narrator: What does the speaker say about family members inheriting the alcoholic trait?

31. Narrator: Does the speaker indicate that everybody with the reaction to beta-endorphin will become alcoholic?

CD B, Track 14

Narrator: Listen to the following conversation about a law class.

Woman: Did you go to class today? What happened?

Man: We began talking about torts.

Woman: About what? I've never heard that word in my life.

Man: A tort is a civil wrong. You know, like not a criminal matter. Something somebody does negligently that harms somebody else.

Woman: A tort? T-O-R-T?

Man: Yep, that's it. We're going to talk about torts for the next couple of weeks, so you'd better get used to it.

Woman: Okay, tell me what was discussed about these torts.

Man: A guy is driving down the street and strikes a kid on his bicycle, and the kid is injured or dies. The driver may have committed a tort — negligence — or worse. What if the kid just ran out in front of him, and he had no way to avoid it? If he wasn't drunk or anything, he wouldn't be charged with a crime, and he wouldn't have committed a tort. But let's say that the driver hit the kid on the sidewalk or in a protected crosswalk or something. The driver could be guilty of a crime if what he did was outrageous, or if he was drunk or something. But if he wasn't — if it was just a bad accident, but the driver was at fault — that would be a tort. Even though it's not a crime, the kid's family could sue the driver for negligence, wrongful death, and stuff like that. They could collect money damages. That's what a tort is — civil law as opposed to criminal law.

Woman: I'm still not sure I get it. Let's look at a legal dictionary. Okay, here — from the Latin "torquere," meaning "to twist or twisted." What? That's really weird. "A private or civil wrong or injury for which a court will grant a remedy in the form of money or other damages." I guess that's just what you said, isn't it?

Man: Yes. Continue.

Woman: "A violation of a duty imposed by law upon all persons occupying the relation to each other that is involved in a given matter. Three elements of every tort action are: existence of legal duty from defendant to plaintiff, breach of the duty, and damage as proximate result."

Man: So apply that definition to the car accident.

Woman: First, it must be found that the driver had a duty to drive carefully, a duty not to hit the boy. It must then be shown that he breached the duty. If he had a duty to drive carefully, and he didn't, he breached the duty. And, if the child was injured or died, there was damage. I don't know what a "proximate result" is.

Man: It's kind of like a direct consequence. There were some cases we studied where all kinds of things happened as the result of one little accident, and basically you couldn't get damages against the guy for all of them because they weren't foreseeable. For example, the kid's father sees the accident and has a heart attack. The man can't be responsible for that too, because how could he know that would happen just because he drove carelessly?

Woman: I guess I'd better read some of this stuff. It's pretty complicated. But I appreciate what you've told me. I guess I understand some of it.

32. Narrator: Why is the woman asking the man for help?

33. Narrator: What do the speakers say is the difference between a tort and a crime?

34. Narrator: According to the man, how long will the class be studying torts?

35. Narrator: What does the man imply would happen if the driver drove carefully and the child darted out in front of him?

36. Narrator: According to the man, is it possible to commit both a crime and a tort?

37. Narrator: According to the definition read by the woman, which of the following could be a tort?

38. Narrator: What is the woman probably going to do?

CliffsNotes

LITERATURE NOTES

Absalom, Absalom!
The Aeneid
Agamemnon
Alice in Wonderland
All the King's Men
All the Pretty Horses
All Quiet on Western Front
All's Well & Merry Wives
American Poets of the 20th Century
American Tragedy
Animal Farm
Anna Karenina
Anthem
Antony and Cleopatra
Aristotle's Ethics
As I Lay Dying
The Assistant
As You Like It
Atlas Shrugged
Autobiography of Ben Franklin
Autobiography of Malcolm X
The Awakening
Babbit
Bartleby & Benito Cereno
The Bean Trees
The Bear
The Bell Jar
Beloved
Beowulf
The Bible
Billy Budd & Typee
Black Boy
Black Like Me
Bleak House
Bless Me, Ultima
The Bluest Eye & Sula
Brave New World
Brothers Karamazov
Call of Wild & White Fang
Candide
The Canterbury Tales
Catch-22
Catcher in the Rye
The Chosen
The Color Purple
Comedy of Errors...
Connecticut Yankee
The Contender
The Count of Monte Cristo
Crime and Punishment
The Crucible
Cry, the Beloved Country
Cyrano de Bergerac
Daisy Miller & Turn...Screw
David Copperfield
Death of a Salesman
The Deerslayer
Diary of Anne Frank
Divine Comedy-I. Inferno
Divine Comedy-II. Purgatorio
Divine Comedy-III. Paradiso
Doctor Faustus

Dr. Jekyll and Mr. Hyde
Don Juan
Don Quixote
Dracula
Electra & Medea
Emerson's Essays
Emily Dickinson Poems
Emma
Ethan Frome
The Faerie Queene
Fahrenheit 451
Far from Madding Crowd
A Farewell to Arms
Farewell to Manzanar
Fathers and Sons
Faulkner's Short Stories
Faust Pt. I & Pt. II
The Federalist
Flowers for Algernon
For Whom the Bell Tolls
The Fountainhead
Frankenstein
The French Lieutenant's Woman
The Giver
Glass Menagerie & Streetcar
Go Down, Moses
The Good Earth
Grapes of Wrath
Great Expectations
The Great Gatsby
Greek Classics
Gulliver's Travels
Hamlet
The Handmaid's Tale
Hard Times
Heart of Darkness & Secret Sharer
Hemingway's Short Stories
Henry IV Part 1
Henry IV Part 2
Henry V
House Made of Dawn
The House of the Seven Gables
Huckleberry Finn
I Know Why the Caged Bird Sings
Ibsen's Plays I
Ibsen's Plays II
The Idiot
Idylls of the King
The Iliad
Incidents in the Life of a Slave Girl
Inherit the Wind
Invisible Man
Ivanhoe
Jane Eyre
Joseph Andrews
The Joy Luck Club
Jude the Obscure
Julius Caesar
The Jungle
Kafka's Short Stories
Keats & Shelley
The Killer Angels
King Lear
The Kitchen God's Wife
The Last of the Mohicans

Le Morte Darthur
Leaves of Grass
Les Miserables
A Lesson Before Dying
Light in August
The Light in the Forest
Lord Jim
Lord of the Flies
Lord of the Rings
Lost Horizon
Lysistrata & Other Comedies
Macbeth
Madame Bovary
Main Street
The Mayor of Casterbridge
Measure for Measure
The Merchant of Venice
Middlemarch
A Midsummer-Night's Dream
The Mill on the Floss
Moby-Dick
Moll Flanders
Mrs. Dalloway
Much Ado About Nothing
My Ántonia
Mythology
Narr. ...Frederick Douglass
Native Son
New Testament
Night
1984
Notes from Underground
The Odyssey
Oedipus Trilogy
Of Human Bondage
Of Mice and Men
The Old Man and the Sea
Old Testament
Oliver Twist
The Once and Future King
One Day in the Life of Ivan Denisovich
One Flew Over Cuckoo's Nest
100 Years of Solitude
O'Neill's Plays
Othello
Our Town
The Outsiders
The Ox-Bow Incident
Paradise Lost
A Passage to India
The Pearl
The Pickwick Papers
The Picture of Dorian Gray
Pilgrim's Progress
The Plague
Plato's Euthyphro...
Plato's The Republic
Poe's Short Stories
A Portrait of Artist...
The Portrait of a Lady
The Power and the Glory
Pride and Prejudice
The Prince
The Prince and the Pauper
A Raisin in the Sun

The Red Badge of Courage
The Red Pony
The Return of the Native
Richard II
Richard III
The Rise of Silas Lapham
Robinson Crusoe
Roman Classics
Romeo and Juliet
The Scarlet Letter
A Separate Peace
Shakespeare's Comedies
Shakespeare's Histories
Shakespeare's Minor Plays
Shakespeare's Sonnets
Shakespeare's Tragedies
Shaw's Pygmalion & Arms...
Silas Marner
Sir Gawain...Green Knight
Sister Carrie
Slaughterhouse-Five
Snow Falling on Cedars
Song of Solomon
Sons and Lovers
The Sound and the Fury
Steppenwolf & Siddhartha
The Stranger
The Sun Also Rises
T.S. Eliot's Poems & Plays
A Tale of Two Cities
The Taming of the Shrew
Tartuffe, Misanthrope...
The Tempest
Tender Is the Night
Tess of the D'Urbervilles
Their Eyes Were Watching God
Things Fall Apart
The Three Musketeers
To Kill a Mockingbird
Tom Jones
Tom Sawyer
Treasure Island & Kidnapped
The Trial
Tristram Shandy
Troilus and Cressida
Twelfth Night
Ulysses
Uncle Tom's Cabin
The Unvanquished
Utopia
Vanity Fair
Vonnegut's Works
Waiting for Godot
Walden
Walden Two
War and Peace
Who's Afraid of Virginia...
Winesburg, Ohio
The Winter's Tale
The Woman Warrior
Worldly Philosophers
Wuthering Heights
A Yellow Raft in Blue Water